Lecture Notes in Artificial Intelligence   4775

Edited by J. G. Carbonell and J. Siekmann

Subseries of Lecture Notes in Computer Science

Anna Esposito Marcos Faundez-Zanuy
Eric Keller Maria Marinaro (Eds.)

Verbal and Nonverbal Communication Behaviours

COST Action 2102 International Workshop
Vietri sul Mare, Italy, March 29-31, 2007
Revised Selected and Invited Papers

 Springer

Series Editors

Jaime G. Carbonell, Carnegie Mellon University, Pittsburgh, PA, USA
Jörg Siekmann, University of Saarland, Saarbrücken, Germany

Volume Editors

Anna Esposito
Second University of Naples, Department of Psychology and
IIASS, International Institute for Advanced Scientific Studies
Via Pellegrino, 19, Vietri sul Mare (SA), Italy
E-mail: iiass.annaesp@tin.it

Marcos Faundez-Zanuy
Escola Universitària Politècnica de Mataró
Avda. Puig i Cadafalch 101-111, 08303 Mataro (Barcelona), Spain
E-mail: faundez@eupmt.es

Eric Keller
Université de Lausanne, Faculté des Lettres IMM/LAIP
1015 Lausanne, Switzerland
E-mail: eric.keller@unil.ch

Maria Marinaro
Università di Salerno, Dipartimento di Fisica "E.R. Caianiello" and
IIASS, International Institute for Advanced Scientific Studies
Via Pellegrino, 19, Vietri sul MAre (SA), Italy
E-mail: iiass.direzione@tin.it

Library of Congress Control Number: 2007938045

CR Subject Classification (1998): I.2.11, I.2, H.5, H.4, K.4, K.3

LNCS Sublibrary: SL 7 – Artificial Intelligence

ISSN	0302-9743
ISBN-10	3-540-76441-0 Springer Berlin Heidelberg New York
ISBN-13	978-3-540-76441-0 Springer Berlin Heidelberg New York

Springer is a part of Springer Science+Business Media

springer.com

© Springer-Verlag Berlin Heidelberg 2007

Typesetting: Camera-ready by author, data conversion by Scientific Publishing Services, Chennai, India
Printed on acid-free paper   SPIN: 12184859   06/3180   5 4 3 2 1 0

Preface

This volume brings together the invited papers and selected participants' contributions presented at the COST 2102 International Workshop on *"Verbal and Nonverbal Communication Behaviours"*, held in Vietri sul Mare, Italy, March 29–31, 2007.

The workshop was jointly organized by the Faculty of Science and the Faculty of Psychology of the Second University of Naples, Caserta, Italy, and the International Institute for Advanced Scientific Studies "Eduardo R. Caianiello"(IIASS), Vietri sul Mare, Italy. The workshop was a COST 2102 event, and it was mainly sponsored by the COST (European Cooperation in the Field of Scientific and Technical Research) Action 2102 in the domain of Information and Communication Technologies (ICT) http://www.isca-speech.org/, as well as by the above-mentioned organizing Institutions.

The main theme of the workshop was the fundamental features of verbal and nonverbal communication and their relationships with the identification of a person, his/her socio-cultural background and personal traits.

In the past decade, a number of different research communities within the psychological and computational sciences have tried to characterize human behaviour in face-to-face communication by several features that describe relationships between facial, prosodic/voice quality, formal and informal communication modes, cultural differences, individual and socio-cultural variations, stable personality traits and degrees of expressiveness and emphasis, as well as the individuation of the interlocutor's emotional and psychological states. There has been substantial progress in these different communities and surprising convergence, and this growing interest makes the current intellectual climate an ideal one for the organization of a workshop devoted to the study of verbal and nonverbal aspects of face-to-face communication and of how they could be used to characterize a more friendly human-machine interaction.

Key aspects considered are the integration of algorithms and procedures for the recognition of emotional states, gestures, speech and facial expressions, in anticipation of the implementation of useful applications such as intelligent avatars and interactive dialog systems.

Due to the multidisciplinary character of the workshop, the scientific contributions stem from computer science, physics, psychology, statistics, mathematics, electrical engineering, and communication science. The contributors to this volume are leading authorities in their respective fields. We are grateful to them for accepting our invitation and making (through their participation) the workshop such a worthwhile event.

The contributions in the book can be said to cover five scientific areas according to a thematic classification, even though all the areas are closely connected and all provide fundamental insights for cross-fertilization of different disciplines.

The introduction presents the aims and goals of COST 2102 and describes its major objectives.

The first area, *verbal* and *nonverbal coding schema*, deals with the theoretical and practical issue of defining variables and identifying models to describe verbal and nonverbal expressions in the realization of communicative actions. It includes the contributions of some leading experts such as Niels Ole Bernsen and Laila Dybkjær, and the papers of Zsófia Ruttkay, and Uwe Altmann et al., on the search for variables describing relationships between gestures and speech.

The second area, *emotional expressions*, is devoted to underlining the importance of emotional communication and reports on advanced experiments for the recognition of emotional nonverbal expressions in music and speech. It includes the contributions by Anna Esposito and Manuela Serio; Jiří Přibil and Anna Přibilová; and Eva Navas et al.

The third area, *gestural expressions*, deals with prosody, intonation, and the use of gesture in conveying key aspects of a message in face-to-face interactions. The section starts with a theoretical paper by Eric Keller and Wolfgang Tschacher on prosodic and gestural expressions and goes on to describe gesture-prosody, gesture-lexicon interaction and an original set of Egyptjan gestural expressions in the papers by Ewa Jarmolowicz et al. and Aly El-Bahrawy.

The fourth area, *analysis and algorithms for verbal and nonverbal speech*, introduces the concept of modelling linguistic and paralinguistic signals as well as new algorithms for speech processing. The section contains outstanding papers by Nick Campbell; Robert Vich and Martin Vondra; György Szaszák and Klára Vicsi; Zdeněk Smékal and Petr Sysel; Peter Murphy; Bernd Kröger and Peter Birkholz; Amir Hussain et al.; and Rüdiger Hoffmann et al.

The fifth area, *machine multimodal interaction*, deals with psychological, pedagogical and technological issues related to the implementation of intelligent avatars and interactive dialog systems that exploit verbal and nonverbal communication features. It includes the papers by Jerneja Žganec Gros; Markku Turunen and Jaakko Hakulinen; Pantelis Makris; Jonas Beskow; Björn Granström and David House; Dirk Heylen et al.; Marcos Faundez-Zanuy et al.; Matúš Pleva et al.; Matej Rojc et al; and Guilherme Raimundo et al.

The editors would like to thank the COST ICT Programme for its support in the realization and publication of this volume, and in particular the COST Science Officer Afonso Ferreira for his constant guidance and encouragement. Our deep gratitude goes to Prof. Raffaele Martone, Vice-Rector of the Second University of Naples, for taking part in the meeting and for his enthusiasm and appreciation for the proposed lectures. Great appreciation goes to the Dean of the Faculty of Science at the Second University of Naples, Prof. Nicola Melone, for his interest and support of the event, and to Prof. Luigi Maria Ricciardi, Chairman of the Graduate Programme on Computational and Information Science, University of Naples Federico II, for his involvement and encouragements. The help of Profs. Alida Labella and Giovanna Nigro, respectively Dean of the Faculty and Director of the Department of Psychology at the Second University of Naples, is also acknowledged with gratitude.

Special appreciation goes to Michele Donnarumma, Antonio Natale, and Tina Marcella Nappi of IIASS whose help in the organization of the workshop was invaluable.

Finally, we are most grateful to all the contributors to this volume and all the participants in the COST 2102 International Workshop for their cooperation, interest, enthusiasm and lively interaction making it not only a scientifically stimulating gathering but also a memorable personal experience.

This book is dedicated to the unknown driving all our lives. Thinking of it motivates our perseverance and appreciation for research work, love and friendship.

August 2007

Anna Esposito
Marcos Faundez-Zanuy
Eric Keller
Maria Marinaro

Based on Manuscripts Submitted to COST Action 2102 International Workshop on

Verbal and Nonverbal Communication Behaviours

Vietri sul Mare, Italy
29 - 31 March 2007

The support and the sponsorship of:

- European Cost Action 2102 "*Cross Modal Analysis of Verbal and Nonverbal Communication*" www.cost2102.eu;
- Second University of Naples, Faculty of Psychology (Italy)
- Second University of Naples, Faculty of Science (Italy)
- International Institute for Advanced Scientific Studies "E.R. Caianiello" (IIASS), Italy
- Regione Campania (Italy)
- Provincia di Salerno (Italy)

  is gratefully acknowledged

International Advisory and Organizing Committee

Anna Esposito, Department of Psychology, Second University of Naples and IIASS, Italy
Macos Faundez-Zanuy, University of Mataro, Barcelona, Spain
Amir Hussain, University of Stirling, UK
Eric Keller, IMM, University of Lausanne, Switzerland
Maria Marinaro, Department of Physics, University of Salerno and IIASS, Italy
Nicola Melone, Department of Mathematics, Second University of Naples, Italy

Local Organizing Committee

Anna Esposito, Second University of Naples and IIASS, Italy
Alida Labella, Second University of Naples, Italy
Maria Marinaro, Salerno University and IIASS, Italy
Nicola Melone, Second University of Naples, Italy
Antonio Natale, Salerno University and IIASS, Italy
Giovanna Nigro, Second University of Naples, Italy
Francesco Piazza, Università Politecnica delle Marche, Italy
Luigi Maria Ricciardi, Università di Napoli "Federico II", Italy

International Scientific Committee

Uwe Altmann, Technische Universität Dresden, Germany
Nikos Avouris, University of Patras, Greece
Gérard Bailly, ICP, Grenoble, France
Ruth Bahr, University of South Florida, USA
Jean-Francois Bonastre, Université d'Avignon, France
Niels Ole Bernsen, University of Southern Denmark, Denmark
Jonas Beskow, Royal Institute of Technology, Sweden
Horst Bishof, Technical University Graz, Austria
Nikolaos Bourbakis, ITRI, Wright State University, Dayton, OH, USA
Maja Bratanić, University of Zagreb, Croatia
Paola Campadelli, Università di Milano, Italy
Nick Campbell, ATR Human Information Science Labs, Kyoto, Japan
Antonio Castro Fonseca, Universidade de Coimbra, Coimbra, Portugal
Aleksandra Cerekovic, Faculty of Electrical Engineering, Croatia
Mohamed Chetouani, Université Pierre et Marie Curie, France
Gerard Chollet, CNRS-LTCI, Paris, France
Muzeyyen Ciyiltepe, Gulhane Askeri Tip Academisi, Ankara, Turkey
Anton Cizmar, Technical University of Kosice, Slovakia
Thierry Dutoit, Faculté Polytechnique de Mons, Belgium
Laila Dybkjær, University of Southern Denmark, Denmark
Engin Erzin, Koc University, Istanbul, Turkey
Francesca D'Olimpio, Second University of Naples, Italy
Aly El-Bahrawy, Faculty of Engineering, Cairo, Egypt
Anna Esposito, Second University of Naples, and IIASS, Italy
Sascha Fagel, Technische Universität Berlin, Germany
Nikos Fakotakis, University of Patras, Greece
Marcos Faundez-Zanuy, Escola Universitaria de Mataro, Spain
Dilek Fidan, Ankara Universitesi, Turkey
Carmen García-Mateo, University of Vigo, Spain
Björn Granström, Royal Institute of Technology, KTH, Sweden
Mohand-Said Hacid, Université Claude Bernard Lyon 1, France
Jaakko Hakulinen, University of Tampere, Finland
Ioannis Hatzilygeroudis, University of Patras, Greece
Immaculada Hernaez, University of the Basque Country, Spain
Javier Hernando, Technical University of Catalonia, Spain
Wolfgang Hess, Universität Bonn, Germany
Dirk Heylen, University of Twente, The Netherlands
Rudiger Hoffmann, Technische Universität Dresden, Germany
David House, Royal Institute of Technology, KTH, Sweden
Amir Hussain, University of Stirling, UK
Zdravko Kacic, University of Maribor, Slovenia
Maciej Karpinski, Adam Mickiewicz University, Poznan, Poland
Eric Keller, Université de Lausanne, Switzerland
Adam Kendon, University of Pennsylvania, USA
Stefan Kopp, University of Bielefeld, Germany

Jacques Koreman, University of Science and Technology, Norway
Robert Krauss, Columbia University, New York, USA
Bernd Kröger, Aachen University, Germany
Alida Labella, Second University of Naples, Italy
Borge Lindberg, Aalborg University, Denmark
Wojciech Majewski, Wroclaw University of Technology, Poland
Pantelis Makris, Neuroscience and Technology Institute, Cyprus
Maria Marinaro, Salerno University and IIASS, Italy
Raffaele Martone, Second University of Naples, Italy
Dominic Massaro, University of California - Santa Cruz, USA
David McNeill, University of Chicago, IL, USA
Nicola Melone, Second University of Naples, Italy
Peter Murphy, University of Limerick, Limerick, Ireland
Antonio Natale, Salerno University and IIASS, Italy
Eva Navas, Escuela Superior de Ingenieros, Bilbao, Spain
Géza Németh, University of Technology and Economics, Budapest, Hungary
Giovanna Nigro, Second University of Naples, Italy
Anton Nijholt, University of Twente, The Netherlands
Igor Pandzic, Faculty of Electrical Engineering, Croatia
Harris Papageorgiou, Inst. for Language and Speech Processing, Greece
Ana Pavia, Spoken Language Systems Laboratory, Portugal
Catherine Pelachaud, Université de Paris 8, France
Bojan Petek, University of Ljubljana, Slovenia
Harmut R. Pfitzinger, University of Munich, Germany
Francesco Piazza, Università Politecnica delle Marche, Italy
Neda Pintaric, University of Zagreb, Croatia
Jiří Přibil, Academy of Sciences, Czech Republic
Anna Přibilová, Slovak University of Technology, Slovakia
Kari-Jouko Räihä, University of Tampere, Finland
Giuliana Ramella, Istituto di Cibernetica – CNR, Napoli, Italy
José Rebelo, Universidade de Coimbra, Coimbra, Portugal
Luigi Maria Ricciardi, Università di Napoli "Federico II", Italy
Matej Rojc, University of Maribor, Slovenia
Algimantas Rudzionis, Kaunas University of Technology, Lithuania
Zsófia Ruttkay, Pazmany Peter Catholic University, Hungary
Yoshinori Sagisaka, Waseda University, Tokyo, Japan
Silvia Scarpetta, Salerno University, Italy
Jean Schoentgen, Université Libre de Bruxelles, Belgium
Stefanie Shattuck-Hufnagel, MIT, Cambridge, MA, USA
Zdeněk Smékal, Brno University of Technology, Czech Republic
Stefano Squartini, Università Politecnica delle Marche, Italy
Piotr Staroniewicz, Wroclaw University of Technology, Poland
Vojtěch Stejskal, Brno University of Technology, Czech Republic
Johne Tao, Chinese Academy of Sciences, P.R. China
Jure F. Tasič, University of Ljubljana, Slovenia
Kristinn Thórisson, Reykjavík University, Iceland
Isabel Trancoso, Spoken Language Systems Laboratory, Portugal

Table of Contents

IV – Analysis and Algorithms for Verbal and Nonverbal Speech

V – Machine Multimodal Interaction

COST 2102: Cross-Modal Analysis of Verbal and Nonverbal Communication (CAVeNC)

Anna Esposito[1,2]

[1] Seconda Università di Napoli, Dipartimento di Psicologia, Via Vivaldi 43, Caserta, Italy
anna.esposito@unina2.it, iiass.annaesp@tin.it
[2] IIASS, Via Pellegrino 19, 84019, Vietri sul Mare, Italy, INFM Salerno, Italy

Abstract. In the following are described the fundamental features and the major objectives of COST 2102: Cross-Modal Analysis of Verbal and Nonverbal Communication (CAVeNC) as they have been expressed in the Memorandum of Understanding. COST (European Cooperation in the Field of Scientific and Technical Research) is "*one of the longest-running instruments supporting co-operation among scientists and researchers across Europe*" www.cost.esf.org. In this framework, COST 2102 is an initiative founded in the Domain of Information and Communication Technologies that has become operative on Dec 2006. Details on the on-going activities as well as the structure and the organization of COST 2102 can be found on www.cost2102.eu. I want to express my gratitude to all researchers which have joined COST 2102 for making real the dream of sharing knowledge and research work with leading experts in the field of multimodal communication.

Keywords: cross-modal analysis of speech, gaze, face and gestures.

1 Prelude

Two channels have been distinguished in human interaction. One conveys messages with a specific semantic content (verbal channel); the other (the non-verbal channel) conveys information related to both the image content of a message and to the general feeling and emotional state of the speaker. Enormous efforts have been undertaken in the past to understand the verbal channel, whereas the role of the non-verbal channel is less well understood. Emotional speech as well as facial expressions, gestures, and gaze constitute the main form of non-verbal information that can be captured and analyzed in a multi-sensory environment, providing the motivation to integrate information from various sources that have tended to be kept separate until now. To understand non-verbal information, advanced signal processing and analysis techniques have to be applied, and psychological and linguistic analyses must be performed. Moreover, understanding the relationship between the verbal and non-verbal communication modes, and progress towards their modelling, is crucial for implementing a friendly human computer interaction that exploits of synthetic agents and sophisticated human-like interfaces and will simplify the user access to future telecommunication services.

A. Esposito et al. (Eds.): Verbal and Nonverbal Commun. Behaviours, LNAI 4775, pp. 1–10, 2007.

2 Background

Human language, gestures, gaze, facial expressions and emotions are not entities amenable to study in isolation. Converging and interweaving cognitive processes are linked in ways that cannot be totally untangled. These links can only be understood by identifying **meta-entities** of mental processes that are more complex than those devoted to the simple peripheral pre-processing of received signals. To understand how human communication exploits information from several channels that all potentially contribute, act and support the speaker's communicative goal, requires the definition and constitution of a cross-modal and cross-cultural database comprising verbal and non-verbal (gaze, facial expressions, and gestures) data. Gathering data across a spectrum of disciplines in a structured manner will reinforce our ability to portray the underlying **meta-structure** and will lead to new mathematical models describing their functioning, thus permitting new approaches to the psychology of the language itself, as well as to the content of any message, independently from its overt semantic meaning.

The scientific study of speech, gestures, gaze, and emotion as an integrated system has taken great strides in the last 20 years, but progress has been slowed by the time-consuming nature of the perceptual analysis. A significant bottleneck is the determination of boundaries between gestures phases, speech, facial and gaze expressions. We may now begin to automate this process.

The major initiative within the Action is to bundle the analyses of all communicative aspects, and to identify physical and psychological features capable of describing the socio-emotional content of a message, as well as to arrive at satisfactory mathematical descriptions, in order to facilitate ultimate computational processing in anticipation to future telecommunication systems that go beyond purely factual and task-oriented applications.

In tune with these research objectives, the Action aims to assemble researchers working in different fields and to create a common public data framework for a large variety of applications that may range from medical diagnosis to entertainment devices (speech, face expression, gaze, and gestures), profiting from a large-scale framework for interaction with other groups that are concerned with developing psychological and software models of face-to-face communication.

2.1 Related European Initiatives

It is felt that this COST Action is of general importance and complementary to other EU activities, specifically the Networks of Excellence SIMILAR, HUMAINE, and ECESS, and the European Integrated Project CHIL, AMI, and PASION. The Action shares some thematic research topics with the above initiatives. In particular HUMAINE also deals with signal analysis for emotion and has identified a working area on data collection and annotation, and SIMILAR also deals with cross-modal analysis of signals, as does ECESS.

But even though the themes show the above similar points, they do not focus on the same elements. For example, in this Action, WG1 deals mainly with motion capture data and the semi-automatic annotation of corpora, and these points are not dealt within HUMAINE. The focus research interest of SIMILAR is on e-interface applications, while this Action, being more research-oriented, aims to develop a deeper analytical understanding of the mechanisms underlying the multimodal aspects of human communication. AMI is concerned "with new multimodal technologies to support human interaction, in the context of smart meeting rooms and remote meeting assistants" while this Action is concerned with analyzing human interaction in the context of face-to-face communication. In contrast to this COST project, ECESS does not propose to work on manual and conversational gestures. PASION shares with the Action the objective of identifying implicit social communication cues that are not usually explicitly shared by people communicating with one and other, but is not particularly focussed on their emotional states. Moreover, all the other themes proposed by the Action (MPEG-7 standardization, cultural differences, personality traits, individual and socio-cultural variations, correlations between verbal and non-verbal entities) are not tackled at all within HUMAINE, SIMILAR, CHIL, AMI or ECESS. Therefore, the research developed by the Action research groups is very much complementary to that developed by the above initiatives. In addition, emotion and multimodal communication are so complex, that having several complementary groups working on them from different perspectives (such as that engineering oriented of CHIL, AMI and SIMILAR, and the theoretical and algorithmic perspective of this Action and HUMAINE), would only be of great advantage to the field of communication technologies and would contribute to speed up the advance of the scientific knowledge and the development of innovative applications in telecommunication.

It must be mentioned that COST 2102 transcends the present EU boundaries and opens collaborative opportunities to a number of European countries that are not presently part of the EU. Finally, since COST has a successful tradition of supporting complementary work to the Framework Programmes, and the overlaps with these EU initiatives is in the nature and scope of a COST Action, COST 2102 aims also to encourage and strengthen the collaboration of EU groups wishing to define related IT projects.

2.2 Related Cost Actions

There are three COST Actions that appear to share some features with this Action: COST 219, COST 287, and COST 298. However, this is not the case since these Actions should better be considered as strongly complementary to the present Action.

The main objectives of COST 219 is to increase the accessibility of the next generation of communication network services to elderly people and people with disability by designing or adapting them to the needs of all kind of users. It shares with this Action few features related to what communication characteristics are impaired in elderly and disabled people. However, while in COST 219 the elderly and disabled people behaviours are investigated from the point of view of their ability to use specific technological interfaces, this Action investigates them from the point of view of which signals are missing in their multimodal communication, and which communication tools need to be developed to add the missing information to their message.

COST 287 focuses on audio systems controlled by gestures and it is strongly complementary to this Action, since the Action does not foresee any activity for music and audio systems. Moreover, in COST 287, the gestures exploited to control such systems are *manipulative* gestures and therefore strongly different from those used in a spontaneous communication. It would be interesting to compare the two categories of gestures for similarities and differences.

The main objectives of COST 298 is to create new knowledge about user creativity when dealing with an aggregate technology comprising several technical solutions such as IPv6, xDSL, ISDN, Bluetooth, UMTS, and to investigate how worthwhile and useful they are for potential users. It intersects with the themes of this Action, to the extent that it moves from the features of spontaneous communication to the features exploited when the communication is implemented through technological tools. In this sense, the two Actions are again strongly complementary.

3 Objectives and Benefits

The main objective of COST 2102 is to develop an advanced acoustical, perceptual, and psychological analysis of verbal and non-verbal communication signals originating in spontaneous face-to-face interaction, in order to identify algorithms and automatic procedures capable of identifying the human emotional states. Several key aspects will be considered, such as the integration of the developed algorithms and procedures for application in telecommunication, and for the recognition of emotional states, gestures, speech and facial expressions, in anticipation of the implementation of intelligent avatars and interactive dialog systems that could be exploited to improve user access to future telecommunication services.

The Action profits from two former COST Actions (COST 277 and COST 278) that identified new appropriate mathematical models and algorithms to drive the implementation of the next generation of telecommunication services such as remote health monitoring systems, interactive dialog systems, and intelligent avatars, realizing the following objectives:

a) Implement a cross-modal analysis (i.e. an analysis that takes into account several communicative signals and their relationships) of audio and video recordings to define distinctive cross-modal communication features for identifying emotional states through signals from speech, gestures and gaze;

b) Define and implement algorithms for processing multimodal signals in order to supply encoded information at a higher semantic level;

c) Identify analysis features to suggest an extended MPEG 7 annotation and define a framework to share these specific MPEG 7 data with the scientific community;

d) Identify analysis features for modelling cultural differences, personal traits, and socio-pragmatic adaptation of speech styles.

3.1 Main Outcomes and Benefits

The expected results of the Action will be threefold:

1. It will contribute to the establishment of quantitative and qualitative features describing both verbal and non-verbal modalities;

2. It will advance technological support for the development of improved multimodal (i.e. exploiting signals coming from several modalities) systems;

3. It will contribute to new theories to clarify the role of verbal and non-verbal modalities in communication, and their exploitation in telecommunication services.

The Action will define, produce and analyse corpora of multimodal communication, both in support of specific COST projects and to serve the research community at large. In the past, corpora for textual natural language processing and speech recognition have spurred robust progress in these sciences. It is therefore expected to incite similar activity in this fields, all while keeping in mind that the field of cross-modal conversational interaction is still in its seminal stages. The Action thus provides a bootstrap mechanism by gathering researchers whose scientific questions will drive the definition and generation of the experimental corpora, which in turn guarantees that these corpora will be scientifically efficacious. The corpora are expected to incite other researchers to use the data and to advance both the field of telecommunication technology and the field of human and social sciences because of the highly multidisciplinary and interdisciplinary character of the proposed research.

As an added value at a European level, this research aims at contributing to the development of intelligent telecommunication services, such as remote health monitoring systems, that taking into account psychological aspects, personal traits, sociocultural differences and individual variations, simplify the everyday-life man-machine interaction by offering natural ways of communication. The Action is also open to research groups that are working on automatic recognition or automatic modelling of speech of Sign Language and aims to establish a close link with them.

3.2 Milestones (in Bold) and Outputs of the Action

The milestones and outcomes of the Action will advance both the basic and technological research in communication and are listed below:

1. An in-depth analysis of the existing methods and procedures that involve different stages of verbal and non-verbal communication. This analysis should furnish new theoretical results to identify and link the different communication channels, to define the amount of information brought to the several communication modes by each channel, and to feed into a mathematical model of their interaction;

2. A multimodal database for the analysis of interactions between the different communication channels and how they integrate in the communication gestalt. The database would also allow cross-linguistics and cross-cultural comparisons between the different communication modalities for defining the degree of cultural and individual specificity to be applied in order to identify meaningful models of user's behaviour;

3. A database of free software and a description of techniques and procedures developed by the Working Groups as well as guidelines for their use;

4. The standardization of the encoding of multimodal human communication features as an extension of the current encoding standard MPEG-7;

5. A yearly international book based on the contributions from the Action's members and working partners, as well as those from experts of related

disciplines and related initiatives, containing the currently developed applications, the update research results, and the future research directions;

6. The understanding and the identification of the effects related to personal traits and cultural background on the face-to-face communication and the role that they play in setting up a successful dialogue;
7. The introduction of a common methodological approach in order to develop an appropriate assessment benchmark that could be a reference for the scientific community;
8. The definition of new algorithms based on the new mathematical models of human interaction and their experimental software implementation in order to ensure their effectiveness for future applications;
9. The identification of new research areas and fusion methods that will serve both for future research projects and for technological exploitations.
10. The implementation of graphical interfaces and intelligent agents capable of implementing a human-like man-machine interaction, exploiting information from gestures, facial expressions, gaze and speech to recognize and synthesize emotional states;
11. A series of scientific publications on international journals, and conference proceedings as well as technical reports of the activities.

4   Scientific Programme

The activities to be carried out in order to implement the above issues will be the following:

TASK 1: Cross Modal Analysis of Audio and Video: This activity will be related to the collection of experimental data through different elicitation techniques for generating spontaneous dialogues as well as assessing experiments with subjects wearing appropriate sensors and cyber-gloves, and facial markers to allow the collection of natural and biofeedback data. Subjects will be from different cultural backgrounds. The Action will ensure synchrony and homogeneity in the data collected by collaborating groups, as well as standard formats for dissemination to the entire research community.

TASK 2: Data Analysis and Feature Correlations: This activity will examine the synchronization of acoustic features (such as waveform, F0 contour; speech energy) with hand movements, gaze and facial expression, to identify relationships between acoustic/prosodic, syntactic and non-verbal features, exploiting, and/or working on improving, already developed systems for time-locking video with multiple lines of transcription such as SignSTREAM and ELAN (Max Plank Institute for Psycholinguistics, Nijmegen), ANVIL (Michael Kipp, DFKI), TRANSANA (Wisconsin Centre for Education Research, etc). Assessment will be provided through statistics and through the implementation of prototyping applications.

TASK 3: Cultural Differences and Individual Socio-Cultural Variations: Since there is really not very much existing research in the area, the Action will define a set of small pilot projects that help clarify which cultural differences deserve further investigation in the European context. For example, do we need a different feature list for Sweden and for Italy? Or are we merely addressing strength-of-parameter setting issues when we speak of cultural differences in facial/speech/gestural expression? How a given communication intent is realized in one country or in another? Cultural differences is a major issue that a COST Action can address powerfully, given its multicultural constitution.

TASK 4: Emotional States: It is evident that the same words may be used as a joke, or as a genuine question seeking an answer, or as an aggressive challenge. Knowing what is an appropriate continuation of the interaction depends on detecting the register that the speaker is using, and a machine communicator that is unable to acknowledge the difference will have difficulty in managing a natural-like conversation. From an acoustic viewpoint, emotions, along with prosody, has been studied within the narrow confines of f0, amplitude and duration. From an image processing viewpoint emotions have been studied within the narrow confines of static positions capable of being displayed in a still image capturing the apex of the expression, i.e. the instant at which the indicators of emotion are marked as prominent.

The Action aims to move beyond this level of representation to include features able to express relationships between emotional speech, accompanying gestures, gaze and facial expressions and other features such as a source-filter representation of emotional speech. This activity will examine how to integrate audio and video data and what should be modelled in order to develop interfaces capable of analyzing users' emotional states, speech style, informal versus formal speech, as well as degree of expressiveness and emphasis. Moreover, the Action aims to go beyond the recognition of the six (almost universally accepted) primary emotions to include some secondary emotions such as boredom, interest, etc., because of their relevance in the human-like machine interaction.

TASK 5: Video and Audio Relationships - Synthesis and Recognition: While speech contributes semantic content to the message, gestures engage the *image content*. This activity will address the following questions: (1) Are there any gestural equivalents of speech entities such as filled and empty pauses, repairs, prosody, voice quality, and personal traits? (2) Assuming that related gestural entities are found, to what degree do they synchronize with speech? (3) Can any video and audio feature describe these relationships? (4) Are there algorithms able to extract such features? (5) How can mathematical models and avatars implement and reproduce these relationships? More specifically to the Information Technology (IT) field, this activity is devoted to the recognition of gestures' shapes and dynamic properties and will provide mathematical models for combining and exploiting verbal and non-verbal signals with the aim to exploit the differences and the similarities in the implementation of synthetic agents that should be able to understand multimodal signals as well as to reproduce them during the interaction with humans.

TASK 6: Data Encoding (Video and Audio) and Definition of an Extended MPEG7 Standard Annotation: In this activity, algorithms for the encoding of dialogues and associated gestures and emotional states will be defined. Video and audio data will be processed and acoustic and video features will be extracted, using standard and new algorithms derived from the knowledge acquired through the perceptual and acoustic analysis of the collected dialogues. Moreover, this task will set the basis for the definition of an extended MPEG7 Standard Annotation.

Formally named *Multimedia Content Description Interface*, MPEG-7 (an ISO standard till 2001) provides a rich set of tools for multimedia annotations aimed at production and use by both humans and machines. In general, MPEG-7 descriptions do not depend on the way content is coded or stored, and MPEG-7 does not call for specific extraction algorithms, but is only concerned with the encoding format for interoperability purposes. These aspects are clearly of interest to this Action, but they need to be integrated with newly multimodal human communication features provided by other Tasks described above. The results will be proposed as an extension to the current standard, possibly through the appropriate normative process, and will serve both for future research projects and for technological exploitation. Moreover, in order to share MPEG 7 data with the entire scientific community, suitable network frameworks will be studied to fully exploit its Internet potential, such as distributed (P2P) or MPEG-7 dedicated server-based schemes.

4.1 Working Groups

Working groups will be organized around the main Tasks as follows:
WG1:

> ➢ TASK 1: Cross modal analysis of audio and video;
> ➢ TASK 2: Data Analysis and Feature Correlations.

WG2:

> ➢ TASK 3: Cultural Differences and Individual and Socio-Cultural Variations;
> ➢ TASK 4: Emotional States;

WG3:

> ➢ TASK 5: Video and Audio Relationships Synthesis and Recognition;
> ➢ TASK 6: Data Encoding and Definition of an Extended MPEG7 Standard Annotation;

In addition, conferences, workshops, and short-term missions will be employed for cooperation and discussion of the results, and will be scheduled carefully in order to achieve the Action's main objectives.

5 Organisation

The achievements of the proposed objectives rely on the interdisciplinary cooperation of the laboratories joining the Action and on the appropriate exchange of data, software tools, algorithms and procedures through the presentation and the discussion of the research implemented by the participating laboratories. To ensure an efficient control and an effective structure, the Action will be broken down into three Working Groups (WG1, WG2, WG3) and responsibilities and workloads will be distributed among them. For each working group there will be a Working Group Coordinator that will be responsible for planning, coordinating and reviewing the scientific and technical contribution of his group, as well as for exchanging results and to ensure interactions with the other working groups. The Management Committee will meet three times per year in order to efficiently organize the research and monitor the expected results.

6   Timetable

The total duration of the Action will be 4 years. During these years the relevant meetings of the Action are scheduled according to the activities described in the table below:

Table 1. Description of the activities carried out during COST 2102 meetings

ACTIVITIES	DURATION
A: Election of chair, vice-chair, and working group co-ordinators and initial planning	1 meeting (Management Committee + Working Groups)
B: Action Management	8 one day meetings 2 per year for preparation and follow up on work plan (Management Committee)
C: Current state of art and applications	1 meeting (Management Committee + Working Groups)
D: Establishment of liaisons and experts network	1 meeting (Management Committee + Working Groups)
E: Co-ordination for research, explanation of results, etc.	8 meetings (Management Committee + Working Groups) (2 per year)
F: Dissemination of results through a conference, arrangement of seminars, development of printed and multimedia information	4 meetings (1 per year)
G: Reviews of the Action	4 meetings (Management Committee + Working Groups) (1 per year)

7   Dimensions

The following 24 COST European countries actively participate to the Action's activities: Belgium, Croatia, Cyprus, Czech Republic, Denmark, Finland, France, Germany, Greece, Hungary, Ireland, Iceland, Italy, Netherlands, Poland, Portugal, Slovakia, Slovenia, Spain, Sweden, Switzerland, United Kingdom, Norway, Turkey. These countries sums up to 47 European participating Institutions. Moreover, 5 overseas Laboratories, from China, Egypt, India, Japan, and USA are involved.

8 Dissemination Plans

Dissemination in COST 2102 will be implemented with the following means:

a) The implementation of a web site (www.cost2102.eu) regularly updated with Action initiatives (meetings, short-term missions, workshops, conferences, etc.) progress reports, agenda and minute meetings;

b) The diffusion of the research results through publications in international journals where the cooperation and the Action support is acknowledged;

c) An annual conference aimed at consolidating the current results and identifying the future research directions. Representatives of the Action's working groups will be the main contributors and lecturers. The contributions will be collected in an international book that synthesizes the main results. The event may be held in conjunction with other related workshops and conferences. This year the event will be held in conjunction with the IEEE Conference on Tools with Artificial Intelligence (ICTAI, **ictai07.ceid.upatras.gr**)

d) The participation to special conference sessions in other international related conferences (as NOLISP07 and those reported above) organized by other complementary European Research Projects such as the Networks of Excellence HUMAINE and SIMILAR, and the IST Projects CHIL, AMI, and PASION;

e) A series of annual progress reports describing major achievements, problems encountered, procedures employed and/or developed, the data collected and their availability (according to the rules defined by the COST regulations), details on the findings obtained, related publications, and remarks and implications for future work;

f) Special issues in international journal reporting the research results of the working groups involved in the Action.

Acknowledgements

This work has been partially funded by COST 2102 "*Cross Modal Analysis of Verbal and Nonverbal Communication*", www.cost2102.edu. Acknowledgements go to **Francesco Piazza** for writing the MPEG7 paragraph, **Eric Keller** for his patience in revising several versions of the proposal, **Robert Vich** and **Zdenek Smékal** for their support and encouragements, and to all the COST 2102 researchers for joining the Action and contributing to it with their research work.

Annotation Schemes for Verbal and Non-verbal Communication: Some General Issues

Niels Ole Bernsen and Laila Dybkjær

NISLab, Denmark
nob@nis.sdu.dk, laila@nis.sdu.dk

Abstract: During the past 5-10 years, increasing efforts have been put into annotation of verbal and non-verbal human-human and human-machine communication in order to better understand the complexities of multimodal communication and model them in computers. This has helped highlight the huge challenges which still confront annotators in this field, from conceptual confusion through lacking or immature coding schemes to inadequate coding tools. We discuss what is an annotation scheme, briefly review previous work on annotation schemes and tools, describe current trends, and discuss challenges ahead.

1 Introduction

Few, if any, of us actually code many different aspects of verbal and non-verbal human-human or human-machine communication on a daily basis. Rather, we tend to be occupied for long stretches of time annotating a single aspect of a single modality, such as when doing spoken dialogue transcription, or, increasingly, annotating a single aspect, such as emotion expression, across a range of modalities. Data coding tends to be hard work, and difficult, too. One often has to first design and create the data resource to be used before having something appropriate to code, possibly after having spent considerable time looking for re-usable data without finding any. As existing coding schemes often turn out to be inappropriate for the purpose at hand, coding scheme creation might follow, which is often hard theoretical work and for which, moreover, a single data resource is rarely sufficient for creating a new consolidated coding scheme. And coding tools constitute a world of their own, with learning-how-to-use difficulties, programming challenges and sometimes tool inadequacy for what one wants to do. It is tempting to think that things are easier for coders of other types of verbal and non-verbal communication phenomena than one's own and that their world is far more well-organised conceptually. Only an attempt to take a global look can contribute to balancing the picture and provide a common view of what it is that we are all involved in as explorers of the only partially charted land of verbal and non-verbal communication.

In this paper we look at previous and current work on annotation and provide a glimpse of what lies ahead. Section 2 seeks to establish common ground by describing what is a coding scheme and defining the notions of general and consolidated coding schemes. Section 3 briefly refers back to previous work on creating surveys of

A. Esposito et al. (Eds.): Verbal and Nonverbal Commun. Behaviours, LNAI 4775, pp. 11–22, 2007.
© Springer-Verlag Berlin Heidelberg 2007

data, coding schemes, and coding tools for natural interactive communication, and Section 4 addresses current trends in the field. Section 5 discusses future challenges and concludes the paper.

2   What Is a Coding Scheme?

In the context of coding verbal and non-verbal communication, a coding (annotation, markup) scheme is basically a theory of the members (types) of a class of phenomena (tokens) to be found in the data. The data itself may be represented in acoustic – speech and other – files, video files, logfiles, hand-written notes or otherwise. A coding scheme may be based on, or has to be able to support the annotation of, one or several data sets, data resources, or corpora. Within the wealth of information represented in the data, a coding scheme focuses on a single generic kind of information, such as the facial expressions of the participant(s), the parts-of-speech they produce, or the behavioural cues to their emotions whether expressed in speech, facially, in gesture or otherwise. In fact, these three examples, although perfectly legitimate, are far too neat to adequately convey what a coding scheme might be targeting, so let's also include examples, such as nose scratchings, looking carefully around to see if anybody is watching, or increasing heart rate because of sensing danger. You might object that these behaviours, although non-verbal all right, do not constitute communication, but see Section 5. The point we wish to make is that the generic kind of information targeted by a coding scheme solely reflects the scheme's underlying coding purpose, which is why such generic kinds of information are unlimited in number. Quite simply, there is an unlimited number of coding purposes one might have when coding a particular data resource.

To be useful, a coding scheme should include three kinds of information which we might call theory, semantics, and meta-data, respectively. These are discussed in the following Sections 2.1, 2.2 and 2.3.

2.1   Theory and Completeness

The first kind of information a coding scheme should include is a theory of the number and nature of the types of phenomena, relevant to the coding purpose, to be found in the data. If that theory is wrong, so that the data includes more or other types of relevant phenomena than those acknowledged by the coding scheme, more types will have to be added to the scheme. This is a perfectly normal situation for the originator or co-developer of an emerging coding scheme: you approach the data with a theory of the number and nature of the phenomena it includes, discover that there are more, other, or even sometimes fewer types than hypothesised, and revise the coding scheme accordingly. By the same token, however, the coding scheme represents a theory under development and the coding scheme is not yet, at least, a consolidated one.

We use the word "theory" above but "theories" may, in fact, be of two different kinds. The first kind is a scientific theory or hypothesis which aims to categorise all possible types of phenomena of a particular kind as determined by the coding purpose, such as all phonemes in a particular language. We call coding schemes based on a scientific theory general coding schemes, whether consolidated or not. The second kind of theory is a pragmatic theory or hypothesis which merely aims to be complete in the sense of capturing all phenomena that happen to be relevant for a given coding purpose. Since a coding purpose may be nearly anything, such as the speech acts people generally use to agree on meeting dates and times [1], or the speech and pointing gesture combinations used to manipulate 2D geometrical shapes [14], the theory underlying coding purposes such as these might not stake any claim to scientific generality or depth of justification – at least not unless or until backed by deeper theory which might explain why these and only these types of phenomena could be used for some purpose. Admittedly, the distinction between scientific and pragmatic theory is thin in some cases. For instance, no existing scientific theory probably explains why English has exactly the set of phonemes it has. But at least our knowledge about English phonemes constitutes a stable scientific generalisation which can be applied in many different contexts. However, no matter which kind of theory is involved, coding aims at completeness relative to coding purpose.

2.2 Coding Scheme Semantics, Criteria

The second kind of information which must be included in a coding scheme is a set of criteria according to which each phenomenon (or each token) in the data can be determined to belong to a particular type among the types of phenomena acknowledged by the coding scheme. These criteria should be made perfectly explicit, clear, and unambiguous as part of the coding scheme representation. This is done by describing criteria for deciding to which type any token belongs and providing useful examples of tokens of each type. Otherwise, coding scheme users will have difficulty applying the coding scheme consistently and in the same way across coders because they will be missing guidance on how to classify the phenomena observed in the data. Coding scheme semantics development is hard work and cannot be done too well.

2.3 Meta-data

The third kind of coding scheme information is meta-data information on the scheme itself. There is no general standard for such meta-data although various initiatives are working towards standardisation, such as the Dublin Core Metadata Initiative (http://-dublincore.org) and the Open Language Archives Community (OLAC) (http://www.-language-archives.org/OLAC/metadata.html). However, it is easy to illustrate the kinds of meta-data that are normally required as well as which additional kinds might be needed in a particular case: What is the coding purpose? Is that a rather unique purpose or could the coding scheme be used more generally, for which other purposes, for instance? Who created the scheme? When? Using which corpora? How well-tested is it, i.e., on how many and/or which corpora has it been applied and with which results? How reliable is it, has inter-coder agreement been measured and with which results? How difficult is the coding scheme to use, are there any specific problems that should be mentioned, how is it applied in coding practice, how much training/domain experience does it require, are codings from two independent coders needed for obtaining reasonably reliable results? Has annotation based on the coding scheme been automated and with which results compared to human coders? Is the coding scheme underpinned by scientific theory, which theory? How (well) is the scheme documented? How can it be accessed, i.e., at which Internet site, by emailing who, is it for-free, are there any conditions on its use? Whom to contact with questions about the coding scheme? Are there any coding tools that could be used? Are coded corpora available, how, under which conditions? Etc.

2.4 Consolidated Coding Schemes

We can now define a consolidated coding scheme. A consolidated coding scheme is one which has been proved reliable for coding a representative variety of corpora under reasonably achievable conditions to be stated, such as coder experience and training, coding procedure, generic kind of corpora, etc. A consolidated coding scheme may or may not be underpinned by deep scientific theory. It may also have problems, such a inherent difficulties in classifying tokens of particular types, as long as these are well described in the coding manual. In other words, we cannot require, at this stage of coding verbal and non-verbal communication, that coding schemes termed 'consolidated' are perfect in all respects.

Interestingly, the fact that a coding scheme can be underpinned by scientific theory does not, by itself, guarantee that the coding scheme is a consolidated one. Data coding may constitute a hard test of the theory underlying the scheme. Scientific theories themselves need justification and they sometimes compete in accounting for phenomena in a particular field. Attempts at data coding based on each of them may contribute to selecting the theory which best accounts for the data. We saw that ourselves some years ago when we developed a coding scheme for communication problems in spoken dialogue. Having done that, we compared the results with Grice's theory of conversational implicature and its typology of cooperativity issues that may arise in spoken dialogue [8]. In the literature at the time, the scope of Grice's theory had been subject to various proposed reductions but none of the critics had raised serious doubt with respect to the theory's validity for human-human shared-goal dialogue, i.e., dialogue in which the interlocutors try to cooperatively solve a problem. Nonetheless, we found that Grice's theory had to be extended in order to account for the types of phenomena which we found in our data from human-computer shared-goal dialogue [3].

Despite the possible imperfections of consolidated coding schemes, it is a great advantage for the coder to use a consolidated coding scheme which comes with the three kinds of information described above. The advantage is that you can simply follow the coding manual and code the data in the expectation that that's it. The alternative of using an unconsolidated coding scheme may carry a range of implications depending on what's in the data. At the very least, the coding task becomes the double one of (i) coding the data and (ii) testing the coding scheme. If the test turns out reasonably well, you will have accomplished two things, i.e., coded your data and contributed, however slightly, to making the coding scheme a consolidated one, possibly contributing useful observations for its coding manual as well. But if the test fails, for instance because a large fraction of the phenomena in your corpus cannot be coded using the scheme, you are left with no coded data and the choice of whether to (iii) look for an alternative coding scheme that might work better, (iv) become a coding scheme co-developer who tries to extend the scheme to cover your corpus, (v) try to develop an alternative coding scheme from scratch, or give up coding the data, which may not be an option because other work depends on the planned annotation.

However, in order to use an existing coding scheme – consolidated or not – you need to find it first, which may not be easy since there are no catalogues available.

3   Previous Work

Some years ago, we were involved in carrying out global surveys of natural interactivity data, coding schemes and coding tools in EU-projects MATE, NITE and ISLE. MATE made a survey of annotation schemes for aspects of spoken dialogue, e.g., prosody and dialogue acts [11]. NITE described a number of gesture, facial expression and cross-modality schemes [18], drawing heavily on ISLE which had reviewed 21 different coding schemes of which 7 concerned facial expression possibly combined with speech, and 14 concerned gesture possibly accompanied by speech [12]. In two other reports, ISLE reviewed multimodal data resources [13] and coding tools [5].

In the period since around the turn of the century, others have looked at verbal and non-verbal communication coding schemes and tools as well. Some did this as part of comparing their own coding scheme to the state of the art or related schemes, e.g., [16], or while looking for a tool to use, e.g., [6]. Others did it as part of surveying multimodality and natural interaction without specifically focusing on annotation [7]. Other examples are the following. Until around 2002 the Linguistic Data Consortium (LDC) maintained a web page with brief descriptions of linguistic annotation schemes and tools (http://www.ldc.upenn.edu/annotation/). Michael Kipp, the developer of the Anvil multimodal annotation tool, maintains a page listing users of Anvil (http://www.dfki.de/~kipp/anvil/users.html). This list mentions various coding schemes which are being applied using Anvil.

To our knowledge, however, there has not been any large-scale initiative in surveying multimodal and natural interaction annotation schemes since ISLE. Maybe the task has simply grown too complex as will be discussed in the next section.

4   Current Trends

While MATE looked at aspects of spoken dialogue annotation, ISLE focused on gesture-only annotation, gesture combined with speech, facial expression-only and facial expression combined with speech. Multimodal annotation, more generally, is a vast area. An interest in any combination of two or more communication modalities requires a multimodal annotation scheme or some cross-modal annotation to see the interactions between the modalities. This adds up to very many possible combinations, such as, e.g., speech and hand gesture, head and eye brow movements, lip movements and speech, gaze and speech, speech, body posture and facial expression, to mention but a few, and it would take considerable effort to compile an overview of the annotation schemes that have been proposed in recent years for all possible combinations, especially since activity in the field would seem to continue to increase. We discuss the increasing activity and some project examples in the following where we also briefly mention consolidation and standardisation efforts.

4.1 Increasing Coding Activity

Since natural interactivity and multimodality gained popularity and became buzz-words in the late 1990s, many initiatives have addressed the construction of increa-singly sophisticated systems incorporating various aspects of human communication. This typically requires data resources and annotation of phenomena which in many cases have not been studied in great detail before, implying a strong need for new coding schemes with a heavy emphasis on multimodal or cross-modal markup.

4.2 Project Examples

In recent years, several large-scale projects have been launched in focused areas of natural interactivity and multimodality, such as emotion or multi-party interaction. We will look at multimodal corpus annotation work done in a couple of these projects and stress that several other projects could have been mentioned instead.

The European HUMAINE Network addresses emotion and human-machine interaction (http://emotion-research.net/). Researchers in the network have proposed EARL (http://emotion-research.net/earl, the HUMAINE Emotion Annotation and Representation Language), an XML-based language for representing and annotating emotions. The language is aimed for use in corpus annotation as well as for recognis-ing and generating emotions. Figure 1 shows an example of audio-visual annotation from the EARL website. The annotation can be done using, e.g., Anvil (Section 3).

```
<emotion category="pleasure" probability="0.4" start="0.5"
end="1.02"/>
<emotion modality="voice" category="pleasure" probability="0.9"
start="0.5" end="1.02"/>
<emotion modality="face" category="neutral" probability="0.5"
start="0" end="2"/>
<emotion modality="text" probability="0.4" start="0.5" end="1.02"
arousal="-0.5" valence="0.1"/>
```

Fig. 1. EARL markup

Face-to-face communication is multimodal and may include emotions in one or several participants. Magno Caldognetto et al. [15] use – within the framework of three different projects - the Multimodal Score annotation scheme implemented in Anvil to synchronously mark up speech, prosody, gesture, facial (mouth, gaze, eyes, eyebrows), and head and body posture in order to facilitate analysis of cross-modal interactions. The investigation aims at better understanding the elements of human communication. Figure 2 only shows part of this enormous coding representation which, in fact, represents several dozens of coding schemes at various stages of devel-opment combined into a single coding representation. The top tier shows the common timeline followed by three tiers presenting the speech signal, the words spoken and their segmentation. Then follows the pitch and intensity aspects of prosody (5 tiers each). Since the right hand does nothing, this tier is greyed out whereas the left hand's behaviour is described in 7 tiers, the last of which relates the gesture to what is being spoken at the same time. The gesture type (Tier 2) is labelled "other" which is typical

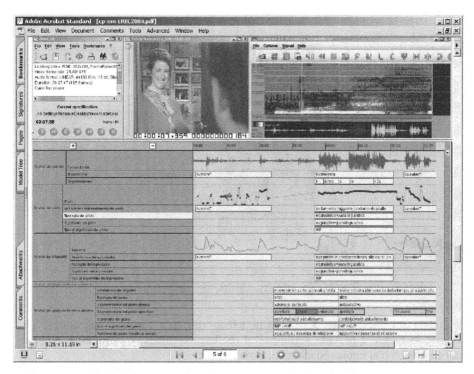

Fig. 2. Multimodal Score annotation in Anvil

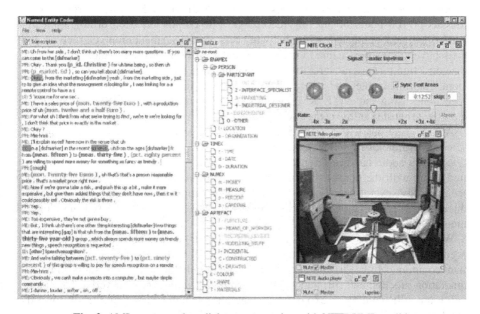

Fig. 3. AMI corpus spoken dialogue annotation with NITE XML toolkit

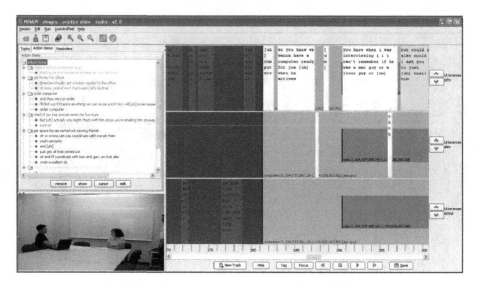

Fig. 4. Meeting topic segmentation annotation with Nomos

of coding schemes under development which still lack complete semantics. The codings in Figure 2 provide a glimpse of the huge complexity of future codings of human-human and human-machine communication.

The European AMI (Augmented Multiparty Interaction) project (http://www.amiproject.org) is one among several large projects in the area of multi-party meeting interaction. One project result is the AMI video Meeting Corpus which consists of 100 hours of meeting recordings. The corpus has been orthographically transcribed and annotated with dialogue acts, topic segmentation, extractive and abstractive summaries, named entities, the types of head gesture, hand gesture, and gaze direction that are most related to communicative intention, movement around the room, emotional state, and where heads are located in the video frames. Markup has been done using the NITE XML toolkit (http://www.ltg.ed.ac.uk/NITE/). Figure 3 shows a screenshot of the coding representation.

A similar corpus is the ICSI Meeting Corpus collected at International Computer Science Institute at Berkeley, CA, which contains 75 meeting recordings (audio and video). The audio has been transcribed at word level and the transcription is distributed along with the corpus (http://www.idiap.ch/mmm/corpora/icsi). The corpus has been used by several people who have annotated various phenomena, such as hierarchical topic segmentation and action items, see, e.g., [9] who have used the Nomos annotation software (Figure 4) [17].

What this small list of projects illustrates is that (i) corpus annotation groundwork is going on in order to better understand multimodal and cross-modal aspects of human communication; (ii) annotation tools are highly desirable for supporting the annotation process; and (iii) annotation schemes for verbal and non-verbal communication are still often at an exploratory stage although steps are being taken towards standardisation, common formats, and consolidation as briefly discussed next.

4.3 Towards Consolidation and Standards

For most multimodal and natural interactive areas there are no standards and few consolidated annotation schemes. At the same time it is acknowledged that consolidated coding schemes, standardisation, and common formats could significantly facilitate analysis and data reuse. The problem is that it is not an easy task to consolidate annotation schemes in the areas we are talking about but there are ongoing attempts in this direction. An example is the W3C incubator group on emotions (Emotion XG) (http://www.w3.org/2005/Incubator/emotion/) proposed by the HUMAINE Network (Section 4.2). As there is no standard annotation scheme or markup language for emotions, the purpose of the Emotion XG is to "discuss and propose scientifically valid representations of those aspects of emotional states that appear to be relevant for a number of use cases. The group will condense these considerations into a formal draft specification" for an emotion annotation and representation language. Clearly, the scope of the planned result will very much depend of the collective representativity of emotional behaviour in general of the use cases selected.

Another example is the International Standards Organisation (ISO) TC37/SC4 group on Language Resources Management (http://www.tc37sc4.org). Focus is on language resources and aspects of their standardisation. To this end, the Linguistic Annotation Framework (LAF) has been established [10]. It aims to provide a standard infrastructure for representing language resources and their annotation. The underlying abstract data model builds on a clear separation of structure and contents. The goal is to achieve an internationally accepted standard that will enable far more flexible use, reuse, comparison, and evaluation of language resources than is the case today.

It is worth noting that, in both cases just mentioned, the aim is a theoretically well-founded, consolidated or even standardised representation and annotation language rather than a particular coding scheme with a fixed set of tags. We agree that, in many cases, this is the right level of abstraction to aim for at this stage given that (i) theoretically complete coding schemes are still a long way off in many areas of multimodal annotation of verbal and non-verbal communication, and (ii) in some cases completeness is not even theoretically feasible because of the open-ended nature of what is being coded, such as human action or iconic gesture. Common formats will facilitate the construction and use of common tools and the reuse/further use of existing data resources never mind the theoretical completeness of the coding schemes supported.

5 Future Challenges

We have discussed the notion of an annotation scheme, briefly presented previous work on annotation schemes and tools, and discussed current trends in coding verbal and non-verbal communication. The work described suggests that we are to a great extent exploring new land where general and/or consolidated coding schemes often do not exist. However, as we have said far too little about what lies ahead, we will try to add some more glimpses in the following.

At first glance, the question of what we annotate when coding verbal and non-verbal communication might appear to have a rather straightforward answer: we code all the different kinds of observable behaviour which humans use to communicate intended meaning to other humans and/or machines, including speech, facial expression and gaze, gesture, head and body posture, and body action as part of the communication. However, this answer is radically incomplete because (i) humans communicate more than deliberately intended meaning and (ii) machines are capable of perceiving information that humans cannot perceive. For instance, (i) our voice may unintentionally reveal our mood, or (ii) bio-sensing is becoming an important source of information for computers during interaction. Moreover, (iii) one-way "communication" is common among humans and is emerging between humans and machines as well, such as in surveillance and friendly observation aimed at learning more about the user. In Figure 5 from [4], we replace "communication" by the more inclusive "information presentation and exchange" and propose a taxonomy of the many different types of the latter which annotators may have to deal with.

A second way in which to put into perspective future challenges in annotating verbal and non-verbal information presentation and exchange is to consider the media and modalities involved. Modality theory [2, 4] provides an exhaustive taxonomy of the large numbers of possible modalities in the three media of light/vision, sound/hearing or audition, and mechanical impact/touch sensing or haptics. Basically, they are all relevant to annotation and their combinatorics is staggering, as Figure 2 is beginning to illustrate. Bio-sensing is becoming important as well, and even smell (olfaction) and taste (gustation) should be kept in mind even though they are not (yet) being much used by machines and normally don't play any significant role in human-human information exchange.

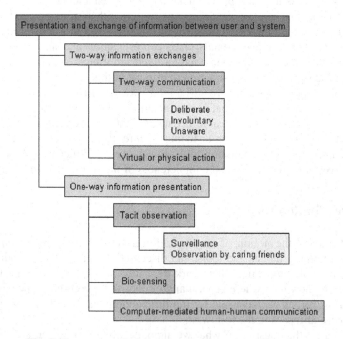

Fig. 5. Taxonomy of information representation and exchange

We need a third typology as well, orthogonal to the one in Figure 5 and to the modality taxonomy, which describes the different possible levels of annotation from low-level, non-semantic, such as phonemes and mouth shapes, through non-semantic structures, such as the phases of some types of gesture, to basic semantics, such as words or smiles, composite semantics, cross-modal semantic combinations, and the semantics of global personal states, such as emotion or cognition, see [4] for a proposal. In addition, there is a strong need for standardised concepts and terminology as even basic terms like 'gesture' have no agreed definition.

Although very different, all three typologies just mentioned as well as the fact that even basic terms lack common definitions, suggest the same conclusion. It is that there is a long way to go before we have anything like a comprehensive and systematic grasp of how to annotate full human-human and human-machine presentation and exchange of information in context, and before we have general and consolidated coding schemes for more than a small fraction of what humans do when they communicate and observe one another during communication.

Acknowledgements

This paper was written as part of the collaboration in COST Action 2102 Cross-Modal Analysis of Verbal and Non-verbal Communication (CAVeNC). We gratefully acknowledge the support.

References

1. Alexandersson, J., Buschbeck-Wolf, B., Fujinami, T., Kipp, M., Koch, S., Maier, E., Reithinger, N., Schmitz, B., Siegel, M.: Dialogue Acts in VERBMOBIL-2, 2nd edn. Report 226, Saarbrücken, Germany (1998)
2. Bernsen, N.O.: Multimodality in Language and Speech Systems - From Theory to Design Support Tool. In: Granström, B., House, D., Karlsson, I. (eds.) Multimodality in Language and Speech Systems, pp. 93–148. Kluwer Academic Publishers, Dordrecht (2002)
3. Bernsen, N.O., Dybkjær, H., Dybkjær, L.: Cooperativity in Human-Machine and Human-Human Spoken Dialogue. Discourse Processes 21(2), 213–236 (1996)
4. Bernsen, N.O., Dybkjær, L.: Multimodal Usability (to appear)
5. Dybkjær, L., Berman, S., Kipp, M., Olsen, M.W., Pirrelli, V., Reithinger, N., Soria, C.: Survey of Existing Tools, Standards and User Needs for Annotation of Natural Interaction and Multimodal Data. ISLE Deliverable D11.1 (January 2001)
6. Garg, S., Martinovski, B., Robinson, S., Stephan, J., Tetreault, J., Traum, D.: Evaluation of Transcription and Annotation Tools for a Multi-modal, Multi-party Dialogue Corpus. In: Proceedings of LREC, pp. 2163–2166 (2004)
7. Gibbon, D., Mertins, I., Moore, R. (eds.): Handbook of Multimodal and Spoken Dialogue Systems. Kluwer Academic Publishers, Dordrecht (2000)
8. Grice, P.: Logic and conversation. In: Cole, P., Morgan, J.L. (eds.) Syntax and Semantics. Speech Acts, vol. 3, pp. 41–58. Academic Press, New York (1975) Reprinted in Grice, P.: Studies in the Way of Words, Harvard University Press, Cambridge, MA (1989)

9. Gruenstein, A., Niekrasz, J., Purver, M.: Meeting Structure Annotation: Data and Tools. In: Proceedings of the Sixth SIGdial Workshop on Discourse and Dialogue, Lisbon, Portugal, pp. 117–127 (2005)
10. Ide, N., Romary, L.: Towards International Standards for Language Resources. In: Dybkjær, L., Hemsen, H., Minker, W. (eds.) Evaluation of Text and Speech Systems. Text, Speech and Language Technology Series, vol. 37, pp. 263–284. Springer, Heidelberg (2007)
11. Klein, M., Bernsen, N.O., Davies, S., Dybkjær, L., Garrido, J., Kasch, H., Mengel, A., Pirrelli, V., Poesio, M., Quazza, S., Soria, C.: Supported Coding Schemes. MATE Deliverable D1.1 (July 1998)
12. Knudsen, M.W., Martin, J.-C., Dybkjær, L., Ayuso, M.J.M: N., Bernsen, N. O., Carletta, J., Kita, S., Heid, U., Llisterri, J., Pelachaud, C., Poggi, I., Reithinger, N., van ElsWijk, G., Wittenburg, P.: Survey of Multimodal Annotation Schemes and Best Practice. ISLE Deliverable D9.1 (2002)
13. Knudsen, M.W., Martin, J.-C., Dybkjær, L., Berman, S., Bernsen, N.O., Choukri, K., Heid, U., Mapelli, V., Pelachaud, C., Poggi, I., van ElsWijk, G., Wittenburg, P.: Survey of NIMM Data Resources, Current and Future User Profiles, Markets and User Needs for NIMM Resources. ISLE Deliverable D8.1 (2002)
14. Landragin, F.: Visual Perception, Language and Gesture: A Model for their Understanding in Multimodal Dialogue Systems. Signal Processing 86(12), 3578–3595 (2006)
15. Magno Caldognetto, E., Poggi, I., Cosi, P., Cavicchio, F., Merola, G.: Multimodal Score: An ANVIL Based Annotation Scheme for Multimodal Audio-Video Analysis. In: Proceedings of LREC Workshop on Multimodal Corpora, Models of Human Behaviour for the Specification and Evaluation of Multimodal Input and Output Interfaces, Lisbon, Portugal, pp. 29–33 (2004)
16. Martell, C.: FORM. In: van Kuppevelt, J., Dybkjær, L., Bernsen, N.O. (eds.) Advances in Natural Multimodal Dialogue Systems. Text, Speech and Language Technology, vol. 30, pp. 79–95. Springer, Heidelberg (2005)
17. Niekrasz, J.: NOMOS: A Semantic Web Software Framework for Multimodal Corpus Annotation. In: Renals, S., Bengio, S., Fiscus, J.G. (eds.) MLMI 2006. LNCS, vol. 4299, Springer, Heidelberg (2006)
18. Serenari, M., Dybkjær, L., Heid, U., Kipp, M., and Reithinger, N.: Survey of Existing Gesture, Facial Expression, and Cross-Modality Coding Schemes. NITE Deliverable D2.1 (September 2002)

Presenting in Style by Virtual Humans

Zsófia Ruttkay

Dept. If Information Technology, Pázmány Péter Catholic University, Budapest, Hungary
Dept. of Computer Science, University of Twente, The Netherlands
Zsofia.Ruttkay@cs.utwente.nl

Abstract. The paper addresses the issue of making Virtual Humans unique and typical of some (social or ethnical) group, by endowing them with style. First a conceptual framework of defining style is discussed, identifying how style is manifested in speech and nonverbal communication. Then the GESTYLE language is introduced, making it possible to define the style of a VH in terms of Style Dictionaries, assigning non-deterministic choices to express certain meanings by nonverbal signals and speech. It is possible to define multiple sources of style and maintain conflicts and dynamical changes. GESTYLE is a text markup language which makes it possible to generate speech and accompanying facial expressions and hand gestures automatically, by declaring the style of the VH and using meaning tags in the text. GESTYLE can be coupled with different low-level TTS and animation engines.

Keywords: Virtual humans, nonverbal behavior, multimodal communication, style, markup language.

1 Introduction

In every-day life, we perceive and comment on the style of each other. We talk about an 'arrogant style', 'a style being not appropriate for the situation', or simply a 'person with style'. Though these statements do not require further explanation, we fall short when trying to establish a definition of style. The Merriam-Webster Online Dictionary[1] describes three meanings:

1. a distinctive manner of expression (as in writing or speech) <writes with more attention to *style* than to content> <the flowery *style* of 18th century prose>;
2. a distinctive manner or custom of behaving or conducting oneself <the formal *style* of the court> <his *style* is abrasive>;
3. a particular manner or technique by which something is done, created, or performed <a unique *style* of horseback riding> <the classical *style* of dance>.

The above three meanings, though not entirely distinct, suggest that in every-day life language usage, behavior and the subtle details of performance are the three aspects of style, as long as they are distinctive, characteristic of the person. These aspects can

---

[1] http://www.m-w.com/

A. Esposito et al. (Eds.): Verbal and Nonverbal Commun. Behaviours, LNAI 4775, pp. 23–36, 2007.

also be identified in Raymond Queneau's famous work, "Exercises in Style" [38]. In this ingenious literary work, the French author takes a few-line banal story happening in a crowded bus, and tells it in 99 exercises, each in different style. The exercises differ not only in language usage, but in what is commented upon in the monologues, and how the objective facts get interpreted. In addition, while reading the pieces, the look and the acting expressions get almost to life. This can be the reason why the texts made a success on the stage and on the screen too.

Another example of the power of style is "Creature comforts", an Oscar-winning animation film [1], in which animals talk and gesture in the well-recognizable style of some human groups (of certain nationality, social status). We conducted a research on comparing the gestures used in this film and by real people. Our exploratory study involved the analysis of a segment by the leopard in the film and the presentation of the same text by humans [40]. It was concluded that:

- in the clay animation film, more hand gestures, and with bigger amplitudes were used, in line with the exaggeration of the extrovert personality of the leopard and the fictional, artistic medium of the clay animation;
- the dictionary of the used hand gestures was similar;
- people could remember and reproduce easily the more expressive gesturing of the leopard.

Thus the style is a source of information on the identity of the speaker, as well as of variety and joy (or annoyance) when communicating with real people. Using the proper style may be even decisive in the success of the communication. Nowadays one can find a multitude of printed and electronic resources on teaching the relevance and best practice of style in business, international peace keeping missions, patient-nurse relationship, etc.

The complexity of the problem is manifested, e.g. in the communicative act of greeting. Factors like culture, gender, age, personality, physical state and mood of the speaker, as well as characteristics of the situation (level of noise/visibility, meeting in a hurry or while taking a stroll) all contribute if the greeting will be verbal and/or non-verbal, if head nod and/or handshakes will be used and in what way: who takes the initiative, how long and firmly the hands are kept, etc. What makes the usage of style more complicated is that the different "sources of style" often describe conflicting behavior: in certain social occasions the style code may be different from the one a person follows normally. It is also a matter of personality and several other factors how these conflicts are resolved.

Style could play an equally powerful role when one is conversing with a virtual character or with a robot. This assumption is justified by the general "computers are social actors" metaphor, and the several subtle studies showing that such factors as the ethnicity and the personality (introvert/extravert) of a synthetic character – even if manifested in a simple, static feature – do have consequences on the subjective judgment and objective performance of the user [24].

In this paper we report on our own work on endowing virtual humans (VHs) [33], or as also called, embodied conversational agents (ECAs) [5] or life-like characters [37] with style.

First we give an overview of related work on VHs with personality, emotions and some variety of nonverbal behavior; and discuss markup-based scripting languages to control their multimodal behavior. Then in Chapter 3 we focus on the definition of style. Chapter 4 is devoted to the computational model of style, and of our GESTYLE language to declare the style of a VH from different aspects, which then is used to resolve meaning markup tags in the text to be uttered by the character. The usage of GESTYLE is illustrated by two examples. In-depth discussion of the language is to be found in [26]. We also developed a markup language for emotional speech, to express in a personal or culture-dependent way emotions, emphasis, hesitation which can be seen as extension of GESTYLE [47], and will be used in the examples. Finally we sum up our results and discuss further research scenarios.

2 Related Work

There has been extensive research going on to study the affective power of VHs, by endowing them with the capability of showing emotions [12]. There are more and more subtle descriptions of the bodily expressions of single or mixed emotions, manifested in the different modalities such as facial expressions [4,10], hand gestures [6, 14, 15] and of course in speech (for an overview, see [47]). There have been computational models to update the emotional state of the VH, devised based on psychological models and using AI frameworks like e.g. his believes, intentions and desires (BDI cognitive model) and his encounters with the inanimate world and other VHs or a real person interlocutor, which is a 'state of the mind' matter. Subtle issues like the impact of social role [36], culture [9, 28] and personality [3] have been addressed independently. Non-verbal signals have been used, in the first place, to turn VHs more expressive, believable and engaging [6, 21, 22, 29, 42]. The fact that people react to VHs as they do to real humans is yet a manifestation of the CASA (Computers Are Social Actors) paradigm by Nass and Reeves [39].

Up to recently, the presentation has been fully deterministic, and has been a matter of a low-level 'animation engine', or left for a professional animator. As of modeling and controlling the subtle characteristics of facial expressions and gestures in order to achieve variety, individuality or expressivity, Perlin [30, 31] demonstrated the importance of non-repetitiveness, by using some random selection criteria and noise to generate different instances of face and body motion of the character. Badler and his colleagues have developed EMOTE [7], a computational framework to modify expressiveness of hand, body and face gestures of VHs [4], which was followed by a parameterized, generative approach for hand gestures [14]. In [41] we have defined a constraint-based framework which allows the conceptual definition and on-the-fly generation of variants of facial expressions.

The traditional [45], as well as the computer animation world it has been recognized how important it is to 'add style' to (captured or synthesized) motion. In case of using motion capture data, several works have using some signal processing methods to retarget 'style' from one captured motion to another. E.g. if a drunken walk has been recorded, then somebody else's captured motion could be turned into 'drunken' by applying the details of the 'drunkenness' in the first motion to the second one [16]. Another direction is to apply 'cartoon' motion style to realistic mocap or video recorded motion [49]. These works have been looking at style as characteristics of motion manner, manifested in the time functions of motion.

With the development of the VH technology, the need arose to have high-level control mechanisms, particularly, XML-based markup languages, to 'instruct' the VH what to present, in speech and with nonverbal gestures [44], VHML [46], APML [8], RRL[32], CML and AML [2], MURML [20]. Each of these representation languages act either at the discourse and communicative functions level (APML, RRL, CML, MURML) or at the signal level (AML, VHML). In the first category one can use markup tags like "emphasis", "get attention" while tags at the signal level may be "smile", "turn head left". In each case the semantics of the control tags are given implicitly, expressed in terms of the parameters (MPEG-4 FAP or BAP, muscle contraction, joint angles and the like) used for generating the animation of the expressive facial or hand gestures. They provide a direct link between what is often called the *mind* and the *body* of the agent. In an ongoing joint work, one single, powerful enough markup language for behavior is being developed [19]. Even in this framework, the mind and body issues are taken care of two components, each with own markup tags and mechanisms, and there is no place to define nonverbal behavioral habits.

Until now none of the mark-up languages has addressed the *style* of the agent. In our view, style is a necessary additional level to be introduced to connect the communicative and the signal layer, allowing the explicit definition and manipulation of the mapping from the communicative tags to the signal tags. In this paper we address how the higher level information of the character (such as culture, age) and of the situation (such as characteristics of the listener, physical circumstances in the environment) affect the choice and the performance of behaviors.

3   Styled Virtual Humans

The development of style for VHs requires tackling the following tasks:

- Identify aspects and parameters of style in human-human interaction.
- Provide a model to deal with conflicting style codes, as well as with the dynamical effects of the situation.
- Use these findings to define a language for style of VHs.
- Identify characteristics of gesturing and provide appropriate parameters to generate gestures which manifest certain aspects of the style.

We have designed and implemented GESTYLE, a hierarchical representation language that can express all the above aspects for creating multi-modal styled VHs, bridging the gap between our earlier work on the highest and lowest levels of nonverbal communication.

3.1   What Decides the Style?

We define style as the *typical way* of a person *expressing* himself. By typical we mean two things:

- distinctive, making the person 'recognizable';
- is characteristic of the person's behavior, in some probabilistic sense: in most of the cases, the person will react in this distinctive manner.

By multimodal behavior, one conveys some meaning, in a conscious or unconscious way [35]. No question, the verbal channel plays a major role in communication, and style is manifested very much in language usage. We focus on the nonverbal channels, and limit the discussion of style to the usage of nonverbal signals: gaze, facial and hand gestures and posture. These, though harder to control consciously, contribute much to the overall impression of a person. In many cases, nonverbal signals extend or even substitute verbal messages.

The *meaning* of a nonverbal signal may concern some factual knowledge about the world (form, time, location of objects), express emotions and cognitive state of the speaker, punctuate speech or regulate the flow of conversation (back-channeling, turn taking) or stand for concepts and acts (e.g. greeting by hand-wave, showing victory) [18, 23, 34].

The mapping of meaning to nonverbal behaviors is many to many: for a single meaning, there are different alternatives expressing it, and the very same nonverbal behavior may have different meanings, depending on the context. For instance, emphasis may be expressed by: eyebrow raise, head nod, hand beat, or a combination of these signals. On the other hand, a raised eyebrow and direct gaze may express emphasis, surprise or waiting for the partner to speak.

One's nonverbal communication repertoire is learnt as a child, similarly to how mother-tongue is learnt (though there is much professional debate in behavioral psychology on to what extent is gesturing innate, and how it is learnt). But just as one may acquire multiple languages, one may learn to nonverbal communications protocols which may be 'dialects' of the basic *cultural conventions* valid in specific *social settings* (e.g. business-like meeting, or flirting) or *subgroups* (e.g. slang of teenagers), or may be of another culture (e.g. body language of Japanese). The *personality* of the speaker influences both the usage of modalities and the subtle details of a nonverbal gesture. E.g. a shy, introvert person conveys less nonverbal signals, uses less space around him, and e.g. gaze contacts are shorter. There are some *biologically determined* characteristics as well, like handedness, the muscle intensity (less with age, or with increased weight). The availability of affordances of the person's bodily means (e.g. with hands full, you cannot greet by handshake) and of his environment (e.g. visibility conditions).

Finally, there may be characteristics of a person's communication which are totally *idiosyncratic* and cannot be related to any of the dimensions above. The way of performing a common gesture can be typical of an individual.

Summing up, there are multiple factors which contribute to the actual style manifested. An extrovert young person, when at a job interview, may do his best to behave as expected in a professional situation. He may try consciously not to betray his nervousness or uncertainty by nonverbal signals like drumming with fingers or tapping feet. Or, in course of a friendly discussion he may forget about the official setting and behave more according to his own, natural style. Thus the different aspects of style may prescribe *conflicting behavior protocols*, and it may vary with time which aspect will be the most dominant.

3.2 Style Displayed in Nonverbal Behavior

The nonverbal behavior of a person can be described along three dimensions: *what* gesture repertoire one uses, *when* one uses gestures, and *how* a gesture is performed.

Repertoire. A gesture repertoire is the set of "known/used" gestures of a person. For a single meaning, different alternative gestures may be used. Some people have a richer repertoire of gestures than others. This is due partly to cultural factors (the repertoire of symbolic gestures in Italy, for instance, is presumably wider than in Great Britain), partly to personality and partly to individual factors.

Usage. Some people use gestures only to substitute words, others gesture a lot, almost constantly, using hands often as redundant means of conveying meaning. Possible motivations to be redundant are the low cognitive capacity of the listener, or the noise in the verbal and/or visual channels, or the high motivation of the speaker to be understood/noticed.

Performance. The last, but not least stylistic difference is in the motion characteristics, that is the way of performing gestures. A hand gesture can be expressed in terms of some formational parameters [14, 43], like handshape, wrist orientation, start- and end-location, path traced by the wrist, and movement characteristics between the two locations, expressed in terms of speed and smoothness profile. While some parameters are determined by the semantics of the gesture (that is, these characteristics are essential to convey the meaning), others, determining the final movement, are free to manifest the style. Specifically, the style is expressed by the following *characteristics of the motion*:

amplitude: the spatial size of the gesture, in terms of the extreme positions;

smoothness: the function describing the motion of the hand along a path may be smooth or jerky;

tempo: slow or fast.

4 The GESTYLE Language to Declare Style

For designing and controlling the gesturing behavior of synthetic humans, we designed the GESTYLE language which can express all factors contributing to the non-verbal style as described in the previous section. GESTYLE has constructs to express the identity of the VH, the meanings to be conveyed in the text to be spoken, the temporal changes in emotional state and communicative affordances available. The final nonverbal behavior is determined by translating the indicated meanings to a (may be multimodal) gesture and deciding its performance characteristics; taking into account the protocols corresponding to the static characteristics, the modifications enforced by temporal changes in the situation and the speech tempo.

The CHARACTER MARKUP language defines the virtual character's *static* characteristics, *culture* (having values of ethnic group or sub-group of an ethnic group like "educated British" or "Napoletanian") *personality* (e.g. extrovert/introvert), *social role* (having value as profession and/or social status), *age* and *sex* to capture biological aspects, and eventual *individual characteristics* like handedness, special gesture usage. This information may be considered invariant during the period the agent is conversing.

The SITUATION MARKUP specifies a situation, by setting dynamical aspects of the speaker (mood, physical state, momentarily available communicative modalities) and the environment (characteristics of the addressee, the social relation between the agent and the addressee, the objects in the environment,...) Some situation characteristics (like those of the listener or the location) may be set for a certain time interval (even the entire duration of the conversation), while emotional aspects may be triggered by an event, an action or people [27].

The COMMUNICATIVE MARKUP tags are used to annotate the text with information the agent desires to communicate (consciously or unconsciously); this information will (potentially) be accompanied by some gesture. The information may be about the world (characteristics of objects), the speaker's state, the discourse state. Accordingly, these markups are tags like *emphasis, enumeration, size big, greeting, get-attention* (at the beginning of a turn taking).

The GESTURE MARKUP specifies a gesturing sequence, by specifying what gestures are to be expressed at certain points of time: raised eyebrow, head nod, wave right hand, etc. Some parameters may be numerical or qualitative (short/long duration, big/small amplitude), and specific for a gesture, like amplitude, duration, start/end time, and motion-manner. Time parameters may be left partially undefined, assuming synchrony to the final speech timing.

In course of compiling the text marked-up with the first three types of tags, the final, lowest-level form is the text with particular GESTURE MARKUP tags. However, it is also possible to insert GESTURE MARKUP tags explicitly to the text, in order to define characteristics of the gestures of a given modality (e.g. to make the motion of the right-hand slow) for some time interval, or even to overwrite or extend the generated gestures.

In order to 'run' the multimodal behavior produced by GESTYLE, an interface must be present translating the low-level and fully specified GESTURE MARKUP tags to the control parameters of the animation player. These parameters may be any animation parameters (e.g. muscle contraction for facial physically-based model, joint angle for articulated body). We have used interfaces to MPEG-4 facial animation parameters [17] and/or MPEG-4 body animation parameters with H-Anim standards [13], depending on the body model in question.

The character and the situation defining parameters may provide complementary entries (e.g. using specific gestures as a weather reporter), but may result in conflicting values for gesturing characteristics. In GESTYLE, there is a built-in default preference for the different high-level parameters (e.g. personal is preferred over professional, which is preferred over cultural). However, this may be overwritten by giving the preferences explicitly, by using a partial ordering of preferences, for details see [24].

4.1 The Definition of Multimodal Gestures

A single-modal *basic gesture* involves only one, elementary body part (e.g. the eye, the mouth, the right arm). The basic gestures may be combined to single-modal composite gestures, which involve a single body part like head, face, hands or trunk. The *single-modal gestures* can be composed into *multimodal* gestures. A composite gesture is defined as the combination of other gestures using two operators: for *parallel combination* (with the possibility for subtle timing synchronization); for *sequential concatenation*.

The formulation of basic hand gesture is based on defining arm configuration (elbow and shoulder joints), wrist orientation and hand shape. For facial gestures, we use the common definitions of emotional and cognitive facial expressions.

4.2 Gesture Dictionaries

A gesture dictionary encodes the characteristic of a single aspect of a character. Hence for a single character, there may be dictionaries used for his cultures (to encode Italian or British gesturing protocols), for different subgroups he belongs to (professional, geographical), for his personality (extrovert versus introvert), or even one for him as an individual person. In a dictionary, the characteristics of usage of gestures expressing the same communicative act by assigning probabilities to the individual gestures in a collection of *gesture dictionary* entries of the format:

$Meaning$ $(parameters_1,$ $Gesture_1,$ $P_1),$ $...$ $(parameters_n,Gesture_n,$ $P_n)$

In the above definition, $Gesture_1,...,$ $Gesture_n$ are gestures used to express the given *Meaning*, covering the alternatives of expressing the communicative function, and $P_1,...$ P_n are probabilities of using the specific gesture in this role. The optional gesture modifying *parameters* specify the motion characteristics of the gesture.

When making a VH gesture with style, a single gesture has to be selected form the possible alternatives, prescribed by different gesture dictionaries according to different CHARACTER specification parameters of the character. The choice may be further influenced by the current SITUATION parameters. The selection of a single gesture from (partly) conflicting choices can be done based on more or less sophisticated reasoning about the decisive factors. For each moment, a current gesture dictionary is composed from the ones prescribed by parameters in the CHARACTER and SITUATION definition. In the style definition reference is made to multiple gesture dictionaries, some with a weight factor and others in a strict tree-like hierarchy [26]. From these a single current dictionary is compiled by first including all communicative acts which only occur in strictly one of the source dictionaries. Then for conflicting prescriptions, that is meaning entries which occur in more then one dictionary, the hierarchy or the explicitly given weights are used to select one.

In the gesture generation stage, all the given CHARACTER, SITUATION and GESTURE parameters having an effect on the motion of a gesture which has to be produced will be taken into account. E.g. an introvert person will make less articulated gestures, while a typical asymmetric eyebrow-usage will have an effect on all facial signals involving eyebrows. The effect of high-level CHARACTER and SITUATION parameters on the motion characteristics are given in terms of low-level GESTURE parameters. Here possible conflicts are dealt with in a similar way as in the gesture selection stage. When nesting occurs, the locally defined, deepest GESTURE parameters override all other prescriptions.

4.3 Different and Varied Nondeterministic Behavior

A major feature of GESTYLE is that it does not provide exactly the same, repetitive behavior. The high-level tags of the CHARACTER MARKUP make it possible that just by changing a single attribute of personality, the very same text gets presented in an entirely different way, reminiscent of an introvert person. Hence by changing the header for different characters, we can produce an inter-personal variety.

The temporal changes (in emotions, in the physical circumstances) are taken care of by embracing certain parts of the text by SITUATION tags, and thus realizing changes in the basic presentation style.

Last but not least, the behavior generated by GESTYLE is non-repetitive. The very same marked-up text will be translated to slightly variant multimodal behavior, due to the probabilistic nature of assigning a meaning tag to some multimodal gesture. We believe that this is very reminiscent requirement for life-likeness, as opposed to repetitive, machine-like behavior. The latter can be perceived even if real-life motion captured, canned data is used, but the same one for each communicative function.

When GESTURE parameters are to be applied to the 'standard' definition of a gesture, they are expressed in terms of modifying certain constraints. E.g. the amplitude increase of the smile will be expressed as increase of the extreme positions. However, as in the definition of smile the limitation of application/release speed are incorporated, the increase of amplitude may result in increase of duration too. The constraint framework allows the generation of different instances of a gesture, including random variants, as different solutions for the same constraint satisfaction problem. That is, when a 'standard smile' is to be made, smiles with slight variations (allowed by the constraints defining the smile) will be produced.

4.4 Implementation and Examples

The GESTYLE language has been implemented in C++. We created two demonstrators, with appropriate gesture dictionaries. In the first one, CharToon is used as the low-level animation engine [25], and a piece from Shakespeare's Hamlet is presented by a 2d cartoon virtual Hamlet, in an extrovert or introvert style. The animation engine takes care of facial expressions, gaze and some hand gestures, rendered in a simple way in 2d.

The difference, resulting from changing a single attribute in the character declaration part (line 4 in Figure 1a) of the entire marked-up text, is to be noticed:

- in the *modality usage* (introvert Hamlet uses less nonverbal expressions, and less hand gestures especially),
- in the *performance* of gestures (smaller amplitude), and
- in the *speech* (introvert Hamlet speaks slower, in lower pitch, some syllable are elongated).

The marked up text and piece of the dictionary used are shown in Figure 1.

Another demo is a 3d full-body avatar, implemented in the STEP language [11], and meant to be used on the web. In this case, we demonstrated how meanings are mapped to specific hand gestures from an alternatives corresponding to choices in dictionaries for an extrovert and introvert style, see Figure 2.

```
1  <StyledText>
2  <StyleDeclaration>
3     <style aspect="biology" dict="Biological"/>
4     <style aspect="personality" dict="Extravert"/>
5  </StyleDeclaration>
6  <TextBody>
7  <Meaning Name="Enthusiastic">
8     <Meaning Name="GetAttention"> What a piece of work is a
9  man! </Meaning>
10 How <Meaning Name="Emphasize">noble </Meaning>in reason!
11 The paragon of animals!
12 </Meaning>
13 <Meaning Name="Contrast"> And yet, </Meaning>
14 <Meaning Name="Sad">
15    <Meaning Name="PointingAtSelf">to me,</Meaning>
16 what is <Meaning Name="EyeM" gesture_length="300"/>
15 this quintessence of
16    <Meaning Name="Emphasize">dust? </Meaning>
17 </Meaning Name="Sad">
...
18 </TextBody>
19 </StyledText>
```

Fig. 1. (a) Marked up text for Hamlet with defining the style of the character (line 2-5), several meaning tags and one tag indicating temporal change to sadness (line 14)

```
1  <StyleDictionary Name = "Extravert">
2  <Speechmode Name="="ExtravertSpeechMode">
3  <Meaning Name="Emphasize" CombinationMode="DOMINANT">
4  <GestureSpec>
5     <ExpressiveSpeech emotion="emph_mild"/>
6     <UseGest Name="nod_and_beat"/><PAR/>
7        <UseGest Name="LookAtPerson"/>
8        <Probability P="0.7"/>
9  </GestureSpec>
10 <GestureSpec>
11    <ExpressiveSpeech emotion="emph_strong"/>
12    <UseGest Name="beat"/>
13       <Probability P="0.3"/>
14    </GestureSpec>
15 </Meaning>
16 </StyleDictionary>
```

Fig. 1. (b) Segment of the Style dictionary for Extrovert personality, with alternatives to express Emphasize meaning in two different ways. Note the usage of the embedded definition of a composite gesture (line 6) and the indication of expressive speech (line 5 and 11).

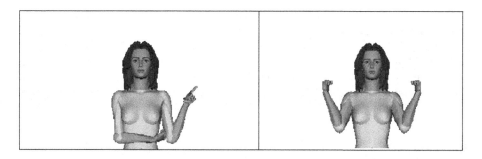

Fig. 2. Two hand gestures to express emphasis. The basic gestures are taken care of the STEP animation engine, the two-handed gesture is defined in GESTYLE as a compound one.

5 Summary and Further Work

We presented the GESTYLE markup language. It is not simply yet another language to author nonverbal presentation for VHs, but has distinctive features:

- It can be used to define the presentation style as of the nonverbal modalities and speech, by giving style aspects and corresponding dictionaries, and preferences for their usage in case of conflicts.
- It distinguishes meaning and gesture markups, and has built-in mechanism to 'translate' meanings to multimodal presentation with low-level gesture and speech tags.
- The gesture dictionaries contain probabilistic alternatives to express meanings, thus a text may be presented differently in subsequent executions, making sure that the presentation is non-repetitive.

We have been using GESTYLE in different demonstrators and for generating material for experiments on perception of VHs.

The implementation was not optimized, so currently it is not possible to feed a VH with marked-up text and generate the output in real-time. The basic bottleneck is in the 2-pass processing needed by the TTS engine, to provide timing of gestures and alterations for expressive speech.

GESTYLE could be a handy environment to author and test different presentation styles. However, the appropriate dictionaries need to be defined from psychological and sociological studies to find out what the distinctive gesture types and manners are for certain groups (divided by culture, profession, age and so on). The GESTYLE language provides a computational framework to define and use different aspects of style. It is a challenging question for behavioral psychology and cultural anthropology to find out basic low-level units of style, and thus decomposing e.g. the cultural aspects to living conditions and social values.

Ultimately, one would like to have an VH which manifests style also in the verbal modality. Style is manifested very strongly in choice of words and sentence structures. It is a challenge to generate styled NL content too, relying on related research [48].

On a longer term, it is a challenging task to develop VHs which have consistent style in all their modalities.

Acknowledgements. We acknowledge the work of Han Noot on implementing GESTYLE. We are thankful for Cartherine Pelachaud and Isabella Poggi for fruitful discussions on related topics. This paper was written in the framework of the EU FP6 COST 2102 action.

References

1. Aardman Studios, Creature Comforts, URL:
   http://atomfilms.shockwave.com/af/content/atom_221
2. Arafa, Y., Kamyab, K., Kshirsagar, S., Guye-Vuilleme, A., Thalmann, N.: Two Approaches to Scripting Character Animation. In: Falcone, R., Barber, S., Korba, L., Singh, M.P. (eds.) AAMAS 2002. LNCS (LNAI), vol. 2631, Springer, Heidelberg (2003)
3. Ball, G., Breese, J.: Emotion and personality in a conversational agent. In: Cassell, et al. (eds.) pp. 189–219 (2000)
4. Byun, M., Badler, N.: FacEMOTE: Qualitative parametric modifiers for facial animations. In: Proc. of the Symposium on Computer Animation, San Antonio, TX (2002)
5. Cassell, J., Sullivan, J., Prevost, S., Churchill, E.: Embodied Conversational Agents. MIT Press, Cambridge, MA (2000)
6. Cassell, J., Bickmore, T., Billinghurst, M., Campbell, L., Chang, K., Vilhjálmsson, H., Yan, H.: Embodiment in Conversational Interfaces: Rea. In: ACM CHI 1999 Conference Proceedings, Pittsburgh, PA, pp. 520–527 (1999)
7. Chi, D., Costa, M., Zhao, L., Badler, N.: The EMOTE Model for Effort and Shape. In: Proc. of Siggraph, pp. 173–182 (2000)
8. De Carolis, Carofiglio, Bilvi, M., Pelachaud, C.: APML, a Mark-up Language for Believable Behavior Generation. In: Proc. of the AAMAS Workshop on Embodied conversational agents – Let's specify and evaluate them (2002)
9. De Rosis, F., Poggi, I., Pelachaud, C.: Tanscultural Believability in Embodied Agents: a Matter of Consistent Adaptation. In: Trappl, R., Petta, P. (eds.) Agent Culture: Designing Virtual Characters for a Multi-Cultural World, Lawrence Erlbaum Associates, Mahwah (2004)
10. Ekman, P.: Facial Expressions. In: Dalgleish, T., Power, T. (eds.) The Handbook of Cognition and Emotion, pp. 301–320. John Wiley & Sons, Ltd, Chichester (1999)
11. Eliens, A., Huang, Z., Visser, C.: A platform for Embodied Conversational Agents based on Distributed Logic Programming. In: Proc. of the AAMAS Workshop on Embodied conversational agents – Let's specify and evaluate them! (2002)
12. Gratch, J., Marsella, S.: Tears and Fears: Modeling emotions and emotional behaviours in synthetic agents. In: Proc. of AA 2001, pp. 278–285 (2001)
13. H-anim 2002, Humanoid animation working group,
    http://www.h-anim.org/ Specifications/H-Anim1.1/
14. Hartmann, B., Mancini, M., Pelachaud, C.: Formational parameters and adaptive prototype instantiation for MPEG-4 compliant gesture synthesis. In: Proc. of Computer Animation 2002, pp. 111–119. IEEE Computer Society Press, Los Alamitos (2002)
15. Huang, Z., Ruttkay, Z.: Gesturing avatars with STEP. In: Gesture Workshop 2003 (2003)
16. Hsu, E., Pulli, K., Popovic, J.: Style Translation for Human Motion. In: Proc. of Siggraph (2005)

17. ISO Information Technology – Generic coding of audio-visual objects – Part 2: visual, ISO/IEC 14496-2 Final Draft International Standard, Atlantic City (1998)
18. Kendon, A.: Human gesture. In: Ingold, T., Gibson, K. (eds.) Tools, Language and Intelligence, Cambridge University Press, Cambridge (1993)
19. Kopp, S., Krenn, B., Marsella, S., Marshall, A.N., Pelachaud, C., Pirker, H., Thórisson, K.R., Vilhjálmsson, H.: Towards a Common Framework for Multimodal Generation: The Behavior Markup Language. In: Gratch, J., Young, M., Aylett, R., Ballin, D., Olivier, P. (eds.) IVA 2006. LNCS (LNAI), vol. 4133, Springer, Heidelberg (2006)
20. Krandsted, A., Kopp, S., Wachsmuth, I.: MURML: A Multimodal Utterance Representation Markup Language for Conversational Agents. In: Proc. of the AAMAS Workshop on Embodied conversational agents – Let's specify and evaluate them! (2002)
21. Lundeberg, M., Beskow, J.: Developing a 3D-agent for the August dialogue system. In: Proceedings of AVSP 1999, Santa Cruz, USA (1999), http://www.speech.kth.se/august/
22. Martin, J.-C., Niewiadomski, R., Devillers, L., Buisine, S., Pelachaud, C.: Multimodal complex emotions: Gesture expressivity and blended facial expressions, International Journal of Humanoid Robotics, Special Edition Achieving Human-Like Qualities in Interactive Virtual and Physical Humanoids (2006)
23. McNeill, D.: Hand and Mind: What Gestures Reveal about Thought. The University of Chicago Press (1991)
24. Nass, C., Isbister, K., Lee, E.-J.: Truth is beauty: Researching embodied conversational agents. In: Cassell, et al. (eds.), pp. 374–402 (2000)
25. Noot, H., Ruttkay, Zs.: CharToon 2.0 Manual, CWI Report INS-R0004, Amsterdam (2000)
26. Noot, H., Ruttkay, Zs.: Style in Gesture. In: Camurri, A., Volpe, G. (eds.) GW 2003. LNCS (LNAI), vol. 2915, Springer, Heidelberg (2004)
27. Ortony, A., Clore, G.L., Collins, A.: The cognitive structure of emotions. Cambridge University Press, Cambridge (1998)
28. Payr, S., Trappl, R. (eds.): Agent Culture - Human-agent Interaction in a Multicultural World. Lawrence Erlbaum Associates, Mahwah (2004)
29. Pelachaud, C., Poggi, I.: Subtleties of Facial Expressions in Embodied Agents. Journal of Visualization and Computer Animation 13, 301–312 (2002)
30. Perlin, K.: Real time responsive animation with personality. IEEE Transactions on Visualization and Computer Graphics 1(1) (1995)
31. Perlin, K.: Improving Noise. In: Proc. of Siggraph (2002)
32. Piwek, P., Krenn, B., Schröder, M., Grice, M., Baumann, S., Pirker, H.: RRL: A Rich Representation Language for the Description of Agent Behaviour in NECA. In: Proceedings of the AAMAS workshop on conversational agents - let's specify and evaluate them! (2002)
33. Plantec, P.: Virtual Humans. In: AMACOM (2004)
34. Poggi, I.: Mind Markers. In: Mueller, C., Posner, R. (eds.) The Semantics and Pragmatics of Everyday Gestures, Berlin Verlag Arno Spitz (2001)
35. Poggi, I., Pelachaud, C.: Facial Performative in a Conversational System. In: Cassell, et al. (eds.), pp. 155–188 (2000)
36. Prendinger, H., Ishizuka, M.: Social role awareness in animated agents. In: Proc. of Autonomous Agents Conference, pp. 270–277 (2001)
37. Prendinger, H., Ishizuka, M. (eds.): Life-Like Characters. Tools, Affective Functions, and Applications. Cognitive Technologies Series. Springer, Berlin Heidelberg (2004)
38. Queneau, R., Wright, B. (translator): Exercises in Style, New Directions (1981)

39. Reeves, B., Nass, C.: The Media Equation: how peopletreat computers, televsions and new media like real people and places. Cambridge University Press, Cambridge (1996)
40. Rookhuiszen, R.: Do people gesture as a leopard does? In: Proceedings of the Bref. Student Conference, University of Twente, Enschede (2007)
41. Ruttkay, Zs.: Constraint-based facial animation. Int. Journal of Constraints 6, 85–113 (2001)
42. Ruttkay, Zs., Pelachaud, C.: From Brows to Trust – Evaluating ECAs. Kluwer, Dordrecht (2004)
43. Stokoe, W.C.: Sign language structure: An outline of the communicative systems of the American deaf, Linstock Press (1978)
44. Tsutsui, T., Saeyor, S., Ishizuka, M.: MPML: A Multimodal Presentation Markup Language with Character Agent Control Functions. In: Proc. (CD-ROM) WebNet 2000 World Conf. on the WWW and Internet, San Antonio, Texas (2000)
45. Thomas, F., Johnston, O.: Disney animation: The illusion of life. Abbeville Press, New York (1981)
46. Virtual Human Markup Language (VHML), http://www.vhml.org
47. Van Moppes, V.: Improving the quality of synthesized speech through mark-up of input text with emotions, Master Thesis, VU, Amsterdam (2002)
48. Walker, M., Cahn, J., Whittaker, S.: Improvising linguistic style: Social and affective bases for agent personality. In: Proc. of Autonomous Agents Conference (1997)
49. Wang, J., Drucker, S., Agrawala, M., Cohen, M.: Proceedings of SIGGRAPH 2006 (2006)

Analysis of Nonverbal Involvement in Dyadic Interactions

Uwe Altmann, Rico Hermkes, and Lutz-Michael Alisch

Technische Universität Dresden, Faculty of Education
Weberplatz 5, 01217 Dresden, Germany
{uwe.altmann,rico.hermkes,lutz-michael.alisch}@mailbox.tu-dresden.de
http://tu-dresden.de/die_tu_dresden/fakultaeten/erzw/

Abstract. In the following, we comment on the assignment of the dynamic variable, its meaning, indicators and furthermore its dimensions. We examine some interaction models which incorporate nonverbal involvement as a dynamic variable. Then we give a short overview of two recently undertaken studies in advance of dyadic interactions focusing on nonverbal involvement measured in a multivariate manner. The first study concentrates on conflict regulation of interacting children being friends. The second study examines intrapersonal conflict and its social expression through "emotional overinvolvement" (EOI) of patients in psychotherapy. We also mention a pilot-study in which the proxemic behaviour between two children in a conflict episode is analysed focusing here on violation of personal space and its restoration through synchronisation. We end with some comments on multiple dimensions and scaling with respect to involvement including thoughts about multidimensional interaction data (MID).

Keywords: nonverbal involvement, conflict, synchronisation.

1 Nonverbal Involvement and Interaction Modelling

The study of nonverbal involvement in interpersonal interactions in a certain sense started with the "equilibrium model" (1965) by Argyle & Dean [4]. Nonverbal involvement was used as a dynamic variable to capture both, (i) a person's involvement in interaction (personal level) and (ii) involvement as the regulation of interaction (interaction level). According to the equilibrium model, interacting partners attempt to hold their own equilibrium level. In addition, the partners establish a common level of intimacy which seems to be acceptable to both of them. Argyle [5] addresses these two levels of scaling when he mentions the distinction between intimacy as the request of a person and intimacy as an interaction variable. Accordingly, involvement is analysed as (i) nonverbal involvement which means the request of a person to involve in an interaction (personal level) and in contrast to that as (ii) the variable to be regulated (interaction level). Note that nonverbal involvement and intimacy (also immediacy) will be treated as functional synonymous [3]. Interaction models of this type

A. Esposito et al. (Eds.): Verbal and Nonverbal Commun. Behaviours, LNAI 4775, pp. 37–50, 2007.
© Springer-Verlag Berlin Heidelberg 2007

share the assumption that the regulation of some relevant interaction variable (involvement, intimacy or immediacy) is necessary to keep the interaction running. Patterson [27], [29] in his arousal model of interpersonal intimacy assumes that a change in involvement is always communicated, based on an arousal potential and some physiological reactions (concerning e.g. heart frequency and respiratory rhythm). Whether a reaction is positive or not, the opposite partner shows closeness or avoidance. However Andersen & Andersen [3] object that the arousal model could not explore different arousal activations as possible reactions that could follow from identical partner's behaviour and that the model depends on the particular interaction phase. Burgoon [10] assumes an "expectancy violations model". Accordingly, interaction happens automatically without conscious awareness as long as no discrepancy to previous expectations appears. If this instead happens, an arousal-activation and behavioural reaction would be initiated. For example, Burgoons model proposes that interacting partners have expectations with respect to their interpersonal distances. Breaking the distance (e.g. invading in a person's own intimate space) leads to arousal-activations and conscious awareness of what happens in the interaction.

Recently, verbal and paraverbal parameters have been used to measure the involvement. In his "sequential functional model", Patterson [28] is listing the relevant verbal and nonverbal involvement dimensions. Moreover, in addition to the common five dimensions (interpersonal distance, body position and orientation, facial expressions, head and eye movements), Patterson mentioned (1) lean, (2) postural openness, (3) relational gestures, (4) speech duration, (5) interruptions, and (6) paralinguistic cues. Similar to this, the "discrepancy arousal model" Capella & Green [11] includes verbal and nonverbal dimensions for exchange patterns in interaction. They assume that during an interaction the involvement increases or decreases very fast, because each actor has no time enough for an adequate choice of a reaction therefore evoking so-called rapid-action-sequences. The behaviour which results from an arousal-activation (leading to increased or decreased involvement) is not an effect of a conscious cognitive process but an immediate affective reaction. Andersen & Andersen [3] emphasise "a strong role to arousal as a direct precursor of affect" (p. 440).

Alternative modelling is used to capture an extended concept of involvement. Coker & Burgoon [14] conceive conversational involvement as the 5-dimensional dynamic variable under study with the dimensions expressiveness, interaction management, immediacy, altercentrism and social anxiety. In psychotherapy research, the extended involvement concept is applied to describe pathological kinds of generators of (social) behaviour (e.g. patients' intrapersonal conflicts). These pathological phenomena are termed emotional overinvolvement (EOI) respective emotional underinvolvement. EOI covers one subscale of the Expressed Emotion Scale (EE). On the one hand, EOI refers to the global quality of a relationship, e.g. married couples or parent-child-relations [7], on the other EOI is related to the patients' involvement into interactions with others to which they are closely related (e.g. family members in family therapy settings) or into interactions with the therapist, when he addresses sensitive themes (concerning the basic intrapersonal conflict) [18].

In the first case, EOI could be measured psychometrically. Leff & Vaughn [21] developed an instrument consisting of three scales (1) care, (2) sacrifice and (3) intrusion. Another way is to measure EOI as some quality of a relationship by observing the open behaviour in psychotherapy. Furthermore, McCarthy et al. [24] study EOI according to an assessment of parent-child-relationship in clinical settings (e.g. while they are solving of a conflict between them). If parents express (1) self-sacrificing behaviour, (2) overprotection or (3) excessive emotion (e.g. crying) towards their child or if they direct more than five positive remarks to the child combined with statements of affection or excessive details about the child's past, higher EOI ratings result as a rule. It is the aim to design EOI as an indicator of quality of relationship using behaviours and patterns of interaction. McCarthy et al. [24] point out that "it is difficult to find clearly and reliably observable behaviours that reflect EOI" (p. 90).

For EOI as a variable regarding the interaction (the second type of EOI), Merten [25] looks for nonverbal indicators. He reports that facially expressed affective behaviour is suitable to capture EOI of parent-child-interactions in therapeutic settings (schizophrenic vs. healthy children in interaction with their parents). In our own research we explore prosody as another nonverbal indicator of EOI. Scherer [34] and Juslin & Scherer [20] denote prosodic and speech quality features as nonverbal vocal attributes.

2   Dynamic Patterns of Prosody in Patient-Therapist-Interactions

Among other subjects of research, we also study nonverbal features of the coping process following the psychotherapeutic treatments which evoke intrapersonal conflicts. Roughly spoken, the study is based on three fundamental components: (i) measurement of multimodal interaction data, (ii) identification of prosodic and speech quality features in sequences of expressed intrapersonal conflicts using EOI, (iii) statistical analysis of all prosodic processes of the interacting pair during a complete individual therapy course. Our final goal here is to find some indicators with respect to the patient-therapist-interaction that may be used to predict psychotherapy to be successful or not. We are using the EOI attributes mentioned above according to component (ii).

2.1   Intrapersonal Conflicts Expressed Through Emotional Overinvolvement

The use and meaning of the concept of intrapersonal conflict vary according to the respective psychotherapeutic frameworks. In a psychoanalytic context, an intrapersonal conflict is thought of as a kind of discrepancy which generates pathological symptoms (e.g. compulsions or extreme anxiety). In most cases, it depends on the earlier history of the entire parent-child-relationship or on traumatic events not yet mastered adequately. Often it is possible that specific stimuli symbolizing the central features of the trauma trigger off emotions connected with intrapersonal conflicts.

Yet, intrapersonal conflicts could be expressed through emotional overinvolvement, e.g. whilst somebody is talking about the matters related to the conflict. Giving utterance to the emotion, the involvement is higher than in the normal case. Note that EOI could be applied under normal circumstances too, for example, if a football fan speaks about a questionable action of the referee. According to the work by Batliner et al. [6], van den Broek [8] and Yu et al. [36] we apply EOI with the use of acoustic features such as tone, pitch, tempo, intensity, voice/silence relation, and voiced/unvoiced relation.

To give an impression, let us consider some facts about patients with social phobia (social anxiety disorder). Their intrapersonal conflicts could be described by discrepancies between less self-esteem and lower engagement in social life or between strong separation anxiety and the necessity to be autonomous in a certain way. Often patients with social phobia believe that they are undesired children who are not good enough with respect to their parental expectations. Therefore, typical symptoms of the disorder are social phobia and dysphoria, when the clients are criticised by others. Accordingly, they tend to avoid those social situations which seem to be unsafe. If the therapist addresses critical relationships, then as a rule the patients are emotionally overinvolved.

2.2   Design and Method

In our study we have to control the factors (i) gender of patients (only women and in addition all natural speakers), (ii) age (from 20 to 35), (iii) psychological disorder (only social phobia) combined with the triggers of EOI (iv) the frame of interaction (e.g. the same room, persons, seating arrangements), and (v) psychotherapeutic treatment. This treatment is based on the work of Luborsky [22] and is organized according to three phases that could be explained as follows: First phase (session 1-8) anamnesis, further exploration and supporting interventions, second phase (session 9-18) intervening in the intrapersonal conflict, and third phase (session 19-25) termination.

This treatment allows for controlled studying those speech characteristics being pertinent to the expression of intrapersonal conflicts through emotional overinvolvement. In the first phase, the therapist focuses on the patient's intrapersonal conflict including any related emotions and situation specific behaviour. During this phase, episodes including EOI to be observed are most likely. Of course, if the psychotherapeutic treatment has been efficiently successful at the end of the third phase, then the patient's utterances are no longer affected by EOI even if he is confronted with the same trigger given first in the beginning phase. Therefore, the design allows for contrasting those episodes accompanied by EOI and those without EOI.

From a technical point of view, our research is based on several new tools recently developed in the fields of our cooperation partners (see below, Acknowledgements):

1. Data collection: Video and high-level acoustics audio records of all interactions in the psychotherapy sessions are applied simultaneously completed by manually labelling the conflict episodes.
2. EOI identification: Prosodic and speech quality parameters are measured and processed with hidden Markov models (HMM; for a detailed discussion see Hoffmann et al., this volume).
3. Analysis of therapy courses: Based on the time-varying data concerning prosody and speech quality parameters, the statistical analysis of any individual therapy course uses the machinery of Functional Data Analysis (FDA) [17], [30], [31] followed by comparing the sample of individual curves statistically (e.g. using a regression theoretic approach with intensity of EOI as input and therapy effect as output).

Note that the variables of interest are nested. Accordingly, psychological treatment, session, and utterance are located on different levels. The term nested refers to (i) the hierarchical ordering of the levels and (ii) the framing of a lower level by a higher one. Here, a certain part of the so called multiscaling problem arises. The time-scales of the measured variables differ from level to level and although in a modest manner within a level too.

3   Conflict Regulation in Children's Interactions Being Close Friends

In this research, we study interaction conflicts. Here conflict means out of sync sequences in nonverbal involvement occurring in interactions of children being close friends. In general, interaction data are collected with 3D videography.

3.1   Nonverbal Involvement and Interaction Conflicts

As mentioned above, nonverbal involvement is used as a variable to describe some states of interaction as well as individual behaviours of the partners. In our study we are interested in the former. So the dynamics of interaction could be characterised using involvement data (more exactly using the synchronised or desynchronised involvement curves). Recent conceptualizations of conflicts in interaction are often based on assumptions borrowed from the theory of dynamical system theory distinguishing between dynamics of cooperation and dynamics of conflict [15]. Accordingly, cooperation is indicated by an involvement coordinated by the partners. However, conflict is in relation to desynchronisation [35] which could succeed certain discrepancies between the interacting partners. In general, we use the concept of conflictuality to denote a global feature of the entire situation in order to express the possibility of conflict in interactions.

3.2   Design and Method

In general, the sampled best friends (aged 9 to 11) participate in an experiment. Part of the experiment is a game called "space flight simulation". One of the friends runs the up-down control of a space shuttle, whilst the other one controls its left-right motion. Collisions with asteroids are possible e.g. a background mechanism is controlling the collisions as an independent variable. Furthermore, the friends are confronted in a certain way with information about "bad playing" which is used to control the increase of conflictuality. Of course, the game consists of several rounds and the friends could reach a more or less high score, although the level, too, is experimentally controlled. In addition, one child and only this one is always the loser and this increases the conflictuality even more. Now the question is which child has to be chosen to play this role. Here, attachment theory gives us a clue, precisely that securely attached children (denoted as type B) tend to be the leader of the relationship (e.g. in interactions) in a probably more distinctive style than insecurely attached children (type A). In our research, we only sample pairs of so-called complementary friends (one being type A and the other type B). Type B children always play the role of the loser in our experiment the last part of which is called the "relaxing phase". In general, each pair of friends is winning the final level of the game achieving the high score in this phase. Of course, this ending is necessary to decrease the evoked conflictuality and to handle the children with integrity.

The children's interactions are recorded using 3D videography. The conflict episodes have to be rated manually. In addition, all trajectories of marked body points have to be calculated. Capturing the involvement dimensions, these points are used to reconstruct the children's bodies and the trajectories give their motions during the interaction.

We hypothesise that the friends tend to evoke synchronised interaction. In contrast, interaction conflicts correspond with more and longer out of sync regions which assume that the solution of a conflict is based on resynchronisation.

3.3   Pilot Studies

Here, the goal is to get some preliminary information about separate dimensions of nonverbal involvement:

1. interpersonal distance, especially the violation of personal space (for first results, see the next section),
2. body position, especially turning towards the partner and away from him,
3. eye movements, especially threatened gaze and gaze avoidance,
4. facial expressions and head position, especially aggressive and negatively indicated expressions.

In any case, each specific synchronisation measure, which has to be chosen, depends on the involvement dimension under study. To simplify our approach, certain episodes are selected inherent conflicts which are visible particularly in one dimension. Accordingly, our succeeding research will be concentrated on the interplay of two and more dimensions.

4   Conflict Episode in Dyadic Child Interaction

In order to simplify the prima facie complexity of the interaction process of the children, we select a simple episode incorporating a conflict between the children which is measurable through the interpersonal distance and its regulation. The beginning of the conflict is marked by a personal space violation. The leading questions of this pilot study are:

1. What about the relation between distance regulation (restoring personal space) and synchronisation?
2. Which of the children is the leader of the interaction (the invader or restorer)?

4.1   Method

Data Collection and Preprocessing. The data of our pilot-study had been collected by 2D-videographic tools; however 3D measurement is the main goal of our research. The conflict episode was recorded in the kindergarten with a (low quality) camcorder (about 32 seconds, exactly 823 frames).

Photogrammetric tracking algorithms had been used to compute the head trajectories. According to this method, a certain point of interest (feature) could be matched throughout an image sequence using its unique nearest neighbourhood. Other applications of the photogrammetric tracking algorithms are, for example, the measurement of the motion of a glacier [23] or bridge deformation [1]. The chosen feature to be tracked in our pilot-study is the middle of the head of each child. In case of our pilot-study, the camera sometimes had not been in a fixed position. Therefore, the motions of the children had to be filtered by using fixed points in the background (e.g. the corner of a window). Low quality of video results in little jumps of the tracking points. To handle this, trajectories were smoothed with locally weighted regression [12], [13]. In order to allow for an analysis of phase synchronisation, the signal was filtered. Therefore, the trajectories had been smoothed as slightly as possible (11 frames = 0.44 sec as bandwidth). The results are shown in figure 1.

Note that the children were acting on a virtual line which is strictly orthogonal to the camera position. Assuming that the differences of x-coordinates of fixed head-points are sufficiently good approximations to capture the interpersonal distance, one constraint here is not to take into account the circumferences and heights of the heads (see figure 2). The regulation of its body distance by a person is related to its forward and backward motions. With respect to our data we define these motions as follows

$$x^*_{\text{girl}}(t) = x_{\text{girl}}(t+1) - x_{\text{girl}}(t) \tag{1}$$
$$x^*_{\text{boy}}(t) = -(x_{\text{boy}}(t+1) - x_{\text{boy}}(t)) \ . \tag{2}$$

The values of x^*_{girl} and x^*_{boy} are related to the speed of the motions. Positive values of two variables indicate movements toward the other person, negative values mark backward movements. Note that t is the video frame and x_{girl} and x_{boy} are measured in pixels. The plots of x^*_{girl} and x^*_{boy} time series are shown in figure 4.

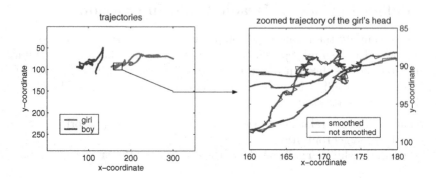

Fig. 1. Left: trajectories of head points. Right: the trajectory of the girl's head point (thin line) and smoothed trajectory (broad line).

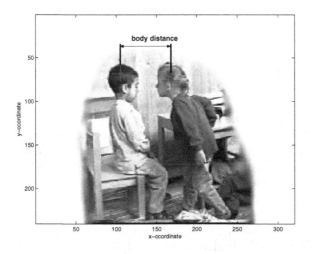

Fig. 2. Body distance

Synchronisation. Considering that two or more weakly interacting systems ajust their behaviour, synchronisation results as an effect of tuning or coordination. Possible measures could be the mutual information, cross correlation, cross spectra or phase synchronisation. Rosenblum et al. [32] point out that the first three are symmetric measures and merely suitable to a limited extent in case of directionality of interaction.

Phase synchronisation could be defined as phase interaction with $m : n$ frequency ratio (m and n integers) or in the presence of (small) noise as[1]

$$|m\phi_1(t) - n\phi_2(t)| < \text{const.} .$$ (3)

---

[1] Here and in what follows below, we are using the index 1 to abbreviate boy and index 2 for girl.

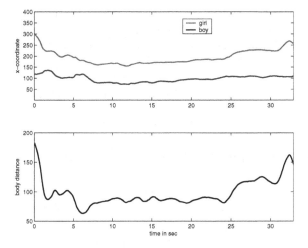

Fig. 3. X-coordinates of heads (upper plot), body distance (lower plot)

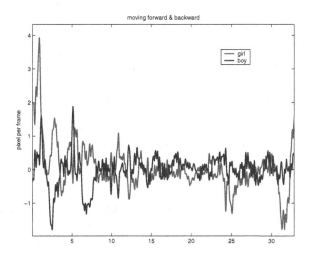

Fig. 4. Time series of x^*_{girl} and x^*_{boy}

If relation (3) is fulfilled with respect to a time interval given we talk about a phase synchronisation region corresponding to a plateau in the plot of the generalised phase difference curve ($\varphi_{m,n}(t) = \phi_1(t) - \phi_2(t)$).

Assuming that the system dynamics could be reduced to its phase dynamics (ϕ), phases could be set as the composition of the frequency of the uncoupled system (ω, a constant) with the phases coupling (f) as the function of the two systems and some noisy perturbation (ξ) [32]:

$$\dot{\phi}_1 = \omega_1 + f_1(\phi_1, \phi_2) + \xi_1(t) \tag{4}$$
$$\dot{\phi}_2 = \omega_2 + f_2(\phi_2, \phi_1) + \xi_2(t) . \tag{5}$$

Here, we are not considering the differences of the amplitude.

A measure related to the phase is the directionality index $d^{(1,2)}$ [32], [33], given the signals being smoothed curves (e.g. finite Fourier series F_1 and F_2). Cross connections of the phase dynamics are defined as

$$c_1{}^2 = \int \int_0^{2\pi} \left(\frac{\partial F_1}{\partial \phi_2}\right)^2 d\phi_1 \, d\phi_2 \tag{6}$$

$$c_2{}^2 = \int \int_0^{2\pi} \left(\frac{\partial F_2}{\partial \phi_1}\right)^2 d\phi_1 \, d\phi_2 \tag{7}$$

and the directionality index

$$d^{(1,2)} = \frac{c_2 - c_1}{c_1 + c_2}. \tag{8}$$

This index takes values in the interval $[-1, 1]$. If $d^{(1,2)}$ is close to zero then bidirectionality is given. If $d^{(1,2)} \approx 1$ or $d^{(1,2)} \approx -1$ then unidirectionality (system 1 leads system 2 or system 2 leads system 1) occurs. To obtain the instantaneous phase one could apply the Hilbert transform [26] (stationarity is not required).

4.2   Results

With respect to forward and backward movements, a region of phase synchronisation was found covering about three seconds in the beginning of conflict episode (see figure 5). Initially the girl invades the personal space of the boy. Accoringly his efforts to restore his personal space (backward motions) are succeeded by the girls invading forward motions. The synchronisation region reflects these coordinated actions. Now, the question is why this region does extend only in a short time interval? In a little while, in the middle of the episode the children change the modality of their nonverbal involvement (not measured here, e.g. the girl wags one's finger at the boy).

Which child is the leader of the interaction? The estimated parameters ($c_1 = 8.29$, $c_2 = 4.97$ and $d^{(1,2)} = -0.25$) suggest bidirectionality with the boy modestly leading the interaction. Bidirectionality means that the children are influencing each other in their reactions. During the episode chosen, the girl initiates the conflict invading the personal space of the boy. However, in general, the boy seems to be the leader of the distance regulation as a whole, because his backward movements regularly are followed by invading forward movements of the girl. As mentioned above, the computed directionality index does not consider the change of modality (from head-head-distance to head-hand-distance).

5   Summary and Outlook

In our research group we study dyadic interaction. We have mentioned here two cases: at first, emotional overinvolvement as an indicator of intrapersonal conflicts of patients with social phobia, and secondly, conflicts in children's friendship interactions. We think that there exists a connection between conflicts and

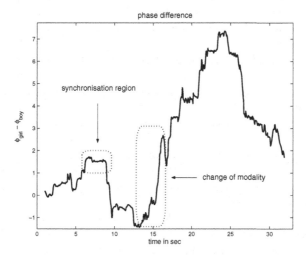

Fig. 5. Phase difference over time

involvement desynchronisation, whereas the solution of a conflict should come along with resynchronisation. In a pilot-study, a short conflict episode between children was analysed, more precisely the distance regulation as a feature of nonverbal involvement. One synchronisation region with respect to restoring and directionality in interaction have been identified and change of modality was observed too (from head-head-distance to head-hand-distance).

Our future research will focus on (i) point tracking and analysis with multiple body points, (ii) other features of involvement, and (iii) the cross-connections between them. Our aim is to model the dynamics of interaction processes (in terms of synchronisation and conflicts) by utilising functional statistics (FDA). Possibly that will result in an analysis of stability (attractors) and change (bifurcations) in interactions. According to this, some measurement of MID seems to be indispensable. Note that there is a link between MID and the problems of multiscaling and configuration phenomena.

In empirical research, the problem of multiscaling occurs when measured data are located on another level than those according to the hypotheses under consideration. Could facial expression as a muscular phenomenon does explain anything with respect to the involvement in interaction? There are different ways to answer this question. Firstly the data could be seen as instances of a certain bottom up process which is generating social meaning or secondly the data could be understood as indicating top down macro level phenomena. According to the first case, a facial action unit (see Ekman & Friesens [16] "Facial Action Coding System") assigned with number 10, occurs together with another facial action unit called 17. This could be an expression of the affect anger. Moreover, in the course of this expression a body movement occurs. Coding the marked body points and reconstructing a body model, all of this could indicate a turn towards the interaction partner. This turn could stand for intimacy or increasing involvement but also for a violation of the partner's personal space. In many cases the facial expression can give some context information to validate the meaning of the body movement. However, in general, multiple behavioral expressions in multiple modalities are shown at the same time (a person speaks or moves its eyes and head). An additional question is whether there are redundancies in the communication channels just activated. Here, the multiscaling problem is added (i) by trying to merge a holistic meaning aggregating the single features of behaviour and (ii) by considering the different sensitivities for a change in the dimensions under study. A spatial position (e.g. a seating position) covers more time than the expression of a prosodic feature or a facial expression. This is because the different dimensions of behaviour are nested. Now, whether the focus is on the global state of a person or the interaction, research is only conducted by using manual ratings which require high efforts and are associated with lower objectivity and loss of reliability.

The main idea is to measure the lower scale-orders exactly and with high frequency in order to construct trajectories and furthermore, identify regions of equilibria and change points in interaction. The general question here is how do variables (which furthermore are at different levels) form a configuration. How are neuronal activity, facial expression, gaze, proximity connected to form an ensemble which corresponds to an emotion or a state of interaction? If the multiscaling problem is solved, questions of this type could be answered.

Acknowledgments. With respect to the research on "Prosodic Patterns of Patient-Therapist-Interactions" our thanks go to our cooperating partners Prof. R. Hoffmann (Technische Universität Dresden, Institute of Acoustics and Speech Communication) and Prof. P. Joraschky (Universitätsklinikum Carl Gustav Carus, Clinic for Psychotherapy and Psychosomatic).

In our research on "Conflict Regulation in Children's Friendship-Interactions", we cooperate with Prof. H.-G. Maas & Dipl.-Ing. P. Westfeld (Technische Universität Dresden, Institute of Photogrammetry and Remote Sensing). We especially appreciate the help of P. Westfeld in tracing the body points.

References

1. Albert, J., Maas, H.-G., Schade, A., Schwarz, W.: Pilot studies on photogrammetric bridge deformation measurement. In: Kahmen, H., Niemeier, W., Retscher, G. (eds.) Proceedings of the 2nd symposium on geodesy for geotechnical and structural engineering, pp. 133–140. Berlin (2002)
2. Alisch, L.-M.: Sprache im Kontext sozial- und humanwissenschaftlicher Forschung (Speech in the context of social and human sciences.). In: Hoffmann, R. (ed.) Elektronische Sprachsignalverarbeitung. Tagungsband der 17. Konferenz Elektronische Sprachsignalverarbeitung, Freiberg/Sachsen, 28.-30.08.2006, pp. 9–10. TUDpress, Dresden (2006)
3. Andersen, P.A., Andersen, J.F.: The Exchange of Nonverbal Intimacy: A Critical Review of Dyadic Models. In: Petronio, S., Alberts, J.K., Hecht, M.L., Buley, J. (eds.) Contemporary Perspectives on Interpersonal Communication, pp. 433–448. Brown & Benchmark Publishers, Dubuque, Iowa (1993)

4. Argyle, M., Dean, J.: Eye-contact, distance and affiliation. Sociometry 28(2), 289–304 (1965)
5. Argyle, M.: Soziale Interaktion. Kiepenheuer & Witsch, Köln (1980)
6. Batliner, A., Fischer, K., Huber, R., Spilker, J., Nöth, E.: How to find trouble in communication. Speech Communication 40, 117–143 (2003)
7. Boye, B., Bentsen, H., Notland, T.H., Munkvold, O.G., Lersbryggen, A.B., Oskarsson, K.H., Uren, G., Ulstein, I., Bjorge, H., Lingjaerde, O., Malt, U.F.: What predicts the course of expressed emtion in relatives of patients with schizophrenia or related psychoses? Social Psychiatry & Psychiatric Epidemiology 34(1), 35–43 (1999)
8. van den Broek, E.L.: Emotional prosody measurement (EPM): A voice-based evaluation method for psychological therapy effectiveness. Medical and Care Componatics 1, 118–125 (2004)
9. Burgoon, J.K., Jones, S.B.: Toward a theory of personal space expectations and their violations. Human Communication Research 2(2), 131–146 (1976)
10. Burgoon, J.K.: A communication model of personal space violation: Explication and initial test. Human Communication Research 4(2), 129–142 (1978)
11. Capella, J.N., Green, J.O.: A discrepancy-arousal explanation of mutual influence in expressive behavior for adult and infant-adult interaction. Communication Monographs 49(2), 89–114 (1982)
12. Cleveland, W.S., Devlin, S.J.: Locally weighted regression: An Approach to Regression Analysis by Local Fitting. Journal of the American Statistical Association 83, 596–610 (1988)
13. Cleveland, W.S., Loader, C.L.: Smoothing by local regression: Principles and methods. In: Härdle, W., Schimek, M.G. (eds.) Statistical theory and computational aspects of smoothing, pp. 10–49. Springer, New York (1996)
14. Coker, D.A., Burgoon, J.K.: The nature of conversational involvement and nonverbal encoding patterns. Human Communication Research 13(4), 463–494 (1987)
15. Coleman, P.T., Vallacher, R., Nowak, A., Bue Ngoc, L.: Intractable conflict as an attractor: Presenting a dynamical model of conflict, escalation, and intractability. In: IACM 18th Annual Conference, June 1, 2005 (2005), Available at SSRN http://ssrn.com/abstract=734963
16. Ekman, P., Friesen, W.V.: Manual for the Facial Action Coding System (FACS). A technique for the measurement of facial action. Consulting Psychologists Press, Palo Alto (1978)
17. Ferraty, F., Vieu, P.: Nonparametric functional data analysis. Springer, New York (2006)
18. Gassmann, D., Grawe, K.: General change mechanisms: The relation between problem activation and resource activation in successful and unsuccessful therapeutic interactions. Clinincal Psychology & Psychotherapy 13(1), 1–11 (2006)
19. Hermkes, R.: Zur Synchronisation in Kinderfreundschaftsbeziehungen. Begriffsbestimmung, Bedeutung und Untersuchungsperspektiven (Synchronisation in child friendships. Concepts and perspectives for empirical interaction studies.). In: Alisch, L.-M., Wagner, J.W.L. (eds.) Freundschaften unter Kindern und Jugendlichen. Interdisziplinäre Perspektiven und Befunde, pp. 107–118. Juventa, Weinheim (2006)
20. Juslin, P.N., Scherer, K.R.: Vocal expression of affect. In: Harrigan, J.A., Rosenthal, R., Scherer, K.R. (eds.) The new handbook of methods in nonverbal behaviour research, pp. 65–135. Oxford University Press, Oxford (2005)
21. Leff, J., Vaughn, C.: Expressed emotions in families: Its significance for mental illness, pp. 37–63. Guilford Press, New York (1985)

22. Luborsky, L.: Principles of psychoanalytic psychotherapy: A manual for supportive-expressive treatment. Basic Books, New York (1984)
23. Maas, H.-G., Dietrich, D., Schwalbe, E., Bäßler, M., Westfeld, P.: Analysis of the motion behaviour of Jakobshavn IsbræGlacier in Greenland by monocular image sequence analysis. International Archives of Photogrammetry, Remote Sensing and Spatial Information Sciences 36(5), 179–183 (2006)
24. McCarthy, C.A., Lau, A.S., Valeri, S.M., Weisz, J.R.: Parent-child interactions in relation to critical and emotionally overinvolved expressed emotion (EE): Is EE a proxy for behavior? Journal of Abnormal Child Psychology 32(1), 83–93 (2004)
25. Merten, J.: Context analysis of facial affective behavior in clinical populations. In: Katsikitis, M. (ed.) The human face, pp. 131–147. Kluwer, Boston (2003)
26. Oppenheim, A.V., Schafer, R.W., Buck, J.R.: Discrete-time signal processing. Prentice-Hall, Englewood Cliffs (1998)
27. Patterson, M.L.: An arousal model of interpersonal intimacy. Psychological Review 83(3), 235–245 (1976)
28. Patterson, M.L.: A sequential functional model of nonverbal exchange. Psychological Review 89(3), 231–249 (1982)
29. Patterson, M.L.: Intimacy, social control, and nonverbal involvement: A functional approach. In: Derlega, V.J. (ed.) Communication, intimacy, and close relationships, pp. 105–132. Academic Press Inc. New York (1984)
30. Ramsay, J.O., Silverman, B.W.: Functional data analysis. Springer, New York (2006)
31. Ramsay, J.O., Silverman, B.W.: Applied Functional Data Analysis. Springer, New York (2002)
32. Rosenblum, M., Cimponeriu, L., Bezerianos, A., Patzak, A., Mrowka, R.: Identification of coupling direction: Application to cardiorespiratory interaction. Physical Review E 65:041909, 1–11 (2002)
33. Rosenblum, M., Cimponeriu, L., Pikovsky, A.: Coupled oscillators approach in analysis of bivariate data. In: Schelter, B., Winterhalder, M., Timmer, J. (eds.) Handbook of time series analysis, pp. 159–180. Wiley, Weinheim (2006)
34. Scherer, K.R.: The functions of nonverbal signs in conversation. In: Clair, R.S., Giles, H. (eds.) The social and psychological contexts of language, pp. 225–244. Lawrence Erlbaum Associates, Hillsdale (1980)
35. Shaw, M., Gaines, B.: Knowledge support systems for constructively channeling conflict in group dynamics. In: Klein, M., Landers, S. (eds.) AAAAI-94 workshop on models of conflict management and cooperative problem solving. AAAI Technical Report pp. 107–116 (1994)
36. Yu, C., Aoki, P.M., Woodruff, A.: Detecting user engagement in everyday conversations. In: Proceedings of the 8th International Conference on Spoken Language Processing (ICSLP), pp. 1329–1332. Jeju Island, Korea (2004)

Children's Perception of Musical Emotional Expressions

Anna Esposito[1,2] and Manuela Serio[2]

[1] Seconda Università di Napoli, Dipartimento di Psicologia, Via Vivaldi 43, Caserta, Italy
anna.esposito@unina2.it, iiass.annaesp@tin.it
[2] IIASS, Via Pellegrino 19, 84019, Vietri sul Mare, Italy, INFM Salerno, Italy

Abstract. This study investigates on children's ability to interpret emotions in instrumentally-presented melodies. 40 children (20 males and 20 females) all aged six years, have been tested for the comprehension of emotional concepts through the correct matching of emotional pictures to pieces of music. Results indicate that 6-year-old emotional responses to orchestral extracts considered full of affective cues are similar to those demonstrated by adults and that there is no gender effect.

Keywords: Emotion, music perception, children, affective cues, vocal expressions.

1 Introduction

Music is regarded as an effective nonverbal means for conveying emotions [15, 45], and several proposals have been made to support a close relationship between music and vocal expression [5, 24, 28]. The identification of these cross-modal emotional similarities in the two domains, if they really exist, would be important both from a theoretical and practical point of view. Theoretically, the existence of a close relationship between music and vocal expression could shed light on how these two channels shape and rise emotional feelings and which performance variables (such as speaking rate and pitch contour for vocal expression, or tempo and mode for music) play a leading role, helping to derive a code, effective in both domains, governing the rise and fall of emotional feelings. Practically, this code could be applied to develop improved interactive dialog systems and intelligent avatars which show human-like behaviors in order to ameliorate human-machine interaction as well as human communication through machine.

There is an evolutionary perspective on which research on music perception relies in order to parallel the perception of emotion in music to that in vocal expression. Vocal expression is the oldest form of nonverbal communication and emotions are considered as adaptive reactions to relevant changes in the environment which are communicated through a nonverbal code from one organism to another [41]. It is suggested that music makes use of the same code in order to arouse emotional feelings in the perceiver [24, 39]. This perspective is based on several assumptions, among which, the most important is that it exists a small set of discrete emotional categories universally shared from which other emotions can be derived [11-12,

A. Esposito et al. (Eds.): Verbal and Nonverbal Commun. Behaviours, LNAI 4775, pp. 51–64, 2007.

22-23, 42]. This small set of emotional categories includes happiness, anger, sadness, and fear, which can be reliably associated to basic survival problems such as nurturing offspring, earning food, competing for resource, avoiding and/or facing dangers. In this context, basic emotions are brief, intense and adapted reactions to urgent and demanding survival issues. These reactions to goal-relevant changes in the environment require "readiness to act" and "prompting of plans" in order to appropriately handle (under conditions of limited time) the incoming event producing suitable mental states, physiological changes, feelings, and expressions [13-14].

The categorization of emotions is, however, debated among researchers and different theories have been proposed for its conceptualization, among these dimensional models [43, 46]. Such models envisage a finite set of primary features (dimensions) in which emotions can be decomposed and suggest that different combinations of such features can arouse different affective states. Bringing the dimensional concept to an extreme, such theories suggest that, if the number of primary features extends along a continuum, it would be possible to generate an infinite number of affective states. This idea, even though intriguing, hurts with the principle of economy that seems to rule the dynamic of natural systems, since in this case, the evaluation of affective states may require an infinite computational time. Moreover, humans tend to categorize, since it allows to make associations, rapid recovering of information and facilitate handling of unexpected events, and therefore, categories may be favored in order to avoid excessive processing time. Furthermore, this discrete evolutionary perspective of basic emotions has been supported through several sources of evidence, such as the findings of (1) an emotion specific Autonomic Nervous System's (ANS) activity[1] [4, 26-27]; (2) distinct regions of the brain tuned to handle basic emotions [9, 29, 36]; (3) presence of basic emotional expressions in other mammalian species (as the attachment of infant mammals to their mothers) [35, 38]; (4) universal exhibition of emotional expressions (such as smiling, amusement, and irritability) by infants, adults, blind and sighted [35] (5) universal accuracy in recognizing facial and vocal expressions of basic emotions by all human beings independently of race and culture [11-22].

Assuming, at the light of the above considerations, that there are some basic emotions from which other affective states can be derived, what has this to do with the parallel between music and vocal expression stated before? Since vocal expressions are the best tool for communicating basic emotions and music makes use of the same code in order to rise similar emotional feelings in the perceiver, we would assume that vocal expressions and music share acoustical features that are innately recognized and do not need to be learned. Therefore we expect that young children should be sensitive to the expression of emotion in music since they are equipped with an innate program to decode it, which has to do with the phylogenetic continuity of vocal expressions and the evolutionary perspective proposed for justifying the existence of basic emotions.

There is a large debate on children's abilities to detect affective expressions in music. According to some authors they are principally intrinsic in the sense that young

---

[1] It should be noticed that not all these findings proved to be strong enough, as for example Caccioppo et al. [6] and Bermond et al. [3] disconfirmed the existence of an autonomic specificity and distinctive ANS's activity patterns for each basic emotion.

children and infants possess enough musical abilities as adults to detect emotional expression in music [51]. These abilities may exploit acoustical properties of the tempo and modes [8], and/or musical scales (such as preference on equal-step scales over equal-step scales [52]; and/or consonance [47], and/or spectral slope[2] differences [53], as well as they can be due to the musical sensitivity of some sub-cortical circuits of the human brain that seem to be fundamental for generating affective responses [36-37].

On the other hand, for some authors, appreciation of emotional expressions in music is considered a learned skill. This is mostly due to the controversial results as to what age children become sensitive to some musical properties such as tempo, and modes which have been proved to be the most salient features adults exploit in music in order to perceive emotional feelings [8, 15, 18-19, 24-25, 30-31, 44, 50-53].

According to Imberty [21] this ability does not develop until the age of 8, whereas Kastner and Crowder [25] showed that children younger than 8 may experience affective responses to the major and minor modes. Dolgin and Adelson [10], investigating age changes in the ability to interpret affect in songs and instrumentally-presented melodies, showed that preschool children recognise emotion in music correctly, even though this ability seems to improve with age. In contrast, Terwogt and van Grinsven [49] showed that preschool children were able to differentiate happy and sad excerpts, but they confused fear and anger. Gregory et al. [17] proved that 3 year-old children do not show significantly different emotional responses to changes in the major and minor modes as 7 year-olds, suggesting that emotional responses develop between the ages of 4 and 7. McCulloch [30] also confirm that 4 and 5 year-olds are generally unable to distinguish between the affective character of major and minor mode in music, while 6 and 7 year-olds do. Dalla Bella et al. [8] reported that emotional responses of 6-8 year-old children are affected by tempo and mode manipulations, 5 year-old responses are affected only by tempo, whereas, neither tempo and/or modes are able to elicit affective responses in 3 year-old children. However, Baruch and Drake [1] as well as Pickens and Bahrich [40] reported sensitivity to detect small changes of tempo in children of about 1 year-old. Finally, Nawrot [32] found that 4 year-old children match correctly photographed emotional facial expressions to pieces of music, whereas Cunningham and Sterling [7] found no reliable evidence that 4 year-olds could attribute basic emotions to orchestral extracts which were considered full of affective cues. Geradi and Gerken [16], in repeating Cunningham and Sterling's experiment, confirmed their results showing that affective responses to music did not appear until the age of 8.

In this paper, we tested the sensitivity of 6 year-olds in perceiving emotional responses to orchestral extracts considered full of affective cues as well as the effect of gender on this sensitivity in order to have a clear picture of the development of such responses in children. The experiment proposed was set up assuming an evolutionary perspective for the emotions and therefore the testing was made on four basic

---

[2] Spectral slope is defined in Tsang & Trainor [54] as "*a global property of the spectral envelope representing the linear component of change in relative intensity level across spectral frequency*".

emotions that are considered to be adaptive reactions to survival problems as peril (fear), bereavement (sadness), collaboration (happiness) and rivalry (anger).

2 Materials and Methods

2.1 Participants

The experiment involved three groups of participants at several stages, all with no musical education. However, the data discussed here are on the performance of 40 children, 20 males and 20 females, attending the first grade of primary school. Their mean age was 6 ± 6 months for females and 6 ± 5 months for males.

The remaining two groups of subjects, consisting of 18 adults (9 males and 9 females from 18 to 30 years old,) and 10 children (5 males and 5 females, from 4 to 8 years old), were involved in order to assess the stimuli selected.

2.2 Stimuli

Two sets of stimuli were used in the experiment. A set of musical stimuli and a set of visual ones. The stimuli were considered representative of happiness, sadness, fear and anger.

Visual Stimuli
The visual stimuli included 15 colour illustrations extracted from primary school books, scanned at high resolution, and printed on high quality photo paper of 13x18 centimetres. They represented cartoon characters of children engaged in several activities like playing, walking, discussing. According to the authors, they clearly expressed emotional states. In particular, 5 illustrations represented happiness, 4 sadness, 3 fear and 3 anger. The illustrations were preferred to photos of human faces, generally used in other similar experiments, to facilitate the children's task, since human faces, being richer in details, are more difficult to be emotionally interpreted by children.

Musical Selections
The musical stimuli consisted of eight 20 second-long musical pieces (two for each of the basic emotions considered) which were already verified by other authors [2, 32-33] as able to rise emotional feelings. In particular the happy condition included *Beethoven's Symphony No.6* (piece P1) Pastoral selection from *Awakening of happy feelings on arriving in the country* [2, 32], and the *Eine Kleine Nachtmusik, Divertimento n. 36* (piece P2) by Mozart [33].

The sad musical selections were *Adagio for Strings* (piece P3) from *Platoon* by Barber [2, 32-33] and the A*dagio from Piano Concerto No.2 in Do Minor* (piece P4) by Rachmaninov [33]. Pieces for fear were selected from *Alexander Nevsky* (piece P5) by Prokofiev [32] and from *Concerto for Piano No.2 Op. 18 in Do Minor* (piece P6) by Rachmaninov. The anger music selections were from *Beethoven's Symphony No.9 in Re Minor Op. 125* (piece P7) and from *Alexander Nevsky* (piece P8) by Prokofiev [32]. All the musical pieces came from digital recordings.

2.3 Procedure

The 18 adults participating to the experiment were individually tested, both on the visual and musical stimuli. Adults' participation was required for comparing adult and child responses to musical selections, as well as for selecting from the 15 illustrations identified by the authors those to be proposed to the children in the subsequent test. The adults were asked to label the 15 illustrations according to the emotional states displayed by the characters. No mention was made and no label was given on the emotional state represented in the illustrations.

As a result of this procedure, 8 illustrations from the original group of 15 (those that obtained the highest score) were selected to be proposed to the children, two for each of the four emotional states under examination.

After the selection of the illustrations, the adults were asked to listen to the musical selections and label them according to the feeling that the musical piece arouse in them. When they were uncertain on which label to assign, they were asked to indicate which illustration was more close the aroused feeling.

The adult labelling of the 8 illustrations was validated by proposing them to a group of 10 children aged from 4 to 8. As in the adults' case, children were asked to look at the illustrations and verbalize what the cartoon character was expressing without mentioning any emotion label. The comparison revealed a different interpretation of the children on two illustrations labelled by the adults as happy and angry. These two illustrations are reported in Figure 1.

Figure 1a was labelled as happy by all the adults, whereas 6 children labelled it as happy and 4 as sad. Figure 1b was labelled as angry by 89% of the adults, whereas 3 children labelled it as angry, 3 as sad and the remaining weren't able to label it. The children were then asked to verbalize, among the remaining happy and angry illustrations scored lower by the adults, the feeling of the cartoon characters, identifying two new illustrations that substituted those reported in Figure 1a and 1b.

The definitive illustrations used for the final experiment are displayed in Figure 2, and were associated respectively with the feeling of happiness (2a and 2b), sadness (2c and 2d), fear (2e and 2f) and anger (2g and 2h). The percentage of correct identification of the feeling displayed in each illustration is reported in Figure 3 both for adults and children.

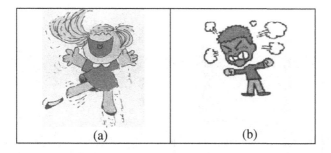

(a)   (b)

Fig. 1. The two illustrations discarded due to a different interpretation of the displayed feeling by the children with respect to the adults

20 children enrolled into the first grade of the primary school "Giousè Carducci" in Casoria (Naples, Italy) participated to the final experiment. The experimenter was introduced to the children as a music teacher.

Before running the experiment, she spent two months with the children in order to become familiar with them. To ensure that each child could correctly match the musical pieces to the emotional state, also these children were asked to label the feeling of the cartoon characters displayed in the 8 illustrations previously selected.

The percentage of correct identification was high and was in accord with the results obtained from the adults and the previous group of children. These percentages are reported in Figure 3.

After the labelling, the eight illustrations were laid out on a table in front of the child. Children were told they would listen to eight pieces of music and would have to point to the illustrations that better went with the music.

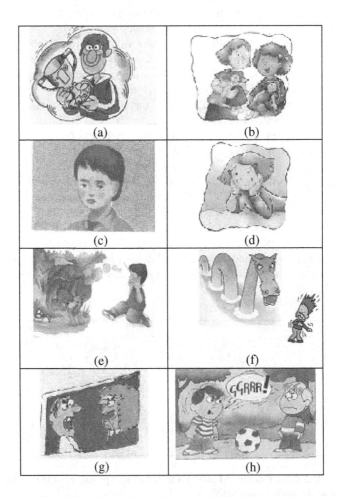

Fig. 2. The illustrations selected for the final experiment

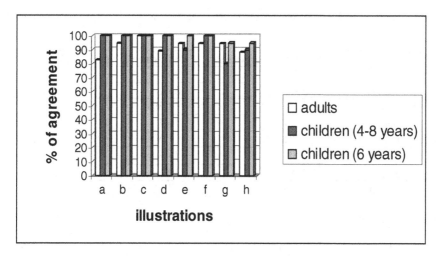

Fig. 3. Percentage of agreement among the three groups of subjects in labelling the emotional feeling displayed in the illustrations used to allow the correct matching of musical pieces to emotional feelings of happiness (illustrations *a* and *b* in Figure 2), sadness (illustrations *c* and *d* in Figure 2), fear (illustrations *e* and *f* in Figure 2), and anger (illustrations *g* and *h* in Figure 2)

3 Results

The majority of adults and children recognised the intended emotions in the proposed musical pieces, except for the pieces 4 and 6 that were poorly identified by the children. Table 1 reports the percentage of correct agreement for adults and children.

It should be noticed that the general distribution of children's and adults' responses was similar, with high recognition scores for happiness and sadness and lower scores for fear and anger. Figure 4 displays the percentage of agreement among subjects (adult males and females and children males and females) to the emotional feeling aroused by each musical piece. It should be noticed that musical pieces labelled with the same emotional feeling did not always received the same percentage of agreement. In particular there are some differences in the interpretation of some musical pieces between adult males and females and children males and females. For example, a low number of adult females interpreted the musical piece P1 as happy as well as a low number of children males interpreted the musical piece P4 as sad.

Generally fear and anger were poorly recognized by the children. Specifically, children interpreted the musical piece P6 as anger in 48% of the cases. This piece received a low correct recognition score also by the adults suggesting that there could be some perceptual features that were not strictly related to the feeling of fear. The musical pieces P7 and P8 intended to arouse the feeling of anger were generally confused with fear both by children and adults, even though the children's performance was worse than the adults'.

For each musical piece, a χ-square statistic ($\alpha = .05$) was computed to determine whether the children's and adults' choices were significantly different and whether the musical perception differs between male and female subjects. The χ-square between adults and children for each musical piece is reported in Table 2.

Table 1. Adults' and children's percentage of agreement in associating emotional feeling to musical pieces

Musical Pieces	Adults' Agreement	Children's Agreement
P1 Happy	72.2%	90%
P2 Happy	100%	65%
P3 Sad	83.3%	72.5%
P4 Sad	88.9%	70%
P5 Fear	72.2%	67.5%
P6 Fear	55.5%	35%
P7 Anger	72.2%	40%
P8 Anger	61.1%	47.5%

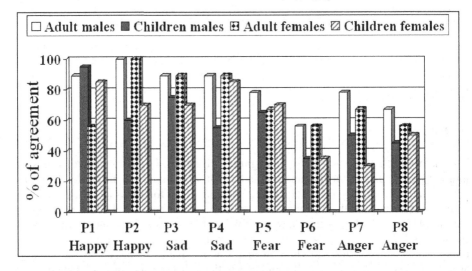

Fig. 4. Percentage of agreement among the four groups in labelling the emotional feeling raised by the musical pieces

As it can be seen in Table 2, the perception of emotional feelings raised by the selected musical pieces does not differ significantly except for the musical pieces P2 and P7 associated to happy and angry feelings respectively.

The significant perceptual difference is due to low scores in the children's labelling of the feeling aroused by the musical pieces P2 and P7 with respect to the adults. P2 selection was perceived as happiness only by 70% of the female and 60% of the male children whereas the adults labelled it as happy in 100% of the cases. P2 was perceived by 20% of the male children as sad, 10% as angry and 10% as fear. 20% of the female children perceived P2 as angry, and 10% as fear. Only 40% of the children, against 72% of the adults, attributed a feeling of anger to the musical piece P7. This selection was confused with fear by 40% of the male and 60% of the female children.

The children's labelling of P6 and P7 was in general below the chance and while P7 (originally labelled as an anger piece) was confused with fear, P6 (originally labelled as a fearful piece) was confused with anger, perhaps implying, in agreement with previous reports [17, 49] that children may use an egocentric perspective and respond to the expression of anger with their own personal reaction to fear and vice-versa. However, even though with a lower score, also adults confused fear with anger and vice-versa when listening to P6 and P7. In particular adult females explicitly used the label "fear", whereas males generally used the label "danger", suggesting perhaps that anger and fear are hardly to be discriminate in musical pieces and it may depend on the listener's perspective.

Table 2. χ^2-square values for adults and children

Musical Pieces	χ^2-square value	$\chi^2_{Critical}$ -square value
P1 Happy	2.99	3.84
P2 Happy	**8.30**	3.84
P3 Sad	0.80	3.84
P4 Sad	2.42	3.84
P5 Fear	0.13	3.84
P6 Fear	2.16	3.84
P7 Anger	**5.16**	3.84
P8 Anger	0.92	3.84

It should also be pointed out that no emotional label was mentioned during the experiment. The adults were left free to verbalize the emotion attributed to the musical pieces since they were simply asked to verbalize which feelings better went with the listened musical piece. Therefore, in some cases, adults used labels as "danger", "quietness", "relaxing". In analyzing the data, however, we categorized these labels as "other" trying to avoid re-interpreting the subject's judgments.

The children instead were forced to choose among the available illustrations, since rather than verbalizing the emotion they were asked to indicate which of the 8 available illustrations better fitted the musical piece they were listening to. This different approach can also explain the statistical difference between children and adults observed for the pieces P2 and P7.

By analyzing the pattern of the subjects' responses rather than the correctness of the majority of their choice however, it becomes apparent that adult and child responses are consistent enough to conclude that there is no difference between them in perceiving similar emotional feelings from music. Figure 5 better illustrates this reasoning. Figure 5 displays, for each musical piece, the confusion pattern of adult and child responses to the four categorical emotions under examination. Note that, in the graph, a further category labeled as "other" is displayed. This category refers to emotional labels different from the four basic emotions considered.

For each musical pieces, a χ^2-square statistic ($\alpha = .05$) was also computed to determine differences between male and female responses both in adults and children. No difference was found for adults.

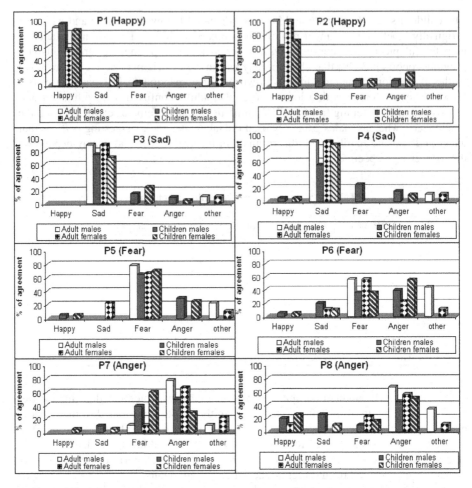

Fig. 5. Distribution of the emotional labels used by the subjects for describing the emotions raised by each musical piece. The category "other" indicates a label different from those considered in the present experiment.

Among children, a significant difference was found only for the piece P4 ($\chi^2(1) =$ 4.29, $\rho=.0384$, $\chi^2_{crititcal}$ (1) = 3.84). Despite these differences, the children (males and females) consistently attributed the same emotional quality to almost all the proposed musical selections. Therefore, we can confidently infer that there is no gender difference in perceiving emotional states from music both for adults and children.

An experiment similar to the present study and based on almost the same musical selections was performed by Nawrot [32] on a group of 24 English children (ranging in age from 3 to 5 year-olds) and adults (ranging in age from 18 to 37 year-olds). Table 3 compares the percentage of agreement between adults and children obtained in the two studies for the same musical selections. As it can be seen from the data displayed in Table 3, analyzing the response's distribution rather than the differences in percentage

Table 3. Comparison with Nawrot's data [32]. Displayed are the percentages with which adults and children correctly recognized the four basic emotions from music.

Emotions	Nawrot's data		Present data	
	Adults	*Children*	*Adults*	*Children*
Happy	90%	38%	72,2%	90%
Sad	60%	22%	83,3%	72,5%
Fear	50%	35%	72,2%	67,5%
Anger	50%	26%	61,1%	47,5%

values, the two different cultural groups show a similar pattern, suggesting that there are no cultural differences in attributing feelings to music between Italian and English subjects and supporting the idea of some universals in music perception.

4 Conclusions

This study was devoted to investigate differences (if there exist) in perceiving emotional feelings from music between adults and children, between gender and between culture. The major aim was to bring support to the few researches proposed in literature designed to determine the age at which affective responses to musical pieces first appear, but we also considered gender and cultural differences comparing our results with a similar study by Nawrot [32]. The attempt was made without deconstructing the music in basic structural elements (such as tempo, timing, mode, consonance) to which several authors have attributed the characteristic to arouse emotional states [8, 15, 18-19, 24-25, 30-31, 44, 50-53]. This was done since the search of a single or a group of musical features to which attribute the arousing of emotional feeling is at its early stage and details about how musical components are extracted, as well as how structural relations among them are computed, are still not well understood. Therefore we simply chose to use orchestral extracts considered full of affective cues. We found that children, as young as six, could interpret basic emotions by matching musical pieces to emotional illustrations and that gender did not play any role in this ability. We also found that there were no cultural differences between Italian and English (both adults and children) in interpreting emotions in the same musical pieces.

There are only two musical pieces, among those selected, where we found a significant difference between children's and adults' judgments. These inconsistencies, as pointed out by different authors [see 32] can be attributed to the emotional communicative value of the particular musical piece, as well as to the influence of the responding individual. This influence however, should be interpreted as a distinct physiological response to music [34, 54] rather than a cultural and/or learning issue since, given the fact that music arouses emotions, it is well known that emotions arouse several autonomic changes [20, 38, 48]. We should then expect individual differences in the incidence and strength with which specific musical selections evoke emotional responses. However, the most salient issue here is that human (whether adults or children) sensitivity to emotional sounds is shared across cultures and ages suggesting that it may be related to the survival benefits that emotional communication had during our evolutionary history. We are clearly speculating at this stage and more work should be done to support this theory. More research is needed to clarify the relations and differences between adults and children in the perception of musical expressions. However, even under the current state of knowledge, it appears that musical expressions are understood and processed like adults by children with no musical experience.

Acknowledgements

This work has been partially funded by COST 2102 "Cross Modal Analysis of Verbal and Nonverbal Communication", www.cost2102.edu. Acknowledgements go to **Miss Tina Marcella Nappi** for her editorial help.

References

1. Baruch, C., Drake, C.: Tempo Discrimination in Infants. Infant Behavior and Development 20(4), 573–577 (1997)
2. Baumgartner, T., Esslen, M., Lutz Jäncke, L.: From Emotion Perception to Emotion Experience: Emotions Evoked by Pictures and Classical Music. International Journal of Psychophysiology 60, 34–43 (2006)
3. Bermond, B., Nieuwenhuyse, B., Fasotti, L., Schuerman, J.: Spinal Cord Lesions, Peripheral Feedback, and Intensities of Emotional Feelings. Cognition and Emotion 5, 201–220 (1991)
4. Bradley, M.M., Cuthbert, B.N., Lang, P.J.: Startle Reflex Modification: Emotion or Attention. Psychophysiology 27, 513–523 (1990)
5. Brown, S.: The "Musilanguage" Model of Music Evolution. In: Wallin, N.L., Merker, B., Brown, S. (eds.) The Origins of Music, pp. 271–300. MIT Press, Cambridge, MA (2000)
6. Cacioppo, J.T., Berntson, G.G., Larsen, J.T., Poehlmann, K.M., Ito, T.A.: The Psychophysiology of emotion. In: Lewis, J.M., Haviland-Jones, M. (eds.) Handbook of Emotions, 2nd edn. pp. 173–191. Guilford Press, New York (2000)
7. Cunningham, J.G., Sterling, R.S.: Developmental Changes in the Understanding of Affective Meaning in Music. Motivation and Emotion 12, 399–413 (1988)
8. Bella, S.D., Peretz, I., Rousseau, L., Gosselin, N.: A Developmental Study of the Affective Value of Tempo and Mode in Music. Cognition 80, B1–B10 (2001)
9. Damasio, A.R., Grabowski, T.J., Bechara, A., Damasio, H., Ponto, L.L.B., Parvizi, J., Hichwa, R.D.: Subcortical and Cortical Brain Activity During the Feeling of Self-Generated Emotions. Nature Neuroscience 3, 1049–1056 (2000)
10. Dolgin, K.G., Adelson, E.H.: Age Changes in the Ability to Interpret Affect in Sung and Instrumentally-Presented Melodies. Psychology of Music 18, 87–98 (1990)
11. Ekman, P.: An Argument for Basic Emotions. Cognition and Emotion 6, 169–200 (1992)
12. Ekman, P.: Expression and the Nature of Emotion. In: Scherer, K., Ekman, P. (eds.) Approaches to emotion, pp. 319–343. Lawrence Erlbaum, Hillsdale, N.J (1984)
13. Frijda, N.H.: Moods, Emotion Episodes, and Emotions. In: Haviland, M., Lewis, J.M. (eds.) Handbook of Emotion, pp. 381–402. Guilford Press, New York (1993)
14. Frijda, N.H.: The Emotions. Cambridge University Press, Cambridge (1986)
15. Gabrielsson, A., Juslin, P.N.: Emotional Expression in Music. In: Davidson, R.J., Goldsmith, H.H., Scherer, K.R. (eds.) Handbook of Affective Sciences, pp. 503–534. Oxford University Press, New York (2003)

16. Gerardi, G.M., Gerken, L.: The Development of Affective Responses to Modality and Melodic Contour. Music Perception 12(3), 279–290 (1995)
17. Gregory, A.H., Worrall, L., Sarge, A.: The Development of Emotional Responses to Music in Young Children. Motivation and Emotion 20(4), 341–349 (1996)
18. Heinlein, C.P.: The Affective Characteristics of the Major and Minor Modes in Music. Journal of Comparative Psychology 8, 101–142 (1928)
19. Hevner, K.: The Affective Character of the Major and Minor Modes in Music. American Journal of Psychology 47, 103–118 (1935)
20. Hodges, D.A. (ed.): Handbook of Music Psychology. IMR Press, San Antonio (1995)
21. Imberty, M.: L'Aquisition des Structures Tonales Chez l'Enfant. Paris: Klinsiek (1969)
22. Izard, C.E.: Organizational and Motivational Functions of Discrete Emotions. In: Lewis, M., Haviland, J.M. (eds.) Handbook of Emotions, pp. 631–641. Guilford Press, New York (1993)
23. Izard, C.E.: Basic Emotions, Relations among Emotions, and Emotion–Cognition Relations. Psychological Review 99, 561–565 (1992)
24. Juslin, P.N., Laukka, P.: Communication of Emotions in Vocal Expression and Music Performance: Different Channels, Same Code. Psychological Bulletin 129(5), 770–814 (2003)
25. Kastner, M.P., Crowder, R.G.: Perception of the Major/Minor Distinction: IV. Emotional Connotations in Young Children. Music Perception 8(2), 189–202 (1990)
26. Levenson, R.W.: Autonomic Nervous System Differences Among Emotions. Psychological Science 3, 23–27 (1992)
27. Levenson, R.W.: Human Emotion: A Functional View. In: Ekman, P., Davidson, R.J. (eds.) The Nature of Emotion: Fundamental Questions, pp. 123–126. Oxford University Press, New York (1994)
28. Levman, B.G.: Western Theories of Music Origin, Historical and Modern. Musicae Scientiae 4, 185–211 (2000)
29. MacLean, P.: Cerebral Evolution of Emotion. In: Lewis, M., Haviland, J.M (eds.) Handbook of Emotions, pp. 67–83. Guilford Press, New York (1993)
30. Mcculloch, R.: Modality and Children's Affective Responses to Music. (1999), www.ms.cam.ac.uk/ ic108/PandP/McCulloch99/McCulloch99.html
31. Madison, G.: Properties of Expressive Variability Patterns in Music Performance. Journal of New Music Research 29(4), 335–356 (2000)
32. Nawrot, E.S.: The Perception of Emotional Expression in Music: Evidence from Infants, Children and Adults. Psychology of Music 31(I), 75–92 (2003)
33. Niedenthal, P.M., Setterlund, M.B.: Emotion Congruence in Perception. Personality and Social Psychology Bullettin 20, 401–410 (1993)
34. Nyklicek, I., Thayer, J.F., Van Doornen, L.J.P.: Cardiorespiratory Differentiation of Musically-Induced Emotions. Journal of Psychophysiology 11, 304–321 (1997)
35. Oatley, K., Jenkins, J.M.: Understanding Emotions, pp. 96–132. Blackwell Publishers (1996)
36. Panksepp, J.: Emotions as Natural Kinds Within the Mammalian Brain. In: Lewis, J.M., Haviland-Jones, M. (eds.) Handbook of Emotions, 2nd edn. pp. 137–156. Guilford Press, New York (2000)
37. Panksepp, J., Bernatzky, G.: Emotional Sounds and the Brain: The Neuro-affective Foundations of Musical Appreciation. Behavioural Processes 60, 133–155 (2002)
38. Panksepp, J.: At the Interface of the Affective, Behavioral, and Cognitive Neurosciences: Decoding the Emotional Feelings of the Brain. Brain and Cognition 52, 4–14 (2003)
39. Peretz, I.: The Nature of Music from a Biological Perspective. Cognition 100, 1–32 (2006)

40. Pickens, J., Bahrick, L.E.: Infants Discrimination of Bimodal Events on the Basis of Rhythm and Tempo. British Journal of Developmental Psychology 13, 223–236 (1995)
41. Plutchik, R.: Emotions as Adaptive Reactions: Implications for Therapy. Psychoanalytic Review, LIII 2, 105–110 (1966)
42. Plutchik, R.: Emotion and their Vicissitudes: Emotions and Psychopatology. In: Haviland, M., Lewis, J.M. (eds.) Handbook of Emotion, pp. 53–66. Guilford Press, New York (1993)
43. Russell, J.A.: A Circumplex Model of Affect. Journal of Personality and Social Psychology 39, 1161–1178 (1980)
44. Salgado, A.G.: Voice, Emotion and Facial Gesture in Singing. In: Woods, C., Luck, G., Brochard, R., Seddon, F., Sloboda, J.A. (eds.) Proceedings of the Sixth International Conference for Music Perception and Cognition [CD-ROM]. Keele, England: Keele University (2000)
45. Scherer, K.: The Psychological Structure of Emotion. In: Smelser, N.J., Baltes, P.B. (eds.) International Encyclopaedia of the Social and Behavioural Sciences, pp. 4472–4477. Pergamon Press, Oxford (2002)
46. Schlosberg, H.: Three Dimensions of Emotion. The Psychological Review 61(2), 81–88 (1953)
47. Schellenberg, E.G., Trehub, S.E.: Natural Musical Intervals. Psychological Science 7(5), 272–277 (1996)
48. Steinberg, R. (ed.): Music and the Mind Machine. Springer, Berlin (1995)
49. Terwogt, M.M., Van Grinsven, F.: Musical Expression of Mood-states. Psychology of Music 19, 99–109 (1991)
50. Trainor, L.J., Heinmiller, B.M.: The Development of Evaluative Responses to Music: Infants Prefer to Listen to Consonance over Dissonance. Infant Behavior and Development 21(1), 77–88 (1998)
51. Trehub, S.E.: The Origins of Music Perception and Cognition: A Developmental Perspective. In: Deliège, I., Sloboda, J.A. (eds.) Perception and Cognition of Music, pp. 103–128. Hove Psychology Press (1997)
52. Trehub, S.E., Schellenberg, E.G., Kamenetsky, S.B.: Infants' and Adults' Perception of Scale Structure. Journal of Experimental Psychology: Human Perception and Performance 25(4), 965–975 (1999)
53. Tsang, D.C., Trainor, J.L.: Spectral Slope Discrimination in Infancy: Sensitivity to Socially Important Timbre. Infant Behavior and Development 25, 183–194 (2002)
54. VanderArk, S.D., Ely, D.: Biochemical and Galvanic Skin Responses to Music Stimuli by College Students in Biology and Music. Perceptual and Motor Skills 74, 1079–1090 (1992)

Emotional Style Conversion in the TTS System with Cepstral Description

Jiří Přibil[1] and Anna Přibilová[2]

[1] Institute of Photonics and Electronics, Academy of Sciences CR, v.v.i.,
Chaberská 57, CZ-182 51 Prague 8, Czech Republic
umerprib@savba.sk
[2] Slovak University of Technology, Faculty of Electrical Engineering & Information
Technology, Dept. of Radio Electronics, Ilkovičova 3, SK-812 19 Bratislava, Slovakia
pribilova@kre.elf.stuba.sk

Abstract. This contribution describes experiments with emotional style conversion performed on the utterances produced by the Czech and Slovak text-to-speech (TTS) system with cepstral description and basic prosody generated by rules. Emotional style conversion was realized as post-processing of the TTS output speech signal, and as a real-time implementation into the system. Emotional style prototypes representing three emotional states (sad, angry, and joyous) were obtained from the sentences with the same information content. The problem with the different frame length between the prototype and the target utterance was solved by linear time scale mapping (LTSM). The results were evaluated by a listening test of the resynthetized utterances.

Keywords: speech synthesis, emotional style, text-to-speech system.

1 Introduction

The requirements on *text-to-speech* (TTS) systems grow increasingly. In addition to the tendency for better speech quality and possibility of multi-voice realization (including male, female, and childish voices) [1] more speaking styles (formal/informal, expressing emotions – sadness, anger, joy, etc.) are required. According to [2], performance of synthetic speech systems can be measured by their intelligibility, variability (capability to change the characteristics of the voice), and naturalness. However, the factors affecting intelligibility correlate negatively with those affecting naturalness. There are three ways to improve the naturalness of synthetic speech: voice quality, speaking style (e.g. the speaker is consciously trying to speak more intelligibly, express his/her social standing relative to the audience, etc.), and emotion (mood).

Emotional influence on prosodic speech characteristics has been studied by phoneticians [3]. Complication in expressing emotions is that the phonetic correlates appear not to be limited to the major prosodic variables (pitch, duration, energy) alone. Besides these, phonetic effects in the voice such as jitter (inter-pitch-period microvariation), or the mode of excitation may be important [4]. One of the first TTS systems producing recognizable emotional speech [5] uses emotion-dependent pitch

A. Esposito et al. (Eds.): Verbal and Nonverbal Commun. Behaviours, LNAI 4775, pp. 65–73, 2007.

and duration rules based on the human vocal emotion effects described in literature for six relevant emotions: anger, happiness, sadness, fear, disgust, and grief. In their system HAMLET (Helpful Automatic Machine for Language and Emotional Talk) the emotion effects are taken as additive to any existing prosodic or voice quality effects in the synthetic speech, as the prosodic features which indicate the various levels of word accent and sentence-level stress must remain recognizable whatever the emotion (in order that the stress is still conveyed correctly). For corpus-based concatenative speech synthesis [6], [7] different speech corpora must be created for different emotions. The system of [6] uses three read-speech emotional corpora with emotions grouped according to similarity:

1. anger, rage, disgust, unwillingness;
2. joy, gratitude, happiness, pleasantness, elation;
3. sadness, disconsolation, loneliness, anxiety.

The system proposed by [7] should generate the "big six" emotions: anger, disgust, fear, joy, sadness, and surprise.

2 Emotional Style Conversion Method

The melody of speech utterances is given by the *fundamental frequency* (F0) contour. Together with the intensity and the speech unit duration it plays an essential role in the transmission of the prosodic information. The F0 contour is obtained during the utterance's analysis in the frames with the length of 10-30 ms, where the speech can be supposed to be stationary. According to the energy of the analyzed speech signal, several beginning and ending frames are not included in the F0 contour. As the basic F0 contour is not continuous curve, the *virtual contour* (VF0) must be obtained by linear, cubic, or another interpolation in the unvoiced parts of the speech. The problem with the different frame length between the *emotional style prototype* (ESP) and the target utterance can be solved by using *linear time scale mapping* (LTSM) of the VF0, energy, and time duration contours.

Developed emotional style conversion method is based on modification of the F0, the energy, and the frame length (time duration) contours of the target (output) synthesized sentence by the parameters of the selected ESP from the database. The ESP relative contours and parameters were created in dependency of the current frame voiceness – separate contours exist for voiced and unvoiced parts of a speech signal. Because the ESPs contain relative values, they can be applied to various types of voices (male, young male, female, childish) with different basic F0 values (105, 160, 230, and 300 Hz). The practical realization of this method can be divided into two phases:

1. Preparation of emotional style prototypes database.
2. Application of ESPs to the synthetic speech generated by the TTS system with basic flat prosody by rules realized as post-processing operation on the speech utterances produced by the TTS system, and as a real-time implementation directly to the TTS system.

2.1 Building of the ESP Database

The database of ESPs was based on the sentences with the same information content: the basic style (neutral) and three emotional styles (joyous, sad, and angry). Designed ESP preparation process will be explained in the following example for the joyous emotional style. The Czech declarative sentence *"Vlak už nejede"* (No more train leave today) pronounced by the male speaker was used. The prototype sentence was analyzed in 24-ms overlapping frames shifted by 12 ms. Preparation of the SSP consists of eight steps:

1. Cepstral analysis of the basic (neutral) and target (joyous) sentences – the values of the fundamental frequency F0 and the energy E_n (calculated from the first cepstral coefficient c_0) are mainly used for next processing. For resynthesis of the source sentence after emotional style conversion, in addition to N_0 values of the minimum phase cepstral coefficients $\{\hat{s}_n\}$ the spectral flatness S_F values are also applied [1]. The whole cepstral analysis scheme is shown in Fig. 1. The determined F0 and energy E_n contours of the basic sentence are shown in Fig. 2.
2. Removal of the low energy beginning and ending frames by the threshold E_{nmin} to obtain the limited F0 contour; definition of ESP working length WL_{LR} in frames.
3. Calculation of VF0 values from the limited F0 contour by cubic interpolation in the position of unvoiced frames (Fig. 3 left); definitions of minimum, maximum, and mean values.
4. Calculation of *relative values* of the VF0 contour (RVF0) as the first output parameter of ESP (Fig. 3 right).

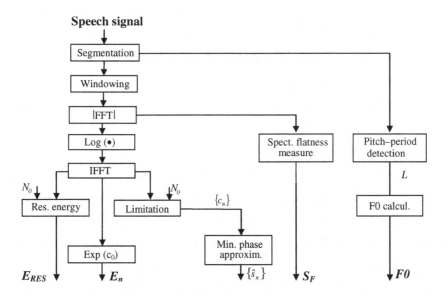

Fig. 1. Block diagram of used cepstral analysis method (for $f_s = 16$ kHz, $N_0 = 50$)

5. Determination of the time *relative duration ratio* (RDUR) between the basic and the target emotional style parts in dependence on voiceness (voiced/unvoiced); calculation of mean ratio values.
6. Calculation of *virtual relative time duration* contours (VRDUR) by cubic interpolation separately for voiced and unvoiced frames as the second output parameter – see Fig. 4.
7. Determination of the energy ratio between basic and target emotional style speech parts in dependence on voiceness; calculation of mean ratio values.
8. Calculation of virtual relative energy contours (VREn) by cubic interpolation as the third output parameter (for voiced and unvoiced frames) – see Fig. 5.

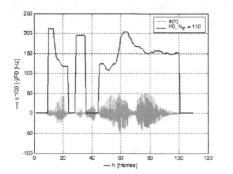 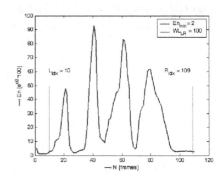

Fig. 2. Input speech signal of joyous sentence together with F0 contour (left), E_n contour and ESP WL_{LR} determination (right)

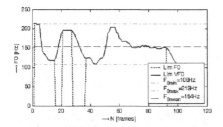 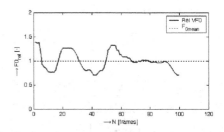

Fig. 3. Virtual F0 contour by cubic interpolation (left), resulting relative VF0 contour (right)

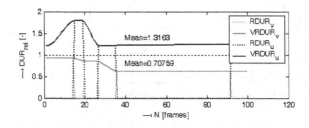

Fig. 4. Determination of time duration ratio between basic and target emotional styles

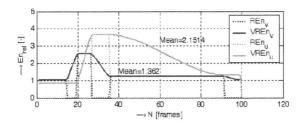

Fig. 5. Determination of energy ratio between basic and target emotional styles

As follows from previous description, each of the ESPs in the database consists of five virtual contour files and one parameter record (containing values of frame length L_F in samples, working length WL_{LR}, energy threshold E_{nmin}, minimum, maximum, and mean values of F0).

2.2 Application of ESP in TTS Synthesis

For description of ESP application the Czech declarative sentence *"Mraky plují oblohou"* (Clouds float on the sky) generated by the TTS system was used. Synthesis parameters were set as follows: male voice, $f_s = 16$ kHz, $F_{0basic} = 110$ Hz, speech rate = 130 %.

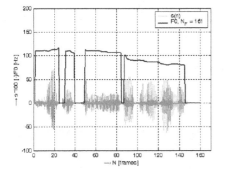
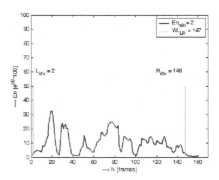

Fig. 6. Speech signal of processed sentence together with F0 contour (left), E_n contour and sentence WL_{LR} determination (right)

The first three steps are the same as in ESP preparation: cepstral analysis of synthesized speech signal, F0 and energy determination, removal of low-energy frames, working length definition (see Fig. 6), and definition of minimum, maximum, and mean F0 values from the calculated VF0 contour. In general, the frame length of the processed sentence is different from the WL_{LR} of the applied ESP.

The *time modification factor* γ corresponding to the ratio of the number of segments of the target utterance N_{target} and the prototype N_{prot} must be determined. For $\gamma > 1$ ($\gamma < 1$) the time compression (expansion) is performed.

Next steps of the ESP application process are:

- RVF0 prototype contour multiplication by the current F_{0mean} value and linear time scale mapping of the prototype to the target sentence – see Fig. 7.
- Transposition of the F0 contour from the ESP – see Fig. 8.
- Pitch-synchronous resynthesis of the target sentences with applied transposed F0, energy, and time duration contours (in dependence on voiceness).

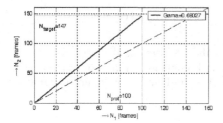
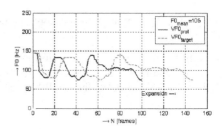

Fig. 7. Linear time scale mapping function (left) for prototype VF0 contour after multiplication by mean F0 value (right)

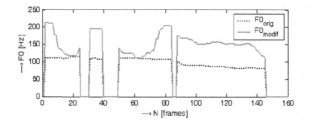

Fig. 8. Final transposition of the F0 contour by the joyous ESP

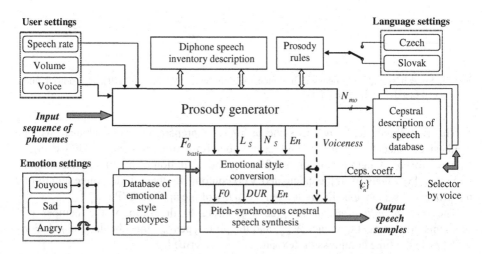

Fig. 9. Block diagram of Czech and Slovak multi-voice TTS system with cepstral description

The second emotional style application method consists of addition a new function block to the real-time TTS system (between the prosody generator and the output speech synthesizer – see Fig. 9). This approach leaves out the cepstral analysis steps, because parameters of cepstral description are available for each frame together with information about voiceness, frame length, pitch-period, and energy. The application of the ESP lies in modification of prosody parameters used for control of the output speech synthesis. For multiplying of RVF0 contour the F_{0basic} value corresponding to the selected voice type is used and the LTSM operation of the selected ESP must be also applied.

3 Experiments and Results

The first experiments with emotional styles application were performed with realization in the form of post-processing operation on the speech utterances generated by the TTS system (see processed speech signals in Fig. 10).

For evaluation of emotional style conversion the listening test called *"Determination of emotional style type"* has been processed. In this test, fourteen listeners (9 Czechs and 5 Slovaks, 8 men and 6 women) chose the emotional voice style from *"Joyous"*, *"Sad"*, *"Angry"*, or *"Not recognized"*.

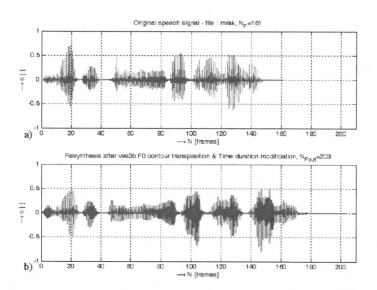

Fig. 10. Processed speech signals: original sentence generated by the TTS system (a), after cepstral resynthesis with transposed emotional style by "Joyous" prototype (b)

The testing corpus was created with the help of the Czech and Slovak TTS system realized as the speech synthesizer for MS SAPI 5 standard. It consists of 75 short sentences in the Czech language (with the average time duration of 1.5 seconds), male voice, $f_s = 16$ kHz. Every time the listening test is performed, ten speech examples are selected randomly from the testing corpus. The developed testing program automatically generates the text protocol about the test. Output test values are stored in separate files for final statistical post-processing and evaluation of the results in a graphical (see Fig. 11) and numerical form (see values in Table1).

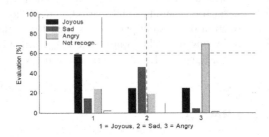

Fig. 11. Listening test summary results in the graphical form

Table 1. Summary results of listening test *"Determination of emotional style type"*

Emotional style	Correct	Wrong or not recognized
Joyous	59.2 %	40.8 %
Sad	46.2 %	53.8 %
Angry	69.8 %	30.2 %

4 Conclusion

In our described experiments, the F0, energy, and time duration contours of three emotional styles (joyous, sad, and angry) were converted always on the sentences with the same information content. The results were evaluated by the listening test of the resynthetized utterances using the cepstral speech description. From the performed listening test it follows that there are always audible differences between the basic sentences generated by the TTS system and those modified by emotional style conversion, and ESPs can be applied on the sentences regardless of their information content and lexical context; significant results are for *"Angry"* style.

The developed ESP conversion method is characterized by low computational complexity. It is very important for real-time speech applications such as speech coders and decoders or TTS systems, implemented especially in small mobile devices. In near feature, this ESP conversion method will be practically implemented in the special aid for blind and partially sighted people – Braille notetaker based on the Pocket PC with the special Braille keyboard connected via wireless Bluetooth standard [8]. Then, we intend to build a larger database of ESPs for increasing the naturalness of generated synthetic speech.

Acknowledgments. The paper was realized within the framework of the research project AVOZ 20670512 and has been supported by the Grant Agency of the Academy of Sciences of the Czech Republic (1QS108040569), and the Ministry of Education of the Slovak Republic (AV 4/0012/07, 1/3107/06).

References

1. Přibilová, A., Přibil, J.: Non-linear Frequency Scale Mapping for Voice Conversion in Text-to-Speech System with Cepstral Description. Speech Communication 48, 1691–1703 (2006)
2. Murray, I.R., Arnott, J.L., Rohwer, E.A.: Emotional Stress in Synthetic Speech: Progress and Future Directions. Speech Communication 20, 85–91 (1996)
3. Vlčková-Mejvaldová, J.: Prosodic Changes in Emotional Speech. In: Vích, R. (ed.) Proc. of the 16th Conference Electronic Speech Signal Processing Joined with the 15th Czech-German Workshop Speech Processing, Prague, pp. 38–45 (2005)
4. Huang, X., Acero, A., Hon, H.-W.: Spoken Language Processing: A Guide to Theory, Algorithm, and System Development. Prentice Hall, New Jersey (2001)
5. Murray, I.R., Arnott, J.L.: Implementation and Testing of a System for Producing Emotion-by-Rule in Synthetic Speech. Speech Communication 16, 369–390 (1995)
6. Iida, A., Campbell, N., Higuchi, F., Yasumura, M.: A Corpus-Based Speech Synthesis System with Emotion. Speech Communication 40, 161–187 (2003)
7. Navas, E., Hernáez, I., Luengo, I.: An Objective and Subjective Study of the Role of Semantics and Prosodic Features in Building Corpora for Emotional TTS. IEEE Transactions on Audio, Speech, and Language Processing 14, 1117–1127 (2006)
8. Přibil, J., Přibilová, A.: Czech TTS Engine for BraillePen Device Based on Pocket PC Platform. In: Vích, R. (ed.) Proc. of the 16th Conf. Electronic Speech Signal Processing Joined with the 15th Czech-German Workshop Speech Processing, Prague, pp. 402–408 (2005)

Meaningful Parameters in Emotion Characterisation

Eva Navas, Inmaculada Hernáez, Iker Luengo, Iñaki Sainz, Ibon Saratxaga,
and Jon Sanchez

Departamento de Electrónica y Telecomunicaciones, University of the Basque Country,
Alda. Urquijo s/n, 48013 Bilbao, Spain
eva.navas@ehu.es, inma.hernaez@ehu.es, iker.luengo@ehu.es,
inaki@aholab.ehu.es, ibon@aholab.ehu.es, jon.sanchez@ehu.es

Abstract. In expressive speech synthesis some method of mimicking the way one specific speaker express emotions is needed. In this work we have studied the suitability of long term prosodic parameters and short term spectral parameters to reflect emotions in speech, by means of the analysis of the results of two automatic emotion classification systems. Those systems have been trained with different emotional monospeaker databases recorded in standard Basque that include six emotions. Both of them are able to differentiate among emotions for a specific speaker with very high identification rates (above 75%), but the models are not applicable to other speakers (identification rates drop to 20%). Therefore in the synthesis process the control of both spectral and prosodic features is essential to get expressive speech and when a change in speaker is desired the values of the parameters should be re-estimated.

1 Introduction

With the progress of new technologies and the introduction of interactive systems, there has been a sudden increase in the demand of user friendly human-machine interfaces. The field of natural interfaces is experimenting increasing activity, showing a wide application market, from avatars and modern interactive entertainment toys to automatic customer service systems, and many researches are being held in this field [1][2][3]. As speech is the natural way of communication for humans, providing these interfaces with speech generation and recognition mechanisms is a must in order to achieve a comfortable interface.

Nowadays, one of the major challenges in the development of oral interfaces is providing naturalness to the communication channel between human and machine. Humans tend to express their emotional and affective state through the voice, therefore capability to generate emotional speech and to recognize the mood of the speaker are also needed.

Many studies indicate that prosodic parameters such as fundamental frequency, intensity and speaking rate are strongly related with the emotion expressed in speech [4][5]. However, voice quality and short-term spectral features have also to be considered when studying emotional or affective speech [6][7][8]. Within this work we aimed at establishing a set of meaningful parameters to identify emotion in the speech when no linguistic information is available. This set of parameters should be

A. Esposito et al. (Eds.): Verbal and Nonverbal Commun. Behaviours, LNAI 4775, pp. 74–84, 2007.

appropriate to be applied to the generation of synthetic emotional speech. At the same time, it has been of interest the comparison between the speakers, to investigate the stability of the parameters across them. A complementary goal of the performed experiments was to validate the emotional content of the databases, since our purpose was to use them for speech synthesis purposes such as prosody modelling of the emotions and as voices for a corpus-based TTS system.

The remainder of the paper is organised as follows: section 2 describes the databases used, and the results of the subjective evaluation tests. Section 3 presents the parameters chosen to perform the classification experiments. The results for the two used databases of these experiments using different parameter sets are presented in section 4., finally, section 5 presents the conclusions of the work.

2 Databases

We have created two emotional databases '*Idoia*' and '*Pello and Karolina*'. Both databases include the following emotions: anger, disgust, fear, joy, sadness and surprise, that are considered the basic ones [9][10]. This set has been used in different studies related with speech, both for emotion recognition [11] and for emotion generation [12]. In addition, neutral style was also considered in both cases.

Both databases were developed for TTS purposes, basically for prosody modelling and corpus-based expressive speech synthesis in standard Basque. They include acted speech and the speakers are professional dubbing actors and actresses.

Following we present a description of these databases and the results of their subjective evaluation.

2.1 Database Description

2.1.1 Idoia
This was the first emotional database recorded in our laboratory and it contains both video and speech. A complete description of the recording details can be found in [13]. This database was also used to validate the use of neutral texts for the study of emotional prosody [13][14]. Appropriately expressing emotion when the text has not emotional content can be a difficult task for the speaker, but it allows an easier comparison among styles. This database was build using two different textual corpora:

Common corpus: it consists of emotion independent texts, which are common for all the emotions, as well as for the neutral style. The texts have neutral semantic content and were phonetically balanced.

Specific corpus: it includes texts semantically related to each emotion, and therefore, the texts are different for each of the emotions considered in the database. Neutral style was not considered in this part of the corpus. In this case, the collection of suitable texts to be recorded is more laborious.

Both text corpora included isolated words and sentences of different complexity and syntactical structure. The structure of Common and Specific corpora is shown in table 1.

The texts were read by a professional dubbing actress. The recording was made using a laryngograph to capture also the glottal pulse signal. Speech and glottal pulse signals were sampled at 32 KHz, and quantified using 16 bit per sample.

The recording was made at a professional recording studio, during two days. The first day the texts related with the emotion were recorded, and the second day the common texts. Within a recording session, every emotion was recorded without interruption, to avoid the speaker loosing concentration. The speaker was allowed to rest between the recordings of texts corresponding to different emotions.

Although both corpus have been analysed and used in different experiments, the results presented in this work are related only to the Common corpus.

Table 1. Data of Common and Specific corpora in *Idoia* database

Type of item	Common corpus	Specific corpus
Isolated digits	20	-
Isolated words	20	20
Isolated sentences	55	55
Total number of items per emotion	95	75
Total number of items	665	450
Total number of words	3,815	2,554
Total number of phonemes	24,058	14,548

2.1.2 Pello and Karolina

This database, containing data from two speakers, was developed with the purpose of being used as voices for a corpus-based expressive speech synthesis system. A detailed description of the recording process and the database contents can be found in [15]. The corpus includes only semantically neutral texts. The main section of the corpus is formed by 702 isolated sentences that were recorded for every emotion and neutral style. Additionally a continuous text was also recorded for every emotion and neutral style to provide for a long speech signal that would enable the study of intersentence breaks. Finally, a short text, uttered in neutral style at the beginning, at the middle and at the end of each session with the purpose of having a recording reference point. In this work all the experiments have been done using only the main part of the corpus (isolated sentences). The main features of this part of the corpus are presented in table 2.

The database was recorded by two professional actors, one male (Pello) and one female (Karolina). A limited casting was done in order to guarantee that the speaker was able of expressing the selected emotions, and also that the speakers´ voices should produce good results when using them for synthesis. Records from different professional speakers were listened and tested by means of Praat resynthesis [16][17]. With the help of this tool original voices were manipulated trying to foresee their suitability to be used for speech synthesis.

The speech and laryngograph signals were sampled at 48 kHz, and quantified using 16 bits per sample. The recording was made at a semi-professional recording studio, during 6 sessions for the female voice and 4 sessions for the male one. Recordings were made emotion by emotion recording every emotion without interruption.

Table 2. Data of Main Corpus

Characteristic	Value
Number of isolated sentences	702
Total number of words	6,582
Number of different words	4,308
Total number of phonemes	39,767
Number of distinct phonemes	35
Total number of diphonemes	40,917
Number of distinct diphonemes	897

2.2 Subjective Evaluation

To prove the ability of the speakers to accurately simulate emotions, a subjective test was prepared. With this test, we wanted to check whether listeners could identify the intended emotion above chance level, assessing this way the validity of the obtained data.

A forced choice test was designed, where users had to select one of the proposed styles. Thus, it was a test for discriminating emotions rather than identifying them. The six emotions contained in the databases were proposed to the listeners. In the case of *Idoia* database, neutral style was also proposed. There was not an option of "Not identified" for use in cases in which the emotion is not clear.

The subjects taking part in the experiment were selected among the students and staff of the Electronics and Telecommunication Department of the University of the Basque Country. All of them were native of Basque, or at least fluent in standard Basque. None of them reported speech or hearing problems. Some of them were used to TTS systems, but none of them had received a special phonetic training.

The tests were performed in the quasi silent environment of a research laboratory. Stimuli were presented to listeners over high quality headphones and reproduced with a standard Sound Blaster soundcard.

The stimuli were presented to subjects by means of electronic forms that grouped ten stimuli to be evaluated. Listeners made no training session and they got no feedback about their performance. Participants could hear the signals by clicking the adequate buttons and they had to choose the emotion they identified in the signal from a six or seven item list. Listeners could hear each stimulus as many times as they wanted. They had to label all the signals presented in a form before starting evaluating the stimuli present in the following one. Once a form had been completed they could not go back to modify it. The order of the stimuli presented was randomised in all the tests.

In the case of the subjective evaluation of *Idoia* database, a total of 15 participants (11 males and 4 females with ages varying from 20 to 36 years) took part in the experiments. The results are presented in table 3.

19 evaluators took part in the subjective evaluation of *Karolina* and *Pello* database. The results for the speaker *Karolina* are presented in table 4 and those for *Pello* in table 5.

Table 3. Confusion matrix of the subjective test in *Idoia* database. Columns contain true values and rows values selected by listeners. Best and worst scores have been emphasized.

Emotion	Anger	Disgust	Fear	Joy	Neutral	Sadness	Surprise
Anger	**85.7%**	4.0%	0.3%	0.0%	7.3%	0.0%	3.3%
Disgust	9.0%	**51.3%**	1.0%	0.0%	3.3%	0.3%	0.0%
Fear	0.0%	7.0%	80.3%	0.0%	0.7%	5.7%	0.7%
Joy	0.3%	0.3%	0.0%	82%	1.3%	0.0%	4.7%
Neutral	3.3%	23%	0.0%	14%	78.7%	17.7%	7.0%
Sadness	0.0%	12.7%	18%	0.0%	0.0%	73.7%	0.0%
Surprise	1.7%	1.7%	0.3%	4.0%	8.7%	2.7%	84.3%

Table 4. Confusion matrix of the subjective test in *Karolina* database. Columns contain true values and rows values selected by listeners. Best and worst scores have been emphasized.

Emotion	Anger	Disgust	Fear	Joy	Sadness	Surprise
Anger	74.7%	13.7%	0.0%	1.1%	0.0%	10.5%
Disgust	14.7%	73.7%	0.0%	0.0%	0.0%	0.0%
Fear	1.1%	0.0%	**60.0%**	0.0%	20.0%	1.1%
Joy	0.0%	1.1%	1.1%	**95.8%**	1.1%	21.1%
Sadness	3.2%	9.5%	34.7%	0.0%	79.0%	0.0%
Surprise	6.3%	2.1%	4.2%	3.2%	0.0%	67.4%

Table 5. Confusion matrix of the subjective test in *Pello* database. Columns contain true values and rows values selected by listeners. Best and worst scores have been emphasized.

Emotion	Anger	Disgust	Fear	Joy	Sadness	Surprise
Anger	87.4%	16.8%	1.1%	0.0%	0.0%	2.1%
Disgust	3.2%	**61.1%**	0.0%	0.0%	1.1%	2.1%
Fear	4.2%	7.4%	66.3%	1.1%	21.1%	3.2%
Joy	0.0%	4.2%	1.1%	**91.6%**	1.1%	15.8%
Sadness	0.0%	5.3%	29.5%	0.0%	74.7%	0.0%
Surprise	5.3%	5.3%	2.1%	7.4%	2.1%	76.8%

All emotions are recognized over the chance level: the minimum identification rate is 51.3% for Disgust in Idoia database which is far above the 14.3% chance level for the test. In Idoia database Anger is the best identified emotion while in Pello and Karolina database is Joy for both speakers. In Idoia database the results for Joy are very good (82%) too. Disgust has the worst results for Idoia and Pello (51.3% and 61.1% respectively) and for Karolina Disgust is also among the worst identified emotions with a 73.3% identification rate. This emotion has also been the most difficult to identify in other experiments made for different languages [18][19][20]. Neutral style was the second preferred option for the worst rated emotions (Disgust and Sadness) in Idoia database. Sadness and Neutral style have been confused in other studies too [5][18]. In the three subjective evaluation processes Fear's second option was Sadness and Sadness' second option was Fear (in Idoia database Neutral and then

Fear). The same phenomenon is observed between Joy and Surprise which are also mutually confused. This confusion between Fear and Sadness, Sadness and Fear and Surprise and Joy has also been observed in Interface database for Spanish [21].

3   Meaningful Parameters to Represent Emotion

In expressive speech synthesis the goal is to produce synthetic speech with a style that could be identified by listeners. We wanted to know which are the meaningful parameters that have to be controlled during the synthesis process to get an expressive synthetic voice. This work aims at answering the following questions: Is it enough to control prosody or spectral content has also to be taken into account in order to obtain expressive synthetic speech? Do speakers use the same parameters to express all the emotions or do they apply different parameters to express each emotion? Does every speaker use prosody and spectral content in the same way to express emotion or do we have to study the value of the parameters for the speaker we are using for synthesis?

In previous studies we already concluded that intonation is not enough to identify emotions [13][14]. In a copy synthesis experiment using *Idoia* database, applying the intonation curve of the emotions to the neutral speech signal the results showed that some emotions, like Fear and Sadness are well identified, but some others, like Anger, Disgust and Joy are not. Results of this experiment are shown in table 6.

Table 6. Identification rate in the copy synthesis experiment with *Idoia* database

Copy synthesis	Best identified			Worst identified		
	Fear	Sadness	Surprise	Anger	Disgust	Joy
	60.0%	59.0%	38.0%	32.3%	31.5%	24.6%
	1.00	0.97	0.38	0.22	0.20	0.00

Therefore controlling the pitch curve is not enough to create expressive synthetic speech, although in some cases it can help. To ascertain which set of parameters do we have to control in synthetic speech to express emotion a series of automatic emotion recognition experiments have been performed using those databases:

In the first experiment short-term spectral features have been used. We refer as "short-term features" to those features calculated every short-time frame of speech, frequently using a short length windowing. We use 18-MFCC and their first and second derivatives. A GMM with 256 gaussian mixtures has been built for each emotion in each database.

In the second experiment long-term prosodic features have been used. "Long-term features" refer to different statistics calculated from speech parameters during a long time interval. The advantage of this kind of parameterization is that the features do not need to form a smooth curve across time. In this way, parameters that can only be calculated over long windows (such as the statistics of some feature) or those that are hard to estimate in a frame-to-frame basis (such as jitter) can be used. These long term features consist of different statistics calculated from the pitch curve and its first and second derivatives, as well as the first and second derivatives of the power curve. The extracted statistics have been mean, variance, minimum, range, skewness and kurtosis. Additionally jitter and shimmer values are also estimated and appended to the feature vector, resulting in 32 features on the whole. The extraction procedure for all this features is shown in figure 1. An SVM has been trained with this information.

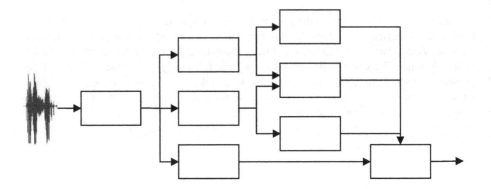

Fig. 1. Long term prosody features extraction procedure

4   Classification Experiments

The results of the classification experiments are shown in tables 7, 8 and 9, for *Idoia*, *Karolina* and *Pello* respectively. All the tables compare the identification results of the two automatic classification systems with the performance of humans measured in the subjective test presented in section 0. Emotions have been ordered from the best identified to the worst identified one and the last row in each sector presents the identification results normalized to the range [0,1] for the sake of an easier comparison.

Using short time spectral features the best identified emotion is Anger in all databases. Also Disgust has very good identification rates for *Pello* and *Karolina*, but not for *Idoia*.

The best identified emotions with the system using long time prosodic features in *Idoia* database are Fear and Sadness, which were also the best identified ones in the copy synthesis experiments. This means that *Idoia* speaker makes use of prosody to express those two emotions. Sadness is also the best identified emotion for *Pello* considering only prosodic information, but Fear is the worst one. In *Karolina* database the opposite is found: Fear gets well identified with prosody, but the results for Sadness are the worst ones.

Figure 2 compares the mean identification rates obtained in each database by humans and by the two automatic systems. Both automatic systems perform better than humans in all databases, except long term prosodic system for *Pello* that is slightly worse than humans, but the difference is not statistically meaningful. The results of the system using spectral information are better than the ones of the system using prosodic information in all cases.

Table 7. Identification rate in the automatic emotion identification experiments compared with the subjective evaluation results for *Idoia* database

	Best identified				Worst identified		
Humans	Surprise	Joy	Neutral	Sadness	Anger	Fear	Disgust
	82.7%	82.0%	78.7%	73.3%	73.0%	66.0%	18.7%
	1.0	1.0	0.9	0.9	0.8	0.7	0.0
ST spectrum	Anger	Sadness	Surprise	Fear	Neutral	Joy	Disgust
	100.0%	100.0%	100.0%	98.8%	97.9%	96.9%	93.8%
	1.0	1.0	1.0	0.8	0.7	0.5	0.0
LT prosody	Fear	Sadness	Anger	Neutral	Joy	Surprise	Disgust
	96.9%	95.9%	94.8%	94.8%	90.7%	90.5%	82.5%
	1.0	0.9	0.9	0.9	0.6	0.6	0.0

Table 8. Identification rate in the automatic emotion identification experiments compared with the subjective evaluation results for *Karolina* database

	Best identified			Worst identified		
Humans	Joy	Sadness	Anger	Disgust	Surprise	Fear
	95.8%	79.0%	74.7%	73.7%	67.4%	60.0%
	1.0	0.53	0.41	0.38	0.21	0.0
ST spectrum	Anger	Disgust	Joy	Surprise	Sadness	Fear
	100%	100%	100%	100%	98.7%	96.7%
	1.0	1.0	1.0	1.0	0.6	0.0
LT prosody	Surprise	Fear	Disgust	Anger	Joy	Sadness
	96.7%	95.3%	93.3%	92.7%	92.0%	85.3%
	1.0	0.88	0.70	0.64	0.59	0.0

Table 9. Identification rate in the automatic emotion identification experiments compared with the subjective evaluation results for *Pello* database

	Best identified			Worst identified		
Humans	Joy	Anger	Surprise	Sadness	Fear	Disgust
	91.6%	87.4%	76.8%	74.7%	66.3%	61.1%
	1.0	0.86	0.51	0.45	0.17	0.0
ST spectrum	Anger	Disgust	Sadness	Joy	Surprise	Fear
	98.0%	98.0%	96.7%	94.7%	91.3%	90.7%
	1.0	1.0	0.82	0.54	0.1	0.0
LT prosody	Sadness	Surprise	Disgust	Joy	Anger	Fear
	80.0%	78.7%	78.7%	78.7%	72.7%	66.0%
	1.0	0.90	0.90	0.90	0.48	0.0

To further study the dependency of the results with the speaker, we have performed some cross speaker emotion identification experiments. The results are presented in table 10. Identification rates drop drastically when changing the speaker. Our models have been trained for one speaker and learn the way this specific speaker express emotion. When the speaker changes the models perform badly because expression of emotions is speaker dependent [21][22][23].

The prosodic system is more robust to speaker changes. The models trained with prosodic information for *Pello* get better results when the speaker is changed although when they are applied to Pello's own signals they get worse results than the models for *Karolina* and *Idoia*. They are probably less adapted to the speaker, so when tested with another speaker their performance is better.

The spectral systems lose their very good performance when the speaker is changed. As expected, the system trained for *Karolina* gets better results when applied to *Idoia* who is also a female speaker than when applied to *Pello*. The models trained for *Pello* have a similar performance both for *Karolina* and *Idoia*. This agrees with other studies that have found that gender specific emotion recognizers perform better than those with both genders mixed [24][25].

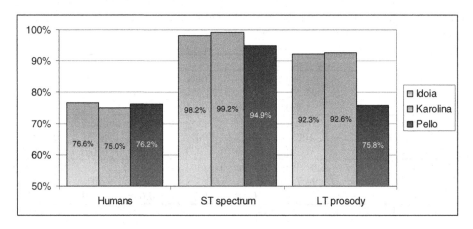

Fig. 2. Mean emotion identification rates for the three databases

Table 10. Mean identification rates for the cross speaker identification experiments

Data for training	Karolina		Pello	
Data for verification	Idoia	Pello	Idoia	Karolina
ST spectrum	27.8%	19.8%	24.7%	24.2%
LT prosody	28.7%	28.8%	51.0%	46.0%

5   Conclusion

Our emotional databases have been validated through a subjective evaluation process. This test has shown that all the emotions recorded are well identified, far above the chance level, for the three speakers; therefore, they can be used to extract the models of emotional speech needed for speech synthesis.

The automatic classifications experiments have shown that spectral information as well as prosodic information are suitable to classify emotions. Both automatic systems perform better than humans in the task of classifying emotions without any linguistic help. Spectral information gets better results for the speaker who trained the system, but behaves worse when the speaker is changed. Prosody is used in a more consistent way by all the speakers hence the results of the automatic classification system based in prosodic information degrade less when the speaker is changed. The different results obtained for each speaker indicates that each speaker interprets emotion in a different way.

The next step in this work will be to consider other long term prosodic features, like speaking rate that has proven to be valuable for the characterization of emotion in other languages [5][26]. The consideration of short time prosodic information could also be interesting to model emotional speech. To validate the results obtained in this work, it is necessary to make speech synthesis experiments, applying these parameters to evaluate the identification rate in synthetic speech.

Acknowledgements

This work has been partially founded by Spanish Ministry of Education and Sciences under grant TEC2006-13694-C03-02 (AVIVAVOZ project, http://www.avivavoz.es/) and by Basque Government under grant IE06-185 (ANHITZ project, http://www.anhitz.com/).

The authors would also like to thank all the people that took part in the subjective evaluation processes.

References

1. Hozjan, V., Kacic, Z.: Improved Emotion Recognition with Large Set of Statistical Features. In: Proc. Eurospeech 2003, pp. 133–136 (2003)
2. Petrushin, V.A.: Emotion Recognition in Speech Signal: Experimental Study, Development and Application, Proc. ICSLP 2000, pp. 222–225 (2000)
3. Seppänen, T., Väyrynen, E., Toivanen, J.: Prosody Based Classification of Emotions in Spoken Finnish. In: Proc. Eurospeech 2003, pp. 717–720 (2003)
4. Yanushevskaya, I., Gobl, C., Ní Chasaide, A.: Voice quality and f0 cues for affect expression: implications for synthesis. In: Proc. INTERSPEECH, pp. 1849–1852 (2005)
5. Yildirim, S., Bulut, M., Lee, C., Kazemzadeh, A., Deng, Z., Lee, S., Narayanan, S., Busso, C.: An acoustic study of emotions expressed in speech. In: Proc. INTERSPEECH pp. 2193–2196 (2004)
6. Gobl, C., Ní Chasaide, A.: The role of voice quality in communicating emotion, mood and attitude. Speech Communication 40(1,2), 189–212 (2003)
7. Johnstone, T., Scherer, K.R.: The effects of emotions on voice quality. In: Proc. XIVth International Congress of Phonetic Sciences, pp. 2029–2032 (1999)
8. Drioli, C., Tisato, G., Cosi, P., Tesser, F.: Emotions and voice quality: experiments with sinusoidal modelling. In: Proc. VOQUAL 2003, pp. 127–132 (2003)
9. Scherrer, K.R.: Vocal Communication of Emotion: A Review of Research Paradigms. Speech Communication 40(1,2), 227–256 (2003)
10. Cowie, R., Cornelius, R.R.: Describing the Emotional States that Are Expressed in Speech. Speech Communication 40(1,2), 2–32 (2003)

11. Lay Nwe, T., Wei Foo, S., De Silva, L.: Speech Emotion Recognition Using Hidden Markov Models. Speech Communication 41(4), 603–623 (2003)
12. Boula de Mareüil, P., Célérier, P., Toen, J.: Generation of Emotions by a Morphing Technique in English, French and Spanish. In: Proc. Speech Prosody, pp. 187–190 (2002)
13. Navas, E., Castelruiz, A., Luengo, I., Sánchez, J., Hernáez, I.: Designing and Recording an Audiovisual Database of Emotional Speech in Basque. In: Proc. of the LREC pp. 1387–1390 (2004)
14. Navas, E., Hernáez, I., Luengo, I.: An objective and subjective study of the role of semantics in building corpora for TTS. IEEE transactions on Speech and Audio Processing 14, 1117–1127 (2006)
15. Saratxaga, I., Navas, E., Hernáez, I., Luengo, I.: Designing and Recording an Emotional Speech Database for Corpus Based Synthesis. In: Basque. Proc. of the LREC, pp. 2127–2129 (2006)
16. Boersma, P., van Heuven, V.: Speak and unSpeak with PRAAT. Glot International 5(9-10), 341–347 (2001)
17. Boersma, P., Weenink, D.: Praat: doing phonetics by computer (Version 4.3.16) [Computer program] (2005), http://www.praat.org/
18. Hozjan, V., Kacic, Z.: Context-Independent Multilingual Emotion Recognition from Speech Signals. International Journal of Speech Technology 6(3), 11–320 (2003)
19. Iida, A., Campbell, N., Higuchi, F., Yasumura, M.: A Corpus-based Speech Synthesis System with Emotion. Speech Communication 40(1,2), 161–187 (2003)
20. Burkhardt, F., Sendlmeier, W.F.: Verification of Acoustical Correlates of Emotional Speech using Formant-Synthesis. In: Proc. ISCA Workshop on Speech and Emotion, pp. 151–156 (2000)
21. Nogueiras, A., Moreno, A., Bonafonte, A., Mariño, J.B.: Speech emotion recognition using hidden Markov models. In: Proc. EUROSPEECH pp. 2679–2682 (2001)
22. Iwai, A., Yano, Y., Okuma, S.: Complex emotion recognition system for a specific user using SOM based on prosodic features. In: Proc. INTERSPEECH, pp. 1341–1344 (2004)
23. Nicholson, J., Takahashi, K., Nakatsu, R.: Emotion Recognition in Speech Using Neural Networks. Neural Computing & Applications 9(4), 290–296 (2009)
24. Ververidis, D., Kotropoulos, C.: Automatic Speech Classification to five emotional states based on gender information. In: Proc. of 12th. EUSIPCO, pp. 341–344 (2004)
25. Vogt, T., André, E.: Improving automatic emotion recognition from speech via gender differentiation. Proc. Language Resources and Evaluation Conference (LREC 2006), pp. 1123–1126 (2006)
26. Theune, M., Meijs, K., Heylen, D., Ordelman, R.: Generating expressive speech for storytelling applications. IEEE Transactions on Audio, Speech and Language Processing 14(4), 1137–1144 (2006)

Prosodic and Gestural Expression of Interactional Agreement

Eric Keller [1] and Wolfgang Tschacher[2]

[1] IMM-Lettres, University of Lausanne, Switzerland
[2] Psychology, University of Bern, Switzerland

Abstract. Conversational interactions are cooperatively constructed activities in which participants negotiate their entrances, turns and alignments with other speakers, oftentimes with an underlying long-term objective of obtaining some agreement. Obtaining a final and morally binding accord in a conversational interaction is of importance in a great variety of contexts, particularly in psychotherapeutic interactions, in contractual negotiations or in educational contexts. Various prosodic and gestural elements in a conversational interaction can be interpreted as signals of a speaker's agreement and they are probably of importance in the emergence of an accord in a conversational exchange. In this paper, we survey the social and psychological context of agreement seeking, as well as the existing literature on the visual and prosodic measurement of agreement in conversational settings.

1 Introduction

In our increasingly complex and interconnected societal structure, obtaining agreements is often a considerable challenge. In comparison to the societal structures predominating in the industrialized countries until World War II, current structures are far more complex, geographically more diffused, and culturally more diverse. As a result, individuals responsible for commercial, governmental or educational decisions are often unknown to individuals working at the periphery of an organization, they may speak a different language, and their value systems may be unlike that of their employees or of their customers. Also, many more families in Europe have been constituted from diverse linguistic and cultural backgrounds. Such differences increase the opportunities for disagreements, which naturally leads to an increased potential for lack of understanding, disagreements and disputes in the execution of joint objectives.

At the same time, individuals in our modern societies have more *options* available to them than in previous generations. It is far easier today to change products, employers or life partners than it was in previous generations. Although many of these options are desirable for personal advancement and for an optimized matching between job offer and employee availability, there is no denying that the diversity of options available to modern individuals frequently complicates obtaining agreements between employers and employees, between vendors and customers as well as between the different members of a family structure.

A. Esposito et al. (Eds.): Verbal and Nonverbal Commun. Behaviours, LNAI 4775, pp. 85–98, 2007.
© Springer-Verlag Berlin Heidelberg 2007

Research on marriage, family and psychotherapeutic issues is probably the context where issues of agreement, disagreement and its various connoted elements (heated discussion, verbal conflict, verbal abuse, verbal attack, verbal aggression, conflictual conversations, etc.) have received the most systematic attention, particularly during the past few years. Research in this specialized field of interpersonal relationships provides some valuable insights into (a) the various categories of agreement, (b) the theoretical position and importance of agreements and disagreements within interpersonal interactions, and (c) the identification of prosodic and visual indicators of agreement.

2 Agreement in Family Relationships and in Organizational Structures

2.1 Chronic Aggressions and Conflicts

The most systematic past research on agreement/disagreement has been conducted from a dysfunctional perspective. A fairly clear trail of relationships has been established between the effects of *long-lasting disagreements (destructive and unhelpful comments, verbal attacks, etc.)* and various degrees of *family dysfunction*. These disruptive effects become most evident over longer periods of time. For example, in Shortt et al.'s study on the relationships of 158 young couples at risk for separation (male and female average 21 years), both physical and verbal forms of aggression were examined over the course of 6 years as predictors of separation of the couple [56]. As expected, the likelihood of relationship dissolution was significantly increased in couples where physical aggression was present; also, psychological aggression[1] was strongly correlated with physical aggression (r of about .5 in the two measured time periods). The relationship between verbal and physical aggression was similarly situated in a study conducted by DeMaris on 3,508 married and cohabiting couples [1]. In these and a number of other studies with smaller population samples, strong verbal disagreement was shown to be less destructive of family relationships than was physical aggression, but it figured as an important contributing factor in family dysfunction.

The harmfulness of chronic verbal disagreement appears to show up most clearly at an older age, after long-term exposure. In a study of 729 adults at least 50 years of age, currently married and in their first marriage, marital quality (defined as agreements/disagreements, positive and negative spousal behaviours, overall quality of relationship and marital communication) predicted to a significant degree measures of physical health, defined as chronic health problems, more disability and poorer

---

[1] Definition of psychological aggression in this study: "Observed psychological aggression was the rate per minute of content codes negative verbal, verbal attack, and coerce during the problem-solving task. Negative verbal behavior was blaming or disapproving of the partner (e.g., 'You really blew that one, didn't you.'). Verbal attack included name-calling, threats, and humiliation of the partner (e.g., 'You're such a loser.'). Coerce was a demand for behavior change that implied impending physical or psychological harm (e.g., 'You'll shut up if you know what is good for you.')."

perceived health [2]. In particular, chronic negative verbal behaviours, such as excessive demands, being too critical or argumentative, being unreliable or continually agitating one's partner was associated with poorer physical health in the respondents. When these negative behaviours were present, they outweighed the positive spousal behaviours with respect to influencing physical health.

These studies place verbal disagreement and aggression in the family core into a chain of events that can be summarized as follows. The original intention behind verbal aggressions is generally an "attack on the self concept of the receiver in order to deliver psychological pain". These attacks are often used to "intimidate, subjugate and control another human being"[2]. In mature adults, verbal aggression ultimately translates into lower degrees of marital satisfaction[3], which leads to negative outcomes in physical and mental well-being in those couples that remain married.

Several elements of this causative translate chain were statistically supported by a study by Gavazzi et al. [3], notably the relationship between (a) the repeated use of *depreciative comments* (i.e., frequent *events*), (b) the establishment of *dissatisfaction* within the relationship (i.e., a stable *state* in which verbal information has been cumulated and has been translated into appreciations and evaluations of a marital condition), and (c) the *negative* physical and mental health effects resulting from this state (i.e., a measurable *outcome*).

Temporary and Non-threatening Disagreements

These references thus indicate that the presence of chronic verbal aggression is an important negative factor in the evolution of personal relationships. Does this also mean that the opposite, verbal support, can act as an important positive factor? Unfortunately, relatively little research has been performed on the benefits of verbal support in family relationships. However, research by Patterson and colleagues on particularly successful enterprises performed in the late 1990's has shown the remarkable impact of successful conversational patterns in organizational structures, and has deepened our understanding of the complex patterns on agreements and disagreements [4].

In the large-scale and long-term research underlying the Patterson et al. account, it emerged that one of the major differences between particularly successful enterprises and other enterprises of similar size orientation was related to the presence of successful internal communication channels (e.g., well-functioning meetings, productive email exchanges and satisfactory face-to-face conversational exchanges, etc.). A fairly extensive network of supportive semantic, emotional and verbal elements was identified in the analyses of such exchanges. It was shown, for example, that above all, an atmosphere of trust and confidence must prevail to enable the discussion of delicate issues (Patterson et al.: "safety in dialog"), that emotions must be bound and be translated into productive verbal statements, that attentive listening and valid interpretation of interlocutors' statements is required to build confidence in the conversational process, and that final conversational accords must ultimately be translated into valid actions. Only when all these elements are present, can a given

---

[2] Infante & Wigley [53] and Jacobson & Gottman [54] respectively, cited in Gavazzi et al. [3].
[3] The relationship between dissatisfaction and separation could not be demonstrated for the younger adults (21 years old [1]).

communication channel make successful contributions to employee satisfaction and enterprise dynamics[4].

2.2 Support and Agreement

It emerges from these and related studies that an important difference must be made between the underlying presence or absence of *support*[5] and the overt presence or absence of *agreement*. Successful communication resulting in generally supported accords involves *both agreements and disagreements formed in the context of support*. In fact, one function of successful social groups is to favour "agreeing to disagree". Nelson & Aboud [5], for example, showed that friends of third- and fourth grade children furnished both more explanations and more criticism of their partners than did non-friends. Also among friends, disagreements provoked more beneficial change on the given experimental tasks than did agreements. Further, the disagreeing friend-pairs presented more mature solutions than did non-friends. Warranted disagreement between well-meaning friends is thus part of a healthy social development pattern which involves an evolution of both agreements and disagreements. The important component of this evolution is that both agreements and disagreements can occur within the framework of a supportive social environment.

Also, some disagreements are imposed by external circumstances. For instance, it has been argued that premature consensus on certain medical treatments has led to standardized treatments that were later shown to be harmful or of doubtful benefit (bloodletting, electroconvulsive therapy, etc.). Also, such premature consensus has led to the marginalization of proponents of opposite views [6]. Warranted disagreement must thus be possible at various levels of societal grouping (families, enterprises, countries, etc.) to favour the evolution of meaningful social solutions, and it should reinforce values that are ethically or morally responsible. As an interesting example of the importance of disagreement, Erath & Bierman [7] showed that children living in violence-favouring families where there was little disagreement between parents showed significantly *more* tendency toward the use of violence outside the family than those where there was disagreement between parents. Apparently, the silent approval of violence by parents reinforced the willingness to use violence outside of the family.

We conclude from this section that successful communication involves patterns of seeking agreements where they are warranted and of permitting, encouraging and supporting disagreements where they are necessary and appropriate. The systematic promotion of supportive communication channels where both agreements and disagreements are welcome can lead to the well-being and a heightened productivity of participants. On the other hand, chronic lack of support in a non-supportive

---

[4] Somewhat similar conclusions were formulated by a team working at the Harvard Negotiation Project [55].

[5] "Support" is taken here in the wider sense of active as well as passive support. In a family situation, support involves the notion of "potential aid in need", while in an enterprise situation, support can be merely "acceptance of common purpose" or "acceptance of divergence". This concept is termed "safety" by Patterson et al. [04]. The crucial elements are that participants in the enterprise must share "mutual purpose" and/or "mutual respect".

environment and the inflictive use of aggressive verbal material have considerable negative long-term effects on psychological and physical welfare of family and organizational participants.

A systematic theoretical structure emerges from these studies that can be summarized in terms of a *tri-phase model* (Table 1). The key dimension is ±*support,* and the three phases are *events, states* and *outcomes.* Productive and sympathetic *communicative interactions* (events) permit to create an environment of *positive or negative rapport* (a state); if the results of conversational exchanges are seen to translate into actual *positive effects* (outcomes), positive rapport is maintained and improved, and increased participant satisfaction results. Failing communicative interactions can be seen as the inverse of this model. Chronically destructive or unhelpful statements or comments showing lack of understanding lead to stable states of negative rapport and distrust; over a certain period of time, such a state can lead to reduced productivity as well as to psychological and physical ill health.

Table 1. An Overall Interactional Model

	Events	**States**	**Outcomes**
+ Support	– constructive or supportive comments – statements showing understanding – constructive or supportive responses	positive rapport	Increased satisfaction and productivity
- Support	– destructive and unhelpful comments – statements showing lack of understanding – aggressive responses – silence, withdrawal	negative rapport	Impaired psychological and physical health

2.3 Agreement in Dyadic Interaction: State of Research in Social and Clinical Psychology

We conclude from the previous sections that conversations contribute in major fashion to an atmosphere of presence or absence of support through complex interplays between manifestations of agreement and disagreement, with the support perceived in such exchanges contributing in crucial manner to important social outcomes. The building blocks of such exchanges are the instances of *agreement* and *disagreement*. Instances of agreement/disagreement provide the basis for support to be perceived or for a pre-existing confidence to be undermined or destroyed.

Although the overall logic governing conversational behaviour is probably reasonably simple, the positive identification and significance of the various socially significant components in a conversation is rarely easy. On lexical and semantic grounds, it is often difficult to make differences between supportive and unsupportive comments (see e.g., neutral and sarcastic comments), and prosodic and visual indicators of presence or absence of support may pre-exist between conversational partners, but be barely noticeable in a given conversation. Also, participants generally pay little attention to such indicators, since they are primarily bent on transmitting their own intentions in the conversation. Even when participants have been trained to become more sensitive to subtle indicators of approval and disapproval, they may still show resistance or ignorance about the use of such information in the midst of a conversation.

It is therefore of interest to explore external technical means of measuring interaction parameters empirically and as automatically as possible. If such indicators can indeed be measured reliably and linked to perceived indications of the presence and absence of support, they could be used in post-hoc sessions to clarify and support the training of beneficial conversational behaviours, particularly in psychotherapeutic and managerial training contexts. The purpose must thus be to elucidate both conscious and non-conscious elements in a conversation, particularly in dyadic exchanges.

Indeed, there is converging evidence in social psychology that the course of a dyadic interaction is shaped in various ways by *non-conscious* influences. Such influences may arise in all channels of communication. Established empirical findings addressed a wide range of variables, e.g. body configurations and postures [8], hand gestures [9, 10], head movements [11] and emotion-related prosodic features [12]. It is generally acknowledged that a substantial portion of behaviour occurs without conscious awareness (e.g. [13]) but nevertheless may have high impact on the course of a conversation. One special domain of nonverbal research in dyadic interaction deals with the correspondence of nonverbal features between two or more people.

This phenomenon of "synchronization" is found both in living systems and even inanimate nature. Flocking birds or a school of fish provide examples of behavioural manifestations of synchrony in the animal kingdom. In animals, these phenomena have been linked with the stability of perception-behaviour links [14]. Analogous mechanisms appear to play a major role in human interactions as well; they may be considered the behavioural underpinnings of higher-level cognitive appraisals of social situations and processes.

Synchrony in Nonverbal Measures

"Behavioural synchronization is a form of coordinative interaction which is thought to be present in almost all aspects of our social lives, helping us to negotiate our daily face-to-face interaction." [15]. Considering human interaction globally, it is evident that some form of coordination or mutual influence plays a crucial role. Cappella [16] summarized that "Coordination is arguably the essential characteristic of every interpersonal interaction. ... Interpersonal communication requires the coordination of behaviour."

Prior to summarizing findings from social and clinical psychology, we wish to clarify the terminology, which presents high heterogeneity. Bernieri & Rosenthal [17] group most of the manifestations of synchrony in the human domain under the term interpersonal coordination, loosely defined as "...the degree to which the behaviours in an interaction are non-random, patterned, or synchronized in both timing and form." Studies that emphasize temporal aspects such as simultaneous movement, rhythm, or meshing of nonverbal behaviour mainly regard quantitative characteristics. Because of this reliance on kinetic qualities we may classify this type of synchrony as *"movement synchrony"*. It deals with "... the precise timing and coordination of movements between individuals ... while the nature or similarity of movements is irrelevant." [18]. Irrespective of which movements are involved, global quantitative variables such as speed, duration, or complexity of movement become synchronized between the two interacting individuals.

In contrast to movement synchrony, the focus may also be put on static or qualitative features of an interaction; postures, mannerisms, and facial displays may thus be categorized as *"behaviour matching"*. Corresponding terms in social psychology are mirroring, mimicry, congruence, or the chameleon effect [13]. In many real world applications, however, these two categories — movement synchrony and behaviour matching — are not disjunctive; commonly a mixture of both categories is observed. If interactants share the same posture (i.e. static synchrony, behaviour matching) and subsequently change their bodily configuration in a temporally coupled manner (dynamic synchrony, movement synchrony), we view synchrony both on quantitative as well as qualitative levels.

Emotional phenomena such as empathy, emotional propagation and emotional contagion have been investigated in a majority of the studies that dealt with synchrony in human interaction. The link between emotional closeness and synchrony has thus received considerable attention. In this vein, Darwin (1872/1965) used the term "sympathy" to refer to imitation based on reflex or habit [19]. Allport [20] stated that "...our understanding of other people is derived from our capacity to imitate, usually in imperceptible ways, the behaviour of the person we are trying to understand ..."; and "empathy becomes simply 'kinaesthetic inference'." The connection of synchrony and empathy has stimulated numerous research efforts. Condon [21] who coined the term interactional synchrony stated that "Synchrony and other forms of behavioural sharing express degrees of closeness or distance between interactants." The notion of nonverbal behaviour correlating with rapport (i.e. a favourable therapeutic relationship) is shared by most psychotherapists [22, 23, 24]. The work of Scheflen [25, 26, 27] suggested ways to conceptualize empathy, rapport and the quality of the therapeutic bond. Yet naturalistic studies have been scarce since many published contributions were descriptive or cited merely anecdotal evidence (e.g. Charny [28]). Empirical research of synchrony in psychotherapy found preliminary evidence in favour of the hypothesis that interactional synchrony is associated with a positive therapeutic relationship and higher agreement between clients and therapists [29, 30, 31].

Taken together, the spectrum of findings in psychology covers various domains of human behaviour and experience. An individual's experience with the phenomenon of synchrony can be traced back to early infancy: Mother-infant studies on imitative behaviour (for a review, see [32]) have shown that even neonates imitate basic facial gestures (see also [33]). Recent neurocognitive research has made a connection between interactional synchrony (including empathy and related psychological phenomena) and a certain system of cortical neurons, the "mirror neurons" [34, 35, 36, 37]. Accordingly, Ramachandran [38] predicted "... that mirror neurons might do for psychology what DNA did for biology: they will create a unifying framework and help explain a host of mental abilities that have hitherto remained mysterious and inaccessible to experiments."

3 Prosodic and Visual Measures of Conversational Interaction Parameters

Past experiments have explored primarily measures of *prosody* and of *visual measures* of head movement in dyadic conversations. The two measures will be discussed separately.

3.1 Prosodic Measures

Prosody is the use of pitch (intonation), amplitude and timing in voice and speech; it is used primarily to signal a person's identity, emotion or attitude, and it can be used secondarily to support other conversational functions, such as agreement/ disagreement. The parameters or greatest relevance to support and agreement are those that have been examined with respect to emotion and attitude. Pittam [39] has summarized the most relevant prosodic parameters relating to emotion in the following list:

Parameter	Phenomena
F0 (fundamental frequency, pitch)	variability, perturbation, contour details
Intensity	mean, range, variability
Formants	means, bandwidth
Temporal	speech rate, pausing
Fluency	slurring of articulation
Spectral	noise, proportion of high frequency energy to low LTS contour and frequency range, short-term spectral envelope measures

Within this list, parameters relating to pitch are probably easiest to analyze and have been used in recent studies on agreement. For example, Roth & Tobin showed a number of pitch patterns emerging in recent naturalistic recordings of well- or ill-integrated teachers in New York Inner City schools [39]. Fairly evident patterns of pitch *disagreements, alignments* and *integration* were shown in this study. The pitch patterns of well-integrated teachers formed continuous patterns with those of their students, while those of ill-integrated teachers showed discontinuous and independent patterns.

Quantitative evaluations of agreement/disagreement in meetings were performed in [40] and [41]. In the first study, 9854 "spurts" (periods of speech without pauses > 500 ms) from seven meetings were labelled as positive, negative, backchannel[6] and "other". One fifth of the spurts was hand labelled, and the rest was labelled with the use of a decision tree classifier using lexical categories (e.g., number of words in a spurt, type of expression, and frequency indicators) as well as prosodic categories (e.g., pauses, fundamental frequency, and duration). Adjacency information (which can be seen to be of importance in Figures 1-4) was not used. Both lexical and prosodic indicators provided encouraging learning rates with 78% and 66% accuracy

---

[6] Phatic or "back-channeling" comments are used to signal events relating to conversational organization, such as signals or invitations to take a turn [39].

respectively. This result was improved upon by the approach used in the subsequent study where an adjacency search was implemented. The result was improved and a score of 86.9% accuracy was attained using an adjacency analysis of a maximum entropy classification for speakers and a reduced number of only three expression types instead of four (positive/negative/backchannel+other).

3.2 Visual Measures

Previous studies of synchrony in psychology predominantly relied on observer ratings. Contemporary multimedia technology, however, makes computerized quantification of movement increasingly accessible. Computer-based systems eliminate several of the problems commonly encountered when assessing nonverbal behaviour by means of observer ratings, especially the high costs (behavioural observation is time-consuming) and the low objectivity of rating procedures.

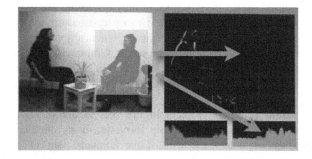

Fig. 6. Frame-to-frame head movements for both participants of a psycho-therapeutic dyad are converted into an amplitude graph. Data from Ramseyer & Tschacher, 2006.

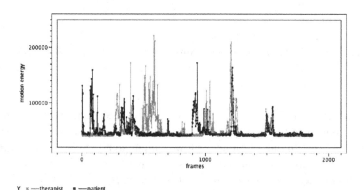

Fig. 7. The delays between head movements are scored. In the left part of the graph, the therapist's movements (grey) follow those of the patient (black), and in the right part of the graph, there is a passage where both participants show coincidental head movements ("synchrony"). Data from [44].

One such automated approach is Motion Energy Analysis (MEA). MEA of a recorded movie is based upon an image differencing algorithm [42, 43]. Each individual image (frame) of a movie has a constant number of pixels that generate a distribution of grey-scale values ranging from 0 (black) to 255 (white). With a fixed camera shot and nothing moving, each pixel retains its grey-scale value from one frame to the next. As soon as any item in a frame moves, the grey-scale distribution changes and can be quantified by differencing subsequent frames. The degree of movement from one frame to the next (the motion energy) equals this difference.

MEA is a simple method to continuously quantify movement in a video stream. Some caveats need to be considered however. First, the camera shot has to remain perfectly steady throughout the sequence; second, lighting conditions must be kept stable; third, the method solely quantifies movement energy, yet is blind to the direction or location of movement. To monitor motion energy of two persons in an interaction setting, two regions of interest (ROI) are defined. Within each ROI, differencing of grey-scale values is performed and recorded separately. If location information is essential, more than two ROIs may be defined (e.g. the faces, hands and arms of interactants). We thus generate two or more continuous time series that encode the amount of movement in these regions. Synchrony is consequently defined as the statistical correlation between the time series. Grammer's research group at the University of Vienna implemented the MEA method in several empirical studies, e.g. of courtship communication [45, 46], physical attractiveness [45] and interpersonal attraction [47].

Recent and current research projects in the second author's department have addressed the process of dyadic relationship formation in psychotherapy. We found synchronization of interactants at the level of questionnaire data (i.e. self-evaluations in post-session reports) [48, 49], in the domain of physiological parameters [50, 51] as well as in nonverbal social behaviour [44].

These findings concern the nonverbal channel. In a pilot study of naturalistic dyadic psychotherapy, we analyzed randomly selected therapy sessions taken from a very large sample of therapies conducted at the psychotherapy research centre of the University of Bern [52]. This database consisted of over 22,000 recorded therapy sessions, each 50 minutes in duration. From this set of sessions, a random sample of 100 sessions displaying different therapy dyads was drawn. An interim analysis at this moment is based on 50 dyads. In their therapeutic interactions, nonverbal synchrony was measured using the MEA approach.

A significant level of synchrony between patient and therapist time series was detected, in comparison to surrogate data. Statistical analyses showed that synchrony computed within the initial 15 minutes of interaction significantly predicted patients' post session evaluations of therapeutic bond quality. In other words, *movement synchrony was linked with therapeutic support and rapport*. Furthermore, the alleged association between the degree of synchrony during therapy and outcome at the end of therapy was corroborated, especially with the outcome measures 'patients' subjective well-being' and 'patients' competence expectancy'. In sum, higher degrees of nonverbal synchrony correlated with better therapeutic relationships as well as with better outcomes at the end of therapy.

4 Conclusion

In this brief review we have considered the process and context of agreement building, as well as the empirical measurement of agreement in the participants. It was seen that the pursuit of agreement building is embedded in and builds upon the pre-existing social framework. If this framework is supportive, or if it is at least characterized by an acceptance of common purpose, conversational transactions have much greater chance of reaching the intended goal of a morally binding agreement. If the framework is non-supportive or conflictual, reaching an agreement may be difficult to impossible.

Prosodic, gestural and postural information may provide a differentiated and independent measure of the process of agreement building which can be of considerable use in clinical and training contexts. Some pilot work has shown excellent correspondence between prosodic indicators of agreement in conversational settings, and between head movement and fundamental accord in psychotherapy settings. The data must be replicated over new studies, and a wider and more precisely circumscribed set of indicators must be defined for this research objective. Also it must be established if these empirical indicators concern overt agreement or relate more to the less evident development of support mechanisms within the conversational relationship.

Acknowledgements

The assistance of the European COST 2102 project as well as the assistance of the Swiss SBF Programme in support of COST is gratefully acknowledged.

References

[1] DeMaris, A.: Till discord do us part: the role of physical and verbal conflict in union disruption. Journal of Marriage and Family 62, 683–692 (2000)
[2] Bookwala, J.: The role of marital quality in physical health during the mature years. Journal of Aging and Health 17, 85–104 (2005)
[3] Gavazzi, S.M., McKenry, P.C., Jacobson, J.A., Julian, T.W., Lohman, B.: Modeling the effects of expressed emotion, psychiatric symptomology, and marital quality levels on male and female verbal aggression. Journal of Marriage and Family 62, 669–682 (2000)
[4] Patterson, K., Grenny, J., McMillan, R., Switzler, A., Covey, S.R.: Crucial conversations: Tools for talking when stakes are high. McGraw Hill, New York (2002)
[5] Nelson, J., Aboud, F.E.: The resolution of social conflict between friends. Child Development 56, 1009–1017 (1985)
[6] Haaga, D.A., Ahrens, A.H.: A disagreement about the benefits of agreement seeking. Psychological Inquiry 3, 244–247 (1992)
[7] Erath, S.A., Bierman, K.L.: Aggressive marital conflict, maternal harsh punishment, and child aggressive-disruptive behavior: Evidence for direct and mediated relations. Journal of Family Psychology 20, 217–226 (2006)
[8] Bernieri, F.J.: Coordinated movement in human interaction: Synchrony, posture similarity, and rapport. Dissertation Abstracts International 49, 4601 (1989)

[9] Bavelas, J.B., Black, A., Chovil, N., Lemery, C.R., Mullett, J.: Form and function in motor mimicry: Topographic evidence that the primary function is communicative. Human Communication Research 14, 275–299 (1988)

[10] Núñez, R., Sweetser, E.: With the future behind them: Convergent evidence from Aymara language and gesture in the crosslinguistic comparison of spatial construals of time. Cognitive Science 30, 401–450 (2006)

[11] Altorfer, A., Jossen, S., Wuermle, O.: Eine Methode zur zeitgenauen Aufnahme und Analyse des Bewegungsverhaltens. Zeitschrift für Psychologie 205, 83–117 (1997)

[12] Neumann, R., Strack, F.: Mood contagion: The automatic transfer of mood between persons. Journal of Personality and Social Psychology 79, 211–223 (2000)

[13] Chartrand, T.L., Bargh, J.A.: The chameleon effect: The perception-behavior link and social interaction. Journal of Personality and Social Psychology 76, 893–910 (1999)

[14] Dijksterhuis, A., Bargh, J.A.: The perception-behavior expressway: Automatic effects of social perception on social behavior. Advances in Experimental Social Psychology 33, 1–40 (2001)

[15] Kendon, A., Harris, R.M., Key, M.R.: The organization of behavior in face to face interaction. The Hague: Mouton and Co. (1975)

[16] Cappella, J.N.: Coding mutual adaptation in dyadic nonverbal interaction. In: Manusov, V. (ed.) The sourcebook of nonverbal measures, Lawrence Erlbaum, Mahwah, NJ (2005)

[17] Bernieri, F.J., Rosenthal, R.: Interpersonal coordination: Behavior matching and interactional synchrony. In: Feldman, R.S., Rime, B. (eds.) Fundamentals of nonverbal behavior, pp. 401–432. Cambridge University Press, New York (1991)

[18] Grammer, K., Honda, R., Schmitt, A., Jütte, A.: Fuzziness of nonverbal courtship communication unblurred by motion energy detection. Journal of Personality and Social Psychology 77, 487–508 (1999)

[19] Darwin, C.: The expression of the emotions in man and animals. University of Chicago Press, Chicago (1965)

[20] Allport, G.W.: Personality: A psychological interpretation. Holt, Rinehart, & Winston, New York (1937)

[21] Condon, W.S.: The relation of interactional synchrony to cognitive and emotional processes. In: Key, M.R. (ed.) The relationship of verbal and nonverbal communication, pp. 49–75. Mouton Publishers, The Hague (1980)

[22] Kriz, J.: Grundkonzepte der Psychotherapie. München: Urban & Schwarzenberg (2001)

[23] Philippot, P., Feldman, R.S., Coats, E.J.: The social context of nonverbal behavior. Cambridge University Press, New York (1999)

[24] Philippot, P., Feldman, R.S., Coats, E.J.: The role of nonverbal behavior in clinical settings. In: Philippot, P., Feldman, R.S., Coats, E.J. (eds.) Nonverbal behavior in clinical settings, Oxford University Press, New York (2003)

[25] Scheflen, A.E.: The Significance of Posture in Communication Systems. Psychiatry 27, 316–331 (1964)

[26] Scheflen, A.E.: Quasi-courtship behavior in psychotherapy. Psychiatry 28, 245–257 (1965)

[27] Scheflen, A.E.: Systems and psychosomatics. An introduction to psychosomatic manifestations of rapport in psychotherapy. Psychosomatic Medicine 28, 297–304 (1966)

[28] Charny, E.J.: Psychosomatic manifestations of rapport in psychotherapy. Psychosomatic Medicine 28, 305–315 (1966)

[29] McDowall, J.J.: Interactional synchrony: A reappraisal. Journal of Personality and Social Psychology 36, 963–975 (1978)

[30] Maurer, R.E., Tindall, J.H.: Effect of postural congruence on client's perception of counselor empathy. Journal of Counseling Psychology 30, 158–163 (1983)

[31] Willis, C.J.: The measurement of mutual nonverbal coordination in the psychotherapeutic process: An exploratory study of the development of an index for clinical use. Dissertation Abstracts International 50, 144 (1989)

[32] Meltzoff, A.N., Prinz, W.: The imitative mind: Development, evolution, and brain bases. Cambridge University Press, New York (2002)

[33] O'Toole, R., Dubin, R.: Baby feeding and body sway: An experiment in George Herbert Mead's. Taking the role of the other. Journal of Personality and Social Psychology 10, 59–65 (1968)

[34] Rizzolatti, G., Fadiga, L., Gallese, V., Fogassi, L.: Premotor cortex and the recognition of motor actions. Brain Research Cognitive Brain Research 3, 131–141 (1996)

[35] Gallese, V., Fadiga, L., Fogassi, L., Rizzolatti, G.: Action recognition in the premotor cortex. Brain 119, 593–609 (1996)

[36] Gallese, V., Keysers, C., Rizzolatti, G.: A unifying view of the basis of social cognition. Trends in Cognitive Science 8, 396–403 (2004)

[37] Boker, S.M., Rotondo, J.L.: Symmetry building and symmetry breaking in synchronized movement. In: Stamenov, M., Gallese, V. (eds.) Mirror Neurons and the Evolution of Brain and Language, John Benjamins Publishing, Amsterdam (2003)

[38] Ramachandran, V.S.: Mirror Neurons and imitation learning as the driving force behind. the great leap forward in human evolution. EDGE 69, (2000), available online: http://www.edge.org/3rd_culture/index.html

[39] Pittam, J.: Voice in Social Interaction: An Interdisciplinary Approach. SAGE, Thousand Oaks, CA (1994)

[40] Roth, W.-M., Tobin, K.: Solidarity and conflict: Prosody as interactional resource in intra- and intercultural communication involving power differences, www.educ.uvic.ca/faculty/mroth/PREPRINTS/Solidarity109.pdf (submitted)

[41] Hillard, D., Ostendorf, M., Shriberg, E.: Detection of agreement vs. disagreement in meetings: training with unlabeled data. Proceedings of HLT/NAACL 2, 34–36 (2003)

[42] Galley, M., McKeown, K., Hirschberg, J., Shriberg, E.: Identifying agreement and disagreement in conversational speech: use of Bayesian networks to model pragmatic dependencies. In: Proceedings of the 42nd Annual Meeting on Association for Computational Linguistics, Article No. 669, Barcelona (2004)

[43] Sonka, M., Hlavac, V., Boyle, R.: Image processing, analysis, and machine vision. Chapman & Hall Computing, New York (1993)

[44] Bobick, A.F., Davis, J.W.: The recognition of human movement using temporal templates. IEEE Transactions on pattern analysis and machine intelligence 23, 257–267 (2001)

[45] Ramseyer, F., Tschacher, W.: Synchrony - A core concept for a constructivist approach to psychotherapy. Constructivism in the Human Sciences 11, 150–171 (2006)

[46] Grammer, K., Keki, V., Striebel, B., Atzmüller, M., Fink, B.: Bodies in motion: A window to the soul. In: Voland, E., Grammer, K. (eds.) Evolutionary aesthetics, pp. 295–324. Springer, Heidelberg (2003)

[47] Grammer, K., Kruck, K.B., Magnusson, M.S.: The courtship dance: Patterns of nonverbal synchonization in opposite-sex encounters. Journal of Nonverbal Behavior 22, 3–29 (1998)

[48] Bechinie, M.: BHS — The "broken heart syndrome". Ethological aspects of lovesickness. Unpublished thesis, University of Vienna (1998)

[49] Tschacher, W., Ramseyer, F., Grawe, K.: Der Ordnungseffekt im Psychotherapieprozess: Replikation einer systemtheoretischen Vorhersage und Zusammenhang mit dem Therapieerfolg. Zeitschrift für Klinische Psychologie und Psychotherapie 36, 18–25 (2007)

[50] Tschacher, W., Grawe, K.: Selbstorganisation in Therapieprozessen Die Hypothese und empirische Pruefung der "Reduktion von Freiheitsgraden" bei der Entstehung von Therapiesystemen. Zeitschrift für Klinische Psychologie 25, 55–60 (1996)

[51] Tschacher, W.: Prozessgestalten. Göttingen: Hogrefe (1997)

[52] Tschacher, W., Scheier, C., Grawe, K.: Order and pattern formation in psychotherapy. Nonlinear Dynamics, Psychology, and Life Sciences 2, 195–215 (1998)

[53] Grawe, K.: Psychological Therapy. Seattle: Hogrefe (2004)

[54] Infante, D.A., Wigley, C.J.: Verbal aggressiveness: An interpersonal model and measure. Communication Monograph 53, 61–69 (1986)

[55] Jacobson, N., Gottman, J.: When men batter nomen: New insights into ending abusive relationships. Simon & Shuster, New York (1998)

[56] Stone, D., Patton, B., Heen, S.: Difficult conversations. Penguin, New York (1999)

[57] Shortt, J.W., Capaldi, D.M., Kim, H.K., Owen, L.D.: Relationship separation for young, at-risk couples: Prediction from dyadic aggression. Journal of Family Psychology 20, 624–631 (2006)

Gesture, Prosody and Lexicon in Task-Oriented Dialogues: Multimedia Corpus Recording and Labelling

Ewa Jarmolowicz, Maciej Karpinski, Zofia Malisz, and Michal Szczyszek

Centre for Speech and Language Processing, Adam Mickiewicz University,
Collegium Novum, Al. Niepodleglosci 4
61-784 Poznan, Poland
ewa@jarmolowicz.art.pl, maciej.karpinski@amu.edu.pl,
zmalisz@ifa.amu.edu.pl, szczysze@interia.pl

Abstract. The aim of the *DiaGest* Project is to study interdependencies between gesture, lexicon, and prosody in Polish dialogues. The material under study comprises three tasks realised by twenty pairs of subjects. Two tasks involve instructional, task-oriented dialogues, while the third is based on a question answering procedure. A system for corpus labelling is currently being designed on the basis of current standards. The corpus will be annotated for gestures, lexical content of utterances, intonation and rhythm. In order to relate various phenomena to the contextualized meaning of dialogue utterances, the material will also be tagged in terms of dialogue acts. Synchronised tags will be placed in respective annotation tiers in ELAN. A number of detailed studies related to the problems of gesture-prosody, gesture-lexicon and prosody-lexicon interactions will be carried out on the basis of the tagged material.

Keywords: dialogue, gesture, lexicon, derivation, prosody.

1 Introduction

While the holistic approach to dialogue analysis, comprising speech and gesture interaction, can hardly be considered "new" or "recent" [7], [29], [30], the attempts to implement it in corpus-based studies of spontaneous communication still face many difficulties and many fundamental questions have not been fully answered yet [35].

Due to substantial technological progress, standard desktop computers offer not only the possibility of detailed, large-scale audio signal analysis, but also video editing and labelling options. On the side of methodology, after the initial period of revolutional chaos, an increasing tendency to define corpus labelling standards can be noticed. Nevertheless, even with the new software, hardware and methodological tools in hand, we can hardly cope with the abundant data coming from completely spontaneous, uncontrolled dialogue situations.

One way to obtain at least partially controlled and more manageable data is to put, indirectly, some constraints on the speakers by assigning them a specific task. Task-oriented dialogues are a frequent subject of study because they provide linguistic material which is both relatively well-structured and contains a certain dose of

A. Esposito et al. (Eds.): Verbal and Nonverbal Commun. Behaviours, LNAI 4775, pp. 99–110, 2007.

spontaneity. Numerous existing corpora provide material for comparative analyses and a view to various solutions of technological problems.

An increasing number of task-oriented dialogue corpora include not only audio but also video data to provide a nearly full picture of the communication act. Taking gestures and facial expression into account may greatly help to find an appropriate explanation for verbal messages and for the entire flow of communication. However, both methodologically and technically, it seems to be a very complex challenge.

2 Project Overview

In our project, we intend to collect and analyse data on the interrelations between gesture, prosody and lexicon in dialogue communication. Our ultimate aim is to create a simple model of multimodal communication that would be able to predict possible sequences of linguistic and extra-linguistic actions in the realization of the studied tasks and would generate a set of most probable lexical, prosodic and gestural components for the most frequently realized dialogue acts. More detailed studies concerning prosodic structure of utterances (with the focus on rhythm and intonation), word formation processes and typical gesture trajectories in task-oriented dialogues will also be conducted.

In order to achieve the main aims of the project, the following steps are undertaken: (a) dialogue task design, testing and recording (completed); (b) the design and testing of multimodal tagging system (in progress); (c) tagging the corpus; (d) the quantitative and qualitative analysis of the tagged data. Currently, we are working on the stage (b), testing theoretical frameworks, existing labelling systems and available software tools for audio-visual material editing and tagging.

3 The Design of the Tasks

The dialogue tasks were intended to involve possibly natural, task-driven communication. Due to the nature of the tasks, the collected material is well-structured in terms of action sequence and dialogue strategies, still preserving much spontaneity, both in speech and gesture. The instructions for participants allowed them to communicate with no restraint but disallowed approaching each other. Any direct suggestions that gestures should be used were avoided. The tasks were designed so that they encourage the use of instructional and illustrating gestures, but many other gesture categories (as listed in, e.g. [37]) occurred during the recorded sessions. Subject A, "the instructor", was asked to stand in front of a small table, while Subject B was sitting at another small table. As it was found during preliminary tests, subjects were more prone to use gestures in the standing position.

In two tasks, the factor of "time pressure" was introduced. The subjects were not informed about the time they had to complete the tasks and they were not equipped with any timer. Shortly before the end of each of these sessions, they were informed about the remaining time. This usually induced more intensive and often more emotional communication, sometimes leading to the introduction of new dialogue strategies.

Task I: Spatial arrangement
A set of objects in everyday use (including ball-pens, a plastic container and its cover, a mug, batteries, a CD) was arranged into an unusual spatial structure. That construction was visible only to Subject A whose task was to instruct Subject B so that s/he re-constructed it on her/his table, using another set of identical items. Necessary actions included putting one thing on, into, under and next to another in various spatial orientations. The time of the session was limited to three minutes. Only one minute before the end of the session, the subjects were informed about the time remaining.

Task II: Origami
A spatial, origami-like figure made of a sheet of paper was placed in front of Subject A. Subject B was handed a sheet of paper and asked to produce a possibly identical figure according to the instructions given by the first subject. Subjects A and B could see each other, but Subject B did not see the original figure. Each session was interrupted after five minutes even if the task had not been completed. One minute before the end of the session the subjects were informed about the remaining time.

Task III: Narration and question-answering
One subject from each pair was presented the same portion of a cartoon: A story about two boys who camped in a forest and met a poacher. Afterwards, s/he was asked to re-tell the story and answer a number of questions. In the part involving question answering, the subjects were first asked a number of questions concerning the details of the cartoon. Then they faced seven short, quickly-asked questions aimed at fast, spontaneous verbal reactions. This was aimed at retrieving a subset of the most easily accessible cartoon-relevant vocabulary from each subject.

4 Video and Audio Recordings

The recording sessions took part in a small anechoic chamber at the Institute of Linguistics, AMU. Two MiniDV camcorders were used for video recording. One of them was placed in front of the standing speaker, over the head of the sitting subject (see section 3). This camcorder was also used in the third task, when the selected speaker stood in front of the interviewers asking questions. The second camcorder was placed on a tripod, approximately in front of the sitting speaker (ca. 20° from the Speaker A - Speaker B axis). In addition to a source of dispersed light attached to the ceiling, two lamps were used for lighting the subjects. To avoid sharp shading, additional white screens were used. The arrangement of the anechoic chamber is shown in Figure 1.

The camcorders were used in fully manual mode. They were focused manually for each pair of subjects and the exposition values were fixed in all of the recordings. This solution proved to be safer during preliminary tests. Auto-focusing tended to fail with rapid body or hand movements as well as with subject dressed in dark, monochromatic clothes. Automatic exposure settings were switched off so that the average lighting level was kept possibly fixed during the entire session. Although the resulting movie recordings seem relatively dark, excessive lighting was consciously avoided to minimize in subjects the stress of being video-recorded. Each camcorder was placed ca. 2.5 metres from the subject. Taking the effective resolution of the equipment (2 Megapixel) into account, the distance allowed for relatively detailed observation of face expression as well as for keeping track of total body movements. The distance between the face of each speaker and the directional light source was roughly two metres.

Since the sound recorded by the camcorders contained perceivable noise coming from the tape mechanism, an additional, independent setup for high-quality sound recording was used. Two large-membrane condenser microphones were placed in front of the subjects. The signal was amplified by a professional mixing console with low-noise microphone pre-amplifiers and sent to a stand-alone CD-Audio recorder. Although not completely acoustically isolated, the subjects were recorded on separate audio channels.

Before each of the tasks, the experimenter entered the chamber, checked the recording equipment and instructed the participants about their roles. Communication during the recording sessions was provided using a monitor speaker placed in the chamber. The quality of the audio signal coming from the microphones was monitored by the recording person during the entire session.

Fifteen pairs of subjects have been recorded so far, but we intend to increase this number to thirty (or even more if some of the currently available recordings show any unacceptable technical flaws). The number of female and male subjects will be kept in balance.

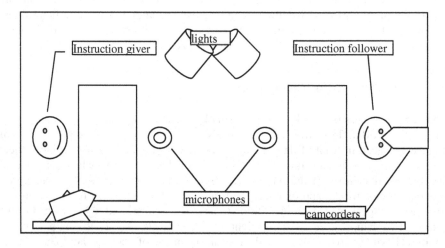

Fig. 1. The arrangement of the anechoic chamber and the recording equipment

5 Labelling System

The corpus of audio and video recordings will be segmented and labelled on several layers for its lexical content, syntactic forms, prosodic realization and gestural component. Most of the segmentation will be carried out "by hand" using adequate software tools. For most purposes, ELAN [23] will be used. For more detailed, phonetic-acoustic and perception-level analyses, Praat [6] will be applied with a number of specialised scripts. Quasi-automatic segmentation will be carried out on the phonetic-segmental level where it will be relevant to the analysis of the intonational and rhythmic structure. As ELAN transcripts are originally in the xml format, additional scripts will be necessary to ensure data transfer between ELAN and Praat. Nevertheless, the xml format will ensure a basic compatibility of the annotation files with many software tools.

5.1 Orthographic Transcription

An extended orthographic transcription system will be applied for the transcription of all the recorded material. The system was developed and tested in *PoInt* [18]and *Pol'n'Asia* (in progress) projects. It offers additional tags for filled and silent pauses, para- and extralinguistic vocal production (e.g., laughter, coughing) as well as other sounds produced by the subjects (e.g., tapping, scratching). This system will offer a direct access to the orthographic forms and will be used in the study of the vocabulary and morphosyntax as well as in the analysis of dialogue act formation. The fact that the orthographic transcription will abstract from the details of the original pronunciation, will have twofold consequences. It will be relatively easy to automatically analyze the vocabulary and its usage, because word forms will be easy to find and tag, which would not be the case if the phonetic transcription would have been used. While this approach would provide a view on the abundance of various phonetic realisations, it would be extremely hard to automatically find and tag different realisations of the same lexical unit. On the other hand, as mentioned, the phonetic variation will be lost in the transcript. Therefore, the applied systems allow for the local use of phonemic/phonetic transcription in order to represent phonetic-segmental phenomena that can have an additional communicative value.

5.2 Dialogue Acts

A dialogue act tier will be introduced for the purpose of further contextualised meaning and an intentional background of various dialogue actions and phenomena can be tracked and analysed. Dialogue acts will be labelled according to the *Pol'n'Asia* scheme which is based on a number of existing systems [1], [9], [10], [13], [28] and complies with standards as suggested in [20], [21], [34], [39]. Each realisation of a dialogue act will be described in four dimensions: *External Action Control, Information Transfer, Dialogue Flow Control* and *Attitudinal Expression*. There is also a slot for *Modality Marker* which refers to the surface-grammatically expressed modality of the labelled phrase (e.g. interrogativity). In each of the four main dimensions, a given act can be described with a limited number of values. For example, for the *External Action Control* dimension, ten values are possible (e.g. *OfferAction, AcceptAction, ConfirmAction*), including *Unmarked* (irrelevant to a given dimension) and *Other* (relevant to a given dimension, but difficult to bound to any of the pre-defined values).

5.3 Lexicon, Derivational System and Syntax

As mentioned in 5.1, the extended orthographic transcription of the dialogues will be a basis for further lexical, morphological and syntactic analyses. The orthographic, time-aligned transcript will be tagged using three specialised tiers. On the syntactic level, parts of sentence and syntactic groups will be tagged. On the lexical level, the system of tags will refer to the parts of speech and their inflectional forms (as Polish is highly inflectional). On the morphological level, the tags will refer to the derivational models applied in particular situations. They will indicate derivational categories to which the described items belong. The details of the tagging system for these layers will be based on the ideas elaborated in [43], [49].

The corpus of the word forms used by the subjects during the task sessions will be created. On this basis, we are going to determine whether stressing, emotional situations enhance or inhibit the derivational activity. In this context, we intend to test the hypothesis that the derivational system develops mainly in the changes of written language. We want to find and describe the principles of derivation which were applied by the subjects. Special attention will be paid to the derivational analogy.

The syntactic analysis will be aimed at the reconstruction of the syntactic schemes typically used by the subjects in the context of task realisation. The reconstruction of the predicative-argumentative structure will provide a link between the morphological and the syntactical structures found in the described dialogues.

5.4 Rhythm

The basic rhythm tier will display segmentation of the signal into vocalic and consonantal events. The C/V segmentation will constitute a time-aligned subdivision within the syllabic tier specifying segments in SAMPA [14]. Segmentation will proceed either manually (using Praat) or preferably automatically using existing scripts for Praat (as applied in e.g. [19], [40]) and later be subjected to human inspection and manual correction.

Once the signal is labelled into C and V events it is fairly simple to extract durations of events given time stamps. The analysis of temporal data provided by syllabic and phrasal tiers may give insights into syntagmatic regularities and paradigmatic structure of rhythm in Polish. It will also add phonetic information to the phonological specification of rhythmic structure specified in the annotation on the phrasal level.

Prominences within a phrase will be annotated on the basis of auditory perception of the signal, inspection of length, amplitude and cross-validation with pitch movements transcribed in INTSINT [25], [36]. A full description of phrasal prominences should include strongly stressed and/or pitch accented syllables as well as syllables which are relatively weaker metrically. The marking used on this level of annotation will be based on the Rhythm and Pitch annotation system [15], [16]. The RaP metrical prominences and phrasing marking conventions will be used. However, the tone mark-up used in labelling of pitch accents will be shared with the intonation layer specified by a separate system (Prosogram or INTSINT, cf. 5.5). Thus, rhythm and intonation marking will exploit and combine different systems which describe events relevant for both levels: phrasal boundaries and pitch movements.

5.5 Intonation

Intonational labelling tends to pose many problems and raise controversies even for deeply-studied languages like English, German or Japanese. There is no standard system for labelling Polish intonation. The most comprehensive description of the Polish intonational system, provided by Steffen-Batogowa [45], is based on concepts and units which differ from the current, widely applied approaches.

According to the framework proposed by Hirst and his colleagues [24] and elaborated by Jassem [27], special attention should be paid to the selection and consequent application of the intonation analysis level. Here, according to the aims of the project, subphonological (perceptual) level was selected for intonational labelling. This will ensure the possibility of studies contrasting different languages in the future, but, which is perhaps even more important, it will leave open the ways of interpretation of the intonational meaning and relevance of intonational units in the context of multi-tiered dialogue analysis.

Although there are many systems which can be applied at this particular level, INTSINT [25] was selected because of the following reasons: (a) it was designed as a system to label the "subphonological level"; (b) consequently, the system is flexible and language independent (which may become crucial as comparative studies are considered in the future); (c) the system is well-documented and has been tested on a number of languages; (d) there are software tools that facilitate, or even automatise, labelling (e.g., a script for Praat which is freely distributed by the authors).

A preliminary intonational transcription that is currently in progress is based on relatively short passages of speech fed as input for the "momelising" script (MOMEL: an intonation modelling procedure [25]). Since all the operations are conducted in Praat, it is easy to resynthesise the analyzed utterances using stylised intonational contours. Since the initial procedure of pitch extraction (based on autocorrelation) frequently fails with spontaneous speech recordings, each portion of the transcription is controlled by ear.

Simultaneously, the use of Prosogram [40] as an intonation analysis tool is taken into account, at least for certain portions of the corpus. Available as a Praat script, Prosogram offers intonation modelling based on the tonal perception model. This means that it takes into account not only the properties of the pitch frequency, but also the way it is perceived. While far from precise pitch perception modelling, it is a tool that may help to keep labelling consistent when the labeller can hardly decide about the choice of a label.

5.6 Gestures

It is likely that annotation systems accurate for Polish data and our purposes will be developed and combined in the process of labelling itself. However, we are currently considering three options as far as the use of an annotating scheme for gestures is concerned: MUMIN [2], CoGesT [22] and the coding system described in Kipp et al. [32].

It seems that the MUMIN scheme would be most appropriate for our dialogue acts coding as it has been developed to capture feedback, turn-management, sequencing and attitudinal properties of dialogue. However, as one of the applied aims of this corpus is to aid in construction of avatars and human-computer interaction systems, coding accuracy of gestures that enables multimodal generation and recognition is of high importance. Each scheme operates with a number of features that influence coding accuracy as well as coding effort. In order to reproduce forms described in the *DiaGest* corpus in subsequent (sub-)projects involving, for example, avatars, we should consider that a reduced form annotating system such as MUMIN could render coarser coding granularity, making appropriate generation more difficult. MUMIN currently exploits only the handedness and trajectory parameters of gesture form annotation and does not employ division into stages of movement [33]. Kipp et al. tries to balance the detail/economy criteria of shape/movement tagging and has been explicitly developed to support generation systems. Coding in CoGesT is more elaborate as it uses criteria based on extended FORM [38] and HamNoSys [42]. However, both do not explore the function dimension to the extent that MUMIN does. In MUMIN, one can find codes for gesture type [41] and for the aforementioned dialogue communication functions that relate gesture and dialogue structuring modalities. The features of MUMIN can be used on a higher level in *DiaGest* demonstrating links between gesture and pragmatic, semantic and discourse structuring properties of phrasing. The lowest level of cross-modal relations in gesture annotation in *DiaGest* will be the lexical level where a possibility exists of combining form accuracy oriented coding systems such as CoGesT and Kipp et al. Semantic relations between word and gesture will require a tier separate from the basic low level tier displaying straightforwardly time-aligned form tagging.

The concept of creating and using a "gesture lexicon" based on reappearing gestures lends space for interesting inter-subject, intercultural and universal observations, as well as for comparisons with the structure of the lexicon in the linguistic modality. CoGesT and the system by Kipp et al. allow for determining gesture lexeme types, which also greatly simplify annotation. The former relates its gesture types to linguistic categories, since in the understanding of the CoGesT authors, gestures have morphology and syntactic structure. Additionally, the choice of a gesture coding scheme partly depends on the choice of the annotating tool.

6   Applications of the Corpus

The *DiaGest* corpus will become a basis for a number of studies in phonetics, linguistics and communication. In our further research, we intend to determine which lexical units, syntactic constructions, prosodic phenomena and gesture configurations (if any) are typical of selected categories of dialogue acts. We are going to determine how they contribute to various aspects of pragmatic meaning. It is also intended to study the role of gestures as delimiters or markers of utterance units and intonational phrases. Our analyses, starting from two different points (speech and gesture) will be aimed at conceptualising dialogue acts as integrated verbal and non-verbal messages.

A number of quantitative and qualitative analyses will be carried out to study the synchronicity (or its absence) in the occurrence of certain phenomena in various modalities of the process of communication [45], [47]. An attempt will be made to answer the question of whether the visual and acoustic aspects of the communication process are based on the same metrical structure (see, e.g. [26], [46]). Hypotheses related to a common, cognitive, "internalised pulse" for speech and gesture will be put forward.

The study of lexical-syntactic level will focus on the structure of the instructional dialogue act. It is intended to describe the word usage patterns typical of task-engaged and emotional utterances. Special attention will be paid to the word formation processes, including the occurrence of derivational neologisms. This will constitute a basis for a minimum dictionary of instructional dialogue which can be applied in the design of task-oriented computer dialogue systems.

The rhythmic and intonational tags, along with the voice recordings, will provide rich material for more detailed, semi-automatic analyses. Wide applications in speech technology are possible, including intonational contour generation in speech synthesis engines and intonational contour recognition or identification in automatic speech recognition (or understanding) systems. The same applies to a model of the rhythmic structures which can be used for the purpose of speech synthesis and recognition.

While numerous studies of speech-gesture interaction have been carried out for other languages, Polish still seems largely neglected in this respect [3], [4], [5]. The project will directly contribute, as a part of basic research, to the extension of the limited knowledge about prosodic properties of Polish spontaneous speech, spontaneous lexicon and syntax. It will also provide a more comprehensive and detailed description of the gestural component of dialogue.

The resulting limited, multidimensional model of task-oriented communication will be tested in the context of the Polish Literacy Tutor project [17] which is closely related to, and based on, the Colorado Literacy Tutor system [11], [12]. As the avatars applied in the original software have been created according to American culture standards, it is highly recommended to "localise" their gestural behaviour and to find appropriate ways for lexical, syntactic and prosodic expression to enhance their positive influence on the Polish learner.

References

1. Alexandersson, J., Buschbeck-Wolf, B., Fujinami, T., Kipp, M., Koch, S., Maier, E., Reithinger, N., Schmitz, B.: Dialogue Acts in VERBMOBIL-2, 2nd edn. (Deliverable) (1998)
2. Allwood, J., Cerrato, L., Dybkjaer, L., Jokinen, K., Navaretta, C., Paggio, P.: The MUMIN Multimodal Coding Scheme. NorFA Yearbook. (2005)
3. Antas, J.: Gest, mowa a mysl. In: Grzegorczykowa R., Pajdzinska A. (eds.) Jezykowa kategoryzacja swiata. Lublin (1996)
4. Antas, J.: Morfologia gestu. Rozwazania metodologiczne. In: Slawski F., Mieczkowska H. (eds.) Studia z jezykoznawstwa slowianskiego. Krakow (1995)
5. Antas, J.: Co mowia rece. Wprowadzenie do komunikacji niewerbalnej. In: Przybylska R., Przyczyna W. (eds.) Retoryka dzis. Teoria i praktyka. Krakow (2001)
6. Boersma, P., Wenink, D.: Praat. Doing Phonetics by Computer (a computer program; version 4.4 and later) (2006)
7. Bolinger, D.: Intonation and Gesture. American Speech 58(2), 156–174 (1983)
8. Bunt, H.: A Framework for Dialogue Act Specification. In: Paper presented at the 4th Joint ISO-SIGSEM Workshop on the Representation of Multimodal Semantic Information, Tilburg (2005)

9. Bunt, H.C., Girard, Y.M.: Designing an Open, Multidimensional Dialogue Act Taxonomy. In: Gardent, C., Gaiffe, B. (eds.) Proceedings of the Ninth International Workshop on the Semantics and Pragmatics of Dialogue (DIALOR 2005), pp. 37–44 (2006)

10. Carletta, J., Isard, A., Isard, S., Kowtko, J., Doherty-Sneddon, J., Anderson, A.: HCRC: Dialogue Structure Coding Manual, Human Communications Research Centre. University of Edinburgh, Edinburgh, HCRC TR – 82 (1996)

11. Cole, R.A., Carmell, T., Connors, P., Macon, M., Wouters, J., de Villiers, J., Tarachow, A., Massaro, D., Cohen, M., Beskow, J., Yang, J., Meier, U., Waibel, A., Stone, P., Fortier, G., Davis, A., Soland, C.: Intelligent Animated Agents for Interactive Language Training. In: STiLL: ESCA Workshop on Speech Technology in Language Learning. Stockholm, Sweden (1998)

12. Cole, R.A., Van Vuuren, S., Pellom, B., Hacioglu, K., Ma, J., Movellan, J., Schwartz, S., Wade-Stein, D., Ward, W., Yan, J.: Perceptive Animated Interfaces: First Steps Toward a New Paradigm for Human–Computer Interaction. Proceedings of the IEEE: Special Issue on Human-Computer Multimodal Interface 91(9), 1391–1405 (2003)

13. Core, M., Allen, J.: Coding Dialogues with the DAMSL Annotation Scheme. In: AAAI Fall Symposium on Communicative Action in Humans and Machines, Cambridge, MA, pp. 28–35 (1997)

14. Demenko, G., Wypych, M., Baranowska, E.: Implementation of Grapheme-to-phoneme Rules and Extended SAMPA Alphabet in Polish Text-to-speech Synthesis. Speech and Language Technology 7, 17. Wydawnictwo PTFon, Poznan (2003)

15. Dilley, L., Breen, M., Bolivar, M., Kraemer, J., Gibson, E.: A Comparison of Inter-Transcriber Reliability for Two Systems of Prosodic Annotation: RaP (Rhythm and Pitch) and ToBI (Tones and Break Indices). In: Proceedings of the International Conference on Spoken Language Processing, INTERSPEECH 2006, Pittsburgh, PA (2006)

16. Dilley, L., Brown, M.: The RaP Labeling System, v. 1.0,ms (2005), http://faculty.psy.ohio-state.edu/pitt/dilley/rapsystem.htm

17. Dziubalska-Kolaczyk, K., Krynicki, G., Sobkowiak, W., Bogacka, A., et al.: The Use of Metalinguistic Knowledge in a Polish Literacy Tutor. In: Duszak, A., Okulska, U. (eds.) GlobE 2004. Peter Lang (2004)

18. Francuzik, K., Karpinski, M., Klesta, J., Szalkowska, E.: Nuclear Melody in Polish Semi-Spontaneous and Read Speech: Evidence from Polish Intonational Database PoInt. Studia Phonetica Posnanensia 7, 97–128 (2005)

19. Garcia, J., Gut, U., Galves, A.: Vocale: A Semi-automatic Annotation Tool for Prosodic Research. In: Proceedings of Speech Prosody, Aix-en-Provence (2002) pp. 327–330 (2002)

20. Gibbon, D., Mertins, I., Moore, R.K. (eds.): Handbook of Multimodal and Spoken Dialogue Systems: Resources, Terminology and Product Evaluation. Kluwer Academic Publishers, Dordrecht (2000)

21. Gibbon, D., Moore, R.K., Winsky, R(eds.): The Eagles Handbook of Standards and Resources for Spoken Language Systems. Mouton de Gruyter (1997)

22. Gut, U., Looks, K., Thies, A., Gibbon, D.: CoGesT: Conversational Gesture Transcription System. Version 1.0. Technical report. Bielefeld University (2003)

23. Hellwig, B., Uytvanck, D.: EUDICO Linguistic Annotator: ELAN, Version 3.0 Manual software manual (2004)

24. Hirst, D.J., Di Cristo, A., Espesser, R.: Levels of Representation and Levels of Analysis for Intonation. In: Horne, M. (ed.) Prosody: Theory and Experiment, Kluwer, Dordrecht (2000)

25. Hirst, D., Espesser, R.: Automatic Modelling of Fundamental Frequency Using a Quadratic Spline Function. Travaux de l'Institut de Phonétique d'Aix-en-Provence 15, 71–85 (1993)
26. Jannedy, S., Mendoza-Denton, N.: Structuring Information through Gesture and Intonation. In: Ishihara, S., Schmitz, M., Schwarz, A. (eds.) Interdisciplinary Studies on Information Structure 03, pp. 199–244 (2005)
27. Jassem, W.: Classification and Organization of Data in Intonation Research. In: Braun, A., Masthoff, H.R. (eds.) Phonetics and its Applications. Festschrift for Jens-Peter Köster. Franz Steiner Verlag, Wiesbaden, pp. 289–297 (2002)
28. Karpinski, M.: Struktura i intonacja polskiego dialogu zadaniowego. Wydawnictwo Naukowe UAM, Poznan (2006)
29. Kendon, A.: Gesticulation and Speech: two Aspects of the Process. In: Key, M.R. (ed.) The Relation Between Verbal and Nonverbal Communication, Mouton (1980)
30. Kendon, A.: Gesture and Speech: How They Interact. In: Wiemann, J.M., Harrison, R.P. (eds.) Nonverbal Interaction, pp. 13–43. Sage Publications, Beverly Hills (1983)
31. Kipp, M.: Anvil: A Generic Annotation Tool for Multimodal Dialogue. In: Proceedings of the 7th European Conference on Speech Communication and Technology, EUROSPEECH 2001, Aalborg pp. 1367–1370 (2001)
32. Kipp, M., Neff, M., Albrecht, I.: An Annotation Scheme for Conversational Gestures: How to Economically Capture Timing and Form. In: Martin, J.-C., Kühnlein, P., Paggio, P., Stiefelhagen, R., Pianesi, F. (eds.) LREC 2006 Workshop on Multimodal Corpora: From Multimodal Behaviour Theories to Usable Models (2006)
33. Kita, S., van Gijn, I., van der Hulst, H.: Movement Phases in Signs and Co-speech Gestures and Their Transcription by Human Coders. In: Wachsmuth, I., Fröhlich, M. (eds.) Gesture and Sign Language in Human-Computer Interaction, pp. 23–35. Springer, Heidelberg (1998)
34. Klein, M.: Standardisation Efforts on the Level of Dialogue Acts in the MATE Project. In: Proceedings of the ACL Workshop: Towards Standards and Tools for Discourse Tagging. University of Maryland, pp. 35–41 (1999)
35. Loehr, D.: Gesture and Intonation. Doctoral Dissertation, Georgetown University, Washington, DC (2004)
36. Louw, J.A., Barnard, E.: Automatic Intonation Modelling with INTSINT. In: Proceedings of the Fifteenth Annual Symposium of the Pattern Recognition Association of South Africa, UCT Press, pp. 107–111 (2004)
37. Malandro, L.A., Barker, L.L., Barker, D.A.: Nonverbal Communication. Addison-Wesley, Reading, MA (1989)
38. Martell, C.: FORM: An Extensible, Kinematically-Based Gesture Annotation Scheme. In: Proceedings of ICSLP, Denver, Colorado (2002) pp. 353–356 (2002)
39. Mengel, A., Dybkjaer, L., Garrido, J.M., Heid, U., Klein, M., Pirrelli, V., Poesio, M., Quazza, S., Schiffrin, A., Soria, C.: MATE: Deliverable D2.1 MATE Dialogue Annotation Guidelines (2000)
40. Mertens, P.: The Prosogram: Semi-Automatic Transcription of Prosody Based on a Tonal Perception Model. In: Bel, B., Marlien, I. (eds.) Proceedings of Speech Prosody 2004, Nara, Japan (2004)
41. McNeill, D.: Hand and Mind: What Gestures Reveal about Thought. University of Chicago Press, Chicago (1992)
42. Prillwitz, S., Leven, R., Zienert, H., Hanke, T., Henning, J.: HamNoSys. Version 2.0. Hamburg Notation System for Sign Languages. An Introductory Guide. Signum, Hamburg (1989)

43. Przepiorkowski, A., Wolinski, M.: A Flexemic Tagset for Polish. In: The Proceedings of the Workshop on Morphological Processing of Slavic Languages, EACL 2003 (2003)
44. Silverman, K., Beckman, M., Pierrehumbert, J., Ostendorf, M., Wightman, C., Price, P., Hirschberg, J.: ToBI: A Standard Scheme for Labeling Prosody. In: Proceedings of ICSLP, pp. 867–869 (1992)
45. Steffen-Batogowa, M.: Struktura przebiegu melodii jezyka polskiego ogolnego. Poznan (1996)
46. Steininger, S., Schiel, F., Louka, K.: Gestures During Overlapping Speech in Multimodal Human-Machine Dialogues. In: International Workshop on Information Presentation and Natural Multimodal Dialogue 2001, Verona, Italy (2001)
47. Swerts, M., Krahmer, E.: The Effects of Visual Beats on Prosodic Prominence. In: Proceedings of Speech Prosody 2006, Dresden (2006)
48. Valbonesi, L., Ansari, R., McNeill, D., Quek, F., Duncan, S., McCullough, K., et al.: Multimodal Signal Analysis of Prosody and Hand Motion: Temporal Correlation of Speech and Gestures. In: European Signal Processing Conference (EUSIPCO 2002) (2002)
49. Wolinski, M.: System znacznikow morfosyntaktycznych w korpusie IPI PAN. Polonica XXII-XXIII, pp. 39–55 (2003)

Egyptian Grunts and Transportation Gestures

Aly N. El-Bahrawy

Faculty of Engineering, Ain Shams University, Cairo, Egypt
`alyelbahrawy@yahoo.com`
`www.alyelbahrawy.com`

Abstract. The paper has two main subjects related to Egyptian culture. The first is a collection of Egyptian grunts used by almost all Egyptians in everyday life, and recognized by almost everybody. The second is another collection of gestures used by passengers of a special kind of public transportation – called microbus- in greater Cairo and outside. Such gestures differ with the geographic location of the microbus route and are used to communicate with the bus driver and his helper. The material of the two collections was provided by students in communication skills classes offered by the author through undergraduate and graduate curricula.

Keywords: grunts, gestures, transportation, Cairo-Egypt.

1 Introduction

The author was inspired by the presentations made during the NATO summer school on the "Fundamentals of Verbal and Nonverbal Communication and the Biometrical Issue" which took place at the International Institute for Advanced Scientific Studies (IIASS) in Vietri, Italy from the 2nd to the 12th of September, 2006. In particular, the lectures given by Nick Campbell [1] on recognizing speech gestures, by David McNeill on gestures and cultures [2], and by Adam Kendon on characteristic of gestural actions [3] were very stimulating. The paper will demonstrate two experiments related to the latter subjects. The first is the compilation of the first Egyptian Grunts dictionary collected by first year engineering students. The second is the use of hand gestures to communicate with the microbus driver collected by post graduate students. The latter collection is an interesting phenomenon related to transportation problems in Cairo, Egypt.

2 The First Egyptian Grunts Dictionary

The importance of non-lexical vocal expressions (grunts) in everyday communication is very obvious if we listen to any recorded conversations. Such grunts express

A. Esposito et al. (Eds.): Verbal and Nonverbal Commun. Behaviours, LNAI 4775, pp. 111–116, 2007.

emotions and feelings that are crucial to interpret the message sent by the speaker. According to Campbell [1], if we consider the audio component of communication, only 15% is expressed as verbal content and 85% is non-verbal speech sounds or grunts. To the author's knowledge, no attempts have been made to collect and document such grunts for the Egyptian language. One of the course projects is to ask the first year students to collect such expressions, suggest a way to write it down, and explain its meaning. The students were very interested in and motivated by this type of exercise. The collected grunts and the way they were written showed a lot of creativity from the students' side. Some of them concentrated on grunts used to communicate with babies, with animals and among Upper-Egyptians. The grunts were collected in what the students called the First Egyptian Grunts dictionary. Figures 1 and 2 show a list of the grunts collected, their supposedly English version, the Arabic version, and the meaning Arabic speakers attribute to them.

English	Arabic	Meaning
Ya3	يع	disgusting, distasteful
Uff	أوف	fed up
Ahh	أه	hurt
Hahaha	هاهاها	laughing
Ekhee	إخبه	disgusting, distasteful
AAAAA	آآآآآ	I understood at last
Ay	أي	feeling pain
E7m E7m	إحم إحم	before entering room to warn ladies
Bekh	بخ	appear suddenly to frighten someone
Youuh	يووه	fed up
Shsh	ششش	stop talking and listen
	بشهق	surprised (suck air inside mouth with little noise)
a'a'a'	أءأءأء	be careful to what you are saying
Ooops	أوبس	retreat after slipping a secret
Hoss	هس	shut up
Eh!	إيه	what is this your are saying
A7'	أح	when you touch something hot
Rololulwiy	زغروئه	noise made by tongue during wedding parties
Yaaah	ياااه	this is too much
Mmm	ممممم	agreeing to what is said
Pesst	بست	calling someone you don't know (inpolite)
dududud	دودودودو	to show that someone is very talkative

Fig. 1. Egyptian grunts: part I

3 Hand Gestures and Transportation in Cairo

Microbuses are small private transportation vehicles used frequently in Cairo and other major cities in Egypt. Such transportation mean is very common since the government was and it is still not able to solve the problems resulting from the overpopulated cities like Cairo and Giza. Such vehicles don't have regular stops, and they stop anywhere where they spot potential passengers. The phenomenon drew the attention of many writers to the extent that some of them [4] coined the expression '*microbus culture*'.

English	Arabic	Meaning
Pssss	بسسس	bicylce rider warding pedestrians from the back
rrrrr or brrrr	ررر/برررر	shivering from the cold
		shocked (air drawn inside - mouth open)
T'	نوأ	no
Akh	أخ	I have forgotten something
Haeeeh	هييه	Happiness (like end of boring class)
Eah	إيه	I could not hear you
mmmah	ممممه	express love to baby or other sex
Local Dialect		
Wah	واه	surprised (upper Egypt)
Ha3	هج	shout of guard
Ehhyy	إهي	really
Ayouhh	أبووه	I made something stupid (Alexandria)
Babies		
Nenah	ننه	let us go to bed
Hosh	هش	stop crying
kutikuti	كوتيكوتي	playing with baby
sewsew	سوسو	make baby smile
Kekh	كخ	stop the baby from doing something wrong
tatah	تاته	urge baby to make his early steps
Animals		
Yess	يس	stop the donkey
Heshsh	هششش	ask animal to leave
Bssbssbss	بسبسبس	ask a cat to come closer
7aaa	حاااا	make the donkey move

Fig. 2. Egyptian grunts: part II

Such culture is responsible for a lot of the unexplainable behavior of the public. In addition to the driver, there is another person who is responsible for shouting to announce the destination of the microbus and collecting the fees. What is interesting to the author is that most passengers use hand gestures to communicate with the driver telling him where they want to go. As part of the course project, the students are asked to collect such hand gestures. The colleted signs depend on the geographical location of the bus route, and are very helpful since the bus doesn't have regular stops. It has also a special importance for female passengers since they can't shout loud enough. Some of the students showed some signs used also in the city of Alexandria. The contributions from the class members were collected and documented as shown in Figures 3 and 4. The regions mentioned in the table are displayed in the map of Greater Cairo shown in Figure 5. The author suggests that such signs can be called gestures according to Kendon [5] words here reported for sake of completeness: << *My approach to gesture starts from the position that gestures, like spoken utterances, are voluntary actions. They are not like emotional reactions and they are not like* digestion or breathing. People engage in gesture, as they engage in speech, as part and parcel of their effort to "say something", to engage in some sort of social action, to play their part in an explicit, willing, fashion in the give and take of social interaction>>.

	Region	Destination	Description	Sketch
1	Elharam	erremaya	index and middle fingers straight while thumb on curled ring and little fingers as if shooting with a pistol	
2	Elharam	ettagneed	same as before but the index and middle fingers touch the other shoulder	
3	Elharam	elharam street	fingers of both hands are pointed upwards to make apex of triangle	
4	Elharam	meshaal	thumb pointed upwards, rest of fingers curled to the inside of palm	
5	Elharam	eggiza	three middle fingers curled inside, thumb and little finger pointed outside moving around arm axis ± 45°	
6	Elharam	eddoki	thumbs pointed upwards, rest of fingers curled to the inside, hand moves up and down as a hammer	
7	06-Oct	elhosary	index finger pointing upwards, thumb over the curled remaining fingers	
8	06-Oct	etawabek	hand open and stretched with all fingers close together and moving up and down	
9	Nasr City	tayaran	two hands, thumbs are entangled, the next four finger are moving back and forth like the wings of a bird	
10	Nasr City	7th district	index and middle fingers are apart while thumb is over the curled ring and little fingers (like the victory sign) denotes seven in Indian numerals	
11	Nasr City	8th district	like the previous sign but upside down, denotes eight in Indian numerals	

Fig. 3. List of Microbus Hand Gestures Part I

	Region	Destination	Description	Sketch	
12	Nasr City	10th district	with both hands closing and opening in a flashing manner to denote the nubmer 10		
13	Nasr City	Rabaa	four fingers stretched while thumb is curled to the inside to denote the number four		
14	Nasr City	6th district	two hands, one open with palm away from body and the other hand, thumb up and fingers curled inside the number six		
15	Shobra	edawaran	index pointed out, rest of fingers curled, index makes a circular orbit		
16	General	same street	index stretched and pointed downwards, rest of fingers curled and moving up and down		
17	General	straight ahead	fingers stretched and close together moving up and down meaning 'along this direction'		
18	General	after the bridge	fingers close together and bent to make a curve movin along a circular path to the front		
19	Alexandria	medan essaa	using one hand to point to the watch around the rist of the other arm		
20	Alexandria	train station	hand open with all fingers close together and moving upwards		
21	Alexandria	victoria	index and middle fingers apart, thumb over the curled ring and little finge denoting the victory sign		

Fig. 4. List of Microbus Hand Gestures Part II

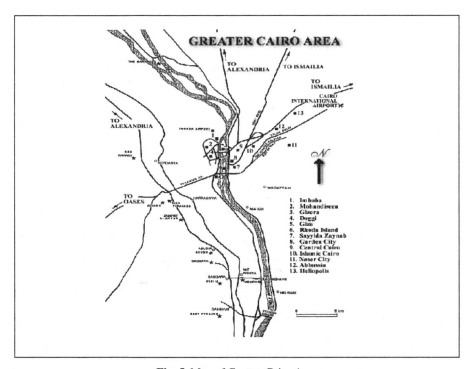

Fig. 5. Map of Greater Cairo Area

4 Conclusions

Out of the interest in nonverbal communication and its relation to culture, two attempts were made to collect and document grunts and special gestures used in Egypt. The first attempt is related to everyday non-lexical vocal expressions used and recognized by Egyptians in their everyday life. The second is a set of special hand gestures frequently used by passengers of microbus living in Greater Cairo and other major cities to communicate with the driver telling him about their destination. The author initiated and introduced these subjects to his students in communication skills classes and asked them to compile the material as part of their course work.

References

1. Campbell, N.: How Speech Encodes Affect and Discourse Information. In: Esposito, A., Bratanic, M., Keller, E., Marinaro, M. (eds.) Fundamentals of Verbal and Nonverbal Communication and the Biometric Issue. NATO Publishing Series, Sub-Series E: Human and Societal Dynamics, vol. 18, pp. 103–114. IOS press, The Netherlands (2007)
2. McNeill, D.: Gesture and Thought. In: Esposito, A., Bratanic, M., Keller, E., Marinaro, M. (eds.) Fundamentals of Verbal and Nonverbal Communication and the Biometric Issue. NATO Publishing Series, Sub-Series E: Human and Societal Dynamics, vol. 18, pp. 20–33. IOS press, The Netherlands (2007)
3. Kendon, A.: Some Topics in Gesture Studies. In: Esposito, A., Bratanic, M., Keller, E., Marinaro, M. (eds.) Fundamentals of Verbal and Nonverbal Communication and the Biometric Issue. NATO Publishing Series, Sub-Series E: Human and Societal Dynamics, vol. 18, pp. 3–19. IOS press, The Netherlands (2007)
4. http://en.wikipedia.org/wiki/Gamal_Alhitani
5. Kendon, A.: An Agenda for Gesture Studies. Semiotic Review 7(3), 8–12 (1996)

On the Use of NonVerbal Speech Sounds
in Human Communication

Nick Campbell[1,2]

[1] National Institute of Information and Communications Technology
[2] ATR Spoken Language Communication Research Laboratory,
Keihanna Science City, Kyoto 619-0288, Japan
nick@nict.go.jp, nick@atr.jp

Abstract. Recent work investigating the interaction of the speech signal with the meaning of the verbal content has revealed interactions not yet modelled in either speech recognition technology or in contemporary linguistic science. In this paper we describe paralinguistic speech features that co-exist alongside linguistic content and propose a model of their function and usage, and discuss methods for incorporating them into real-world applications and devices.

Keywords: interactive speech, social interaction, affect, natural data, statistical modelling, real-world applications.

1 Introduction

"Research on various aspects of paralinguistic and extralinguistic speech has gained considerable importance in recent years. On the one hand, models have been proposed for describing and modifying voice quality and prosody related to factors such as emotional states or personality. Such models often start with high-intensity states (e.g., full-blown emotions) in clean lab speech, and are difficult to generalise to everyday speech. On the other hand, systems have been built to work with moderate states in real-world data, e.g. for the recognition of speaker emotion, age, or gender. Such models often rely on statistical methods, and are not necessarily based on any theoretical models" [1].

In the fields of speech technology and multi-modal interaction, applications are already being developed from these models and data, based on published research findings and on assumed market needs. The developers of these applications might not be experts in paralinguistics or human psychology themselves, and accept the methods and assumptions of researchers in these fields as necessary and proper for the technologies. However, the data and methods required to understand basic human characteristics almost certainly do not equate to the data required to build working applications.

This paper describes some findings from an analysis of a very large corpus of spontaneous everyday conversations and shows that a considerable proportion of the speech is concerned not only with transfer of linguistic content, but also with the display of interpersonal affective information, functioning alongside, and in parallel with, the transfer of linguistic content. Whereas linguistic science and psychology may suffice to describe the content of each utterance and the various affective states of the speaker and listener,

A. Esposito et al. (Eds.): Verbal and Nonverbal Commun. Behaviours, LNAI 4775, pp. 117–128, 2007.

a new branch of communication modelling might be required to describe the social interactions per se and the pragmatic function of many of the speech sounds and speaking styles that were encountered.

Reflecting some of the more recent developments in Conversational Analysis and discourse modelling [2, 3, 4], the findings from this study have confirmed that a large amount, approximately half, of the speech sounds used in normal everyday conversational speech are nonverbal, often simply perceived as 'noise' but functioning to signal important affect-related information. However, because many of these nonverbal speech sounds are typically considered as "fillers" or "hesitations", "performance errors" (sic), or as evidence of lack of preparation of the speech utterance they are frequently edited out of recordings, disregarded in a transcription, or simply not produced at all by the professional speakers (actors, announcers, newsreaders, etc) on whom many researchers rely to produce their data for analysis.

The analysis performed on 1,500 hours of transcribed spontaneous natural spoken interactions recorded over a period of five years in the Kansai region of Japan has provided insights into new challenges for speech synthesis, new features for speech recognition, and raises questions about the need for a new grammar of spoken language which will function both independently and in conjunction with contemporary linguistic grammars. These issues will be addressed separately below.

2   A Database for Paralinguistic Research

It is imperative that any further data we collect on the same scale should be of use both to basic fundamental research issues *and* to application development. The 'Workshop Theme' of Para-Ling'07 [1] poses this question as: "How would a database need to be structured so that it can be used for both research on model-based synthesis and research on recognition?".

Those working from within the statistical approaches might respond that both synthesis and recognition benefit more from an increase in the amount of raw data than from any other type of improvement. However, this may be because both tasks have so far been constrained mainly to produce linguistic information from or for a speech signal, and because neither technology really yet tackles the psychological aspects of personal interaction and discourse management such as are signalled by changes in voice quality and prosody control.

Those working from within the social sciences might answer that a 'corpus' is of more value than a 'database', since the latter is not just a condensed and structured version of the former, but implicitly encapsulates, and is therefore limited by, current assumptions about the ontology of the subject, whereas the former also includes examples of many more features that have not yet been sufficiently understood to be included as explicit database dimensions.

Our own experience of collecting a very large amount of natural conversational speech, in the field, would not be an easy one to replicate; it was both expensive and time-consuming, and the recorded data include much information of a personal and often confidential nature so that the resulting corpus can not be readily distributed or made publically available[1]. However, based on that experience, we do have opinions about what form a research database should take and on ways that it might be more efficiently collected.

The design constraints for collecting a representative corpus of speech should of course incorporate factors that govern size and naturalness. Given a large-enough corpus, we can assume that most *normal* aspects of interactive speech will be covered, but we can also be sure that many marginal or non-typical events will *not* be included, however large the corpus. Solving this problem requires perfecting elicitation methodologies that will provoke a natural reaction to an unnatural stimulus, and at the same time requires serious consideration about the *purpose* of the data collection, i.e., whether it is primarily to collect many examples of what a human speaker might possibly do and say (no matter how rare or unusual they may be) or whether it is to build a database of multiple examples of how they normally respond in a wide range of situations. The former is presumably the goal of the academic, the latter the goal of the engineer. The goal of the community is to establish a common ground between the two.

Labov's Observer's Paradox [5] (wherein the presence of an observer or a recording device has a measurable effect on the performance of the observed) must first be overcome in order to gather representative speech or multimodal interaction data. Furthermore, if we constrain the behaviour of our subjects in *any* way, then the results will also be unnatural, by definition. If we set any bounds at all on the data that are to be collected, then we are constraining our findings to meet our prior expectations, yet if we simply gather all and every sample that comes our way, we will be faced with some very repetitive and monotonous samples of speech. This is the Corpus-Maker's Paradox.

It is a truism that "the data define the application and the application defines the data"; a corpus that is ideal for speech synthesis may not necessarily be of any use at all for speech recognition, and vice versa. Even within the narrow confines of speech synthesis, a corpus of newsreading might be of little use for story-telling. Indeed, it may not be possible to collect all-purpose data any more than it would be reasonable to expect a single human being to be perfect at (for example) combining comedy, professional newsreading, and Shakespearean acting. Just as people specialise and develop strengths in particular areas, so the corpora we collect can only be representative of specific contexts and predetermined social situations. It is necessary first to define the purpose of the data collection.

It is suggested as part of the the workshop theme that "In application-oriented research, such as synthesis or recognition, a guiding principle could be the requirements of the 'ideal' application: for example, the recognition of finely graded shades of emotions, for all speakers in all situations; or fully natural-sounding synthesis with freely specifiable expressivity; etc. [...], and a cross-cutting perspective may lead to innovative approaches yielding concrete steps to reduce the distance towards the 'ideal'." [1]

This suggestion can be taken to imply that the defining characteristic of paralinguistics in human interaction is the (emotional) state of the speaker per se. Now, it may be that the current research needs of both psychology and linguistics can indeed be

---

[1] Note, however, that the ESP corpus *can* be made available, for research use only, to approved institutes and individuals subject to the signing of a non-disclosure agreement.

satisfied by facts about the speaker (or the utterance) in isolation, but the present paper argues strongly that it is instead the *common space between the speaker and the listener* that should be of most interest in terms of understanding paralinguistics for application-based research.

In 'speaker-centric' research, where different emotional states result in different lexical-choices, speaking-styles, and phrasing, the ideal corpus will be one in which the speaker experiences as many emotions of as many different varieties as possible. In 'communication-centred' research, on the other hand, while the speaker's emotional states may vary, it is the varying states of *relationships with the listener* (i.e., with the conversational partner) and the *discourse intentions of the speaker* that become more critical. It is our experience that speakers tend to monitor themselves and suppress or control display of their own emotional states during normal conversational interactions and that they focus instead on projecting an ideal state or 'character' for the current discourse purpose. They do this most obviously through prosodic modulation of feedback utterances.

3   Prosody of Paralinguistic Speech

Some novel aspects of the conversational speech encountered in the ESP Corpus will be discussed in this section. They are presented in support of the claim that at least *two* streams of information are being produced in parallel by the speaker in such interactive situations, and to argue that unless *both* streams are represented in the corpus, or simulated in laboratory data, then it will fail to be representative of typical expressive speaking styles.

The structure of spontaneous speech appears to be fragmented in much the same way as files on a computer disk can be fragmented, with individual fragments containing both inherent meaning and linking information. The discourse as a whole is made up of the combined fragments yet many of them might appear quite unintelligible in isolation. Whereas the linking information present in disk fragments is related to blocks and sectors on the disk, the linking information in a speech fragment relates it to the speaker's discourse intentions through prosody.

Continuing the computer metaphor, while the fragments on the disk are often physically separate, the files we see on the screen appear to be coherent and whole. So on listening to the speech, although we perceive a coherent stream, the phonetic transcription reveals much more fragmentation.

The entire corpus (1,500 hours of speech in all) was transcribed by hand under strict phonetic requirements: the text was to be both human-readable, *and* machine readable, accurately representing each sound that was present in the speech with some form of tag or label. Many of these sounds correspond to words in the language; about half did not (examples have been published elsewhere [6], see also [7]).

Many of the non-word sounds were laughter. In all we counted more than two-thousand types of laugh, many appearing more than a few hundred times each. Many more of these sounds were 'grunts', (equivalent to 'ummh' or 'err' in English) [8]. Others were 'wrappers', frequent phrases such as 'you, know', 'well, ...', 'let me see ...,', serving to break-up the conversation and allow the speaker to express affect through voice-quality and prosodic differences.

It is argued that the very frequent appearance of such simple nonverbal elements interspersed regularly throughout the speech allows the speaker to express not just the linguistic content, but also 'state-of-mind' through 'tone-of-voice'.

3.1   Voice Quality and Paralinguistic Speech

'Tone-of-Voice' is a term often used by the layperson but rarely by the speech professional. David Crystal uses it in "Paralinguistics" ([9], p.173) noting that "babies respond to adult tones of voice very early indeed, from around two months, and it is these which are the first effects to emerge in their own productions - from as early as seven months". Voice quality is certainly an essential part of prosody [10], though not often included in linguistically-based prosodic research or speech technology, which usually confine their interests to the 'big-three', pitch, power, and duration. In paralinguistic research, one might claim that voice-quality is *even more* important than for example segment duration or speech amplitude except in certain marked cases. Dimension-reduction experiments using Principal Component Analysis have shown for several of the speakers in the ESP data that voice-quality appears strongly in either the first or the second principal component, where the first three principal components together account for approximately half of the significant variance in the acoustic parameters of speech that is linguistically similar but functionally diverse. (For example [13, 14]).

Being a parameter that is difficult to control intentionally, voice quality serves as a strong indicator of the affective states of the speaker [11, 12], and is perhaps the most strongly recognised feature of paralinguistic speech, albeit subconsciously.

3.2   Synthesis of Paralinguistic Speech

Several approaches have been suggested to incorporate paralinguistic information in synthesised speech. While many have attempted to model the prosody of expressive speech (e.g., [15]), and even more have concerned themselves with the manipulation of voice quality parameters to distinguish between male and female voices (and very occasionally children), few have attempted to modify voice quality for paralinguistic effect.

There have also been many attempts to model 'emotion' in speech synthesis, from the work of Janet Cahn in the eighties onwards [17, 18], but almost all (see e.g., [19, 20] as notable exceptions) have concentrated on emulating the big-five (or is it six?) emotions of joy, anger, fear, disgust, sadness, and 'neutral' (sic) that have traditionally been used for research into facial expressions [21].

Our experience with the natural-conversations corpus is that such strong and marked emotions are particularly rare in everyday speech. They may present an appealing challenge to the designers of speech synthesis engines, but surely there is little call for them in real-life applications apart from story-telling and games. Much more important for business applications is the need to express interest and boredom, hesitation and politeness, warmth and distance, etc. Yet these dimensions of paralinguistic expression are seldom taken up as challenges.

3.2.1 Model-Based Approaches

Alessandro's work on voice quality modification [22] provides a strong model for the representation and modification of voice quality, where the main dimension of variation is in the range of hard/soft or breathy/pressed voice. Pressed voice being used to express enthusiasm, and creaky voice for more casual speaking styles.

Kawahara's STRAIGHT [23, 24] also provides a mechanism for voice-quality modification and has been used to replicate the expressive voice and speaking styles of Japanese Noh actors [23, 24] as well as for emotion simulation.

However, our human sensitivity to even very fine modifications of voice quality result in clear perception of any damage caused by speech signal warping and we appear to have a low tolerance to model-based speech synthesis where expression of paralinguistic information is concerned.

3.2.2 Data-Driven Approaches

Data-driven approaches, on the other hand, require very large amounts of speech data, and are strongly limited to only one voice and speaking style if high-definition, clear voice quality is a requirement.

Iida et al [25, 26] tested a multi-database approach to concatenative speech synthesis wherein a speaker was recorded for one hour each under four different emotional states and confirmed that the associated voice quality variations can be incorporated in concatenative methods.

Campbell's recent work [27, 28] also attempts to incorporate non-verbal information in the speech through use of speech segments incorporating different voice-quality characteristics. Having a five-year database of one person's speech should provide the ultimate resource for such data-driven synthesis, but in practice, we still lack a clear understanding of all the factors which control these variations and how different voice qualities will be perceived when used for synthesised utterances, so this remains as current and future work which will be reported elsewhere (see e.g. [30]).

3.3 Recognition/Classification of Paralinguistic Properties of Speech

It has proven to be particularly difficult to produce a complete and sufficient set of labels for the ESP corpus, as different labellers perceive different types of information from the same speech signal. This does not, however, imply that what they perceive is random, more that they are attuned to different dimensions of information in the signal. Taken together, the sum of all the labels describe many aspects of the speech, but individually they can be difficult to compare. For example, labeller A may determine that the speaker is 'speaking softly', Labeller B that she is 'being kind', labeller C that she is 'acting cute', and so on. Of course we can constrain the set of terms that the labellers are allowed to use to describe the data and so achieve higher 'consistency' in the labelling, but at the loss of what information?

We can instead explain the apparent confusion as follows: labeller A is being sensitive to the mechanics of the speaking style, labeller B to its pragmatic function, and labeller C more to appearance. There is no contradiction, nor any objective measure of which is more appropriate.

As well as using subjective labels of the types illustrated above, when selecting an utterance variant for concatenative speech synthesis, we also attempt to describe each speech fragment in terms of three slightly more objective dimensions. The first describes the speaker, the second her relationship with the interlocutor, and the third the intention underlying the utterance.

The speaker has at any given time various interacting states of arousal; she may have slept well, be interested in her topic, be healthy, not hung-over, etc., all of which will have an effect on her speaking style. Her relationship with the interlocutor may be close, the situation informal, relaxed, public, quiet, in a pub, etc., all having an effect on her manner of speaking. And she may be performing a greeting, in the morning, politely, etc., which three dimensions taken together collectively determine not only the manner of speaking but also the content of the utterance, its wording and complexity.

So for an ideal paralinguistic concatenative speech synthesiser, all the data would be labelled in such a way. Given five years of someone's conversational utterances preserved in a corpus, it should be feasible to synthesise most of the utterances required for the sixth year from this resource if such a general and comprehensive system of labelling could be applied to all the data. That, however, would require automatic techniques for the detection or estimation of each descriptive parameter (and if we could do that, we would have produced a very exceptional and useful computing device indeed!). This too remains as work in progress, though we now have 10% of our data manually labelled for such details.

3.4 Analysis of Paralinguistic Speech

The first stage of such automatic corpus processing requires recognition of the component speech fragments and annotation of each fragment in terms of its speaking style features. Several techniques are already available for this.

Since the speech has already been transcribed, one could suppose that further automatic labelling would be unnecessary, but that is not the case. We need finely aligned time information, at the phone level if possible, for each speech segment for prosodic analysis and speech synthesis development. Speech recognition tools that can be freely downloaded are widely available for such a task. A dictionary can be created from the transcriptions, which are also useful for training a statistical language model. With such a large amount of closed training data, recognition and alignment performance is very high.

However, as noted above, approximately half of the data is nonverbal, and the speech is also highly fragmented. Non-standard recognition is necessary in this case, for where a standard speech recogniser typically uses a set of 'garbage' models to normalise and filter out the so-called 'non-speech' noises from the speech signal, it is precisely those noises that are of most interest for use in paralinguistic feature detection.

We have therefore produced a further dictionary and language model specifically for the detection of 'grunts', laughs, and other such nonverbal speech events. Here, we treat the lexical speech (i.e., that which can be recognised well by the standard recogniser) as 'garbage', and concentrate instead on the stream of noises, detecting prosodic and voice-quality changes over time from their discrete and simple repetitions.

A dictionary of only 100 items accounts for at least half of the non-lexical speech utterances in the corpus. Our nonverbal dictionary contains several thousand items but many of them only occur very infrequently. Because the small number of common sounds (typical grunts) are so very frequent in conversational speech, these particular sounds facilitate very fine comparison of their prosodic differences. For example, when the speaker (a listener in this case) utters 'umm, umm, umm' every three seconds (which often happens in Japanese conversations), we can tell easily if she is speeding up or slowing down, if her pitch is rising across the series, or falling, if her voice is becoming relatively more or less breathy, etc., and it is from this dynamic prosodic information that our paralinguistic 'understanding' of the speech information is derived.

3.4.1 Acoustics and Physiology

The degree of tension in the voice reveals the degree of relaxation of the speaker. From the settings of the larynx, speed of the speech, range of excursion of pitch and power, etc., that is measured on the stream of nonverbal speech fragments we can form an estimate of the changing psychological and physiological states of the speaker.

We have shown in previous work [31][2] that the settings of these acoustic parameters correlate very well with differences in speaker state (e.g., the 'social' tension associated with politeness) and relationship with the interlocutor (e.g., degree of familiarity).

We have also confirmed for different speakers and for different interlocutors in a balanced conversational setup that basic voice quality settings differ consistently according to familiarity to an extent that can be reliably measured.

3.5   Assessment and Perception of Paralinguistic Speech

Returning then to the initial topic of what form an ideal database should take, we consider in this section what it is that people perceive in so-called paralinguistic speech. Or phrased differently, what aspects of the speech signal should be taken into account when evaluating a conversational utterance as suitable for inclusion in a database of speech samples?

From the above, we can conclude that it may be an oversimplification to associate paralinguistic expression simply with emotion in speech. Rather, we should consider its social function and think of it instead as an indicator of social psychological states (after Crystal, ibid, p.167, and Scherer '94 [29]). Variety in paralinguistic expression serves to indicate such interpersonal relationships as dominance, submission, leadership, and so on ... Crystal links variation in tone-of-voice with factors such as hard-sell vs soft-sell in television marketing - where the emotional state of the speaker is almost irrelevant, compared with the relationship that is being established between the speaker and the listener.

Since paralanguage serves to communicate "grammatical, attitudinal, and social information" (ibid, p.168), so a corpus for paralinguistic research and application development should be balanced not just in terms of speaker arousal, but also in terms of speaker-interlocutor relationships. If we must record such speech in a studio, then perhaps we should arrange for a series of different interlocutors to be present to motivate

---

[2] cf especially our "Gold-Star Slides for Science".

the speaker in different ways. Remote conversations, by telephone, are of course the easiest way to do this, without having the voice of the interlocutor interfere with the recordings of the target speaker. Having the same speaker talk in turn with friends, family members, staff, colleagues, strangers (both male and female) is the easiest way to elicit natural variation in speaking styles.

In assessing and labeling the resulting corpus, we still need to establish a framework wherein aspects of speaking style, interspeaker relationships, perceived speaker character, interpersonal stances, and so forth can be annotated and compared.

3.6   Typology of Paralinguistic Speech

Because there are not the same kinds of clear-cut distinctions between classes and types of paralinguistic information as there are between the words and phones of a language, Crystal was driven to describe paralinguistics as "the 'greasy' part of speech". One can sympathise with his frustration.

A /p/ may not gradually merge into a /b/, but interest can easily merge into boredom, and boredom into frustration. Politeness can merge gradually into familiarity, and laughter into tears. A speaker might sound cute to one listener and at the same time obnoxious to another. The categories of Paralinguistic variation cover all facets of human interaction, yet in attempting to map them we might have to include contradictory subjective descriptors as well as more objective measures based on observation of the signal.

4   Applications

How are we to reconcile this lack of a consistent framework with the concrete demands of application development? Perhaps the needs of the latter can resolve the quandries of the descriptive approach. When designing an application for human interaction, e.g., a speech interface for an advanced translation device, we can list up the situations in which it is expected to be used and precisely enumerate the capabilities required for each type of interaction it is to be built for.

But what of the ECA? Research into embodied communicative agents is now common worldwide and considerable real money is being spent by ordinary people on life in virtual worlds[3]. Here the needs are for truly expressive interactions, and in an environment unmoderated by real-world physical constraints. The expectations of the customers will be very high in such situations, and the information carried by voice quality in these very interactive environments will be (perhaps literally) explosive.

Perhaps because of the high sensitivity to voice-quality and prosody in human (or ECA) interactions it will be better to reduce realism in a way similar to graphic images in cartoons. However, it should be noted that, so far, *NO* cartoons have successfully used artificial voices alongside artificial images. All use human voices distorted to sound less like the original speaker. Perhaps this is because of the innate sensitivity of even the two-month-old baby to paralinguistic information carried by tone of voice.

---

[3] See e.g., "Second Life" [32] where almost six million members spent more than 1.5 million US dollars in the past 24 hours.

5   Conclusions

"Paralanguage describes the nonverbal communication that accompanies verbal communication".

This paper has presented some personal views on the use of nonverbal speech sounds in human communication, based on experiences gained from the continuing analysis of a very large corpus of spontaneous conversations. The paper has suggested that (a) conversational speech encodes two distinct streams of information, (i) linguistic, and (ii) interpersonal. Whereas the Wikipedia defines the Greek prefix 'para' as meaning 'beside', 'near', or 'alongside', this paper inclines towards the view that linguistic and paralinguistic information are intertwined rather than parallel and distinct. They coexist in much the same way that vowels and consonants coexist in speech, alternating in an irregular but well-formed way to jointly create an impression of meaning.

The paper has also suggested (b) that the so-called ill-formed, highly-fragmented nature of spontaneous speech is actually a natural evolution of the two streams, allowing content-filled linguistic fragments to be wrapped in nonverbal adjuncts that by being frequent, simple, and often-repeated, allow the listener, even one not yet personally familiar with the speaker to make fine-grained judgements about small changes in vocal settings and speech prosody.

A unifying theme of the paper has been the function of paralinguistic information, defined here as a means to clarify the speaker's attitudinal stances, to display her affective states, and to establish her relationships with the interlocutor for the purposes of the discourse, which we have modelled as three different dimensions of paralinguistic control: (a) the speaker, (b) her relationship with the interlocutor, and (c) the intention underlying the utterance. These have been tested in speech synthesis applications.

That babies of two-months can understand differences in their mother's tone-of-voice implies that this is a very basic and prelinguistic form of communication. To reduce it simply to a mere display of emotion is an oversimplification, yet we still lack words to do it justice.

Thirty-eight years ago, David Crystal closed his chapter on Paralinguistics with these words (ibid, p.174): "There is still a considerable gap, however, between our intuitive ability to recognise and interpret paralinguistic effect - our 'natural' sense of linguistic appropriateness and taboo - and our ability to state in clear terms what it is that we perceive. The spectre which still haunts papers on paralanguage, including this one, is the extraordinary difficulty of putting into words and diagrams what it is that we hear in order that the effects described be as meaningful as possible to the reader". They are clearly still true today.

Acknowledgements

This work is supported by the National Institute of Information and Communications Technology (NiCT), and includes contributions from the Japan Science & Technology Corporation (JST), and the Ministry of Public Management, Home Affairs, Posts and Telecommunications, Japan (SCOPE). The author is especially grateful to the management of Spoken Language Communication Research Labs at ATR for their continuing encouragement and support.

References

[1] Shröder, M.: Impersonal Communication: from the website of ParaLing 2007. The Workshop Theme, http://www.dfki.de/paraling07/WorkshopTheme/

[2] Allwood, J.: An activity based approach to pragmatics. Technical Report (GPTL) 75, Gothenburg Papers in Theoretical Linguistics, University of Goteborg (1995)

[3] Goffman, E.: Forms of Talk, Philadelphia, University of Philadelphia Press (1981)

[4] Shaw, M.E.: Group dynamics: the psychology of small group behaviour. McGraw Hill, New York (1981)

[5] Labov, W., Yeager, M., Steiner, R.: Quantitative study of sound change in progress, Philadelphia PA: U.S. Regional Survey (1972)

[6] Campbell, N.: How speech encodes affect and discourse information. In: Esposito, A., Bratani ć, M., Keller, E., Marinaro, M. (eds.) Fundamentals of Verbal and Nonverbal Communication and the Biometric Issue, pp. 103–114. IOS Press, Amsterdam (2007)

[7] Ward, N.: Non-Lexical Conversational Sounds in American English. Nigel Pragmatics and Cognition 14(1), 113–184 (2006)

[8] Ward, N.: Pragmatic Functions of Prosodic Features in Non-Lexical Utterances. In: Proc. Speech Prosody 2004, Nara, Japan, pp. 325–328 (2004)

[9] Crystal, D.: Prosodic Systems and Intonation in English. Cambridge University Press, Cambridge (1969)

[10] Pittam, J., Scherer, K.R.: In: Vocal expression and communication of emotion. Guilford, New York, pp. 185–197 (1993)

[11] Scherer, K.R.: Vocal affect expression: A review and a model for future research. Psychological Bulletin 99, pp. 143–165 (1986)

[12] van den Broek, E.L.: Empathic Agent Technology (EAT). In: Johnson, L., Richards, D., Sklar, E., Wilensky, U. (eds.) Proceedings of the AAMAS-05 Agent-Based Systems for Human Learning (ABSHL) workshop, pp. 59–67. Utrecht, The Netherlands (2005)

[13] Campbell, N., Mokhtari, P.: Voice Quality; the 4th prosodic parameter. In: Proc 15th ICPhS, Barcelona, Spain (2003)

[14] Campbell, N., Nakagawa, A.: 'Yes, yes, yes', a word with many meanings; the acoustics associated with intention variation. In: Proc ACII 2007 (Affective Computing and Intelligent Interaction) Lisbon, Portugal (2007)

[15] Hamza, W., Bakis, R., Eide, E.M., Picheny, M.A., Pitrelli, J.F.: The IBM Expressive Speech Synthesis System. In: Proceedings of the International Conference on Spoken Language Processing (ICSLP), Jeju, South Korea (October 2004)

[16] Pitrelli, J.F., Bakis, W., Eide, R., Fernandes, E.M., Hamza, R., Picheny, M.A.: The IBM Expressive Text-to-Speech Synthesis System for American English. IEEE Transactions on Audio, Speech, and Language Processing 14(4), 1099–1108 (2006)

[17] Cahn, J.E.: Generating expression in synthesized speech. Master's thesis, Massachusetts Institute of Technology (1989), http://alumni.media.mit.edu/~cahn/emot-speech.html

[18] Cahn, J.E.: The Generation of Affect in Synthesized Speech. Journal of the American Voice I/O Society 8, 1–19 (1990)

[19] Trouvain, J., Schroeder, M.: How (not) to add laughter to synthetic speech. In: Proc. Workshop on Affective Dialogue Systems, pp. 229–232. Kloster Irsee, Germany (2004)

[20] Schroeder, M.: Dimensional emotion representation as a basis for speech synthesis with non-extreme emotions. In: Proc. Workshop on Affective Dialogue Systems, Kloster Irsee, Germany. LNCS, pp. 209–220. Springer, Heidelberg (2004)

[21] Ekman, P.: Universals and cuntural differences in facial expression of emotion. In: Cole, J.K. (ed.) Nebraska Symposium on Motivation, pp. 207–282. University of Nebrasaka Press, Lincoln (1972)

[22] d'Alessandro, C., Doval, B.: Voice quality modification for emotional speech synthesis. In: Proc. Eurospeech 2003, Geneva, Switzerland, pp. 1653–1656 (2003)

[23] Kawahara, H., de Cheveigné, A., Banno, H., Takahashi, T., Irino, T.: Nearly defect-free F0 trajectory extraction for expressive speech modifications based on STRAIGHT. In: Proc. Interspeech 2005, Lisboa, pp. 537–540 (2005)

[24] Modification of Japanese Noh voices for speech synthesis:
http://www.acoustics.org/press/152nd/kawahara.html

[25] Iida, A., Campbell, N., Yasumura, M.: Design and Evaluation of Synthesised Speech with Emotion. Journal of Information Processing Society of Japan 40 (1998)

[26] Iida, A., Campbell, N., Iga, S., Higuchi, Y., Yasumura, Y.: A speech synthesis system with emotion for assisting communication. In: Proceedings of the ISCA Workshop on Speech and Emotion, Belfast, pp. 167–172 (2000)

[27] Campbell, N.: Specifying Affect and Emotion for Expressive Speech Synthesis. In: Gelbukh, A. (ed.) CICLing 2004. LNCS, vol. 2945, Springer, Heidelberg (2004)

[28] Campbell, N.: Conversational Speech Synthesis and the Need for Some Laughter. IEEE Transactionson Audio, Speech, and Language Processing 14(4), 1171–1179 (2006)

[29] Scherer, K.R.: Interpersonal expectations, social influence, and emotion transfer. In: Blanck, P.D. (ed.) Interpersonal expectations: Theory, research, and application, pp. 316–336. Cambridge University Press, Cambridge and New York (1994)

[30] Campbell, N.: Expressive / Affective Speech tone-of Synthesis. In: Benesty, J., Sondhi, M.M., Huang, Y. (eds.) Springer Handbook on Speech Processing and Speech Communication, Springer, Heidelberg (2007) (in press)

[31] Campbell, N.: Getting to the heart of the matter; speech as expression of affect rather than just text or language. In: Language Resources & Evaluation, vol. 39(1), pp. 109–118. Springer, Heidelberg (2005)

[32] Second Life: a 3-D virtual world entirely built and owned by its residents. Since opening to the public in, it has grown explosively and at the time of writing is inhabited by a total of 5,788,106 people from around the globe (2003), http://secondlife.com/

Speech Spectrum Envelope Modeling

Robert Vích and Martin Vondra

Institute of Photonics and Electronics,
Academy of Sciences of the Czech Republic,
Chaberská 57 CZ-182 52 Prague 8, Czech Republic
{vich,vondra}@ufe.cz

Abstract. A new method for speech analysis is described. It is based on extremes finding in the magnitude spectrum of a speech frame followed by interpolation. The interpolated spectrum envelope can be used for speech synthesis and also for the estimation of the excitation and background noise. In the contribution the proposed method is illustrated using a noisy speech frame and compared with LPC spectrum and spectrum obtained by classical and hidden cepstral smoothing.

Keywords: speech analysis, cepstral analysis, envelope estimation.

1 Introduction

Voiced speech signal is produced in the human speech production system as the convolution of the excitation waveform produced by the glottis and of the impulse response of the vocal tract. In speech analysis we decompose the speech signal back into these two components. As the speech signal is a time varying signal it must be divided into short segments in which it can be supposed to be stationary.

In most of the analysis techniques based on *linear prediction* (LP) [1] the speech signal is modeled as the response of an all-pole system. In the case of voiced signals the calculated parameters are biased by the fundamental frequency of the periodic excitation produced by the vocal folds. That means that the resonant behavior of the vocal tract model can be estimated only with an error. To exclude this systematic error, the so called pitch synchronous analysis should be performed, which consists in the identification of the model parameters from a speech frame between two excitation impulses. Such a procedure involves the localization of pitch pulses in voiced frames, which is not a simple task. In both procedures the frequency spectrum of the vocal tract model can be obtained by evaluation of the identified transfer function of the model. In LP speech analysis the true envelope of the speech spectrum is not obtained.

For comparison of different speech modeling approaches an example of noisy speech frame has been chosen. It is sampled with $F_s = 8$ kHz, the frame length is $N = 1024$, Hamming windowed, analyzed with FFT with the dimension $N_F = 2048$. The length of the temporal window was chosen relative long, which enables to examine the spectral noise. In Fig. 1 the speech frame and the corresponding speech magnitude spectrum together with the frequency response of the LP vocal tract model of the order $p = 12$ are shown.

A. Esposito et al. (Eds.): Verbal and Nonverbal Commun. Behaviours, LNAI 4775, pp. 129–137, 2007.
© Springer-Verlag Berlin Heidelberg 2007

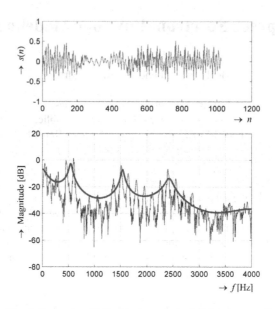

Fig. 1. Example of LP speech analysis, LPC order $p = 12$

Another method of speech analysis is based on *homomorphic* or *generalized homomorphic analysis* [2], [3]. This approach enables the separation of signals which are composed through multiplication or convolution. Homomorphic speech analysis can be divided into following steps:

- Fast Fourier Transform (FFT) analysis of a windowed speech signal frame and calculation of the logarithmic magnitude spectrum. In the case of a voiced speech frame, the logarithmic magnitude spectrum contains an additive periodic component the period of which is equal to the fundamental frequency.
- Inverse FFT of the logarithmic magnitude spectrum yields the real cepstrum in which the cepstrum corresponding to the vocal tract impulse response and the cepstrum corresponding to the periodic excitation produced by the vocal folds occupy approximately disjoint time intervals. The cepstrum of the periodic excitation is also quasi periodic with the fundamental frequency period. By windowing the cepstrum with a rectangular cepstral window of the length M we can separate the two cepstral components.
- Using FFT to the non-periodic low-time portion of the cepstrum we obtain an approximation of the logarithmic magnitude spectrum of the vocal tract impulse response. Also in this cepstral approach the obtained magnitude spectral response of the vocal tract model is not the true spectral envelope, it corresponds more or less to a mean square approximation of the logarithmic magnitude speech spectrum. FFT of the high-time part of the cepstrum yields the logarithmic magnitude spectrum of the periodic excitation and noise.

In Fig. 2 an approximation of the cepstral vocal tract frequency response using cepstrum weighting with a rectangular window of the length $M = 26$ is shown. For comparison in Fig. 3 the result of cepstrum windowing again with a rectangular window but with the length $M = 50$ is depicted. The fundamental frequency of the speech signal is $F_0 = 150$ Hz, which corresponds to the fundamental frequency period $T_0 = 6.6$ ms, or $M_0 = 53$ in samples for $F_s = 8$ kHz.

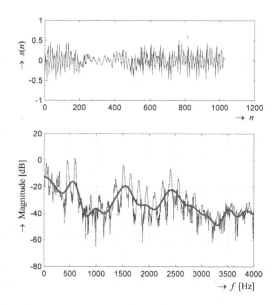

Fig. 2. Example of cepstral speech smoothing with $M = 26$

The weighting of the cepstrum by a rectangular window introduces into the logarithmic spectrum magnitude a degradation given by the Gibbs phenomenon. In this paper a simple procedure based on linear filtering of the logarithmic magnitude spectrum is presented, which tries to minimize the error in the estimated vocal tract model frequency response. In [4] this approach has been called *hidden homomorphic processing*.

In this paper a further approach to de-composing the speech frame spectrum into an approximation of the magnitude spectrum of the vocal tract model impulse response – the envelope and the excitation spectrum is presented. It is based on direct spectrum envelope estimation. Using this spectrum envelope the excitation signal spectrum and spectral noise can be estimated. All mentioned methods can be used for speech analysis, speech coding and speech synthesis and could be also used for continuous noise spectrum estimation in speech enhancement [5] and in base line estimation of the noise level for harmonic-to-noise-estimation for noninvasive assessment of voice pathology [6].

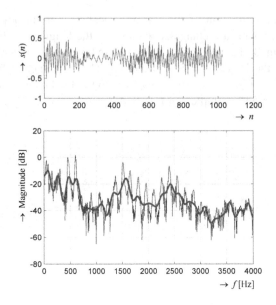

Fig. 3. Example of cepstral speech smoothing with $M = 50$

2   Spectral Smoothing by Hidden Homomorphic Processing

The main idea of this approach consists in the assumption that the periodicity of the logarithmic magnitude spectrum of a voiced speech frame can be suppressed by FIR linear filtering of the logarithmic magnitude speech spectrum, which corresponds to weighting in the cepstral domain using a window given by the frequency response of the FIR filter. This approach has been proposed in 1994 [4] and called *hidden homomorphic processing*. It means that the pass band of the FIR filter is placed in the low-time region of the speech cepstrum and its stop band in the high time cepstrum part corresponding to the harmonic components of the speech spectrum. The aim is to minimize the Gibbs phenomenon, which is caused using a simple rectangular cepstral window for speech deconvolution.

As the pass band width is inversely proportional to the FIR filter length, we must adapt the filter length to the fundamental frequency of the speech signal frame. The estimation of the fundamental frequency is a common part of speech analysis procedure and can be realized in the time or frequency domain [7].

In contrary to the design of FIR filters using windows, we use the window as the impulse response of a FIR filter for filtering the discrete logarithmic magnitude spectrum. It is done using noncausal convolution of a chosen normalized window and the logarithmic magnitude spectrum. That corresponds in the cepstral domain to cepstrum weighting by a cepstral window, which shape is given by the magnitude spectrum of the FIR filter given by the window. The normalization ensures the conservation of the spectrum level.

In this case the total cepstral window length in the cepstral time domain in steps $T = 1/F_s$ is equal to the dimension of the applied FFT. The main lobe width B_c in the cepstral domain is given by

$$B_c = \frac{2N_F}{MF_s},$$ (1)

where N_F is the dimension of the FFT, M is the FIR filter/window length and F_s is the sampling frequency. For suppressing the peaks in the cepstrum, corresponding to the harmonic structure of the logarithmic magnitude spectrum beginning with the first prominent peak, the half main lobe width $B_c/2$ must be smaller or equal to the fundamental frequency period of the voiced speech frame $T_0 = 1/F_0$, where F_0 is the fundamental frequency

$$B_c / 2 \leq T_0 = 1/F_0.$$ (2)

That means that the filter length M must be chosen as

$$M = a\frac{N_F}{F_s}F_0.$$ (3)

Naturally the integer part of (3) is used, preferably the next higher odd number. The coefficient a depends on the type of the applied FIR filter, i.e. on the chosen window, see Table 1. There are summarized some properties of several basic windows [2]. For our purpose of suppressing the cepstrum components corresponding to the harmonic structure of the logarithmic magnitude spectrum, the Hann filter/window seems to be appropriate. The rectangular smoothing filter in the spectral domain introduces the Gibbs phenomenon in the cepstral domain; the Blackman filter/window is too long. The Hamming filter/window has somewhat smaller −3dB main lobe width than the Hann filter/window.

Table 1. Properties of basic FIR filters/windows

FIR filter	Width of main lobe	First cepstral zero coefficient a	Peak amplitude of side lobe [dB]
Rectangular	$2N_F/M$	1	-13
Hann	$4N_F/M$	2	-31
Hamming	$4N_F/M$	2	-41
Blackman	$6N_F/M$	3	-57

As already mentioned, FIR filtering of the logarithmic magnitude spectrum is done using noncausal convolution of the chosen normalized FIR filter impulse response and the logarithmic magnitude spectrum. If the FIR filter is of reasonable length the convolution can be performed directly. For long FIR filters, i.e. for voices with high fundamental frequency, fast convolution using FFT is preferable, which is in fact similar to classical cepstrum windowing, but without the choice of the cepstral window. By subtraction of the logarithmic smoothed spectrum from the logarithmic magnitude speech spectrum the spectrum of the excitation and noise can be obtained.

In Fig. 4 the effect of spectral smoothing by hidden homomorphic processing of the noisy speech frame is presented. For comparison two FIR filters are used, a rectangular smoothing filter with $M = 19$ and a Hann filter with $M = 39$. The application of the Hann filter results in a more smoothed vocal tract frequency response. By comparing Fig. 2, 3 and 4 the differences in smoothing can be realized.

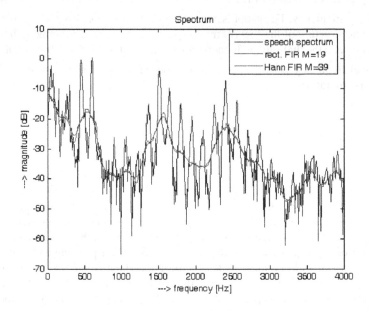

Fig. 4. Spectral smoothing of the noisy speech frame using rectangular and Hann FIR filter

3 Spectral Envelope Estimation

In this section a direct spectrum envelope estimation method is shortly presented. The idea is not new. Paul [8] in 1981 proposed a low-bit-rate spectral envelope estimation vocoder. In his paper the maxima were searched at multiples of the fundamental frequency and linear interpolation was used. In addition to estimating the speech spectrum his approach allows also the determination of a continuous estimate of the background noise spectrum, which he used for noise suppression. The spectral envelope estimator does not have the addition property of homomorphic signal processing.

The proposed algorithm of spectral envelope estimation is simple. In the discrete logarithmic magnitude speech spectrum with the frequency sampling interval $F = F_s/N_F$, the peaks of the spectrum are found and the logarithmic spectral envelope is estimated using a cubic interpolation formula within the peaks and with the same frequency sampling interval. For voiced speech the maxima of the spectrum can be also used for F_0 determination. By subtraction of the logarithmic spectral envelope from the logarithmic magnitude speech spectrum, the spectrum of the excitation and noise can be obtained. The peak estimation algorithm can be used for the second time on the estimated envelope and a new envelope with lower number of details results.

The spectral envelope estimator has many good properties with respect to speech modeling. The spectral peaks are not much influenced by noise. There are no assumptions like all pole or pole/zero model and no model order must be chosen. As already mentioned the fundamental frequency can be estimated as a byproduct. For unvoiced frames the spectral envelope is also obtained with sufficient accuracy. The logarithmic spectral envelope may be used for real cepstrum computation and for the construction of the cepstral speech synthesis model together with the estimated fundamental frequency [9]. The properties of the spectrum envelope estimation method can be easily modified by choosing an appropriate temporal analysis window length before the spectral analysis. Using a short window only the main peaks in the spectrum are used for interpolation, for long windows the spectral noise between the spectral lobes appears and may be evaluated.

In Fig. 5 the result of the described spectrum envelope estimation for the noisy speech sample is presented. Because of a long frame $N = 1024$ with respect to the fundamental frequency period, the envelope imitates mostly the periodic structure of the voiced speech spectrum. Between the lobes the envelope touches the noise spectrum. For comparison in Fig. 6 the envelope is estimated only in multiples of the fundamental frequency, like in the paper by Paul [8].

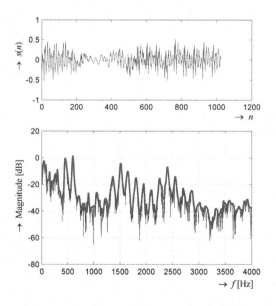

Fig. 5. Example of logarithmic speech spectrum envelope estimation with frame length $N = 1024$

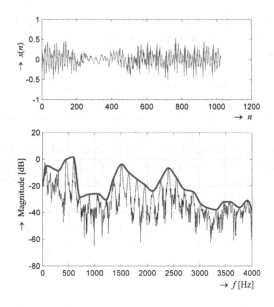

Fig. 6. Example of logarithmic speech spectrum envelope estimation with frame length $N = 1024$ using only peaks at multiples of the fundamental frequency

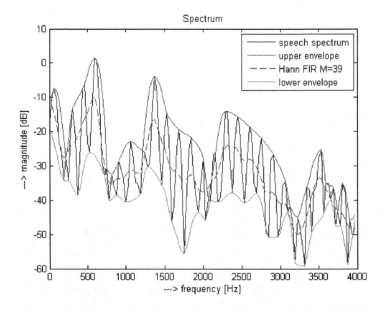

Fig. 7. Example of logarithmic speech spectrum with frame length $N = 256$, with upper envelope, lower envelope and smoothed spectrum using Hann FIR filter

The envelope estimation can be formulated also for spectrum magnitude or for pseudo spectrum [3]. The obtained spectrum envelopes are different. For interpretation of the speech spectrum envelope and the harmonic and noise spectrum the logarithmic magnitude spectrum is preferred.

A similar approach can be formulated also for speech spectrum minima tracking. Than we obtain two envelopes, the upper spectral envelope given by peak finding and the lower spectral envelope, given by the minima, between which the speech spectrum occurs. The ratio of the mean spectral energy of the upper envelope to the mean spectral energy of the lower envelope can be used as a measure of the harmonic-to-noise ratio. In Fig. 7 the upper and lower spectral envelopes together with the smoothed spectrum of the noisy speech frame using Hann FIR filter with $M = 39$ are shown. In this figure for comparison with Figs 5 and 6 a shorter temporal window $N = 256$ was used.

4 Conclusion

The aim of the contribution is to present and compare different approaches of speech deconvolution. The second goal of this investigation is to find a robust and more reliable method of vocal tract modeling for speech synthesis and extraction of the excitation signal and additive noise. The last mentioned task could be used in speech enhancement for continuous noise spectrum estimation.

Acknowledgements. This paper has been supported by the National research program "Information Society" of the Academy of Sciences of the Czech Republic, project number 1ET301710509.

References

1. Markel, J.G., Gray, A.H.: Linear Prediction of Speech. Springer, New York (1976)
2. Oppenheim, A.V., Schafer, R.W.: Digital Signal Processing. Prentice-Hall, Englewood Cliffs (1989)
3. Vích, R.: Pseudo Cepstral Analysis of Czech Vowels. In: Faundez-Zanuy, M., Janer, L., Esposito, A., Satue-Villar, A., Roure, J., Espinosa-Duro, V. (eds.) NOLISP 2005. LNCS (LNAI), vol. 3817, pp. 161–173. Springer, Heidelberg (2006)
4. Vích, R., Horák, P.: Spectral Smoothing of Voiced Speech Signals by Hidden Homomorphic Processing. In: Biosignal 1994 12th International Conf., Brno, pp. 142–144 (1994)
5. Martin, R.: Noise power spectral density estimation based on optimal smoothing and minimum statistics. IEEE Transactions on Speech and Audio Processing 9(5), 504–512 (2001)
6. Murphy, P.J., Akande, O.O.: Noise estimation in voice signals using short-term cepstral analysis. J. Acoust. Soc. Am. 121(2) (2007)
7. Schwarzenberg, M., Vích, R.: Robuste Grundfrequenzbestimmung durch Korrelationsanalyse im Frequenzbereich. In: Fortschritte der Akustik, DAGA 1995, Saarbrücken, vol. II, pp. 1019–1022 (1995)
8. Paul, B.P.: The Spectral Envelope Estimation Vocoder. IEEE Trans. ASSP 29(4), 786–794 (1981)
9. Vích, R.: Cepstral Speech Model, Padé Approximation, Excitation and Gain Matching in Cepstral Speech Synthesis. In: Proc. of the 15th Biennial International EURASIP Conference BIOSIGNAL, Brno, pp. 77–82 (2000)

Using Prosody in Fixed Stress Languages for Improvement of Speech Recognition

György Szaszák and Klára Vicsi

Budapest University of Technology and Economics,
Dept. of Telecommunications and Media Informatics, Budapest, Hungary
szaszak,vicsi@tmit.bme.hu
http://alpha.tmit.bme.hu/speech/

Abstract. In this chapter we examine the usage of prosodic features in speech recognition, with a special attention payed to agglutinating and fixed stress languages. Current knowledge in speech prosody exploitation is addressed in the introduction. The used prosodic features, acoustic-prosodic pre-processing, and segmentation in terms of prosodic units are presented in details. We use the expression "prosodic unit" in order to differentiate them from prosodic phrases, which are usually longer. We trained a HMM-based prosodic segmenter relying on fundamental frequency and intensity of speech. The output of this prosodic segmenter is used for N-best lattice rescoring in parallel with a simplified bigram language model in a continuous speech recognizer, in order to improve speech recognition performance. Experiments for Hungarian language show a WER reduction of about 4% using a simple lattice rescoring. The performance of the prosodic segmenter is also investigated in comparison with our earlier experiments.

Keywords: speech recognition, prosody, agglutinating languages, fixed stress, lattice rescoring.

1 Introduction

Prosodic features are an integral part of every spoken language utterance. They provide cues for the listener for the decoding of syntactic and semantic structure of a message. Moreover, they also contribute to the expression of speaker's emotions and communicative intent. On different linguistic levels, accents, breaks, rhythm, speaking rate, etc. play an important role in syntactic classification of each element of a message. In addition to this, intonation carries information also about sentence modality, which might be very important in several speech applications (like information retreival systems for example, where it is crucial in terms of correct speech understanding to be able to differentiate questions from statements). This information contained in prosody can and should be exploited in automatic speech recognition in order to improve speech recognition and understanding performance by decoding information that is only carried by prosody and also by ensuring a redundant parameter sequence for the whole speech decoding process itself.

A. Esposito et al. (Eds.): Verbal and Nonverbal Commun. Behaviours, LNAI 4775, pp. 138–149, 2007.

This chapter presents how prosodic features can be used to improve speech recognition of agglutinating and fixed stress languages. Finally the results of such an experiment were summarized, in which a prosodic segmenter was integrated into a Hungarian speech recognizer.

The structure of this chapter is as follows: firstly, some more introduction is given in two subsections in order to show an overview of the current usage of prosody in speech technology, and also to present the possible ways of exploiting prosodic information in fixed stress agglutinating languages. Then, acoustical pre-processing of prosodic features is addressed, followed by the presentation of an integrated speech recognizer using also prosodic information. Finally, experimental results, and discussion of possible further work areas are shown. The chapter ends with a short conclusion.

1.1   Usage of Prosody in Speech Technology

In speech synthesis, generating the correct prosody for each utterance is a basic requirement. The integration of prosody in this domain is more succesful than in speech recognition. For example, Venditti and Hirschberg summarised the current state of knowledge in intonation and discourse processing for American English [1]. They described an intonation-discourse interface which can be used in speech technology, mainly for speech synthesis. For Hungarian, modeling and generating prosody based on a syntactic - and hence also on morphological - analysis was descibed by Koutny, Olaszy and Olaszi in [2]. They emphasize that intonation and word accent should not be mixed up.

Using prosodic features in automatic speech recognition is not a trivial task, due to some difficulties summarized by Langlais in his work [3]: the significant contextual variability of prosodic knowledge (type of speech, speaker, structure and content of sentences, nature of the environment, etc.); the complexity of relations between prosodic information and various linguistic organization levels of a message and problems encountered with accurate measurement of prosodic parameters, and their possible integration on a perceptual level.

However, several attempts prooved to be succesful in this domain. Veilleux and Ostendorf [4] presented an N-best rescoring algorithm based on prosodic features and they have significantly improved hypothesis ranking performance. Kompe et al. presented a similar work for German language in [5]. Gallwitz et al described a method for integrated word and prosodic phrase boundary recognition in [6].

1.2   Underlined Role of Prosody in Agglutinating Languages

Exploiting prosodic knowledge can be of great importance in case of many languages, that are characterized by agglutinating or fixed stress. We present this by the example of the Hungarian language.

As a member of the Finno-Ugrian language family, Hungarian is a highly agglutinating language (a noun might even have more than 1000 different forms) characterized by a relatively free word order. Syntactic relations are expressed by a rich morphology, e.g. by case endings (the number of possible case endings is also very high, Hungarian distinguishes about 18 cases). In our opinion, these two characteristics (agglutinating and free word order) of Hungarian highly correlate: in a basic sentence syntax, almost all attributes of the verb are interchangeable, because case endings reflect syntactical relations, no matter where the words are placed within the sentence. This is illustrated in Table 1, where each row contains a correct word order for the sentence *John entered the bank at 8 a.m.* Of course, the meaning of the sentence slightly varies following the word order changes, as the focus position - the most stressed position in a sentence found usually immidiately before the verb - is occupied by different words. This also means that a wide spectra of logical relations and communicative intent can be expressed simply by word order changes, strongly underlined by prosody. A detailed description of these phenomena - including prosodic bearing - are given in details by Hunyadi in [7]. He also investigates to what extent this can be regarded as a universal grammatical quality by involving Finnish and Japanese languages. From our point of view, the fact that prosody and syntax complement each other, is an important observation.

In addition to this, two important characteristics of Hungarian are of importance: firstly, that Hungarian is a fixed stress language, since stress falls always on the first syllable of a word. The second one is rather a trivial remark, namely, that the agglutinating property also results in a relatively higher average word length compared to other non-agglutinating languages (e.g. English for example).

On the base of this introductory analysis of agglutinating languages (such as Hungarian), we conclude that these languages have quite a different linguistic organisation, then the non-agglutinating ones (as English). Agglutinating, free word order and fixed stress underline the role of prosody in syntactical segmentation of a message. This implies that some changes or extension of approaches used in speech technology for these "atypically organized" languages can contribute to a better performance mainly in speech recognition and understanding, but also in natural language processing problems and in several other domains. Especially, as standard methods developed and widely used for speech recognition in English or other Germanic or Indo-European languages are not directly applicable for highly agglutinating languages. Well-known problems are the larger size of vocabulary and the radically increased complexity of statistical language models. We beleive that the extension of speech recognizer systems with prosodic knowledge is a cue to overcome these difficulties.

2   Exploiting Prosodic Information

2.1   Acoustic Prosodic Features

For representation of prosody, fundamental frequency (F_0), energy level and time course were measured. F_0 and energy, measured at the middle of vowels of the utterance, and the duration of the vowels in the syllable (nucleus duration) are presented in a Hungarian sentence in Fig. 1. In this example, the peaks

Table 1. Correct word order possibilities and the accented logical aspect of the information for a Hungarian sentence "János bement a bankba 8 órakor." meaning "John entered the bank at 8 a.m."

Word order	Accented logical aspect
János bement a bankba 8 órakor.	None (standard order without accent)
János ment be a bankba 8 órakor.	It was John and not another person.
János ment be 8 órakor a bankba.	John entered at 8 a.m. Someone else might have also entered at another time.
A bankba ment be 8 órakor János.	The bank and not another place.
8 órakor ment be a bankba János.	It was at 8 a.m. that he entered.
...	...

of energy and fundamental frequency clearly represent the first syllables of the words. Of course, a strict word-level segmentation based on prosody is not always feasible, since usually not all words are accented within a sentence. Such a word level segmentation algorithm was described in [8]. Fig. 1 illustrates that syllable prominence in Hungarian is governed mainly by intensity and F_0 (which per se, highly correlate also for physiologic reasons). It was found that in Hungarian, syllable length is less influenced by the stress and it plays rather a role in sentence level intonation. Pauses, length of pauses or other prosodic features have not been examined yet.

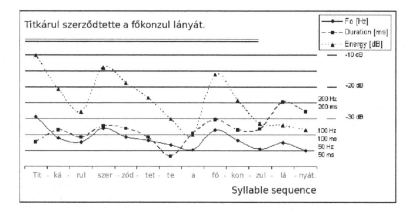

Fig. 1. Fundamental frequency and energy levels measured at the middle of vowels and duration of the vowels in the syllables in a Hungarian sentence 'Titkárul szerződtette a főkonzul lányát.' The syllable sequence is presented on the X axis.

2.2 Acoustic Prosodic Pre-processing

The extraction of prosodic information is performed using the Snack package of KTH [9]. F_0 is extracted by ESPS method using a 25 ms long window. Intensity is also computed with a window of 25 ms. The frame rate for both variables is set to 10 ms. The obtained F_0 contour is firstly filtered with our anti-octave jump tool. This tool eliminates frequency halving and doubling, and also cuts F_0 values associated to the first and last frames of each voiced speech segment. This is followed by a smoothing with a 5 point mean filter (5 points cover a window of about 50 ms) and then the log values of F_0 are taken, which are linearly interpolated. During the interpolation, two restrictions must be fulfilled. Firstly, interpolation should not affect pauses in F_0 longer than 250 ms; secondly, interpolation should be omitted if the initial value of F_0 after an F_0-gap higher than a threshold value. This threshold value depends on the last measured F_0 values and equals the 110 % of the average F_0 value of the three last voiced frames before the gap (unvoiced period). The intensity contour is simply mean filtered, using again a 5 point filter.

After feature extraction and basic shape conditioning described above, delta and acceleration coefficients are appended to both F_0 and intensity streams. These coefficients are computed with a regression-based formula. The regression is performed in 3 different steps with increasing regression window length: firstly with a window of ±10 frames, secondly with a window of ±25 frames, and finally, a window of ±50 frames is used. This means that the final feature vector consists of 14 elements (original F_0 and intensity data + 3-3 delta + 3-3 acceleration components for both of them).

2.3   Prosodic Speech Material

The speech material for acoustic-prosodic features was chosen from the BABEL [10] continuous read speech database. The database was segmented in terms of prosodic features by an expert, reliing on waveform, F_0, intensity and sub-jective judgement after listening to the utterance. Our segmentation technique differs significantly form methods which label high and low accents and/or end-ings (such as the well-known ToBi [11] for example). During the segmentation, prosodically well marked units were looked for, which were found to be tipi-cally short speech segments consisting of one or some more word(s). Later in the article, these units will be called prosodic units in order to differentiate them from prosodic phrases, especially because prosodic units are considerably shorter than prosodic phrases. Prosodic units in Hungarian usually consist of an initially stressed word followed by other, non or slightly stressed words. A syntagm is re-garded as the prototype of the prosodic unit, however, other word groups than syntagms can also form a prosodic unit.

Prosodic units were labelled, based on the following considerations: the typ-ical F_0 - and often also the intensity - contour of such units is a less or more strong accent, followed by a slowly or suddenly falling F_0 (intensity). Of course, higher lingustic levels and their associated prosodic features also influence the prosody, as in case of some questions and phrase endings that do not co-occur with sentence endings, a slowly rising contour is the most likely. In this latter case, intonation often suppresses normal (high) accents which translates into an inversed (low) accent. This means that in this case the first syllable of a word

Table 2. Prosodic units used for segmentation

Prosodic label	Description
me	Sentence onset unit
fe	Strongly stressed unit
fs	Stressed unit
mv	Low sentence ending
fv	High sentence or phrase ending
s	Slowly falling F_0 / intensity (after fv)
sil	Silence

has the lowest F_0 / intensity value. Please note, that due to these phenomena, all labels were placed in a manner that they coincide with word boundaries. The used labels are presented in Table 2. As it can be seen, a total of 6 contour types + silence were distinguished and used during labelling.

A total of 700 (mainly complex) sentences from 14 speakers were selected from the BABEL database [10] for prosodic segmentation, which were used later to train a prosodic segmenter as described in section 2.4.

2.4   Automatic Prosodic Segmentation

In order to carry out prosodic segmentation, a small HMM set was trained for all the 7 prosodic unit types in Table 2. The training methodology of the prosodic segmenter is identical with the one used in [8], the acoustic pre-processing is done as shown in section 2.2. Here, the recognition of prosodic units is based on Viterbi decoding, similar to the case of speech recognition. However, as prosodic features are processed as vectors of 14 elements and a strict prosodic grammar is used, the prosodic decoding process is very fast.

During prosodic recognition, a sophisticated sentence model is used as a constraint. This model suggests that each sentence is built from one or more prosodic phrases, and constituting prosodic phrases are composed from prosodic units. The sentence model requires that each sentence begins with a sentence onset unit (*me*) and end with either a low sentence ending unit (*mv*) or a phrase ending unit (*fv*). Stressed units (*fe* and *fs*) are allowed to appear within a sentence. The *fe* symbol refers to a stronger accent typically found at the beginning of a new phrase within a sentence. The slowly falling unit (*s*) is allowed optionally, but only immediately after a phrase ending (*fv*). Between all sentences, a silence (*sil*) is supposed, eventually substituted by a slowly falling unit (*s*) (if F_0 interpolation filled a shorter silent period).

Later, the trained prosodic segmenter is used for the segmentation of the input speech in parallel with the speech recognition process, which is split into two subsequent stages. Details are explained in section 3.

Since prosodic features (also known as supra-segmental feautures) contain information on higher level than basic recognition units (ie. phonemes), it is worth blurring the boundaries of the prosodic units. This means that the prosodic unit boundaries predicted by the prosodic module are transformed to a probability density function that predicts rather the likelihood of prosodic unit boundaries than their exact location in time. To implement this in an easy way, a cosine function in the $[-\pi, \pi]$ interval is matched against the predicted prosodic unit boundary $\pm \Delta T$ interval. Thus, within the interval of $[t_B - \Delta T, t_B + \Delta T]$ the L_B log likelihood of prosodic unit boundary is defined as:

$$L_B(t) = C * cos(\frac{\pi}{2\Delta T}t) + C \qquad (1)$$

where t_B is the location of the predicted prosodic unit boundary on the time axis, $t \epsilon[t_B - \Delta T, t_B + \Delta T]$, C is a constant. Otherwise the value of L_B is regarded to be 0. During the experiments presented in section 4, ΔT was equal to 10 frames (100 ms).

3   Speech Recognition Using Automatic Prosodic Segmentation

In our speech recognizer with integrated prosodic segmenter module, speech recognition is done in two subsequent stages. In the first stage, an N-best lattice is generated. The output of the prosodic segmenter is then combined with this lattice using a rescoring algorithm presented in section 3.2. The rescored lattice is then used in the second pass recognition that yields the final recognition results. This process is illustrated in Fig. 2.

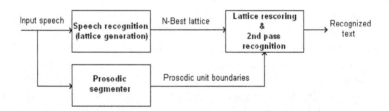

Fig. 2. Speech decoding process using prosodic features

3.1   First Pass Recognition

In the first pass of speech decoding Viterbi algorithm-based standard lattice generation and prosodic segmentation are done in parallel. Currently, the speech recognizer (lattice generator) and the prosodic segmenter modules work independently, hence no information about word or phone alignment hypotheses are transferred from the speech recognizer to the prosodic segmenter module.

In the first pass speech recognition procedure, a bigram language model is also used for recognition. In order to investigate the effect of prosodic information, bigram weights can even be set to an equal value. In this case, the bigram model will contain only binary information whether a word sequence is allowed or not. In this way, a part of the information contained in a statistical bigram is supposed to be replaced by prosodic information. This approach also allows to partly overcome difficulties in bigram language model generation and usage in case of highly agglutinating languages, hence for large vocabulary applications for such languages, generating an N-gram language model is often blocked by data sparsity problems, and the size of language models often balks real-time operation.

3.2   Lattice Rescoring

The rescoring of the N-best lattice created in the first pass speech recognition process is based on the output of the prosodic segmenter. The principle of rescoring is to renumerate word or word-chain candidates whose boundaries match the prosodic segmentation and to punish those which contain a prosodically predicted unit boundary within themselves.

   To do this, all arcs are collected from the word hypotheses graph (in our case, arcs correspond to distinct words in such graphs). Then, for each arc, two additional scores are calculated in addition to the $Sc_{original}$ original score in the lattice given by the speech recognizer. All scores used are interpreted as logaritmic scores.

   The renumerating score (Sc_{renum}) is computed based on the degree of co-occurence of prosodic unit boundaries and the initial and terminal nodes of the arc:

$$Sc_{renum} = w_a L_B(t_{start}) + w_b L_B(t_{end})   \tag{2}$$

where L_B is computed from (1), t_{start} and t_{end} refer to the start ans end nodes (times) of the arc, w_a and w_b are constant weights. For simplicity, $w_a = w_b = 0.5$ in (2).

   A similar punishment (Sc_{punish}) score is computed for in-word frames of each arc:

$$Sc_{punish} = \sum_{i=k+1}^{N-k-1} L_B(i)   \tag{3}$$

where L_B is calculated from (1), N is the number of frames in the arc, k is an integer $2k < N, k = \Delta T$. The reason for the skip in (3) defined by k is to allow prosodic unit boundaries to be a bit shifted. The highest scores will be added to arcs which fit the best the prosodic segmentation. The new score ($Sc_{rescored}$) in the rescored lattice is given by:

$$Sc_{rescored} = w_o Sc_{original} + w_c(Sc_{renum} - Sc_{punish})   \tag{4}$$

where w_o and w_c are the corresponding weights.

   In experiments described in section 4, the weights used were $w_o = 1$ and $w_c = 2.5$.

3.3 Second Pass Recognition

At this final step, the rescored lattice is used as a grammar for speech recognition. Recognition at this stage is very fast, because possible hypotheses are evaluated by simply parsing the word graph defined by the lattice. The final recognition result is output at the end of the second pass.

4 Experimental Tests

4.1 Speech Recognition Experiment Using Prosody

For experimental tests, a special medical application for Hungarian language [12] (medical reports in radiology - abdominal ultrasonography) was chosen. This task has a relatively small vocabulary (5000 words).

The speech recognizer itself was a state of the art speech recognizer trained by the HTK toolkit [13]. This recognizer uses phoneme models (37 models for Hungarian), speech is pre-processed in the "standard" way using 39 coefficients (12 MFCC + energy + 1st and 2nd order deltas) and 10 ms frame rate, the output distribution is described by 32 Gaussians. The recognizer was trained with acoustic data from the Hungarian Reference Database [12] using approx. 8 hours of speech. In addition to this baseline recognizer, the system was extended by the prosodic segmenter module described in 2.4, as presented in section 3.

During experiments, only a simplified bigram language model was used. This means that the bigram model contained only binary information whether a word sequence was allowed. (Constructing a bigram model for highly agglutinating languages - as explained in section 3.1 - is not an easy task, moreover, the use of such bigram models is limited due to the radically increasing computation time). The word insertion log probability was set to -25, the prosodic score scale factor was 2.5 (see equation (4)). These settings were obtained on the basis of empirical optimization.

The performance (ratio of correctly recognized words and WER reduction) of the extended system was compared to the baseline recognizer. Results for 6 selected test sequences are presented in Table 3. The selection of these presented utterances was representative.   As shown in Table 3, rescoring of the N-best lattice based on the output of the prosodic segmenter usually improves the performance of the recognition system. However, in some cases (for example ID 16 in Table 3), performance is worse after rescoring (WER reduction is less than 0). On the other hand, a sometimes very high WER reduction was reached (for example ID 03). In this case we usually found utterances of proper and careful - but of course natural - pronunciation, also in terms of prosodic constituents. The overall results for all 20 test medical reports show total WER reduction of 3.82%.

4.2 Reliability of Prosodic Segmentation

Test utterances which show a slightly higher WER after prosodic rescoring of the word hypotheses graph were further analysed in order to reveal the reason

Table 3. Correctly recognized words in case of the baseline speech recognizer ("Baseline") and of the recognizer extended by the prosodic module ("Prosodic") and WER reduction for 6 representatively selected medical reports

Speaker ID	Words correct [%] Baseline	Prosodic	WER reduction [%]
03	71.2	78.9	10.9
07	78.8	80.6	3.6
08	84.6	84.6	0.0
10	70.8	72.2	2.0
16	68.3	66.7	-2.4
19	83.8	90.5	8.1
All 20	75.99	78.89	3.82

of the increased WER values. It was found, that the higher WER was caused by the errors of prosodic segmentation, in which case prosodic unit boundaries were placed within some words. On the other hand, omission of a prosodic unit boundary by the prosodic segmenter did not influence system performance.

In order to further analyse the performance of speech recognition when system is extended by the prosodic segmenter, we have also investigated the reliability of prosodic segmentation, expressed as the correctness of prosodic segmentation, which is defined as the ratio of the number of correctly placed prosodic unit boundaries and of the number of all placed prosodic unit boundaries. Of course, the correct placement of a prosodic unit boundary should also be defined: a prosodic unit boundary was regarded as correct if it did not deviate more than $\Delta T = 100ms$ from real prosodic unit boundary placed by human expert. In this way ΔT defines the required accuracy of placement of prosodic unit boundaries.

The correctness of prosodic segmentation was compared to our previous experiment described in details in [8]. The difference between the previous and the current experiment was the testing set: in current experiment medical reports recorded in real conditions were used in contrast with the previous experiment, where clear, read speech test utterances were used from BABEL database. Further on, previous experiment will be referred to as *BABEL test*, while current experiment will be called *Medical test*. A comparaison of *BABEL test* and *Medical test* results is given in Table 4. Of course, training and test material were always separated, test utterances were excluded during the training also in *BABEL test*.

As shown in Table 4, the correctness of prosodic segmentation obtained for medical reports is 65.6%, which is worse than in *BABEL test* (76.5%). However, even with this worse prosodic segmentation performance a WER reduction of 3.82% of speech recognition was reached as seen in Section 4.1.

In our opinion, one reason for a part of prosodic segmentation errors in *Medical test* is caused by the real conditions: prosodic segmentation errors can be explained by inproper F_0 contour extraction, caused by fast, less carefully articulated speech of poor intensity or sometimes by hoarse sentence endings not

Table 4. Correctness of prosodic segmentation in case of previous BABEL, and current Medical report tests

Experiment	Training	Testing	Correctness in %
BABEL test	BABEL	BABEL	76.5
Medical test	BABEL	Medical reports	65.6

characteristic in BABEL database used for the training of the prosodic segmenter in both cases. Certainly, the fact that *Medical test* test material was recorded in real conditions - unlike *BABEL test* test data which is read speech of very good quality - also infuences results. However, an important outcome of current experiment is that hoarse or "whispered" parts of speech can be used as cues for detection of prosodic units, as they were found to indicate quite well low sentence endings in several times.

Another source of prosodic segmentation errors was the supra-segmental nature of prosodic features (since the typical duration of a phoneme is about 80-100 ms in Hungarian, and we had to use a severe lattice rescoring in terms of the allowed prosodic unit boundary deviation defined by equation (1)). By allowing communication between prosodic segmenter and first pass speech recognizer modules (ie. by using phoneme - and hence syllable - alignment information in the prosodic segmenter), this error should be decreased.

On the other hand, we should also mention that the advantage and the disadvantage of HMM prosodic segmentation method are the same: HMM structure allows a fine alignment of prosodic units by making relatively soft decisions. This ensures the detection of prosodic unit boundaries, but also causes errors as it is too permissive.

5   Conclusion

In this chapter we presented the use of a prosodic segmenter in speech recognition providing a more detailed prosodic segmentation then detection of phrase boundaries. The output of the prosodic segmenter was used to rescore N-best lattices in parallel with a simplified language model. Obtained results show a WER reduction of 3.8% for a Hungarian medical speech recognition task. The reliability - correctness - of prosodic segmentation was also analysed. Results were compared with our previous results obtained by using good quality read speech for testing of the prosodic segmenter. In real conditions, the prosodic segmentation performance was found to be worse, hence it is important even in terms of prosodic features to use spontanous speech material for the training of the prosodic segmenter used in real conditions. Some other outcomes of the experiments should also be mentioned in the conclusion: firstly, the detailed prosodic segmentation can also help in syntactic analysis of spoken utterances in natural language processing, however, this issue has not been investigated yet; secondly, the prosodic segmentation approach is adaptable to all fixed stress languages, or it means an alternative or additional information source for language modeling in case of agglutinating languages, where N-gram language model generation and usage are sources for several difficulties. Experiments and results shown is this work constitute an initial achievement in this domain, but further work is needed to extend our knowledge on speech prosody and its contribution to the speech recognition process.

References

1. Venditti, J., Hirschberg, J.: Intonation and discourse processing. In: Proceedings of the 15th ICPhS, Barcelona, pp. 107–114 (2003)
2. Koutny, I., Olaszy, G., Olaszi, P.: Prosody prediction from text in Hungarian and its realization in TTS conversion. International Journal of Speech Technology 3 (3-4), 187–200 (2000)
3. Langlais, P., Méloni, H.: Integration of a prosodic component in an automatic speech recognition system. In: 3rd European Conference on Speech Communication and Technology, Berlin, pp. 2007–2010 (1993)
4. Veilleux, N.M., Ostendorf, M.: Prosody/parse scoring and its application in ATIS. In: Human Language and Technology. Proceedings of the ARPA workshop, Plainsboro, pp. 335–340 (1993)
5. Kompe, R., Kiessling, A., Niemann, H., Nöth, H., Schukat-Talamazzini, E.G., Zottman, A., Batliner, A.: Prosodic scoring of word hypothesis graphs. In: Proceedings of the European Conference on Speech Communication and Technology, Madrid, pp. 1333–1336 (1995)
6. Gallwitz, F., Niemann, H., Nöth, E., Warnke, V.: Integrated recognition of words and prosodic phrase boundaries. Speech Communication 36, 81–95 (2002)
7. Hunyadi, L.: Hungarian Sentence Prosody and Universal Grammar. In: Kertész, A. (ed.) Metalinguistica 13, Peter Lang, Frankfurt am Main, Germany (2002)
8. Vicsi, K., Szaszák, Gy.: Automatic Segmentation of Continuous Speech on Word Level Based on Supra-segmental Features. International Journal of Speech Technology 8(4), 363–370 (2005)
9. Sjölander, K., Beskow, J.: Wavesurfer - an open source speech tool. In: Proceedings of the 6th International Conference of Spoken Language Processing in Beijing, China, vol. 4, pp. 464–467 (2000)
10. Roach, P.: BABEL: An Eastern European multi-language database. In: International Conference on Speech and Language Processing, Philadelphia (1996)
11. Silverman, K., Beckman, M., Pitrelli, J., Ostendorf, M., Wightman, C., Price, et al.: ToBi: A standard for labelling English prosody. In: Proceedings of the 1992 International Conference on Spoken Language Processing, Banff, pp. 867–870 (1992)
12. Vicsi, K., Kocsor, A., Tóth, L., Velkei, Sz., Szaszák, Gy., Teleki, Cs., et al.: A Magyar Referencia Beszédadatbázis és alkalmazása orvosi diktálórendszerek kifejlesztéséhez. In: Proceedings of the 3rd Hungarian Conference on Computational Linguistics (MSZNY), Szeged, Hungary, pp. 435–438 (2005)
13. Young, S., Evermann, G., Kershaw, D., Moore, G., Odell, J., Ollason, D., et al.: The HTK Book (for version 3.3). Cambridge University, Cambridge (2005)

Single-Channel Noise Suppression by Wavelets in Spectral Domain

Zdeněk Smékal and Petr Sysel

Department of Telecommunications Brno University of Technology, Purkynova 118,
612 00 Brno, Czech Republic
smekal@feec.vutbr.cz

Abstract. The paper describes the design of a new single-channel method for speech enhancement that employs the wavelet transform. Signal decomposition is currently performed in the time domain while noise is removed on individual decomposition levels using thresholding techniques. Here the wavelet transform is applied in the spectral domain. Used as the basis is the method of spectral subtraction, which is suitable for real-time implementation because of its simplicity. The greatest problem in the spectral subtraction method is a trustworthy noise estimate, in particular when non-stationary noise is concerned. Using the wavelet transform we can achieve a more accurate power spectral density also of noise that is non-stationary. Listening tests and SNR measurements yield satisfactory results in comparison with earlier reported experience.

Keywords: Single-channel Speech Enhancement, Power Spectral Density, Wavelet Transform Thresholding.

1 Introduction

In modern fixed and mobile communication systems (cell phones, modems of the type of ADSL or VDSL, hands-free sets in automobiles, audio transmission over the Internet-VoIP, satellite transmissions, teleconferences, etc.) it is necessary to solve the basic problem of removing interference and noise from speech signal background. The interference is on the one hand interference from the surrounding environment, on the other hand it is interference acquired in the course of transmission or recording. Various methods for enhancing speech hidden in noise are used in practice but none of the available methods is universal since it is always designed for only a certain type of interference that is to be removed. Since enhancing speech masked in noise is of fundamental significance for further speech signal processing (subsequent recognition of the speaker or type of language, compression and processing for transmission or storing, etc.) it is imperative to find a reliable method that will work even under considerable interference and will be modifiable to match different types of interference and noise. The existing methods can basically be divided into two large groups: single-channel methods and multi-channel methods. In single-channel methods the speech signal is detected by one microphone or is acquired from one transmission channel. In most cases the speech is heavily degraded by noise.

A. Esposito et al. (Eds.): Verbal and Nonverbal Commun. Behaviours, LNAI 4775, pp. 150–164, 2007.

Restoring speech from one channel is an exacting job because no information is available on sound intensity, character and positioning of sources of acoustic signals, type of interference, and the like. The most widely applied methods include the method of spectral subtraction [1], the RASTA method [2], the spectrogram mapping method [3], and statistical methods [4]. In the case of multi-channel methods one or more speakers and their environment are detected by several microphones (an ordered field of microphones). The aim of multi-channel methods is to separate the individual detected channels from the mix obtained. This is conditional on the number of detected channels being equal to or greater than the number of partial signals that we want to obtain by the separation. The best-known methods are here beam-forming [5], Blind Source Separation (Independent Component Analysis, Principal Component Analysis) [6, 7], and Multi-channel Blind Deconvolution [8]. Multi-channel methods achieve better results in speech enhancement but they are more demanding as regards the number of calculations. They are particularly utilizable where the microphone field can be deployed in an invariant configuration (inside an automobile, in a production bay, in a telephone booth, etc.). Still, it is necessary to continue solving the problem of single-channel methods of speech enhancement since in many practical situations only one speech recording is available.

The wavelet analysis is a certain alternative to the Fourier representation for the analysis of short-term stationary real signals such as speech [9]. In voiced speech sounds the speech signal has the most energy in the low-frequency region, which however does not carry much information. The greatest part of information is in voiced segments contained in the first several formants. Unvoiced sounds of speech have a considerably lower energy than the voiced ones but their spectrum is distributed into the higher-frequency region of the spectrum. Speech intelligibility is particularly affected by transitions between voiced and unvoiced sounds of speech. For this reason, for example, the standardized frequency band of telephone channel has been chosen in the range from 300 Hz to 3400 Hz at a sampling frequency of 8 kHz. The spectrum components with high energy have been removed, which are below the 300 Hz boundary but which do not carry much information. The upper boundary was chosen such that at least the first 3 formants of voiced sounds of speech appear in the spectrum. These properties of the speech signal form the basis of the method of sub-channel filtering, where banks of quadrature mirror digital filters with perfect reconstruction are used to perform filtering. These digital filter banks are closely connected with the discrete wavelet transform with discrete time [10, 11]. Modern coding systems operate with a sampling frequency of 16 kHz, and there are efforts to increase the processed frequency band from 3.4 kHz to at least 7 kHz [12].

2 Modulation Spectrum and Its Analysis

One of the first methods that began to process the modulation spectrum of speech signal was the RASTA method [2, 13]. It is an enhancement method based on digital filtering of relative temporal changes in the spectrum of finite speech segments. It is based on the idea that all signals that do not correspond to the physiological properties of man can be suppressed, i.e. to the speed with which man is physically able to alter the muscle arrangement of speech organs during speech production. Depending on the estimate of SNR a digital filter of the type of low pass or band pass is selected to suppress the noise.

In Fig. 1 we can see the spectrogram magnitude of a part of the sentence "Please fax this information", which is shown in its development with time. The speech was detected in an anechoic chamber without the presence of noise. It is the temporal development of individual components of the magnitude of speech signal spectrum that is referred to as modulation spectrum. Fig. 2 gives the modulation spectrum of the same sentence, which was recorded while the speech was interfered with by vacuum cleaner operation. As can be seen, the modulation spectrum changed in both the low-frequency region (periodic interference components) and the region close to $f_s/2$ (effect of vacuum cleaner noise and aliasing).

If the noise is of non-stationary nature, then the greatest problem consists in estimating its power spectral density with sufficient frequency resolution. Two types of estimating the power spectral density are known: non-parametric methods and parametric methods. The best-known non-parametric methods include the Barlett method of periodogram averaging [14], the Blackman and Tukey method of periodogram smoothing [15], and the Welch method of averaging the modified periodograms [16]. Although the three methods have similar properties, the Welch method is the most widely used. These methods are called non-parametric because the parameters of the data being processed are not sought in advance. To yield a good estimate of the power spectral density the methods require the application of a long recording of data (at least 10^4 samples).

The periodogram is defined as follows:

$$P_{xx}\left(e^{j2\pi f}\right) = \frac{1}{N}\left|\sum_{n=0}^{N-1} x[n]e^{-j2\pi f n}\right|^2 = \frac{1}{N}\left|X\left(e^{j2\pi f}\right)\right| . \tag{1}$$

The function $X\left(e^{j2\pi f}\right)$ is the Fourier transform of discrete signal $x[n]$. It can be shown that the periodogram is an asymptotically unbiassed estimate but its variance does not decrease towards zero for $N \to \infty$. This is to say that the periodogram itself is not a consistent estimate [17]. To be able to use the FFT, we must choose the discrete frequency values:

$$P_{xx}\left[e^{j2\pi f_k}\right] = \frac{1}{N}\left|\sum_{n=0}^{N-1} x[n]e^{-j2\pi f_k n}\right|^2 = \frac{1}{N}\left|\sum_{n=0}^{N-1} x[n]e^{-jk\frac{2\pi}{N}n}\right|^2 , \tag{2}$$

$$k = 0, 1, ..., N-1 .$$

The periodogram is calculated at N frequency points f_k. For the comparison of the properties of non-parametric methods, the quality factor was proposed:

$$Q = \frac{\left\{E\left(P_{xx}\left[e^{j2\pi f_k}\right]\right)\right\}^2}{\text{var}\left(P_{xx}\left[e^{j2\pi f_k}\right]\right)} , k = 0, 1, ..., N-1 . \tag{3}$$

A comparison of the non-parametric methods is given in Table 1. All the three methods yield consistent estimates of power spectral density. In the Bartlett method a rectangular window is used whose width of the main lobe in the frequency response

"Please fax this information"

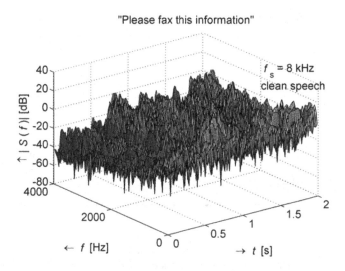

Fig. 1. Modulation spectrum of spectrogram magnitude of finite speech segment without noise

"Please fax this information"

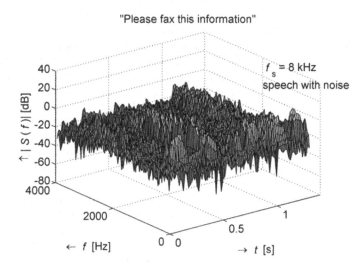

Fig. 2. Modulation spectrum of spectrogram magnitude of finite speech segment, with speech interfered with by vacuum cleaner noise

when the maximum value drops by 3 dB is $\Delta f = 0.9/M$, where M is the length of partial sequences. In the Welch method a triangular window is used whose width of the main lobe in the frequency response when the maximum value drops by 3 dB is $\Delta f = 0.28/M$, where M is again the length of partial sequences and their overlap is 50%. In the Blackman-Tukey method, too, the triangular window is used and $\Delta f = 0.64/M$. As can be seen, in the Blackman-Tukey and the Welch methods the quality factor is higher than in the case of the Bartlett method. The differences are small though. What is important is that Q increases with increasing length of data N.

Table 1. Comparison of the quality of non-parametric methods according to [17]

Method of PSD estimation	Q	Number of complex multiplications
Bartlett [14]	$1.11 \, \Delta f \, N$	$\dfrac{N}{2} \log_2 \dfrac{0.9}{\Delta f}$
Welch [16]	$1.39 \, \Delta f \, N$	$N \log_2 \dfrac{1.28}{\Delta f}$
Blackman-Tukey [15]	$2.34 \, \Delta f \, N$	$N \log_2 \dfrac{1.28}{\Delta f}$

This means that if for a defined value Q we want to increase the frequency resolution of estimate Δf, we must increase N, i.e. we need more data.

The main drawback of non-parametric methods is the fact that they assume zero values of the autocorrelation estimate $r[m]$ for $m \geq N$. This assumption limits the frequency resolution of the periodogram. It is further assumed that the signal is periodic with period N, which is not true either. Since we have at our disposal only a sequence of finite length, there is aliasing in the spectrum.

There are, of course, also other methods that can extrapolate the values of autocorrelation for $m \geq N$. On the basis of the data analysed the parameters of the model are estimated (that is why they are called parametric methods), and using the model the properties of power spectral density are determined. Three types of model are known: AR (Auto Regressive), MA (Moving Average), and ARMA. From the three models, the AR model is the most frequently used. This is because it is well-suited to represent a spectrum with narrow peaks and then the Yule-Walker equation can be used to calculate the model coefficients. Wold [18] derived a theorem that says that any random process of the type of ARMA or MA can be represented uniquely using an AR model of infinite order.

The noise of vacuum cleaner was chosen for the comparison of different methods for estimating power spectral density. Vacuum cleaner noise is no typical random process since in addition to the random signal due to the friction between air current and vacuum cleaner parts it also contains periodic components due to rotor rotation. This noise was chosen because this type of noise is often encountered in speech enhancement. The majority of household appliances (blender, hair drier, etc.) and workshop machines (drilling, grinding, sawing and other machines) produce a similar type of noise.

Fig. 3 gives a comparison of the estimates of power spectral density of vacuum cleaner noise obtained using a periodogram (full line) and a 10th-order AR model (dashed line). As stated above, the periodogram is an asymptotically unbiased estimate but its variance may cause an error of as much as 100% [19]. Moreover, it is inconsistent since it does not decrease with increasing signal length. This is shown in Fig. 3 by the large variance of values given by the full line. By contrast, the AR model provides a smoothed estimate of power spectral density. In the calculation, however, we encounter difficulties when estimating the order of the model. If a very low order of the model is used, we only obtain an estimate of the trend of power spectral density and lose the details, which in this case represent the maxima of the harmonics of periodic interference. If, on the contrary, the order of AR model is high, we obtain statistically unstable estimates with a large amount of false details in the spectrum. The variance of such an estimate will be similar to the estimate obtained using the periodogram. The choice of the order of the model is an important part of the estimation and depends on the statistical properties of the signal being processed. These properties are, however, in most cases also only estimated. For a short stationary signal the value of the order of the model can be chosen in the range:

$$0.05N \leq M \leq 0.2N , \tag{4}$$

where N is the signal length, and M is the order of the model [19]. For segments whose length $N = 200$ samples the minimum order is $M = 10$. But for signals formed by a mixture of harmonic signals and noise this estimate mostly fails.

An estimate obtained using the periodogram can be made more precise via averaging the modified periodograms, which we obtain by dividing the signal into segments and weighting the latter by a weighting sequence. This approach is used in the Welch method for estimating the power spectral density [16]. In Fig. 4 we can see a comparison of the estimates of power spectral density obtained using the Welch method (with 13 segments weighted) and the AR model of 10th order. It is evident from the Figure that in comparison with the estimate obtained using the periodogram the Welch method yields a smoothed estimate, whose variance, moreover, decreases with increasing number of averaged segments (consistent estimate). Dividing the signal into segments naturally results in a reduced frequency resolution of the estimate, which shows up in less pronounced maxima that represent the components of periodic interference. In addition, in the case of non-stationary interference, periodograms may be averaged for segments that include noise of different statistical properties and thus also of different power spectral densities. This further reduces the accuracy of estimating the power spectral density.

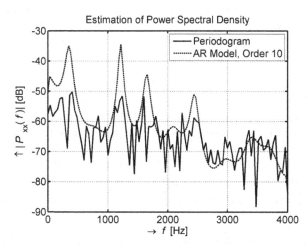

Fig. 3. Estimation of power spectral density of vacuum cleaner noise, using the periodogram and the 10th-order AR model

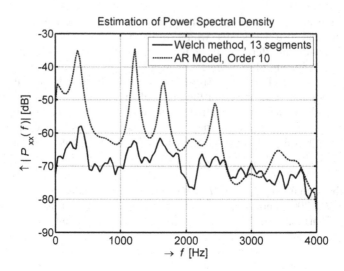

Fig. 4. Estimation of power spectral density of vacuum cleaner noise, using the Welch method of averaging modified periodograms for 13 segments, and the 10th-order AR model

3   Enhancing the Estimate of Power Spectral Density

To enhance the estimate of power spectral density the wavelet transform can also be used. In [20] the non-parametric estimate of the logarithm of power spectral density is made more precise using the wavelet transform. With this method, statistically significant components of the estimate $\ln P_{xx}\left[e^{j2\pi f_i}\right]$ are obtained from thresholding different levels of wavelet decomposition and thus its non-negative values are ensured. The input signal is interfered with by additive non-Gaussian noise, and the wavelet coefficients of additive noise are assumed to be independent of the wavelet coefficients of power spectral density of useful signal. For the processing, type Daubechies wavelets of the 1st, 4th, 6th and 8th orders and type coiflet wavelets of the 2nd and 3rd orders were used. The method does not assume any preliminary knowledge of the type of noise. In [21] the authors endeavour to find a better estimate of power spectral density than the periodogram logarithm itself. To do this, they use the Welch method of modified periodograms, when they first average K periodograms that have first been multiplied by the spectral window. In [22] the method of wavelet transform thresholding is used to estimate noise, and this estimate is used to enhance speech by the spectral subtraction method.

Consider a stationary random process $x[n]$, which has a defined logarithm of power spectral density $\ln G_{xx}\left(e^{j2\pi f}\right)$, $f \le 0.5$. As the function $\ln G_{xx}\left(e^{j2\pi f}\right)$ is periodic by frequency f, it can be expanded into a discrete Fourier series [17]:

$$\ln G_{xx}\left(e^{j2\pi f}\right) = \sum_{m=-\infty}^{\infty} v[m]\, e^{-j2\pi f m} \; . \tag{5}$$

Assuming that $G_{xx}(e^{j2\pi f})$ is a real and even function by f, it holds that $v[m] = v[-m]$. The coefficients of discrete Fourier series are:

$$v[m] = \int_{-0.5}^{0.5} \{ \ln G_{xx}(e^{j2\pi f}) \} e^{j2\pi f m} \, df , \quad m = 0, \pm 1, \pm 2, \ldots \quad . \tag{6}$$

Discrete Fourier series coefficients $v[m]$ are cepstral coefficients and the sequence $v[m]$ is the cepstrum of autocorrelation sequence $\gamma_{xx}[m]$, where the Wiener-Khinchine relation holds:

$$G_{xx}(e^{j2\pi f}) = \sum_{m=-\infty}^{\infty} \gamma_{xx}[m] e^{-j2\pi f m} , \tag{7}$$

where it holds $\gamma_{xx}[m] = E(x^*[n] \, x[n+m])$, and where the symbol * denotes a complex conjugate.

The estimate of autocorrelation sequence equals:

$$r_{xx}[m] = \frac{1}{2N+1} \sum_{n=-N}^{N} x^*[n] \, x[n+m] , \tag{8}$$

and it holds:

$$\gamma_{xx}[m] = \lim_{N \to \infty} r_{xx}[m] . \tag{9}$$

The inverse equation to equation (5) has the form:

$$G_{xx}(e^{j2\pi f}) = \exp\left(\sum_{m=-\infty}^{\infty} v[m] \, e^{-j2\pi f m} \right) = \sigma_w^2 \, H(e^{j2\pi f}) \, H(e^{-j2\pi f}) , \tag{10}$$

where $\sigma_w^2 = e^{v[0]}$ is the variance of white noise sequence $w[n]$.

The transfer function $H(z)$, $z = e^{j2\pi f m}$, is the causal part of discrete Fourier series (5) and $H(z^{-1})$ its non-causal part. In case the AR model is used, it holds for the transfer function:

$$H(z) = \frac{1}{A(z)} = \frac{1}{1 + \sum_{i=1}^{p} a_j z^{-j}} . \tag{11}$$

The power spectral density will be obtained as follows:

$$G_{xx}(e^{j2\pi f}) = \sigma_w^2 |H(e^{j2\pi f})|^2 , \tag{12}$$

where $\sigma^2{}_w$ is the variance of white noise sequence $w[n]$, for which it holds:

$$\sigma_w^2 = E(|w[n]|^2) . \tag{13}$$

The periodogram $P_{xx}(e^{j2\pi f})$, as the estimate of power spectral density $G_{xx}(e^{j2\pi f})$, is defined as follows:

$$P_{xx}\left(e^{j2\pi f}\right) = \sum_{m=-(N-1)}^{N-1} r_{xx}[m]\, e^{-j2\pi f m} = \frac{1}{N}\left|\sum_{n=0}^{N-1} x[n]\, e^{-j2\pi f n}\right|^{2} . \tag{14}$$

Using the periodogram we can determine the power spectral density as:

$$G_{xx}\left(e^{j2\pi f}\right) = \lim_{N\to\infty} E\left(P_{xx}\left(e^{j2\pi f}\right)\right) . \tag{15}$$

4 Application of Enhanced Noise Estimation in the Spectral Subtraction Method, Using the Wavelet Transform

Suppose the input signal $y[n]$ is an additive mixture of speech signal $x[n]$ and noise $\eta[n]$:

$$y[n] = x[n] + \eta[n] . \tag{16}$$

In view of the linearity of discrete Fourier transform the power spectrum of thus formed mixture is equal to the sum of the power spectrum of speech signal $|X[k]|^{2}$, the power spectral density of noise and the mutual power spectral densities:

$$|Y[k]|^{2} = |X[k]|^{2} + G_{\eta\eta}[k] + G_{x\eta}[k] + G_{\eta x}[k] . \tag{17}$$

In case the noise and the speech signal are non-correlated, the mutual power spectral densities are equal to zero. In that case the estimate of power spectrum can be obtained by subtracting the estimate of power spectral density of noise:

$$\left|\hat{X}[k]\right|^{2} = |Y[k]|^{2} - \hat{G}_{\eta\eta}[k] = |X[k]|^{2} + G_{\eta\eta}[k] - \hat{G}_{\eta\eta}[k] . \tag{18}$$

The first member represents the non-distorted power spectrum of speech, the other members represent estimate bias. For unbiased estimate $G_{\eta\eta}[k] - E\{\hat{G}_{\eta\eta}[k]\} = 0$ the mean estimate value $E\left\{\left|\hat{X}[k]\right|^{2}\right\}$ approximates the non-distorted speech signal.

For the unbiased estimate of power spectral density, however, the estimate variance of the power spectrum of speech signal is equal to:

$$E\left\{\left(\left|\hat{X}[k]\right|^{2} - E\left\{\left|\hat{X}[k]\right|^{2}\right\}\right)^{2}\right\} = E\left\{\left(|X[k]|^{2} + G_{\eta\eta}[k] - \hat{G}_{\eta\eta}[k] - |X[k]|^{2}\right)^{2}\right\},$$

$$E\left\{\left(\left|\hat{X}[k]\right|^{2} - E\left\{\left|\hat{X}[k]\right|^{2}\right\}\right)^{2}\right\} = E\left\{\left(G_{\eta\eta}[k] - \hat{G}_{\eta\eta}[k]\right)^{2}\right\} = E\left\{\left(\hat{G}_{\eta\eta}[k] - E\left\{\hat{G}_{\eta\eta}[k]\right\}\right)^{2}\right\}. \tag{19}$$

It is thus equal to the estimate variance of the power spectral density of noise. If for the estimate of power spectral density of noise we use the periodogram, whose variance is as much as 100% of its value, the variance of power spectrum estimate and the reconstruction error will also be of high value. To estimate the power spectral density of noise the method of averaging modified periodograms (the Welch method) or exponential averaging of the estimate is therefore used, both of which have a lower variance than the periodogram. Exponential averaging is performed according to the relation:

$$\hat{G}_{\eta\eta}^{(l)}[k] = \rho\,\hat{G}_{\eta\eta}^{(l-1)}[k] + (1-\rho)\hat{G}_{\eta\eta}[k]\ ,\tag{20}$$

where $\hat{G}_{\eta\eta}^{(l-1)}[k]$ is the estimate from the preceding signal segment, $\hat{G}_{\eta\eta}[k]$ is the estimate from the current segment, $\hat{G}_{\eta\eta}^{(l)}[k]$ is the new estimate of power spectral density of noise, and ρ is a constant.

To reduce the periodogram variance the proposed method uses the procedure of thresholding the wavelet coefficients of a periodogram. The block diagram of this method is given in Fig. 5. The same as with the original method of spectral subtraction, the signal is first divided into segments of $2N = 2^{M+1}$ in length. For each segment the discrete Fourier transform is calculated, and the phase and the magnitude spectra are separated. The magnitude spectrum is used to calculate the power spectrum of the input signal, from which the speech activity is detected using a voice activity detector. A simple power detector or a detector based on spectral distance can be used. In case we are concerned with a speech segment, the estimate of power spectral density is subtracted from the power spectrum of input signal according to relation (21). To guarantee that the estimate of power spectrum will be non-negative, the value is limited from below by the zero value:

$$\left|\hat{X}[k]\right|^2 = \begin{cases} \left|Y[k]\right|^2 - \hat{G}_{\eta\eta}[k]\ , & \left|Y[k]\right|^2 - \hat{G}_{\eta\eta}[k] \geq 0 \\ 0\ , & \left|Y[k]\right|^2 - \hat{G}_{\eta\eta}[k] < 0 \end{cases}\tag{21}$$

The power spectrum is transformed into a magnitude spectrum, joined with the unchanged phase spectrum, and via the inverse discrete Fourier transform the reconstructed signal is obtained.

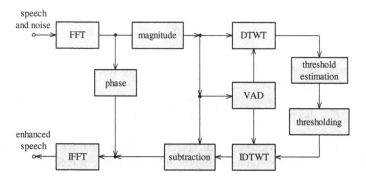

Fig. 5. Block diagram of modified spectral subtraction method with estimation of power spectral density via thresholding the wavelet transform coefficients

The modification of the method consists in changing the estimate of power spectral density of noise. If the segment is marked as a segment containing noise, the current power spectrum represents a noise periodogram. The periodogram is then decomposed into 8 levels using the discrete wavelet transform with the 8th-order Daubechies mother wavelet according to the relation:

$$C_{j,m}[k] = \sum_{k=0}^{2N-1} \left(\ln P_{\eta\eta}[k] \right) \psi_{j,m}[k] \, , \tag{22}$$

where $P_{xx}[k]$ are periodogram samples obtained by a discrete Fourier transform of a noise segment of $2N = 2^{M+1}$ in length. The base functions $\psi_{j,m}[k]$ are derived by temporal shift $j = 0, 1, .. , 2^m - 1$ and by the dilatation (with scale $m = 0, 1, ... , M - 1$) of the mother function $\psi[k]$ according to the relation:

$$\psi_{j,m}[k] = \frac{1}{\sqrt{2^m}} \psi \left[\frac{k}{2^m} - j \right] . \tag{23}$$

To calculate the threshold used for thresholding the wavelet transform coefficients the universal Johnstone-Donoho method [24] can be used (which was proposed for noise with normal distribution) according to the relation:

$$\lambda = \sigma \sqrt{2 \log N} \, , \tag{24}$$

where σ is the standard noise deviation, and N is the length of data. In [23] a method has been proposed for determining the threshold in dependence on scale, which is optimal for thresholding the discrete wavelet transform coefficients of the periodogram. If the scale m is large, then the threshold equals:

$$\lambda_m = \alpha_m \ln N \, , \tag{25}$$

where the constants α_m are from Table 2, and N is the length of data. If the scale is small, $m \ll M - 1$, the threshold is determined according to the relation:

$$\lambda_m = \frac{\pi}{\sqrt{3}} \sqrt{\ln N} . \tag{26}$$

To threshold the wavelet transform coefficient obtained the soft thresholding is used according to the relation:

$$C_{j,m}^{(s)}[k] = \text{sgn} \left(C_{j,m}[k] \right) \max \left(0, \left| C_{j,m}[k] \right| - \lambda_m \right) , \tag{27}$$

where λ_m is the threshold value chosen. Then the smoothed estimate of power spectral density of noise $G_{\eta\eta}[k]$ is obtained using the inverse discrete wavelet transform in the form:

$$\ln \hat{G}_{\eta\eta}[k] = \frac{1}{N} \sum_{m=0}^{M} \sum_{j=0}^{2^m-1} C_{j,m}^{(s)}[k] \, \psi_{j,m}[k] , \ k = 0, 1, ..., N-1 . \tag{28}$$

Table 2. Values of constant α_m for determining the threshold when thresholding the wavelet transform coefficients

scale m	α_m	scale m	α_m
$M-1$	1.29	$M-6$	0.54
$M-2$	1.09	$M-7$	0.46
$M-3$	0.92	$M-8$	0.39
$M-4$	0.77	$M-9$	0.32
$M-5$	0.65	$M-10$	0.27

This estimate is used in spectral subtraction until another segment is marked as noise segment.

Using the proposed technique of thresholding the wavelet transform coefficients of periodogram an estimate of the power spectral density of vacuum cleaner noise was obtained. The estimate is compared with the AR model and with the Welch method of periodogram averaging in Figs 6 and 7. It is evident from Fig. 6 that the estimate using the AR model is more smoothed but less able to localize narrow-band components. By contrast, the estimate using the thresholding of wavelet transform coefficients is less smooth but the pronounced peaks in the power spectrum, which represent the harmonic components of the interference by vacuum cleaner motor, are more easily localized in the frequency axis than in the AR model. This is also apparent from a comparison of the method of thresholding the wavelet coefficients and the Welch method of averaging modified periodograms in Fig. 7.

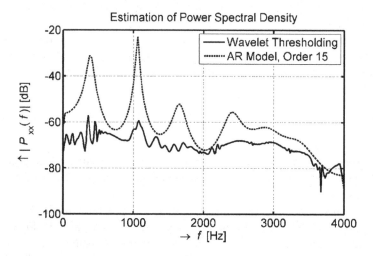

Fig. 6. Estimation of power spectral density of vacuum cleaner noise, via thresholding the wavelet transform coefficients of periodogram and via the AR model of 15th order

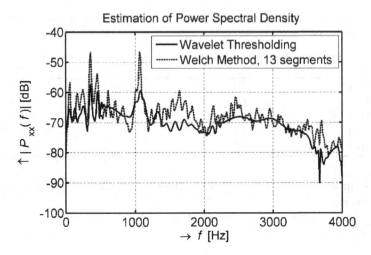

Fig. 7. Estimation of power spectral density of vacuum cleaner noise, via thresholding the wavelet transform coefficients of periodogram and via the Welch method of averaging modified periodograms for 13 segments

5 Experimental Results

The proposed method of spectral subtraction was tested on actual recordings of speech signal interfered with by different types of noise. The speech signal was interfered with by the noise of vacuum cleaner and shower, which have the character of wideband noise almost approximating white noise. In the testing, the speech signal was also exposed to interference by noise from a drilling machine and a Ford Transit, which on the contrary have the character of narrow-band noise. In view of the fact that the recordings were made in a real environment and it was impossible to obtain pure speech signal without noise, the estimation of the quality was performed using the signal-to-noise ratio determined segmentwise according to the relation:

$$SNR_{SEG} = 10\log_{10}\frac{R_s}{R_\eta} \ . \tag{29}$$

The power of signal R_s is determined from a segment containing the speech signal while the power of interference R_η is estimated from a segment that does not contain the speech signal.

A noisy speech signal was enhanced using the proposed modified method of spectral subtraction. For comparison, the speech was also enhanced by the method of spectral subtraction with the power spectral density of noise being estimated using the Welch method. For enhancement, the RASTA method was also applied. The values of SNR of the original signal and of the signal reconstructed by the individual methods are given in Table 3.

Table 3. Estimation of signal-to-noise ratio for four different types of noise and three different methods of speech signal enhancement

Estimation of signal-to-noise ratio SNR_{SEG} [dB]			
Method	Original	Modified	Spectral	RASTA
Type of interference	signal	method	subtraction	method
Vacuum cleaner	12	22	16	16
Shower	13	24	17	16
Drill	0	13	17	14
Ford Transit	3	20	18	17

Compared to the original spectral subtraction method and the RASTA method there was a marked improvement in the SNR in the case of interference of wideband character –vacuum cleaner or shower. Less good results are obtained in the case of interference of narrow-band character, where in addition much depends on the position of narrow-band interference. If interference is in the same frequency band as speech, e.g. drilling machine, the modified method of spectral subtraction exhibits an improvement of SNR which is only a little lower than the improvement in the original method of spectral subtraction or RASTA method. If the position of narrow-band interferences is outside the speech frequency band (low-frequency noise of the Ford Transit engine), then the modified method is comparable with the other methods.

6 Conclusions

For the estimation of power spectral density the proposed method of spectral subtraction makes use of thresholding the wavelet transform coefficients of the interference periodogram. This reduces the variance of the estimate of power spectral density of noise, which reduces the variance of the estimate of signal power spectrum and the signal reconstruction error. It follows from the experiments made that the method is suitable mainly for noise of wideband nature – e.g. shower, vacuum cleaner, etc. In that case the SNR of reconstructed signal is markedly higher than in the original method of spectral subtraction (which uses for the estimation of power spectral density the Welch method of periodogram averaging) or in the RASTA method. For noise of narrow-band character the method is comparable with the other methods. If the narrow-band interference is outside the speech frequency band, the proposed method achieves a slightly higher SNR than the other methods do.

Acknowledgments. This work was supported within the framework of project No 102/07/1303 of the Grant Agency of the Czech Republic and the National Research Project "Information Society" No 1ET301710509.

References

1. Deller, J.R., Hansen, J.H.L., Proakis, J.G.: Discrete-Time Processing of Speech Signals. A John Wiley & Sons, Inc. Publication, New York (2000)
2. Hermansky, H., Wan, E.A., Avenando, C.: Speech Enhancement based on Temporal Processing. In: Proceedings of the IEEE International Conference on Acoustics, Speech and Signal Processing, pp. 405–408. IEEE Computer Society Press, Los Alamitos (1995)

3. Smékal, Z., et al.: Non-Linear Methods of Speech Enhancement. Research Report of COST 277 European Project, Brno (2004)
4. Benesty, J., Makino, S., Chen, J.: Speech Enhancement. Springer, Berlin (2005)
5. Van Trees, H.L.: Optimum Array Processing (Part IV of Detection, Estimation and Modulation Theory). A John Wiley & Sons, Inc. Publication, New York (2002)
6. Te-Won, L.: Independent Component Analysis, Theory and Applications. Kluwer Academic Publishers, Boston (1998)
7. Roberts, S., Everson, R.: Independent Component Analysis, Principles and Practice. Cambridge University Press, Cambridge (2001)
8. Hyvärinen, A., Karhunen, J., Oja, E.: Independent Component Analysis. A John Wiley & Sons, Inc. Publication, New York (2001)
9. Strang, G., Nguyen, T.: Wavelets and Filter Banks. Wellesley-Cambridge Press, Wellesley (1996)
10. Vaidyanathan, P.P.: Multirate Systems and Filter Banks. Prentice Hall P T R, Englewood Cliffs, New Jersey (1993)
11. Fliege, N.J.: Multirate Digital Signal Processing. A John Wiley & Sons, Inc. Publication, New York (1994)
12. Ahmadi, S., Jelinek, M.: On the Architecture, Operation, and Applications of VMR/VW: The New cdma200 Wideband Speech Coding Standard. IEEE Communications Magazine, 74–81 (May 2006)
13. Avenando, C., Hermansky, H.: Temporal Processing of Speech in a Time-Feature Space. Research Report, Oregon (April 1997)
14. Bartlett, M.S.: Smoothing Periodograms from Time Series with Continuous Spectra. Nature (London) 161, 686–687 (1948)
15. Blackman, R.B., Tukey, J.W.: The Measurement of Power Spectra. Dover, New York (1958)
16. Welch, P.D.: The Use of Fast Fourier Transform for the Estimation of Power Spectra: a Method on Time Averaging over Short Modified Periodograms. In: IEEE Trans, vol. AU-15, pp. 70–73. IEEE Computer Society Press, Los Alamitos (June 1967)
17. Proakis, J.G., Manolakis, D.G.: Digital Signal Processing-Principles, Algorithms and Applications, 3rd edn. Prentice Hall, New Jersey (2006)
18. Wold, H.: Study in the Analysis of Stationary Time Series. Reprinted by Almqvist & Wiksell, Stockholm (1954)
19. Uhlír, J., Sovka, P.: Digital Signal Processing. Prague: CVUT Publishing (In Czech) (1995)
20. Moulin, P.: Wavelet Thresholding Techniques for Power Spectrum Estimation. IEEE Transactions on Signal Processing. 42(11), 3126–3136 (1994)
21. Walden, A.T., Percival, D.B., McCoy, E.J.: Spectrum Estimation by Wavelet Thresholding of Multitaper Estimators. IEEE Transactions on Signal Processing. 46(2), 3153–3165 (1998)
22. Sysel, P.: Wiener Filtering with Spectrum Estimation by Wavelet Transform. In: Proceedings of International Conference on "Trends in Communications", Bratislava, Slovakia, pp. 471–474 (2001)
23. Vidakovic, B.: Statistical Modeling by Wavelets. John Wiley & Sons, Inc. Publication, New York (1999)
24. Donoho, D.L., Johnstone, L.M., Kerkyacharian, G., Picard, D.: Wavelet shrinkage: asymptotia (with discussion). J.R. Statist. Soc. B 57, 301–369 (1995)

Voice Source Change During Fundamental Frequency Variation

Peter J. Murphy

Department of Electronic and Computer Engineering
University of Limerick, Limerick, Ireland
`peter.murphy@ul.ie`

Abstract. Prosody refers to certain properties of the speech signal including audible changes in pitch, loudness, and syllable length. The acoustic manifestation of prosody is typically measured in terms of fundamental frequency (f0), amplitude and duration. These three cues have formed the basis for extensive studies of prosody in natural speech. The present work seeks to go beyond this level of representation and to examine additional factors that arise as a result of the underlying production mechanism. For example, intonation is studied with reference to the f0 contour. However, to change f0 requires changes in the laryngeal configuration that results in glottal flow parameter changes. These glottal changes may serve as important psychoacoustic markers in addition to (or in conjunction with) the f0 targets. The present work examines changes in open quotient with f0 in connected speech using electroglottogram and volume velocity at the lips signals. This preliminary study suggests that individual differences may exist in terms of glottal changes for a particular f0 variation.

1 Introduction

In concatenative speech synthesis systems (e.g. sinusoidal [1] or harmonic plus noise [2] models) pitch modification takes the following broad form:

- i) extract the residual signal from an LPC analysis
- ii) scale the residual in the time or frequency domain
- iii) re-synthesise the original vocal tract envelope approximation with the scaled residual signal

Such approaches have been termed shape-invariant pitch scale modification. In terms of voice production the method attempts to keep the transfer function of the vocal tract constant while the source harmonics move under this transfer function. Through maintaining a constant spectral envelope the phonetic information essentially remains unchanged. However, a further issue arises if the problem is considered from a time-domain viewpoint in terms of the underlying glottal flow signal. The LPC residual signal arises from what remains following an analysis of the voiced speech signal that considers the system to be an all-pole filter excited by an impulse train excitation spaced at the pitch period. The prominent feature of the residual signal is a narrow peak spaced at the fundamental period and it is this signal that is scaled for

A. Esposito et al. (Eds.): Verbal and Nonverbal Commun. Behaviours, LNAI 4775, pp. 165–173, 2007.

pitch modification purposes. The true glottal source can be represented as a convolution of an impulse train spaced at the pitch period and the glottal flow waveform. Given the similarity between the impulse train and the residual signal, to a first approximation, the true source can be considered as the glottal flow waveform convolved with the residual signal. Therefore, increasing f0 by bringing the residual pulses closer together is equivalent to shortening the closed phase of the glottal cycle. A hoarse quality in the voice signal (with some aspects of double pulsing) when f0 modification reaches 20% is reported in [1]. This is explained in [3] to be due to consecutive open phase glottal cycles overlapping. The existing synthesis solution to this problem is to record more data at different f0s and modify only within certain limits. In formant synthesis the glottal flow can be scaled directly to ensure that OQ remains constant with f0 and basic aspects of voice quality are retained. The relative height of the glottal harmonics remains the same for the scaled glottal flow signals. This changes the amplitude of the overall speech spectral envelope when measured in actual frequency values. In the former case, the speech spectral envelope remains constant which means that the relative height of the glottal harmonics changes. The advantage of the latter approach is that it can be used for an arbitrarily wide range of f0 variation. Although this approach appears plausible from a production viewpoint it is of interest to find out how the glottal source actually changes with f0 variation in human speech.

2   Voice Source Characterisation

2.1   Measures from the Voice Source Waveform

In order to assess voice source variation with f0 changes the salient features of the source must be extracted. The following features, illustrated in Fig. 1, using the LF-model [4] have been used extensively in voice source parameterisation.

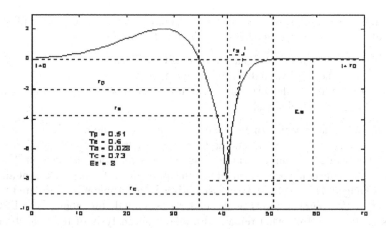

Fig. 1. LF model of the voice source

The parameters derived from the model include:

Effective open quotient: $OQ_i = T_e/T_0$ (effective open time/pitch period)

Effective waveform skewing: $R_k = (T_e - T_p)/T_p$ (effective closing time/opening time)

Negative amplitude of maximum rate of closure: E_e

2.2 Measures from the Speech Spectrum

The voice source can also be indirectly characterized through observation of the spectrum. The following measures are taken form the speech spectrum (expressed in dB):

H1 – amplitude of first harmonic
H2 – amplitude of second harmonic
A1 – amplitude of first formant
A3 – amplitude of third formant

The spectral measures of H1-H2, H1-A1 and H1-A3 have also been extracted from the speech signal with a view to characterising glottal attributes [5]. H1-H2 corresponds with OQ while the spectral tilt measures, H1-A1 and H1-A3 correspond more closely to the skewing of the waveform.

3   Analysis Studies of Glottal Source Variation with Changing Fundamental Frequency

A number of studies have investigated the change in glottal characteristics with variation in f0 during human speech. However, the findings have differed somewhat and are summarised very briefly below.

In [6] a number of studies are cited [7-9] where OQ remains constant as f0 increases. In [10] it is reported that a pitch-accented vowel has greater amplitude than a non-reduced vowel but that glottal waveshape remains similar. In [11] no consistent glottal changes are found as f0 varies. It is stated in [12] that the equivalent of OQ stays constant with an increase in f0 but that the pulse skews more to the right. It is noted in [13] that OQ increases and an increase in pulse skewing towards the right occurs, as f0 increases for a constant voice effort. In [14] it is reported that, in general, H1-H2 covaries with f0. The authors also note that while H1-H2 is positively correlated with OQ, the measure is also strongly affected by glottal pulse skewing.

Some of the differences reported regarding glottal change with f0 may be due to a number of methodological differences: context (e.g. rising/falling f0, where phonation is in relation to f0 range of the speaker) or individual speaker differences. The present study employs an unambiguous measure of OQ derived from the DEGG signal.

4   Method

Previous studies of glottal changes with f0 variation in human speech have employed either inverse filtering or direct analysis of the acoustic waveform and spectrum. The work of the first author's group has looked to advance glottal inverse filtering (GIF) techniques for use on connected speech [15-16] and the process of developing GIF techniques to incorporate detailed source-filter interaction effects is ongoing. In the present study the electroglottogram (EGG) signal (Fig.2) and the integrated speech waveform (which serves as an approximation to the volume velocity at the lips - vvl) are employed to estimate source characteristics.

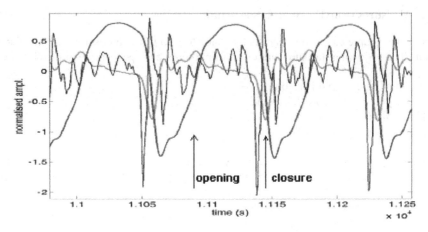

Fig. 2. Timing relationship between Speech (dark line), EGG (dark line – slow varying signal) and DEGG (light line)

Fig. 2 illustrates the electroglottogram signal, together with its first derivative (DEGG) and the corresponding speech waveform. The EGG signal provides a measure of vocal fold contact area or conversely vocal fold impedance (1/contact area) depending on the signal polarity. The present signal is plotted with impedance

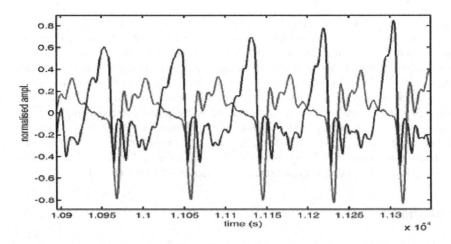

Fig. 3. Timing relationship between volume velocity at the lips (vvl) and differentiated electroglottograph signal (DEGG)

increasing on the y-axis. The EGG signals and the speech waveforms have been manually time-aligned (in practice the speech signal lags the EGG signal due to the propagation time of acoustic signal from glottis to microphone). The OQ is extracted from the DEGG signal, which has a peak corresponding to the points of glottal opening (positive peak) and closure (negative peak).

Fig. 3 illustrates the integrated speech waveform (vvl) together with the time-aligned DEGG signal. The figure suggests that for this vowel (a/) a measure of OQ may also be extracted directly from the vvl estimate.

5 Analysis

The following test sentences from [11] were employed in the analysis: (nuclear pitch accent preceding a non-reduced vowel and nuclear pitch accent following a non-reduced vowel).

The underlined word is accented.

The <u>bat</u> sat here. (x3 repetitions)
The bat <u>sat</u> here. (x3 repetitions)

These sentences were recorded for two male and three female speakers. Also rising pitch and falling pitch for a sustained a/ vowel were recorded. In the analysis f0 and OQ are estimated from the DEGG and vvl signals.

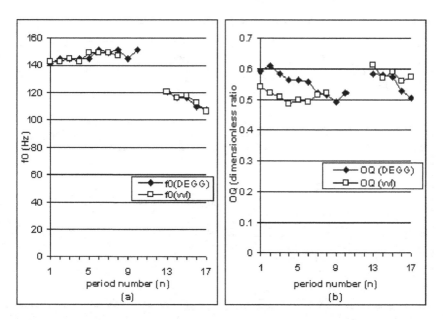

Fig. 4. (a) f0 vs period no. and (b) OQ vs period no. extracted from the test phrase "The bat sat here." (the periods nos. refer to the vowel containing the nuclear pitch accent – a/ in bat, and the following non-reduced vowel – a/ in sat) for speaker 1.

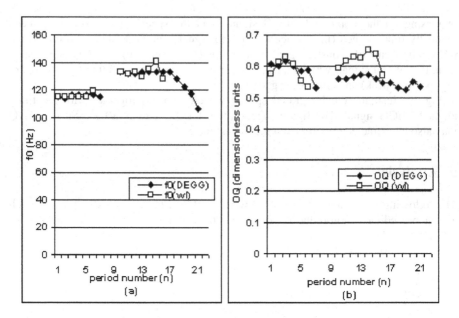

Fig. 5. (a) f0 vs period no. and (b) OQ vs period no. extracted from the test phrase "The bat sat here." (the periods nos. refer to the non-reduced vowel – a/ in bat, followed by a vowel containing the nuclear pitch accent – a/ in sat) for speaker 1.

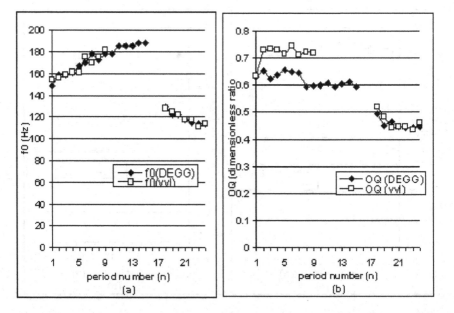

Fig. 6. (a) f0 vs period no. and (b) OQ vs period no. extracted from the test phrase "The bat sat here." (the periods nos. refer to the vowel containing the nuclear pitch accent – a/ in bat, and the following non-reduced vowel – a/ in sat) for speaker 2.

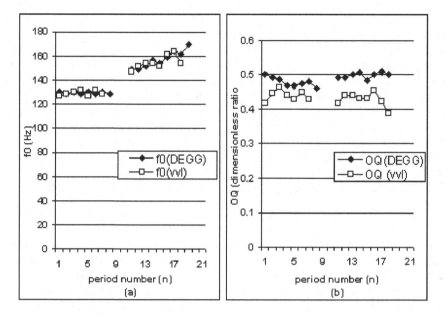

Fig. 7. (a) f0 vs period no. and (b) OQ vs period no. extracted from the test phrase "The bat s<u>a</u>t here." (the periods nos. refer to the non-reduced vowel – a/ in b<u>a</u>t, followed by a vowel containing the nuclear pitch accent – a/ in s<u>a</u>t) for speaker 2.

6 Results

The results indicate f0 and OQ, respectively, plotted against period number, where f0 and OQ are measured using EGG and vvl signals. In Fig. 4 and Fig. 5 the nuclear pitch accent is in the word bat for speaker 1 and speaker 2, respectively.

In Fig.6 and Fig.7 the nuclear pitch accent is in the word sat for speaker 1 and speaker 2, respectively.

Table 1. Approximate average values for f0 and OQ for speaker 1 and speaker 2

	Speaker 1		Speaker 2	
	V́V	VV́	V́V	VV́
f0 (Hz)	146, 110	116, 128	170, 120	128, 156
OQ	0.55, 0.55	0.58, 0.55	0.62, 0.44	0.47, 0.5

V́V indicates that the pitch-accented vowel is the first vowel ('b<u>a</u>t'), while VV́ indicates that the pitch-accented vowel is the second vowel ('s<u>a</u>t').

7 Discussion

This preliminary study of voice source changes with pitch variation investigates OQ variation measured using DEGG and vvl signals for two renditions of the sentence "The bat sat here" for two speakers. In rendition 1 the pitch accent is on the vowel in 'bat', while in rendition 2, the pitch accent is on the vowel in 'sat'. For rendition 1, speaker 1, f0 drops by about 26 Hz going from the nuclear pitch accent (in 'bat') to the non-reduced vowel (in 'sat'), with little change in the corresponding OQ, with average value of 0.55 in each case. For rendition 2, speaker 1, f0 increases by approximately 12 Hz going from the non-reduced vowel (in sat) to the nuclear pitch accent (in bat), while OQ is quite constant, decreasing slightly from 0.58 to 0.55. For rendition 1, speaker 2, f0 drops by about 50 Hz going from the nuclear pitch accent (in 'bat') to the non-reduced vowel (in 'sat'), while OQ changes from an approximate average value of 0.62 to 0.44. For rendition 2, speaker 2, f0 increases by approximately 28 Hz going from the non-reduced vowel (in 'sat') to the nuclear pitch accent (in 'bat'), while OQ increases slightly from 0.47 to 0.5.

In [11] there is a difference in prominence of the F1 amplitude for the pitch-accented vowel compared to the non-reduced vowel. This is about 5.6 dB in the VV́ sequence and 2.2 dB for the V́V sentence (average values for two speakers). In that study H1-H2 and spectral tilt (H1-A3) did not show consistent differences for the vowels in either sentence. For the data of that study it was concluded that the main difference (in going from a pitch accented vowel to a non-reduced vowel - and vice-versa) is the change in amplitude of the glottal source as opposed to a change in its waveshape or spectrum. This largely appears to be the case also in the present study also. For speaker 1, OQ is quite constant for each sentence, while for speaker 2, OQ shows only a small increase from V́ to V́ in the VV sequence. However, in the V́V sequence for speaker 2, OQ reduces markedly from V́ (0.62) to V (0.44). It is noted that in [11] the f0 decrease in V́V is 32% and 20% for each speaker. In the present study it is 33% (speaker 1) and 42% (speaker 2). The greater variation in f0 may account for the glottal changes.

8   Conclusion

The data presented is consistent with what has previously been reported in the literature. Some previous research has suggested that glottal parameters remain constant with changes in f0 while other work reports that OQ increases as f0 increases. In the present study OQ did not vary noticeably when the f0 change was moderate. For a higher f0 in the speaker's range, OQ increased. This suggests that where the speaker is within his/her pitch range plays a part in determining the extent of the corresponding glottal change. A number of further studies employing different prosodic contexts and a larger number of speakers are required in order to draw more general conclusions.

Acknowledgements

This work is supported through an Enterprise Ireland International Collaboration Fund IC/2003/86. The first author wishes to express his gratitude to Professor

Kenneth Stevens and his colleagues, Speech Communication Group, Research Laboratory of Electronics, MIT, for participating in this work and for fruitful discussions on this and related work.

References

1. Quatieri, T., McAulay, R.: Shape invariant time-scale and pitch-scale modification of speech. IEEE Trans. Signal Processing 40(3), 497–510 (1992)
2. Stylianou, Y.: Applying the harmonic plus noise model in concatenative speech synthesis. IEEE Trans. Speech and Audio Processing 9(1), 21–29 (2001)
3. Jiang, Y., Murphy, P.: Production based pitch modification of voiced speech. In: Proceedings International Conference on Spoken Language Processing, Denver, USA (2002)
4. Fant, G., Liljencrants, J., Lin, Q.: A four-parameter model of glottal flow. STL_QPSR 4, 1–13 (1985)
5. Hanson, H.: Glottal characteristics of female speakers: Acoustic correlates. 101(1), 466–481 (1997)
6. Klatt, D.H., Klatt, L.C.: Analysis, synthesis and perception of voice quality variations among female and male talkers. 87(2), 820–856 (1990)
7. Cleveland, T., Sundberg, J.: Acoustic analysis of three male voices of different quality. STL_QPSR 4, 24–38 (1983)
8. Lofqvist, A., Koenig, L.L., McGowan, R.S.: Voice source variations in running speech: A study of Mandarin Chinese tones. In: Fujimura, O., Hirano, M. (eds.) Vocal Fold Physiology: Voice Quality Control, Singular Publishing Group, San Diego, pp. 3–22. Singular Publishing Group, San Diego (1995)
9. Karlsson, I.: Glottal waveforms for normal female speakers. J. Phon. 14, 415–419 (1986)
10. Holmberg, E.B., Hillman, R.E., Perkell, J.S.: Glottal airflow and transglottal air pressure measurements for male and female speakers in low, normal and high pitch. J. Voice 4, 294–305 (1989)
11. Stevens, K.: Prosodic influences on glottal waveform: preliminary data. In: International Symposium on Prosody, Yokohama, Japan, pp. 53–64 (1994)
12. Strik, H., Boves, L.: On the relationship between voice source parameters and prosodic features in connected speech. Speech Communication 11, 167–174 (1992)
13. Pierrehumbert, J.: A preliminary study of the consequences of intonation for the voice source. STL-QPSR 4, 23–36 (1989)
14. Swertz, M., Veldhuis, R.: The effect of speech melody on voice quality. Speech Communication 33, 297–303 (2001)
15. Fu, Q., Murphy, P.: Robust glottal source estimation based on joint source-filter model optimization. IEEE Trans. Audio, Speech and Language Processing 14, 492–501 (2006)
16. Akande, O., Murphy, P.: Estimation of the vocal tract transfer function for voiced speech with application to glottal wave analysis. 46, 15–36 (2005)

A Gesture-Based Concept for Speech Movement Control in Articulatory Speech Synthesis

Bernd J. Kröger[1] and Peter Birkholz[2]

[1] Department of Phoniatrics, Pedaudiology, and Communication Disorders,
University Hospital Aachen and Aachen University, 52074 Aachen, Germany
[2] Institute for Computer Science, University of Rostock, 18059 Rostock, Germany
bkroeger@ukaachen.de
piet@informatik.uni-rostock.de

Abstract. An articulatory speech synthesizer comprising a three-dimensional vocal tract model and a gesture-based concept for control of articulatory movements is introduced and discussed in this paper. A modular learning concept based on speech perception is outlined for the creation of gestural control rules. The learning concept includes on sensory feedback information for articulatory states produced by the model itself, and auditory and visual information of speech items produced by external speakers. The complete model (control module and synthesizer) is capable of producing high-quality synthetic speech signals and introduces a scheme for the natural speech production and speech perception processes.

Keywords: articulation, speech synthesis, speech production, gesture.

1 Introduction

Within the field of cross-modal analysis of verbal as well as nonverbal communication it is feasible to use approaches capable of modeling speech perception and speech production as close as possible to real biological processes. But neural models of speech perception and speech production are rare (e.g. Guenther 2006, Guenther et al. 2006, Kröger et al. 2006b, Kröger et al. 2007). A general approach for modeling speech production and perception is introduced in this paper. We describe a comprehensive, computer-implemented gesture-based model for speech movement control and outline learning procedures for the optimization of control rules within this model. The learning procedures are based on auditory as well as on visual speech perception.

2 Three-Dimensional Model of the Vocal Tract and Acoustic Simulation

From an acoustic point of view, the vocal and nasal tracts constitute lossy tubes of non-uniform cross-sectional area. With regard to a computer simulation of acoustic

A. Esposito et al. (Eds.): Verbal and Nonverbal Commun. Behaviours, LNAI 4775, pp. 174–189, 2007.

propagation within these tubes, as it is needed for an articulatory speech synthesizer, the following simplifying assumptions can be made to keep the numerical calulations tractable (Flanagan 1965): (1) Sound propagates as plane waves, i.e., we assume one-dimensional wave propagation. (2) We neglect tube bendings, especially between the mouth and the pharynx. (3) The tubes are represented in terms of incremental sections of right, elliptical geometry.

With these assumtions, the vocal system can be represented as a branched tube system consisting of short abbutting tube sections as illustrated schematically in Fig. 1. This tube model, in turn, can be represented by an area function, i.e., the cross-sectional areas along the centerline of the tube branches. In our synthesizer, this area function is generated by an articulatory model of the vocal tract and a model of the vocal folds that will be described in Section 2.1. The simulation of acoustic propagation within the tube model and the generation of the synthetic speech signal will be briefly discussed in Section 2.2.

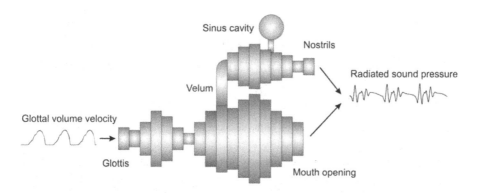

Fig. 1. Schematic representation of the tube model for the vocal tract and the nasal tract

2.1 Vocal Tract Model

The vocal tract is modeled in terms of a number of wireframe meshes that represent the surfaces of the articulators and the vocal tract walls. Fig. 2 gives an overview of the meshes. Two of them, the upper cover and the lower cover, represent the superior-posterior and the inferior-anterior walls of the vocal tract, respectively. The upper cover comprises sub-surfaces for the posterior wall of the larynx and the pharynx, the velum, and the hard palate. The lower cover consists of sub-surfaces for the anterior wall of the larynx and pharynx, and the mandible. The tongue, the upper and lower teeth, the upper and lower lip, the epiglottis, and the uvula are all represented by individual surfaces. Fig. 5 (b) shows a 3D rendering of the vocal tract for the vowel [i:].

All of the surfaces are defined in the fixed reference frame of the hard palate. The teeth, mandible, palate, uvula, and epiglottis are considered as rigid structures, while the velum, the tongue, the lips, and the laryngeal and pharyngeal walls are deformable. The shape of the rigid structures has been adapted to an adult male speaker by

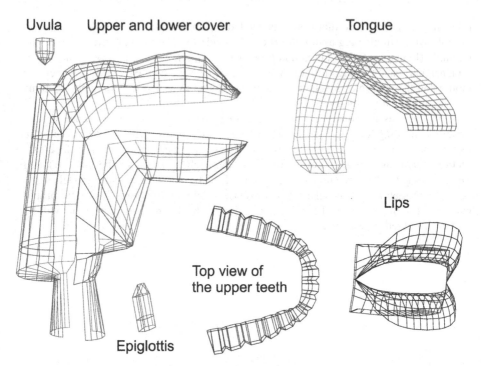

Uvula   Upper and lower cover   Tongue

Lips

Top view of
the upper teeth

Epiglottis

Fig. 2. Wireframe representation of the surfaces defining the vocal tract geometry

means of volumetric Magnetic Resonance Imaging (MRI) data of the vocal tract and
Computer Tomography scans of plaster casts of the jaw and teeth, and therefore
represent his anatomy (Birkholz and Kröger 2006). The position and orientation of the
rigid structures, as well as the shape of the deformable structures, are defined by a set
of 24 vocal tract parameters. Fig. 3 illustrates the influence of the most important
parameters on the shape of the vocal tract. The shape of the lips depends on the
parameters LP and LH that specify the degree of protrusion and the vertical distance
between the upper and lower lip. The actual geometry of the lips is calculated on the
basis of the "laws for lips" by Abry and Boë (1986). The parameter VA determines the
position and shape of the velum that can vary between a maximally raised velum and
a maximally lowered velum. The actual vertex positions are calculated by interpolation between according key shapes. The vertical position of the larynx is defined
by the parameter HY, and the horizontal position of the hyoid by HX. The upper part
of the larynx widens or narrows according to the hyoid position, and the length of the
pharynx wall is stretched or shortened according to HY. The mandible can be
translated in the midsagittal plane by the parameters JX and JY, and can be rotated
by JA.

Most parameters affect the shape of the tongue. In the midsagittal plane, the tongue
contour is modeled by two circular arcs and two second-order Bézier curves. One of
the circles represents the tongue body, and the other one the tongue tip. Their center
positions are defined in Cartesian coordinates by (TCX, TCY) and (TTX, TTY). The

spline curves have two parameters each, (*TRX, TRY*) and (*TBX, TBY*), specifying the positions of their median points. In addition to the parameters defining the midsagittal tongue contour, four parameters specify the relative height of the tongue sides at four equidistant points along the contour.

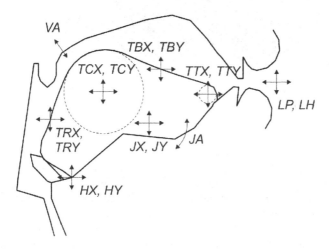

Fig. 3. Midsagittal section of the vocal tract model. The abbreviations (*TCX, TCY*, etc.) denote the vocal tract parameters and the arrows indicate their respective areas of influence on the model geometry.

In order to determine the vocal tract parameters for the realization of the speech sounds of Standard German, the parameters were manually adjusted in such a way that the model derived midsagittal vocal tract outlines closely matched tracings of the corresponding outlines in the MR images of the same subject as above. Fig. 4 (a), (b) and (c) illustrate the determination of MRI tracings by means of the vowel [y:]. Fig. 4 (a) shows the original midsagittal image of the vowel, and (b) shows the edges in the picture that were determined automatically by means of a Sobel operator. The vocal tract outline in (b) was then fitted with Catmull-Rom Splines that are illustrated in (c). Finally, the tracings were rotated and translated into the reference frame of the vocal tract model, and differences in head-neck angles between the subject and the vocal tract model were compensated for by warping the MRI derived outlines (Birkholz and Kröger 2006).

Fig. 5 (a) illustrates the results of the parameter tuning for the vowel [i:]. The dotted and the solid lines represent the MRI outline and the model derived outline, respectively. The dashed line represents the tongue side. Because of the flexibility of the vocal tract parameters, similar good matches could be achieved for all speech sounds in the MRI corpus. Fig. 5 (c) and (d) illustrate the determination of the vocal tract center line and the area function for a given vocal tract geometry. The centerline is calculated similarly to the method by Mermelstein (1973) and additionally smoothed. At 129 equidistant positions along the centerline, the vocal tract surfaces

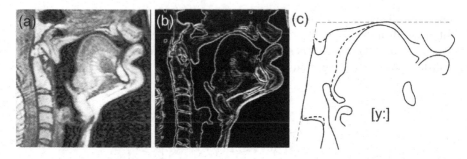

Fig. 4. (a) Midsagittal magnetic resonance image (MRI) for the phone [y:]. (b) Edges detected by a Sobel operator for (a). (c) Tracing results for (b). The thick dashed lines indicate the left side of the tongue.

are intersected with planes perpendicular to the centerline. The areas of the resulting cross-sections are calculated numerically and constitute a high-resolution area function. This area function is low-pass filtered and mapped on the cross-sectional areas and perimeters of 40 abutting elliptical tube sections that comprise the tube model of the vocal tract.

To test the *acoustic* match between the vowels spoken by the MRI subject and the synthesized vowels with the tuned parameters, the first three formants of all vowels in the corpus were compared. The formants of the subject's vowels were determined by a LPC analysis. The formants of the synthetic vowels were extracted from a frequency domain simulation of the vocal system on the basis of the model derived area functions (Birkholz and Jackèl 2004). The error between the natural and synthetic formant frequencies averaged over all vowels was about 12%. This error must be mainly attributed to the resolution-limited accuracy of the MRI tracings as well as to the imperfect matching of the outlines. It is well known that in certain regions of the vocal tract, the formant frequencies are quite sensitive to small variations of articulatory parameters (Stevens 1989). Therefore, the acoustic differences could be caused by only small articulatory deviations due to the above sources of errors. To test how far small corrective variations of the vocal tract parameters can improve the acoustic match, we implemented an algorithm searching the parameter space to minimize the formant errors. With only little articulatory changes of the vocal tract parameters in the sensitive regions, the average formant error reduced to 3.4% (Birkholz and Kröger 2006).

For the voiced excitation of the synthesizer, we implemented a parametric model of the glottal geometry based on Titze (1984). A schematic representation of the model is shown in Fig. 6. The vocal fold parameters are the degree of abduction at the posterior end of the folds at the lower and upper edge, the fundamental frequency F_0, the phase difference between the upper and lower edge, and the subglottal pressure. Based on these parameters, the model generates the time-varying cross-sectional areas at the glottal inlet and outlet opening that are in turn mapped on two glottal tube sections (an upper and a lower one). We extended Titze's original model to account for a smooth diminishment of the oscillation amplitude with increasing abduction and for a parametrization of glottal leakage similar to Cranen and Schroeter (1995).

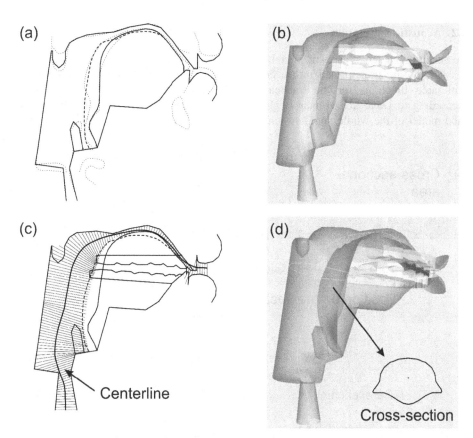

Fig. 5. (a) The vocal tract parameters were adjusted in such a way that the model outline (solid lines) closely matches the MRI tracing for the vowel [i:] (dotted lines). (b) 3D rendering of the vocal tract model for the adapted vowel [i:]. (c) Midsagittal section of the vocal tract model with the centerline. The straight lines normal to the centerline indicate the positions and orientations of the cutting planes. (d) Centerline and cross-section in the pharyngeal region within the 3D geometry of the vocal tract.

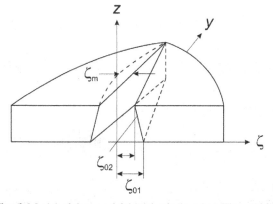

Fig. 6. Model of the vocal folds/glottis based on Titze (1984)

2.2 Acoustic Simulation

To generate the actual acoustic signal, the geometric models of the vocal tract and the vocal folds are transformed into a composite discrete area function and combined with area functions for the trachea, and the nasal tract with paranasal sinuses (according to Dang and Honda 1994). These area functions represent the branched tube model of the whole vocal system as illustrated in Fig. 7 (top). The areas of the

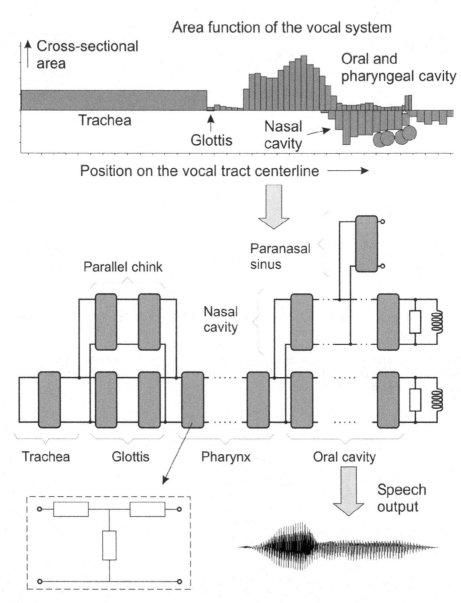

Fig. 7. Generation of the acoustic speech signal (see text)

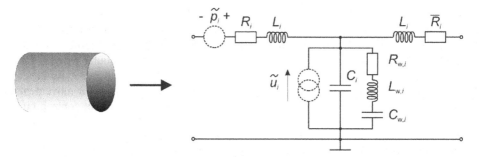

Fig. 8. Correspondence between a short tube section and a two-port network section of an electrical transmission line with lumped elements

nasal cavity are flipped upside down and the paranasal sinuses are drawn as circles. This tube model is then transformed into an equivalent electrical transmission line network as in Fig. 7 (middle). In this network, each tube section is represented by a two-port section as depicted in Fig. 8. On the basis of electro-acoustic analogies, the geometric parameters of the tube sections are transformed into the electrical network components of the two-port sections (Birkholz and Jackèl 2004, Birkholz 2005, Birkholz et al. 2007a). In this network, electrical current corresponds to volume velocity and voltage corresponds to sound pressure. The time-varying distribution of volume velocity and pressure in the tube model is simulated in the time domain based on finite difference equations for the corresponding variables in the network at a sampling rate of 44.1 kHz. Specific algorithms were implemented for the simulation of losses due to friction, sound radiation, and wall vibration, as well as for the generation of noise due to turbulence. The radiated speech signal is approximated as the time derivative of the volume velocity through the mouth opening and the nostrils. At each time instant of the simulation, a new set of parameters for the vocal tract and the vocal folds can be specified, leading to an updated tube model geometry which leads to changes in the acoustic properties of the vocal system. The implemented acoustic simulation is capable of generating speech sounds of all phonetic categories (e.g. vowels, fricatives, plosives, nasals, ...) on the basis of appropriate area functions.

In summary, the presented synthesizer does not only generate a high quality acoustic output, but also the corresponding sequence of 3D vocal tract shapes and area functions. The geometrical output can, for example, be used for the animation of the lip and chin region of a face model of a virtual speaker (avatar). Furthermore both outputs – geometrical information of articulator positions (e.g. palatal contact patterns) and the acoustic speech signal – are essential for learning speech production (motor execution for speech articulation) and may help refining speech perception (place of articulation, see motor theory of speech perception).

3 The Gesture-Based Control Concept

The term *gesture* as used in this paper denotes the concept of *target-directed speech movements realizing speech sounds* (e.g., a lip closing gesture in temporal coordination with a glottal opening-closing gesture for the realization of a voiceless labial stop /p/. From the viewpoint of motor control, gestures are target-directed actions, i.e., prelearned high-level motor programs accomplishing a specific task like lip closure or glottal opening without specifying the concrete muscular activity for each motor unit on the primary motor level (Saltzman and Munhall 1989, Ito et al. 2004). This concept of the *gesture* or *motor action* is widely accepted for movement control of biological systems in general - not only for speech movement control, but also for nonverbal gestures like eye-brow movements as well as for head, arm, and other (speech-accompanying) body movements (Sober und Sabes 2003, Todorov 2004, Paine und Tani 2004, Fadiga und Craihgero 2004).

The gesture-based control concept introduced here is related to the control concept introduced by Saltzman and Munhall (1989) which was extended to a linguistic theory by Browman and Goldstein (1989, 1990, and 1992). A controversial discussion of this concept was stimulated by these papers, mainly due to problems concerning the quantitative implementation of this approach (e.g., Kröger et al. 1995) and due to the fact that perception as a control instance for production is not considered in this approach (Kohler 1992). Especially the control of gestural target positions is actually mainly done in perceptual domains (Perkell et al. 1997, Guenther et al. 1998, Guenther and Perkell 2004).

On the other hand, there are a lot of well-accepted facts privileging a gestural concept above simpler segmental target concepts for describing speech movements and for establishing speech motor control models. In the case of vowels it is well known that their targets need not to be reached completely for producing or perceiving a vowel phoneme. In the case of casual speech or in the case of high speaking rate, vowel realizations often exhibit target undershoot without affecting the perceptual identification and discrimination of the phoneme produced (Lindblom 1963, Strange 1989). That indicates the importance of formant trajectories compared to steady state formant patterns and thus the importance of target-directed articulatory movements instead of pure articulatory target locations. This supports the hypothesis that vocalic targets are perceived rather from the acoustic results of articulatory movements towards an auditory target than from the real achievement of the (articulatory or acoustic) target positions. This underlines that articulatory movement transitions are more important for speech perception than reaching the target positions and thus supports the concept of the speech gesture.

In addition, the gesture-based approach introduced in this paper does not longer exhibit shortcomings of earlier gestural concepts: (i) The quantitative model for describing goal-directed movements is changed; (ii) gesture execution is learned using external auditory and sensory (auditory and somatosensory) feedback information; (iii) learning concepts are used to implement the complete repertoire of speech gestures for a specific language.

The basic assumptions of the gestural concept introduced in this paper are:

(i) Each speech sound (or phoneme realization) consists of one or more gestures distributed over gestural tiers (Tab. 1 and Fig. 9). Vocalic sounds are composed of a tract-shaping gesture determining the vowel quality (high-low, front-back, rounded-unrounded), a glottal closing gesture responsible for voicing (clgl, see Tab. 1), and a velopharyngeal closing gesture (clvp) ensuring that the vowel is not nasalized. The realization of a consonant phoneme is composed of a consonantal near closing or (full)closing gesture determining manner and place of articulation (see Tab. 1), a glottal opening or closing gesture determining whether the consonant is voiced or unvoiced, and a velopharyngeal opening (opvp) or tight closing gesture (tcvp) determining whether the sound is nasal or oral.

(ii) A temporal interval of activation is defined for each gesture (Fig. 9, shaded boxes). This temporal interval comprises a transition portion and (optionally) a target portion if the target is reached (both portions are not separated strictly in Fig. 9). Target portions occur in many types of gestures when articulatory saturation effects occur (e.g. contact of two articulators or contact of an articulator with the vocal tract walls, Kröger 1993 and Kröger 1998). Saturation effects lead to constant effective vocal tract constrictions (or glottal or velopharyngeal constriction) over the target portion time interval while the vocal tract parameter values continue to change towards the target (see non-dashed and dashed line in Fig. 10). For example in the case of contact between the tongue tip and the hard palate during a consonantal apical closing gesture, a time interval for complete closure occurs. Within this time interval the contact area between the articulator and the vocal tract wall changes but the complete closure remains.

Table 1. List of vocalic, consonantal, velopharyngeal, and glottal speech gestures (not complete). Default gestures are marked by an asterisk. Keep in mind that gestures should not be confused with phonemes (e.g., the phoneme /b/ is realized by a {b}-gesutre in combination with a {pho}-gesture; the phoneme /p/ is realized by a {b}- in combination with a {-pho}-gesture; the phoneme /m/ is realized by a combination of a {b}-, a {nas}-, and a {pho}-gesture). Moreover the gestural symbols represent distinctive features or bundles of distinctive features realized by this gesture. The symbol {-nas} means non-nasalized sonorant. The symbol {obs} means obstruent, which is by definition non-nazalised sound and which always needs a velopharyngeal tight closure in order to avoid pressure loss in the mouth cavity.

Abbreviation	Symbol	Name of Gesture
iivt	{i:}	(vocalic) vocal tract ii-shaping
uuvt	{u:}	(vocalic) vocal tract uu-shaping
aavt	{a:}	(vocalic) vocal tract aa-shaping
swvt *	{schwa} *	(vocalic) vocal tract schwa-shaping *
....	....	....
clla	{b}	(consonantal) labial closing
clap	{d}	(consonantal) apical closing
cldo	{g}	(consonantal) dorsal closing
ncld	{v}	(consonantal) labio-dental near closing
ncal	{z}	(consonantal) alveolar near closing
ncpo	{Z}	(consonantal) postalveolar near closing
....	....	....
clvp *	{-nas} *	velopharyngeal closing *
tcvp	{obs}	velopharyngeal tight closing
opvp	{nas}	velopharyngeal opening
....	....	....
clgl *	{pho} *	glottal closing *
tcgl	{?}	glottal tight closing
opgl	{-pho}	glottal opening
....	....	....

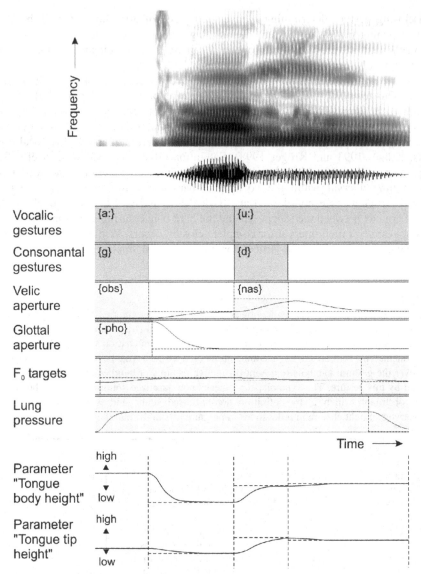

Fig. 9. Gestural score for the utterance /ka:nu:/: Six tiers are given: vocalic tier, consonantal tier, velic tier, glottal tier, fundamental frequency tier, and lung pressure tier. Gestural activation is marked by the shaded boxes. In the case of velic, glottal, and lung pressure gestures only one parameter is controlled (e.g. *VA* for a velic gestures). In the case of vocalic and consonantal gestures many vocal tract paratemers are controlled. As an example, the spatio-temporal trajectories for the vocal tract parameters tongue body height *TBH* and tongue tip height *TTH* are displayed. In the case of both parameters the targets for the {g}-, {a:}-, {d}-, and {u:}-gesture are displayed (dashed lines). If no activation is marked on the vocalic, velic, or glottal tier, the appropriate default gesture becomes activated. If no activation is marked on the consonantal tier, no consonantal gesture is active. The vocal tract is solely determined by vocalic gestures in this case.

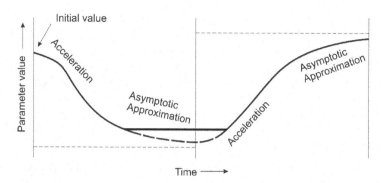

Fig. 10. Spatiotemporal control parameter trajectory for an articulator movement in the case of two successive gestures. Durations and target locations for the gestures are indicated by thin dashed lines. The bold horizontal line indicates a saturation effect (i.e., a constant degree of constriction) while the control parameter further changes (bold dashed line). The distance between the dashed bold line and the solid bold line indicates the degree of articulator to articulator or articulator to vocal tract wall contact.

(iii) Gestural time functions are quantitatively described by a third order cascaded system (Birkholz 2007c and cf. Ogata and Sonoda 2000) which is capable of approximating natural articulatory data better than the critically damped second order system used by Browman and Goldstein (1990b) and Smith et al. (1993) (see also Kröger et al. 1995). Within the quantitative approach by Birkholz (submitted) gestural rapidity (i.e., the time period of the gestural transition portion or the time period needed for approximating the gestural target) is defined controlling the articulatory velocity for each gesture. Target values and gestural rapidity can vary for each gesture, for example with respect to different prosodic conditions of the corresponding syllable.

(iv) In many cases more than one articulator is involved in the gestural movement realization (e.g. upper lips, lower lips, and mandible in the case of a labial closing gesture). A concept of articulatory dominance is used to determine the contribution of each articulator for the realization of a gestural movement (Birkholz 2007c, Birkholz et al. 2006). Also in the case of temporal overlap of gestures on the same or on different tiers, the resulting gestural movement trajectories for each articulator are calculated using the dominance concept.

4 Learning Gesture-Based Control Using Sensory Feedback and External Speech Signals

Over the last decades it became more and more apparent that purely rule-driven formant synthesis systems are not suitable for producing natural sounding speech (i.e., high-quality speech signals) in comparison to data-driven concatenative speech synthesis like the unit-selection approach. Thus, a rule based gestural control module for articulatory speech synthesis does not lead automatically to high quality synthetic speech. To overcome this problem, one idea is to combine unit selection approaches with articulatory speech synthesis (Birkholz et al. 2007b), e.g., to generate crucial control information like segmental durations using unit selection modules. The idea introduced here is different. If we want to model speech production and speech perception as close as possible to real biological processes, it should be tried to extract control rules from learning procedures as toddlers do it during speech acquisition. That means to extract control information (i) from audible feedback signals during self-productions (babbling) and (ii) from external auditory and visual speech signals by imitation.

An outline of learning steps that we implemented to establish control rules for the gesture-based articulatory speech synthesizer is given below (not complete):

(i) In order to cope with the many-to-one articulatory-to-acoustics inversion problem in vowel production, constraints must be introduced regarding the possible articulator configurations for vowel targets (e.g., constraints for jaw position in isolated vowel production). This subset of articulatory configurations must still cover the whole vowel space, i.e., the dimensions low-high, front-back, and rounded-unrounded. It can be learned or trained during babbling (Kröger et al. 2006b).

(ii) In order to consider coarticulatory effects of neighboring consonants on the articulation of vowels (e.g., to allow higher jaw positions for a vowel produced in the context of alveolar fricatives compared to isolated production) rules for compensatory articulation have to be learned during babbling such that the production model is capable of producing comparable vocal tract shapes (or area functions) using different (compensatory) articulator positions (e.g., a decrease in jaw position has to be compensated for by an increase in tongue elevation and lower lips elevation, and vice versa, see Kröger et al. 2006c).

(iii) The production of consonantal closing gestures and the perception of the place of articulation is also learned during babbling in our approach using a V_1CV_2 training set where V_1 and V_2 cover the whole vowel space and C covers lip, tongue tip, and tongue body closures (Kröger et al. 2006a and 2006b). This learning step leads to a database combining perceptual knowledge and articulatory knowledge – i.e. which formant transition in which vocalic context is produced for each place of articulation (labial, dental, alveolar, postalveolar, palatal, velar).

(iv) The production of other types of consonants like fricatives and nasals is also learned during babbling in our approach. For learning optimal friction noise production the degree of constriction is varied at different places of articulation. For learning the difference between nasal and obstruent sound production, different maneuvers of the velum (i.e., wide opening vs. tight closure) are trained in parallel to the oral closing gesture.

(v) During babbling, the model mainly acquired general, language independent phonetic knowledge, like the relation between formants and articulatory positions for vocalic sounds, the relation between formant transitions and consonantal closing gestures in different vocalic contexts, and so on. After this, the model is ready to imitate external productions, i.e., to learn from acoustic and optical data produced by other speakers. This means to learn language specific speech production and in consequence language specific perception, e.g., the perceptual magnet effect (Kröger et al. 2007).

(vi) The next steps of imitation training are (a) to strengthen the articulation of language specific places and manners of articulation, (b) to learn the language specific gestural coordination for consonant clusters and for different syllable structures (simple to complex), and (c) to learn language specific prosodic items like intonation patterns. These training steps have not been modeled so far.

5 Discussion

An articulatory speech synthesizer comprising a three-dimensional vocal tract model and a gesture-based concept for the control of articulatory movements has been described in this paper. The concept of speech gestures for quantitative control of speech articulation introduced here is discussed carefully with respect to other gestural approaches. The gestural model introduced here comprises a quantitative specification for sound targets and for the generation of the spatiotemporal gestural movement trajectories. It has been emphasized that a quantitative concept for describing goal-directed actions is very important because these trajectories define the perceptually important formant trajectories. A modular learning strategy based on speech perception is outlined for the built-up of gestural control rules. Sensory feedback information for defined articulatory items produced by the model itself and auditory and visual information of speech items produced by external speakers are used successively for the generation of the control rules. The complete model (control module and synthesizer) is capable of producing high-quality synthetic speech signals and gives a scheme for speech production and speech perception which is closely related to the human biological speech production and perception mechanisms. Potential applications for this model are (i) high-quality speech synthesis, (ii) establishing models for human speech production and perception, capable of helping to understand normal speech production, normal speech perception, and in addition, the underlying mechanisms of motor speech disorders (Kent 2000).

Acknowledgments. This work was supported in part by the German Research Council DFG grants JA 1476/1-1 and Kr 1439/10-1.

References

Abry, C., Boë, L.J.: Laws for lips. Speech Communication 5, 97–104 (1986)

Birkholz, P.: 3D-Artikulatorische Sprachsynthese. Unpublished PhD thesis. University Rostock (2005)

Birkholz, P.: Control of an articulatory speech synthesizer based on dynamic approximation of spatial articulatory targets. In: Proceedings of the Interspeech 2007 - Eurospeech. Antwerp, Belgium (2007c)

Birkholz, P., Jackèl, D.: Influence of temporal discretization schemes on formant frequencies and bandwidths in time domain simulations of the vocal tract system. In: Proceedings of Interspeech 2004-ICSLP. Jeju, Korea, pp. 1125–1128 (2004)

Birkholz, P., Kröger, B.J.: Vocal tract model adaptation using magnetic resonance imaging. In: Proceedings of the 7th International Seminar on Speech Production, pp. 493-500. Belo Horizonte, Brazil (2006)

Birkholz, P., Jackèl, D., Kröger, B.J.: Construction and control of a three-dimensional vocal tract model. In: Proceedings of the International Conference on Acoustics, Speech, and Signal Processing (ICASSP 2006), Toulouse, France, pp. 873-876 (2006)

Birkholz, P., Jackèl, D., Kröger, B.J.: Simulation of losses due to turbulence in the time-varying vocal system. IEEE Transactions on Audio, Speech, and Language Processing 15, 1218–1225 (2007a)

Birkholz, P., Steiner, I., Breuer, S.: Control concepts for articulatory speech synthesis. In: Proceedings of the 6th ISCA Speech Synthesis Research Workshop. Universität Bonn (2007b)

Browman, C.P., Goldstein, L.: Articulatory gestures as phonological units. Phonology 6, 201–251 (1989)

Browman, C.P., Goldstein, L.: Tiers in articulatory phonology, with some implications for casual speech. In: Kingston, J., Beckman, M.E. (eds.) Papers in Laboratory Phonology I: Between the Grammar and Physics of Speech, pp. 341–376. Cambridge University Press, Cambridge (1990a)

Browman, C.P., Goldstein, L.: Gestural specification using dynamically-defined articulatory structures. Journal of Phonetics 18, 299–320 (1990b)

Browman, C.P., Goldstein, L.: Articulatory phonology: An overview. Phonetica 49, 155–180 (1992)

Cranen, B., Schroeter, J.: Modeling a leaky glottis. Journal of Phonetics 23, 165–177 (1995)

Dang, J., Honda, K.: Morphological and acoustical analysis of the nasal and the paranasal cavities. Journal of the Acoustical Society of America 96, 2088–2100 (1994)

Fadiga, L., Crahighero, L.: Electrophysiology of action representation. Journal of clinical Neurophysiology 21, 157–169 (2004)

Flanagan, J.L.: Speech Analysis, Synthesis and Perception. Springer, Berlin (1965)

Guenther, F.H., Perkell, J.S.: A neural model of speech production and its application to studies of the role of auditory feedback in speech. In: Maassen, B., Kent, R., Peters, H., van Lieshout, P., Hulstijn, W. (eds.) Speech motor control in normal and disordered speech, pp. 29–49. Oxford University Press, Oxford (2004)

Guenther, F.H., Hampson, M., Johnson, D.: A theoretical investigation of reference frames for the planning of speech movements. Psychological Review 105, 611–633 (1998)

Guenther, F.H.: Cortical interactions underlying the production of speech sounds. Journal of Communication Disorders 39, 350–365 (2006)

Guenther, F.H., Ghosh, S.S., Tourville, J.A.: Neural modeling and imaging of the cortical interactions underlying syllable production. Brain and Language 96, 280–301 (2006)

Ito, T., Gomi, H., Honda, M.: Dynamic simulation of speech cooperative articulation by muscle linkages. Biological Cybernetics 91, 275–282 (2004)

Kent, R.D.: Research on speech motor control and its disorders: A review and prospective. Journal of Communication disorders 33, 391–428 (2000)

Kohler, K.J.: Gestural reorganization in connected speech: A functional viewpoint on 'articulatory phonology'. Phonetica 49, 205–211 (1992)

Kröger, B.J.: A gestural production model and its application to reduction in German. Phonetica 50, 213–233 (1993)

Kröger, B.J.: Ein phonetisches Modell der Sprachproduktion. Niemeyer Verlag, Tübingen (1998)

Kröger, B.J., Birkholz, P., Kannampuzha, J., Neuschaefer-Rube, C.: Modeling sensory-to-motor mappings using neural nets and a 3D articulatory speech synthesizer. In: Proceedings of the 9th International Conference on Spoken Language Processing, Interspeech 2006, ICSLP, pp. 565–568 (2006a)

Kröger, B.J., Birkholz, P., Kannampuzha, J., Neuschaefer-Rube, C.: Learning to associate speech-like sensory and motor states during babbling. In: Proceedings of the 7th International Seminar on Speech Production. Belo Horizonte, Brazil, pp. 67–74 (2006b)

Kröger, B.J., Birkholz, P., Kannampuzha, J., Neuschaefer-Rube, C.: Spatial-to-joint coordinate mapping in a neural model of speech production. In: DAGA-Proceedings of the Annual Meeting of the German Acoustical Society. Braunschweig, Germany, pp. 561–562 (2006c)

Kröger, B.J., Birkholz, P., Kannampuzha, J., Neuschaefer-Rube, C.: Modeling the perceptual magnet effect and categorical perception using self-organizing neural networks. In: Proceedings of the International Congress of Phonetic Sciences. Saarbrücken, Germany (2007)

Kröger, B.J., Schröder, G., Opgen-Rhein, C.: A gesture-based dynamic model describing articulatory movement data. Journal of the Acoustical Society of America 98, 1878–1889 (1995)

Lindblom, B.: Spectrographic study of vowel reduction. Journal of the Acoustical Society of America 35, 1773–1781 (1963)

Mermelstein, P.: Articulatory model for the study of speech production. Journal of the Acoustical Society of America 53, 1070–1082 (1973)

Ogata, K., Sonoda, Y.: Evaluation of articulatory dynamics and timing based on cascaded first-order systems. In: Proceedings of the 5th Seminar on Speech Production, Kloster Seeon, Germany, pp. 321–324 (2000)

Paine, R.W., Tani, J.: Motor primitive and sequence self-organization in a hierarchical recurrent neural network. Neural Networks 17, 1291–1309 (2004)

Perkell, J.S., Matthies, M., Lane, H., Guenther, F., Wilhelms-Tricarico, R., Wozniak, J., Guiod, P.: Speech motor control: Acoustic goals, saturaltion effects, auditory feedback and internal models. Speech communication 22, 227–250 (1997)

Saltzman, E.L., Munhall, K.G.: A dynamic approach to gestural patterning in speech production. Ecological Psychology 1, 333–382 (1989)

Smith, C.L., Browman, C.P., Kay, B., McGowan, R.S.: Extracting dynamic parameters from speech movement data. Journal of the Acoustical Society of America 93, 1580–1588 (1993)

Sober, S.J., Sabes, P.N.: Multisensory integration during motor planning. The Journal of Neuroscience 23, 6982–6992 (2003)

Stevens, K.N.: On the quantal nature of speech. Journal of Phonetics 17, 3–45 (1989)

Strange, W.: Dynamic specification of coarticulated vowels spoken in sentence context. Journal of the Acoustical Society of America 85, 2135–2153 (1989)

Titze, I.R.: Parameterization of the glottal area, glottal flow, and vocal fold contact area. Journal of the Acoustical Society of America 75, 570–580 (1984)

Todorov, E.: Optimality principles in sensorimotro control. Nature Neuroscience 7, 907–915 (2004)

A Novel Psychoacoustically Motivated Multichannel Speech Enhancement System

Amir Hussain[1], Simone Cifani[2], Stefano Squartini[2], Francesco Piazza[2], and Tariq Durrani[3]

[1] Department of Computing Science & Mathematics, University of Stirling, Stirling, FK9 4LA, Scotland, UK
ahu@cs.stir.ac.uk
http://www.cs.stir.ac.uk/~ahu
[2] Dipartimento di Elettronica, Intelligenza Artificiale e Telecomunicazioni, Università Politecnica delle Marche, Via Brecce Bianche 31, 60131, Ancona, Italy
http://www.deit.univpm.it
[3] Institute of Communications & Signal Processing, University of Strathclyde, Glasgow, G1 1XW, Scotland, UK
t.durrani@eee.strath.ac.uk

Abstract. The ubiquitous noise reduction / speech enhancement problem has gained an increasing interest in recent years. This is due both to progress made by microphone-array systems and to the successful introduction of perceptual models. In the last decade, several methods incorporating psychoacoustic criteria in single channel speech enhancement systems have been proposed, however very few works exploit these features in the multichannel case. In this paper we present a novel psychoacoustically motivated, multichannel speech enhancement system that exploits spatial information and psychoacoustic concepts. The proposed framework offers enhanced flexibility allowing for a multitude of perceptually-based post-filtering solutions. Moreover, the system has been devised on a frame-by-frame basis to facilitate real-time implementation. Objective performance measures and informal subjective listening tests for the case of speech signals corrupted with real car and F-16 cockpit noise demonstrate enhanced performance of the proposed speech enhancement system in terms of musical residual noise reduction compared to conventional multichannel techniques.

Keywords: Adaptive signal processing, array signal processing, auditory properties, noise reduction.

1 Introduction

Multichannel techniques offer advantages in noise reduction due to their capability to incorporate both spatial and spectral information in the enhancement process. Although the generalized sidelobe canceller (GSC) beamformer was introduced by Griffiths and Jim more than twenty years ago, applications of beamforming to the speech enhancement problem have emerged recently. Gannot et al. [1] presented a

A. Esposito et al. (Eds.): Verbal and Nonverbal Commun. Behaviours, LNAI 4775, pp. 190–199, 2007.
© Springer-Verlag Berlin Heidelberg 2007

linearly constrained GSC beamformer that considers arbitrary transfer functions (TFs) and that can be implemented by estimating only the TFs ratios, namely the TF-GSC. An important issue is how to exploit the spatial information provided by the multiple observations in a postfiltering block to further improve the enhanced signal. An integrated speech enhancement system including the above TF-GSC beamformer, a multichannel signal detection algorithm and a postfiltering stage has been presented by Gannot and Cohen in [2]. The proposed system uses optimally-modified Log-spectral Amplitude (OM-LSA) postfilter, which is an extension of the Ephraim and Malah LSA taking into account speech presence uncertainty. This is accomplished by estimating the speech presence probability exploiting spatial information provided by the GSC.

In relation to psychoacoustically motivated research, Goetze *et al.* presented a multichannel noise reduction approach in [8] for stereo systems, based on a simple delay and sum beamformer and a postfiltering block. Diverse suppression rules were tested, including the perceptually-based rule proposed by Gustafsson [5]. Other perceptually motivated noise reduction techniques have also emerged recently. Most of them propose a heuristic application of psychoacoustic principles to an existing suppression rule [6]. Wolfe and Godsill [7] attempted to integrate these principles into the enhancement process by quantitatively defining a cost function (that explicitly considered auditory masking) and then derived a suppression rule.

In this paper we integrate this perceptually optimal suppression rule with the state-of-the-art TF-GSC beamformer [1] deriving a more flexible and open framework with respect to conventional multichannel speech enhancement systems. This paper is organized as follows: The assumed model and the TF-GSC beamformer are described in section 2. Section 3 is a brief description of the overall proposed system framework. Section 4 describes the multichannel signal detection block and Section 5 summarized the derivation of the perceptually optimal spectral amplitude estimator. Section 6 discusses the evaluation criteria employed and presents preliminary experimental results using a variety of noisy datasets. Finally some concluding remarks are given in section 7.

2 Problem Formulation and GSC Beamforming

The considered model assumes that M microphone signals, $z_1(t),\ldots, z_M(t)$, record a source $x(t)$ and M uncorrelated noise interfering signals $d_1(t),\ldots, d_M(t)$. Thus, the i-th microphone signal is given by

$$z_i(t) = a_i(t) * x(t) + d_i(t), \ 1 \le i \le M \tag{1}$$

where $a_i(t)$ is the impulse response of the i-th sensor to the desired source, and $*$ denotes convolution. Hence, applying the short-time Fourier Transform (STFT) to (1), assuming time-invariant impulse responses [1], and observing that we are not interested in channel-balancing (so we can consider the model where the first channel becomes unity) we have the following:

$$Z_1(k,l) = X(k,l) + D_1(k,l)$$
$$Z_2(k,l) = A_2(k)X(k,l) + D_2(k,l)$$

$$\hbar$$

$$Z_M(k,l) = A_M(k)X(k,l) + D_M(k,l)$$

(2)

where k is the frequency bin index, and l the time-frame index. We can rewrite the set of equations (2) in a more compact matrix form

$$\mathbf{Z}(k,l) = \mathbf{A}(k)X(k,l) + \mathbf{D}(k,l)$$

(3)

where $\mathbf{Z}$, $\mathbf{A}$, X, $\mathbf{D}$ are M-complex vectors.

From Fig. 1 it can be seen that the linearly constrained GSC is composed of three main parts: a fixed beamformer (FBF) $\mathbf{W}(k)$, a blocking matrix (BM) $\mathbf{B}(k)$, and a multichannel adaptive noise canceller (ANC) $\mathbf{H}(k, l)$. The FBF is an array of weighting filters that suppresses or enhances signals arriving from different directions by destructive or constructive interference. The column of the BM can be regarded as a set of spatial filters suppressing any component impinging from the direction of the signal of interest, thus yielding $M - 1$ reference noise signals $U(k, l)$. These signals are used by the ANC to construct a noise signal to be subtracted from the FBF output, in the process attempting to eliminate stationary noise that passes through the fixed beamformer, and thus yielding an enhanced signal $Y(k, l)$. The ANC, $\mathbf{H}$, is updated at each time-frame using the normalized Least Mean Squares (NLMS) algorithm.

Note that in the TF-GSC, the matrices $\mathbf{W}$ and $\mathbf{B}$ are constructed using the TF ratios, which have to be estimated using some system identification procedure. In our current implementation, the TFs have been estimated offline using the algorithm proposed by Shalvi and Weinstein in [12]. A potential improvement considering the uncertainty of desired signal presence in the observed signals and allowing an efficient online estimation was recently proposed by Cohen in [13].

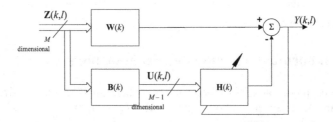

Fig. 1. Generalized Sidelobe Canceller (GSC)

3 Proposed Framework Overview

A block diagram of the proposed framework is shown in Fig. 2. After the beamforming stage, the beamformer (BF) output, $Y(k, l)$, is post-filtered using a perceptually-optimal spectral amplitude (PO-SA) estimator (which is described later in section 5). The PO-SA requires, for its computation, the global masking threshold, $Th(k, l)$, and the *a priori* SNR $\xi(k, l)$, of $Y(k, l)$. Since the global masking threshold is better estimated on a clean signal and as we need to estimate $\xi(k, l)$, the well-known Ephraim and Malah log-spectral amplitude estimator (LSA) [9] is previously applied to $Y(k, l)$, yielding a partially enhanced signal $Y_{en}(k, l)$ and a "decision-directed" estimate of $\xi(k, l)$. The partially enhanced signal and the reference noise signals are used by the multichannel signal detector to distinguish between desired transient components and noise transient components in the estimation of the global masking threshold. The PO-SA estimation is then carried out and the beamformer output, $Y(k, l)$, can finally be post-filtered. In the next section 4, the proposed multi-channel signal detection block is described and the PO-SA block is described in section 5.

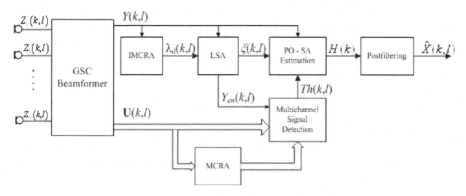

Fig. 2. Proposed System

4 Multichannel Signal Detection

To further improve the postfiltering process, one can capitalize spatial information provided by the beamformer. Generally, each spectral component k of each reference noise signal $U(k, l)$ and of the enhanced signal $Y(k, l)$ is a sum of three components, a nonstationary desired source component, a pseudostationary noise component, and a transient interference. In [2], the authors observed that transient signal components are relatively strong at the beamformer output, whereas transient noise components are relatively strong at one of the reference noise signals and accordingly proposed a detection method based on the ratio between the transient power at the beamformer output and the transient power at the reference noise signals, termed the transient beam-to-reference ratio (TBRR), which indicates whether a transient component is more likely due to speech or interfering noise.

In the proposed method, the multichannel signal detection is carried out on a perceptual basis by means of a psychoacoustic (PA) model. Masking refers to a process where one sound is rendered inaudible because of the presence of another sound. Simultaneous masking may occur when two or more stimuli are simultaneously presented to the auditory system. From a frequency-domain point of view, the absolute threshold of hearing is raised in the frequency regions close to the masker, hiding the presence of other weaker spectral components. A global masking threshold taking into account these masking effects can be estimated using a PA model. Since the global masking threshold, $\hat{Th}(k)$, is better estimated on the cleanest signal as possible, a rough enhancement procedure is firstly performed. The reference noise signals are enhanced using spectral subtraction, while the BF output is cleaned using the LSA estimator [9]. The reasons are twofold: firstly LSA provides better enhancement, and secondly it requires the computation of the *a priori* SNR, $\xi(k)$, which is also needed by the subsequent PO-SA block, which can therefore be estimated only once. To keep the computational load low, only the pseudostationary noise of the BF output is estimated via the so called Improved Minima Controlled Recursive Averaging (IMCRA) algorithm [4], while for reference noise signals a simpler Minima Controlled Recursive Averaging (MCRA) estimation [3] is used. Since the LSA estimation is carried out within the IMCRA algorithm, the LSA block of Fig. 2 can be removed by using the same estimate of $\xi(k)$ for either IMCRA or PO-SA blocks. In doing this, special attention has to be paid to the choice of the weighting parameter in the "decision-directed" *a priori* SNR estimate. The spectrally-subtracted signals are then fed to the psychoacoustic model. A slightly modified version of the ISO-11172 Psychoacoustic model 1 has been used. Assuming that the input signals are in the frequency domain, the model can be divided in four steps: a) identification of tonal and noise maskers, b) decimation and reorganization of maskers, c) calculation of individual masking thresholds, d) calculation of the global masking threshold. Recalling [10], a tonal component is a local maximum in the PSD that exceed neighboring components within a certain Bark distance by at least 7dB. Consequently, the tonal set is defined as:

$$S_T = \{ P(k) \mid P(k) > P(k \pm 1) \ and \ P(k) > P(k \pm \Delta k) + 7dB \} \tag{4}$$

where k varies with frequency. For an 8 kHz sampling frequency we have chosen a constant $k = 2$. Note that hereafter the time-frame index l has been omitted for notational simplicity purposes. A tonal masker is then associated to each spectral peak, according to:

$$P_{TM}(k) = 10 \log_{10} \sum_{j=-1}^{1} 10^{P(k+j)/10} \ [dB] \tag{5}$$

where energy from three adjacent spectral components centered at the peak is combined to form a single tonal masker. Residual spectral energy within a critical band not associated with a tonal masker must, by default, be associated with a noise masker. Thus, for each critical band a single noise masker is computed for remaining spectral lines not within the $\pm \Delta k$ neighborhood of a tonal masker using the sum:

$$P_{NM}(\bar{k}) = 10 \log_{10} \sum_{j} 10^{P(j)/10}, \ \forall P(j) \notin \{ P_{TM}(k, k \pm 1, k \pm \Delta k) \} \tag{6}$$

where

$$\bar{k} = \left(\prod_{j=l}^{u} j \right)^{1/(l-u+1)} \tag{7}$$

with l, u indicating the lower and upper bound of the critical band, respectively.

Therefore, the position of tonal and noise maskers indicates the energy distribution along the frame and, specifically, the tonal set can be regarded as a set containing desired and undesired transient components. Recalling the consideration made at the beginning of this section, these transient components may be detected by comparing tonal maskers between the BF output and the reference noise signals.

Let $\mathbf{TM} = [TM_Y \, TM_{U_1} \dots TM_{U_{M-1}}]^T$ be a $M \times K$ matrix containing the tonal maskers of the BF output signal and the reference noise signals for each time-frame l, respectively. Each row is defined as follows:

$$TM_i(k) = \begin{cases} P_{TM_i}(k) & \forall k : P_{TM_i}(k) \neq 0 \\ 0 & otherwise \end{cases} \tag{8}$$

The comparison of tonal makers is summarized in the following pseudo-code:

```
for each frequency bin k
    if TM(1, k) ≠ 0
        for 2 ≤ i ≤ M
            for Δ₁ (k) ≤ k' ≤ Δᵤ (k)
                if TM(i, k') > TM(1, k)
                    TM(1, k) = ATh(k)
            end
        end
end
```

where $_l(k)$ and $_u(k)$ define the subband interval, $ATh(k)$ is the absolute threshold of hearing and $z(k)$ is an Hz to Bark transformation. In our test the subband intervals are defined in accordance with the critical bands.

Hence, we get a new set of tonal maskers, where those due to interfering noise have been lowered at the corresponding value of the absolute threshold of hearing, $ATh(k)$, which can then be used in the b), c) and d) steps of the PA model to compute the global masking threshold, $\hat{T}h(k)$. A more detailed description of the PA model can be found in [10]. The next section 5 summarized the PO-SA estimation block.

5 Perceptually Optimal Spectral Amplitude (PO-SA) Estimation

The previously estimated global masking threshold, $\hat{T}h(k)$, and *a priori* SNR, $\hat{\xi}(k)$, are used to derive a perceptually-optimal spectral amplitude (PO-SA) estimator. In order to improve the perceived signal quality, masking properties of the human auditory system have been exploited by several researchers. Most perceptually-motivated noise reduction techniques use the global masking threshold to heuristically adjust the parameters of an existing suppression rule [6]. In [7] Wolfe and Godsill showed that the derivation of a suppression rule can be regarded as a Bayesian estimation of a random variables X (the clean speech spectral amplitude) as a function of the observations of some related random variable Y (the noisy speech spectral amplitude). The Bayes estimate minimizes the risk with respect to $f_{X,Y}(X, Y)$, the joint probability density function of X and Y, of a non-negative cost function $C(x, \hat{x})$ of x and its estimate $\hat{x}$ as follows:

$$\hat{X}^{opt} = \arg\min_{\hat{x}} \left\{ \int_{-\infty}^{\infty} C(X, \hat{X}) f_{X|Y}(X|Y) dX \right\} \tag{9}$$

It is interesting to note that, the classical MMSE estimation, for example, can be viewed as a quadratic cost function, $C(x, \hat{x}) = |\hat{x} - x|^2$. Depending on the considered cost and joint probability density functions, one can obtain different estimators. This feature and the possibility to improve or change the global masking threshold estimation make our proposed system extremely flexible to exploiting different perceptually-based post-filtering solutions. In the current implementation we used a cost function that is both simple and efficient and can be seen as a generalization of the well-known MMSE criterion to include a masking threshold Th. The idea is that the cost of an estimation error is always zero if it falls below the masking threshold, namely:

$$C(X, \hat{X}) = \begin{cases} \left(|\hat{X}| - |X| \right)^2 - Th^2, & \text{if } \left\| |\hat{X}| - |X| \right\| > Th \\ 0 & \text{otherwise} \end{cases} \tag{10}$$

Assuming the same statistical model used by Ephraim and Malah in [9] and the cost function (10), the minimization problem (9) can be solved. As an analytical expression is not achievable, the solution is found using numerical methods. However, for the sake of computational efficiency, an approximation can be formulated [9] as follows:

$$H(k) = \begin{cases} \max \left\{ \dfrac{\hat{Th}(k)}{|Y(k)|}, \dfrac{\hat{\xi}(k)}{1+\hat{\xi}(k)} \right\}, & \text{if } |Y(k)| > \hat{Th}(k) \\ 1 & \text{otherwise} \end{cases} \tag{11}$$

The fully enhanced output signal $\hat{X}(k)$ is the finally obtained as follows:

$$\hat{X}(k) = H(k)Y(k) \tag{12}$$

6   Simulations and Results

We tested the system using a five-channels implementation. We used 8 kHz recordings of three different types of noise, namely: Gaussian, car noise and F-16 cockpit noise. Input data had on average -3dB and -6dB overall manufactured SNR. The time-frequency analysis was done with a Hanning window of size 512 samples with 50% overlap. The proposed noise reduction algorithm was applied on a set of voices (both male and female) corrupted with additive noise. For the sake of comparison we also implemented the state-of-the-art multi-channel speech enhancement system proposed by Gannot and Cohen in [2] that integrated the TF-GSC beamformer with the multichannel signal detection algorithm and a postfiltering stage. The enhanced speech was evaluated with objective measures and an informal listening test as well. The objective measures reported here are the segmental SNR and the Log-Likelihood ratio, also referred to as the Itakura distance, each of which is defined as follows [11]:

$$SegSNR = \frac{10}{L}\sum_{l=0}^{L-1}\frac{\sum_{n=0}^{K-1}x_d^2\left(n+lK/2\right)}{\sum_{n=0}^{K-1}\left[x_d\left(n+lK/2\right)-x_\phi\left(n+lK/2\right)\right]^2} \tag{13}$$

$$LLR\left(\overset{\hbar}{a}_d,\overset{\hbar}{a}_\phi\right)=\log\left(\frac{\overset{\hbar}{a}_d R_\phi \overset{\hbar}{a}_d^T}{\overset{\hbar}{a}_\phi R_\phi \overset{\hbar}{a}_\phi^T}\right) \tag{14}$$

where $\overset{u}{a}$ denotes a linear prediction (LP) coefficient vector, R is the autocorrelation matrix, L represents the number of frames in the signal and the subscripts d and ϕ refers to clean and enhanced speech, respectively.

Tables I and II summarize the segSNRs achieved by the conventional system of [2] and by our proposed system for a -3dB and a -6dB overall input SNR, respectively. Sample Figures 3 (a)-(d) respectively show, a -6dB noisy input waveform for a female speaker, corruptive car noise, the enhanced signal using system in [2], the enhanced signal using the proposed system, and the Itakura distance for the proposed system (solid) and the system in [2] (dashed). These, and other similar, results confirm that our proposed system is able to achieve comparable or better SNR values to the conventional system of [2]. Informal listening tests using random presentation of the processed signals to four young male adults and to two female adults showed that the noisy speech signals processed by the proposed system were of better perceived quality in terms of lower perceived musical residual noise compared to the other method of [2].

Table 1. Segmental SNR for –3dB male and female input signals

Noise	Proposed System		System [2]	
	Male	Female	Male	Female
Gaussian	0.1	-1.9	-0.6	-2.8
Car noise	1.0	-0.7	0.6	-2.1
F16-cockpit	-0.3	-1.8	-0.6	-3.8

Table 2. Segmental SNR for –6dB male and female input signals

Noise	Proposed System		System [2]	
	Male	Female	Male	Female
Gaussian	-0.8	-2.7	-1.1	-4.5
Car noise	0.2	-0.9	0.3	-2.4
F16-cockpit	-1.1	-2.8	-1.4	-5.2

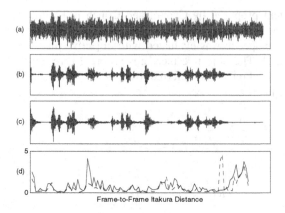

Fig. 3. Noisy input signal (-6 dB, car noise) – (a); Enhanced signal using Cohen system – (b) and using the proposed system - (c); Itakura distance for the proposed system (solid) and for the Cohen system (dashed) – (d).

7   Conclusion

Multi-microphone arrays often suffer when the noise field tends to become more diffused, urging for some postfiltering technique to further reduce the noise at the beamformer output. In this contribution we have presented a new approach to multichannel noise reduction that exploits the state of the art both in array signal processing and perceptually based spectral subtraction deriving a much more flexible and open framework with respect to conventional multichannel speech enhancement systems. In preliminary experiments, the algorithm has been assessed by virtue of objective and subjective quality measures and has proven to be robust, especially in very noisy environments, yielding a comparatively lower musical residual noise compared to [2]. The reduction in perceived musical noise is attributed to the novel introduction of the perceptually optimal suppression rule that works on the output of the state-of-the-art TF-GSC beamformer. A detailed theoretical analysis is now proposed to define the attainable performance along with more formal subjective listening tests.

Note that whilst the preliminary results reported in this paper should be taken with care, they do give interesting information on the limits of such methods as well as on the enhancement brought about by the new scheme. Further experiments will use other extensive real data sets, as well as speech recognizers and normal hearing human subjects in order to further assess and formally quantify the perceived speech quality and intelligibility improvements obtained by use of the proposed multi-channel speech enhancement system. In addition, a real-time sub-band implementation of the GSC beamformer, exploiting ideas from the multi-microphone sub-band adaptive (MMSBA) framework of [14], will also be developed in order to further reduce the computational load.

References

1. Gannot, S., Burshtein, D., Weinstein, E.: Signal enhancement using beamforming and nonstationarity with applications to speech. IEEE Trans. Signal Processing 49(8), 1614–1626 (2001)
2. Gannot, S., Cohen, I.: Speech enhancement based on the general transfer function GSC and postfiltering. IEEE Trans. Speech and Audio Processing 12(6), 561–571 (2004)
3. Cohen, I., Berdugo, B.: Speech enhancement for nonstationary noise environments. Signal Processing 81(11), 2403–2418 (2001)
4. Cohen, I.: Noise spectrum estimation in adverse environments: Improved minima controlled recursive averaging. IEEE Trans. Speech and Audio Processing 11(5), 466–475 (2003)
5. Gustafsson, S., Jax, P., Vary, P.: A novel psychoacoustically motivated audio enhancement algorithm preserving background noise characteristics. In: ICASSP, pp. 397–400 (1998)
6. Virag, N.: Single channel speech enhancement based on masking properties of the human auditory system. IEEE Trans. on Speech and Audio Processing 7(2), 126–137 (1999)
7. Wolfe, P., Godsill, S.: The application of psychoacoustic criteria to the restoration of musical recordings. In: Proc. 108th AES Conv. (2000)
8. Goetze, S., Mildner, V., Kammeyer, K.D.: A psychoacoustic noise reduction approach for stereo hands-free systems. In: Proc. 120th AES Conv., Paris (May 20-23, 2006)
9. Ephraim, Y., Malah, D.: Speech enhancement using a minimum mean-square error log-spectral amplitude estimator. IEEE Trans. Acoustics, Speech and Sig. Proc. 33(2), 443–445 (1985)
10. Painter, T., Spanias, A.: Perceptual coding of digital audio. Proc. of the IEEE 88(4), 451–513 (2000)
11. Hansen, J.H.L., Pellom, B.L.: An effective evaluation protocol for speech enhancement algorithms. In: Proc. of the Int. Conf. on Speech and Language Processing, vol. 6, pp. 2819–2822 (1998)
12. Shalvi, O., Weinstein, E.: System identification using nonstationary signals. IEEE Trans. signal Processing 44, 2055–2063 (1996)
13. Cohen, I.: Relative transfer function identification using speech signals. IEEE Trans. Speech and Audio Processing 12(5), 451–459 (2004)
14. Hussain, A., Squartini, S., Piazza, F.: Novel Sub-band Adaptive Systems Incorporating Wiener Filtering for Binaural Speech Enhancement. In: Faundez-Zanuy, M., Janer, L., Esposito, A., Satue-Villar, A., Roure, J., Espinosa-Duro, V. (eds.) NOLISP 2005. LNCS, vol. 3817, pp. 318–327. Springer, Heidelberg (2006)

Analysis of Verbal and Nonverbal Acoustic Signals with the Dresden UASR System

Rüdiger Hoffmann, Matthias Eichner, and Matthias Wolff

Technische Universität Dresden, Institut für Akustik und Sprachkommunikation
01062 Dresden, Germany
{ruediger.hoffmann,matthias.eichner,matthias.wolff}@ias.et.tu-dresden.de
http://www.ias.et.tu-dresden.de/sprache

Abstract. During the last few years, a framework for the development of algorithms for speech analysis and synthesis was implemented. The algorithms are connected to common databases on the different levels of a hierarchical structure. This framework which is called UASR (Unified Approach for Speech Synthesis and Recognition) and some related experiments and applications are described. Special focus is directed to the suitability of the system for processing nonverbal signals. This part is related to the analysis methods which are addressed in the COST 2102 initiative now. A potential application field in interaction research is discussed.

Keywords: Speech analysis; graph learning; finite state machines; speech analysis; acoustic signal processing.

1 Introduction

Considering the evolving computer technology in the 1960-th, the Dresden University founded a research unit for communication and measurement in 1969. Since then, the acoustic human-computer interaction is one of the main aspects in research and teaching. This unit is now named "Institute of Acoustics and Speech Communication" and includes the chair for Communication Acoustics and the chair for System Theory and Speech Technology.

The main activities at the chair for System Theory and Speech Technology in the past have been directed to the development of speech recognizers and text-to-speech (TTS) systems. In both directions, special effort was concentrated to versions which are suited to be applied in embedded systems. An overview of the activities in speech synthesis was recently given in [1]. Prosody models have been developed and applied for the improvement of speech recognition systems and also of TTS systems. Of course, the development of the speech databases is an essential part of these activities.

At the end of the 1990-th, the collection of algorithms in speech recognition (and speech synthesis also) required the definition of a common experimental platform, and the UASR concept was developed. This paper is intended to give an overview of the projects which were carried out around the UASR.

A. Esposito et al. (Eds.): Verbal and Nonverbal Commun. Behaviours, LNAI 4775, pp. 200–218, 2007.
© Springer-Verlag Berlin Heidelberg 2007

2 Unified Approach to Speech Synthesis and Recognition (UASR)

2.1 System Concept

It was the basic observation which initiated the idea of UASR that the different databases in speech recognition and in speech synthesis were more and more converging at the end of the 1990-th (see Table 1). For companies working in speech technology, the speech databases are much more complicated to acquire and much more valuable than the algorithms. The UASR framework considers this tendency by arranging a combination of speech recognition and speech synthesis modules around common databases in a hierarchical structure. The basic idea which we published firstly in [2] is illustrated in Figure 1.

Table 1. Selected databases in speech recognizers and synthesis

	Recognizer	Synthesizer
Phrase level	Language model (stochastic n-gram grammar and/or regular grammar)	Rules or neural nets for determination of phrase boundaries and accents; language model in special cases, e. g. for concept-to-speech (CTS)
Word level	Pronunciation dictionary (sometimes with pronunciation variants)	Rules or neural nets for grapheme-to-phoneme conversion, complemented by an exception dictionary
Sound level	Phoneme models (monophones, triphones, etc.), normally as HMM	Sounds or sound combinations, represented parametric or as waveforms

The implementation of the UASR was initiated for two reasons. At first (as already mentioned), a platform for the development of speech related algorithms was required. It required in parallel the definition of a suited software technology. For this purpose, the system dLabPro was developed basing on former own solutions. It consists mainly of an object oriented class library. Programming is performed in a special script language or C.

Secondly (and maybe more important), the UASR is an object of basic research. The left part obviously describes the hierarchy of a speech analyzer / recognizer whereas the right part is a text-to-speech system. Both parts are not understood in a completely satisfactory way until now, and the common arrangement offers a way to re-establish the classic approach of analysis-by-synthesis to understand the processes better and optimize the models.

In the bottom up-process of the left side of the model, information is stepwise reduced. The information which is striped off in this way describes preferably the personal features which are included in the speech signal but are not considered because speech recognition should be speaker independent. In Figure 1, this information is summarized as prosody which is, of course, a simplification. The personal features in turn play a more and more important role in the top-down

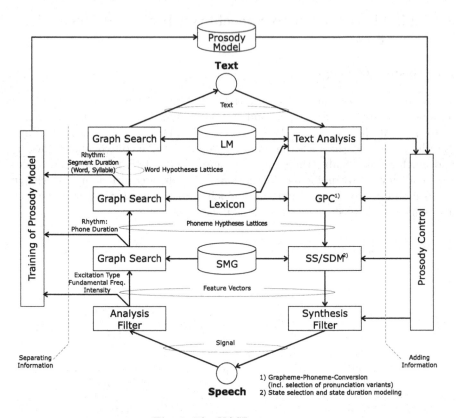

Fig. 1. The UASR structure

process of speech synthesis at the opposite side because synthetic speech should be as personalized as possible. The transfer of the personal features which is illustrated in the model by a separate link is an interesting research object.

2.2 Structure Learning as Core Problem

The knowledge on the different levels of the UASR system can be expressed predominantly by graph structures. Therefore it was necessary to implement a number of graph handling and training algorithms. We mention some graph structures as examples for which the development of training algorithms was performed:

– On the phone level, knowledge is usually expressed by hidden Markov models (HMM). We adopted a special version of HMM called structured Markov graphs which were originally introduced by Wolfertstetter and Ruske to improve the performance of speech recognizers [3]. While the behavior of the HMM states is originally described by mixtured Gauss densities, they are splitted for the SMGs in several states which are described by one Gaussian density only (see Figure 2). This method allows a more explicit modelling

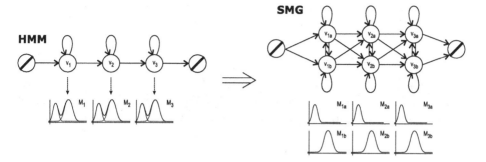

Fig. 2. Converting a HMM into a SMG

of trajectories in the feature space which is useful especially if the phone models are applied in the synthesis branch of the system. We implemented several SMG training procedures which are summarized in [4].

– On the word level, pronunciation dictionaries are required for the analysis branch of the UASR as well as for the synthesis branch. They can be given by definition but also acquired by a training procedure. The latter shows benefits especially if pronunciation variants have to be considered in the dictionary. Following a proposal of Westendorf [5], the training of pronunciation dictionaries formed a research focus of our group for a long time, starting with the German Verbmobil project [6,7] and ending up with a DFG project which aimed to the construction of hierarchical dictionaries [8]. A final overview is given in [9]. An example graph is shown in Fugure 3.

– A higher-level example for considering rules of pronunciation refers to the pronunciation of numbers. In a cooperation project with an industrial partner, a training method had to be developed which allowed learning the pronunciation of numbers in different languages from examples (e. g. that 123 is spelled in English as "one hundred and twenty three") [10].

It became clear that the unification of the training algorithms for the different graph structures on the different levels of the UASR model was necessary. Therefore we adopted the concept of FSMs (Finite State Machines) and

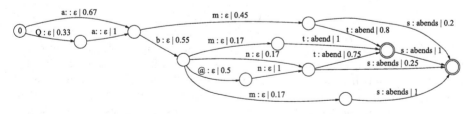

Fig. 3. Pronunciation network for the German word "abends" (*in the evening*). This model was automatically learned from the read speech corpus PhonDat II with the method described in [6].

developed modules which are basing on the relations between graph learning and automata. We describe this approach in the next section.

2.3 FSM Implementation

On virtually every hierarchy level speech may be represented as strings of symbols (see table 2). The deterministic or stochastic relations between these levels can be expressed by finite state machines (FSM) where the symbols on one level form the input of the automata and the symbols of another level are their output.

Table 2. The most essential application fields of finite automata in speech technology

Problem	Knowledge source(s)	Essential algorithms
Command recognition	HMM (Transductor) Word list (Transductor) Regular grammar (Acceptor)	Composition Minimization Synchronous search (DP)
Recognition of continuous speech	HMM (Transductor) Lexicon (Transductor) Stochastic grammar (Acceptor)	Composition Minimization Synchronous search (DP)
Statistical grapheme-to-phoneme conversion	Stochastic grammar (Transductor)	Asynchronous search (A* search)
Unit selection for concatenative speech synthesis	Unit graph (Transductor)	Inference Asynchronous search (A* search)
Acoustic HMM synthesis (state selection)	HMM (Transductor)	Asynchronous search (A* search)

Finite state machines are widely applied. From the standpoint of system theory they fit into the concept of sequential automata (or discrete linear time invariant systems) as shown in figure 4. Such automata have a memory which stores the *internal state* $z(k)$ at time k of the system as well as *input* and *output* terminals $x(k)$ and $y(k)$. State, input and output values are all limited to finite sets (alphabets Z, X and Y). The individual automaton is characterized by its (time invariant) *behavioral function* w which determines for every possible state z and input symbol x the next state z' and an output symbol y

$$w : Z \times X \times Y \times Z \mapsto \mathbb{K}, \qquad (1)$$

where $\mathbb{K}$ stands for a scalar *weight*. A common exemplification of w is an automaton graph. Each automaton state is drawn as a vertex. Each element of w can be interpreted as a transition between two states which "consumes" an input symbol x and "emits" an output symbol y. w also assigns a weight $w(z, x, y, z') \in \mathbb{K}$ to each transition, most simply $\mathbb{K} = \{0, 1\}$ for "transition exists" or "transition does not exist". In general, weights allow stochastic relations between input and output symbols or strings, respectively. State transitions are drawn as edges of the automaton graph (see figure 5 for an example). The mathematical definition of a finite state machine is the 7-tuple

$$\mathcal{A} = \{X, Y, Z, I, F, \mathbb{K}, w\}, \tag{2}$$

where $I \in Z$ and $F \in Z$ denote designated start and final states of the automaton. $\mathbb{K}$ is usually not just a scalar but a semiring including aggregation operations along and across sequences of state transitions (so called *paths*) which are required for computations with automata. Table 3 lists the semirings implemented in the dLabPro FSM library.

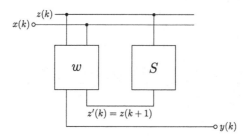

Fig. 4. General sequential automaton with behavioral function w, memory S, input and output terminals $x(k), y(k)$ and current and next internal state $z(k), z'(k)$

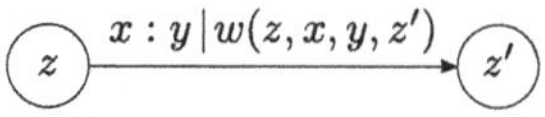

Fig. 5. Example for an automaton graph with states z and z' and transition $e = \{z, x, y, w(z, x, y, z'), z'\} \in w$

Table 3. Weight semirings implemented in the dLabPro FSM library. $x \oplus_{\log} y = -\ln\left(e^{-x} + e^{-y}\right)$ is the log. semiring addition

Semiring	Set	$\oplus$	$\otimes$	$\bar{0}$	$\bar{1}$	$\oslash$	$\oslash$	ext
Boolean	$\{0,1\}$	$\vee$	$\wedge$	0	1	n/a	n/a	n/a
real	$\mathbb{R}$	$+$	$\bullet$	0	1	$<$	$>$	max
probability	$[0,1]$	$+$	$\bullet$	0	1	$<$	$>$	max
logarithmic	$\mathbb{R} \cup \{-\infty, \infty\}$	$\oplus_{\log}$	$+$	∞	0	$>$	$<$	min
tropical	$\mathbb{R} \cup \{-\infty, \infty\}$	min	$+$	∞	0	$>$	$<$	min

As stated above FSMs are capable of bidirectionally translating strings between different hierarchy levels of speech. Figure 3 shows an example for the stochastic relation between phonetic strings (pronunciation variants) and the

Table 4. Automaton operations implemented in the dLabPro FSM library

Set operations	
$\mathcal{A} \cup \mathcal{B}$	Union
$\mathcal{A} \cap \mathcal{B}$	Intersection
$\mathcal{A} \setminus \mathcal{B}$	Difference
Rational operations	
$\mathcal{A}^*$	KLEENE closure
$\mathcal{A} \oplus \mathcal{B}$	Sum
$\mathcal{A} \otimes \mathcal{B}$	Product
Other operations	
$\mathcal{A}^{\leftarrow}$	Reversal
$\mathcal{A}^{-1}$	Inversion
proj $(\mathcal{A})$	Projection
$\mathcal{A} \times \mathcal{B}$	Cartesian product
$\mathcal{A} \circ \mathcal{B}$	Composition
Equivalence transformations: $\mathcal{A} \equiv \mathrm{op}(\mathcal{A})$	
$\langle \mathcal{A} \rangle$	Connection
$\xi(\mathcal{A})$	ε-removal
det $(\mathcal{A})$	Determinization
min $(\mathcal{A})$	Minimization
	Tree expansion
Search and approximation	
	n-best paths (A^* search)
	Dynamic programming
	Pruning

orthographic representations of two words. In this connection FSMs are often called *finite state transducers* (FST) in contrast to *finite state acceptors* (FSA) which do not emit any output and just "check" whether an input string is acceptable. With some generalizations finite state transducers can represent language models as well as lexicons and acoustic models. The latter require a somewhat broader concept of alphabets to allow continous observation vectors as input "symbols" of HMMs. This, however, does not make a difference in principle.

Using FSMs almost all tasks in speech recognition and many tasks in speech synthesis can be solved with a well defined set of automaton operations. As the community has done research on FSMs for many years, there are plenty of highly optimized algorithms available. We implemented the most important FSM operations in our experimental platform dLabPro (see table 4). The implementation is sufficient for

- automatic speech recognition,
- several tasks in speech synthesis (e.g. text pre-processing, grapheme-phoneme-conversion and acoustic unit selection), and
- FSM learning.

3 Some Experiments and Applications

3.1 Speech Server

Selected components of UASR have been used in different projects with practical background. E. g., the implementation of a client-server structure for speech recognition was necessary in an e-learning project. In this structure (Figure 6), the speech recognition system (basing on UASR algorithms) is located at the server completely. A Java applet for sound I/O and for the communication with the server runs at the client which needs no special software.

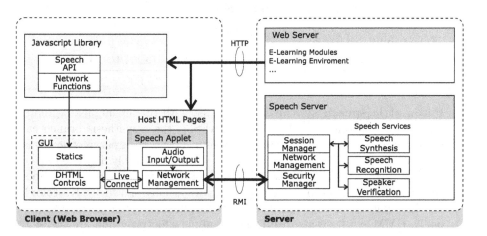

Fig. 6. Client-server architecture

Phoneme recognition rates of the UASR recognizer subsystem were measured in the context of the development of the Speech Server. Table 5 shows the recognition rates (Accuracy (A), Correctness (C), Density (HD)) dependent on the data base, the acoustic analysis (Mel-Cepstrum (MC), Cepstrum (CP), Mel-Log-Spectrum (MF)), and the decoding strategy (best chain vs. hypothesis based). The models include approx. 309600 parameters.

3.2 Parametric Speech Synthesis

The synthesis branch of UASR is potentially useful for a number of investigations:

– **Analysis by synthesis methods:** This was the most interesting aspect of UASR when we were setting up the system. Because very few is known about the reasons of errors in the interior of a complex speech recognizer, the resynthesis of the former input on the different levels of the hierarchy could reveal valuable insights. Until now, the resynthesis mechanisms are implemented up to the word level.

Table 5. Results of phoneme recognition experiments with the recognizer of the Speech Server [4]

Database	Analysis	Best			Hypotheses		
		C	A	HD	C	A	HD
	MF	56.0	35.4	1.0	59.6	53.3	1.6
Verbmobil	CP	50.3	21.3	1.1	55.2	44.7	1.9
	MC	49.3	17.4	1.1	53.6	43.1	1.8
	MF	59.1	51.4	0.8	57.2	55.6	1.1
PhonDAT-II	CP	55.7	46.2	0.8	53.8	51.3	1.2
	MC	53.1	36.8	0.9	50.8	46.5	1.3
	MF	79.4	74.7	1.0	76.6	75.4	1.2
SynDAT	CP	70.7	57.0	1.0	70.0	67.9	1.6
	MC	77.1	67.2	1.0	75.2	72.0	1.5

- **Parametric speech synthesis:** Combined with proper linguistic preprocessing (e. g., from our TTS system DRESS), the resynthesis branch can
  serve as acoustic subsystem of a TTS system. This type of parametric acoustic synthesis is known as HMM synthesis and was probably discussed firstly
  in [12]. HMM synthesis shows interesting features. At first, a very good
  speech quality can be obtained. This was especially shown by K. Tokuda
  [13] in a impressive series of investigations during the last years [14]. Secondly, HMM synthesis algorithms need only low footprint and are therefore
  suited for embedded applications very well.
- **Framework for better personalization:** Speech synthesis will need better
  personalization in the near future. To obtain this, so-called adaptive personal
  features have to be considered in the synthesis process. It seems to be true
  that the suitability of parametric synthesis systems for these adaptation
  processes is essentially better than that of concatenative systems.

The following sequence of processing steps was implemented within the UASR
framework:

- Text processing / Grapheme-to-phoneme conversion / Prosodic processing
  (adopted from our TTS system DRESS)
- Selection of phoneme models (SMGs)
- State selection and state duration modelling
- Extraction of the feature vector sequence
- Inverse feature transformation (PCA)
- Generation of the excitation signal
- Acoustic synthesis

The analysis filter of the recognition branch of the UASR and the synthesis
filter of the synthesis branch must be complementary to each other to fulfill

the purpose of the whole system. In our first version [16], we used MFCC features for the analysis because an inverse filter is known from the literature [15]. Meanwhile, we studied a number of other parametric synthesis methods also because we are interested especially in solutions which are suited for embedded systems [17].

As a first step towards personalization, an inverse VTLN (vocal tract length normalization) algorithm was implemented that allows a male/female transformation of the voice with very low computational expenses [18].

3.3 Applying Speech Models and Pronunciation Dictionaries in Spontaneous Speech Synthesis

While the HMM synthesis refers to the lower levels of the synthesis branch of UASR, the following investigations aimed to study the influence of the higher-level databases to the synthesis process. These databases can be utilized to make the result of the synthesis branch more natural sounding. We tried to apply the available language models and pronunciation dictionaries (which include pronunciation variants) in the preprocessing part of TTS synthesis. The idea which is known from the literature [19,20] is basing on the observation that frequent words are usually pronounced more quickly than rare words. Therefore, the statistics from the language model can be used to control the selection of pronunciation variants of different length from the dictionary. We did it in the UASR framework to make the speech output of our TTS system DRESS more "spontaneous" [21].

Figure 7 shows an example. The graph represents a network of pronunciation variants for the German phrase *"morgens zwischen acht und neun"*. Nodes represent the word pronunciations, edges carry weights obtained from the

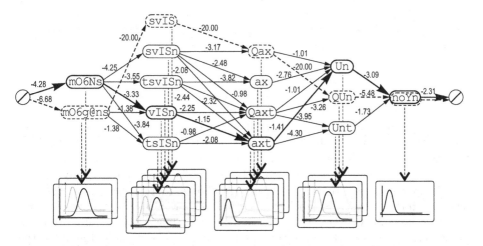

Fig. 7. Network of pronunciation variants for the German phrase "morgens zwischen acht und neun" [21] (explanation in the text)

pronunciation variant sequence model. The bold path denotes the pronunciations selected using the model. The Gaussians illustrate the different statistics
of the duration. The example shows the correct consideration of word boundary effects (e. g., the elision of /t/ and assimilation of /s/ between the first two
words). For comparison, the dashed edges show the path chosen considering only
target durations.

A number of listening experiments confirmed the expectations [22]. However,
the synthesized speech is far from real "spontaneous" speech. It became clear
the algorithms work very well while many unsolved problems are connected to
the databases. Spontaneous speech is not only characterized by pronunciation
variants but also by a large number of non-verbal effects which are not considered at all in our language models and dictionaries. Additionally, there is a
conflict between the databases because pronunciation variants are considered in
the dictionaries but not in the language models due to the restricted amount of
training material.

4   Classification of Non-verbal Acoustic Signals

We have seen from the last example that the expansion of our algorithms and
databases to non-verbal elements of communication has fundamental importance
for future research. This means that we must show the ability of the UASR
components to handle non-verbal signals. The easiest way to demonstrate this
is to apply the algorithms to non-speech signal. This is done in the next section
before we come back to non-verbal components of speech.

4.1   Non-speech Signals

The analysis of acoustic signals other than speech is required in very different
branches. Traditionally, heuristic signal processing and recognition methods are
applied which are mostly basing on numerical pattern recognition. With growing
complexity of the tasks, these classical methods fail or are at least difficult to
handle. The situation can be improved in many cases if the complex signals
are represented as structural models of acoustic events (e.g. through finite state
machines). The structural pattern recognition methods which were developed for
the purposes of speech processing have been successfully applied to the analysis
of such signals. The following table shows selected projects. Those which are
more recent have been solved using our UASR technology.

The quality assessment of musical instruments is one example for the classification of non-speech signals from Table 6. The goal of this study was to
provide a tool to instrument makers that allows to measure the influence of
changes in the production process on the sound characteristics of an instrument.
For this purpose we recorded a database of solo music pieces played on different instruments of the same type under varying conditions and adapted the
UASR concept to process the music signals. Acoustic modelling was done using

Table 6. Projects of the TU Dresden applying methods of speech recognition at nonspeech acoustic signals

Years	Projects	Partners	References
1985-1993	Analysis of livestock sounds	University of Leipzig and Inst. f. Kleintierforschung Merbitz	[23]
1999	Characterization of iron sheets basing on Barkhausen noise	TU Bergakademie Freiberg	[24]
1999-2002	Classification of snoring sounds	nighty electronics, Bad Salzdetfurth	[25]
2002-2004	Analysis of brake sounds	sinus GmbH Leipzig and voiceINTERconnect GmbH Dresden	[26]
2003-2006	Acoustic quality assessment of technical processes	Fraunhofer IZFP Dresden (funded by DFG)	[27]
2004-2006	Classification of Korotkov noise for non-invasive blood pressure measuring	Gesundheitstechnik Stier Neuruppin	[28,29]
2005-2006	Quality assessment of musical instruments basing on solo pieces	Inst. für Musikinstrumenten-bau Zwota (funded by German ministry BMBF)	[30]
2007-2008	Early fault recognition in spinning machinery	Consortium of institutes and companies (funded by German ministry BMWi)	

HMMs trained by a structure learning algorithm (Figure 8). We performed extensive subjective evaluations to study to what extent differences between instruments are perceivable and compared this with the results of the classification experiments.

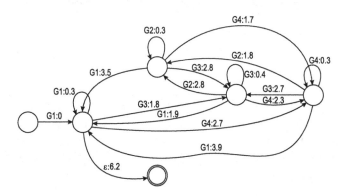

Fig. 8. HMM automaton graph for one individual guitar. The transitions are annotated with the index of a Gaussian PDF defining one state in the feature space and a weight (neg. log. transition probability).

Table 7. Projects in prosody research at TU Dresden

Years	Project	Partners	References
1960-th	Two-level model of German sentence intonation	Academy of Sciences in Berlin	[31,32]
1970-th	German microintonation and its application in speech synthesis	Humboldt University in Berlin	[33]
1980-th	German sentence intonation and its application in speech synthesis and rehabilitation engineering	Humboldt University in Berlin	[34]
1994-1998	Rule based intonation model	University of Tokyo	[35]
1995-1997	Learning intonation models		[37]
1998-2000	Rhythm, hybrid prosody model		[38,39]
2001-2003	Integrated prosody model	TFH Berlin	[40]
2001-2005	Speaking and reading styles		[43,44]
2001-2004	Application of wavelet analysis and evolutionary methods		[43,42]
2002	Multilinguality studies (English, Mandarin, French)	ICP Grenoble	[46,47]
2002-2003	Robust pitch analysis		[45]
2003	Intensity model of German		[48]
2004-2006	Automatic prosodic annotation of databases (English)	Siemens AG Munich	[49]

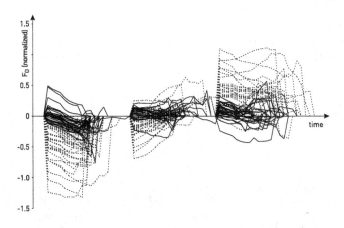

Fig. 9. Pitch contour of different spoken versions of the word "computer", pronounced as keyword (dotted) or in textual context (normal)

4.2   Speech Prosody

Investigating speech prosody plays a central role in the development of speech technology and was considered in the Dresden group since its founding. Table 7 shows the historic roots as well as the more recent activities. The have been directed to the development of the Dresden Speech Synthesis (DRESS) system but also to the utilization of prosodic information in speech recognition.

Figure 9 shows one of the applications of prosodic information in speech recognition. For the e-learning project which was already mentioned, improved keyword recognition was required. We investigated the prosodic differences which appeared between the different pronunciations of the word "computer" which was applied as keyword but also appeared in the normal text. In the figure, the dotted curves show the pitch contour of the keywords while the normal ones describe the pitch contour of the same word but in normal context of fluent

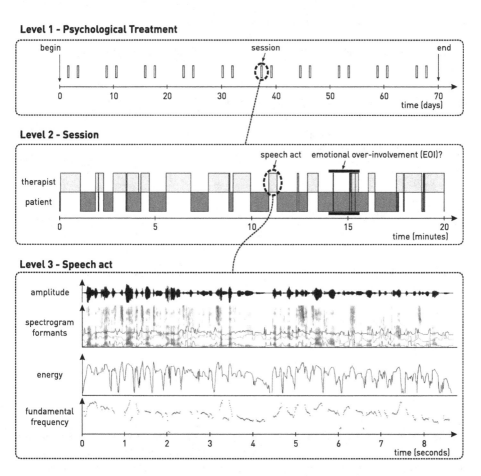

Fig. 10. Hypothetic course of a psychotherapy. Three levels showing different time-related scaling can be distinguished: 1. Treatment (t in days), 2. Session (t in minutes), 3. Speech act (t in seconds). On level 2, there are those sequences of interaction in the course of which the patient is activating his central intrapersonal conflict. This activation could be measured by the prosodic features associated with emotional over-involvement. The automatic identification and prediction is intended to be performed by means of acoustic features (level 3).

speech.Clearly, including the pitch information in the keyword recognizer improved the recognition rate essentially.

4.3   Interaction Research

It is intended now to extend the UASR architecture toward the extraction / addition of non-linguistic information from/to the speech signal. This includes the refinement of the existing prosodic analysis and control, but also the development of new methods which are suited to evaluate certain communication situations. As an example of this kind of analysis, a multidisciplinary project will be started which aims to the identification and prediction of specific situations during the psychotherapeutical treatment[1].

As can be seen in Figure 10, the analysis has to be performed on very different levels of timing (whole therapy / single therapy session / single speech act). Correspondingly, there are different structures which can be revealed by the analysis. In Figure 10, an example is marked by EOI which means emotional over-involvement. Episodes which show EOI are indicators for activated intrapersonal conflicts. A therapy could be successful, e. g., if episodes with EOI appear at the beginning but are disappeared in the final phase.

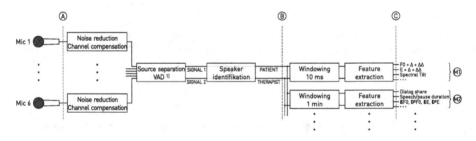

Ⓐ Sound recording of raw signal (6 channels, 16 bits, 16 kHz)
Ⓑ Sound recording of pre-processed signals (2 channels, 16 bits, 16 kHz)
Ⓒ Data recording (multichannel, XML, compressed, approx. 5-25 kbit/s)

Ⓜ1Ⓜ2 Feature data streams
  1) VAD = voice activity detection

Fig. 11. System for recording and feature extraction (acoustic frontend)

The project is also challenging from the acoustic point of view because a scene analysis has to be performed in an "acoustic frontend" which is in certain sense an extension of the lowest level of the UASR structure. According to Figure 11, the following tasks have to be solved for this multi-speaker scenario:

 – Per microphone channel: noise reduction & channel compensation
 – Voice activity detection & source separation
 – Speaker identification (e. g., therapist vs. patient)

---

[1] A detailed discussion is given in the paper of U. Altmann et al. in this volume.

- Extraction of short-time (segmental) features
- Extraction of long-time (suprasegmental) features

As a first step, the algorithms of the ICA (Independent Component Analysis) were implemented in the UASR. First experiments showed very encouraging results with respect to the separation of different acoustic sources.

5 Conclusion

We have shown in this overview that the components which are implemented in the UASR system are suited to handle complex signals which are predominantly speech but also other acoustic signals coming from human, other biological, technical, or musical sources. The common base of all these solutions is learning structures, which is performed now in a newly implemented FST framework. It is intended to apply this framework in interaction research now. To do this, the extension of the acoustic level of UASR by an acoustic frontend will be necessary.

Acknowledgments. The UASR project is one of the main activities of the Dresden group. Many people were engaged in this project over the years in very active way, and the authors would like to thank all of them. Special thanks for contributing material to this paper to Steffen Werner (section 3.3) and Oliver Jokisch (section 4.2).

The DFG (Deutsche Forschungsgemeinschaft) kindly supported the project with the following grants:

- Structural training of hierarchical organized pronunciation dictionaries (Ho 1674/3, 1997–2000)
- Integration of speech recognition and synthesis using common databases (Ho 1675/7, 2001–2005)
- Development of data analysis methods for the quality assessment of technical processes (Ho 1674/8, 2004–2007, cooperation project with the Fraunhofer Institute for Non-destructive Testing)

References

1. Hoffmann, R.: Speech synthesis on the way to embedded systems. Keynote lecture, SPECOM 2006, XI. In: International Conference Speech and Computer, St. Petersburg, Proceedings June 25-29, 2006, pp. 17–26 (2006)
2. Eichner, M., Wolff, M., Hoffmann, R.: A unified approach for speech synthesis and speech recognition using stochastic Markov graphs. In: Proc. 6th Conf. on Spoken Language Processing (ICSLP), Beijing, vol. I, pp. 701–704 (October 16-20, 2000)
3. Wolfertstetter, F., Ruske, G.: Structured Markov models for speech recognition. In: Proc. IEEE Int. Conf. on Acoustics, Speech, and Signal Processing (ICASSP), Detroit, pp. 544–547 (May 7-12, 1995)
4. Eichner, M.: Sprachsynthese und Spracherkennung mit gemeinsamen Datenbasen: Akustische Analyse und Modellierung. PhD thesis, TU Dresden, Dresden: TUD-press 2007 Studientexte zur Sprachkommunikation, vol. 43 (2006)

5. Westendorf, C.-M.: Learning pronunciation dictionary from speech data. In: Proc. Int. Conf. on Spoken Language Processing (ICSLP), Philadelphia, pp. 1045–1048 (October. 3-6, 1996)
6. Eichner, M., Wolff, M.: Data-driven generation of pronunciation dictionaries in the German Verbmobil project – Discussion of experimental results. In: ICASSP. Proc. IEEE Int. Conf. on Acoustics, Speech, and Signal Processing, Istanbul, June 5-9, 2000, vol. III, pp. 1687–1690. IEEE Computer Society Press, Los Alamitos (2000)
7. Eichner, M., Wolff, M., Hoffmann, R.: Data driven generation of pronunciation dictionaries. In: Wahlster, W. (ed.) Verbmobil: Foundations of Speech-to-Speech Translation, pp. 95–105. Springer, Berlin (2000)
8. Wolff, M., Eichner, M., Hoffmann, R.: Measuring the quality of pronunciation dictionaries. In: PMLA. Proc. ISCA Workshop on Pronunciation Modeling and Lexicon Adaptation for Spoken Language, Estes Park, CO, pp. 117–122 (September 14-15, 2002)
9. Wolff, M.: Automatisches Lernen von Aussprachewörterbüchern. PhD thesis, TU Dresden, Dresden: w.e.b. Universitätsverlag 2004 (Studientexte zur Sprachkommunikation, vol. 32) (2004)
10. Flach, G., Holzapfel, M., Just, C., Wachtler, A., Wolff, M.: Automatic learning of numeral grammars for multi-lingual speech synthesizers. In: ICASSP. Proc. IEEE Int. Conf. on Acoustics, Speech, and Signal Processing, Istanbul, June 5-9, 2000, vol. III, pp. 1291–1294. IEEE Computer Society Press, Los Alamitos (2000)
11. Eichner, M., Göcks, M., Hoffmann, R., Kühne, M., Wolff, M.: Speech-enabled services in a web-based e-learning environment. Advanced Technology for Learning 1, 2, 91–98 (2004)
12. Falaschi, A., Giustiniani, M., Verola, M.: A hidden Markov model approach to speech synthesis. In: Proc. European Conf. on Speech Communication and Technology (EUROSPEECH), Paris, pp. 187–190 (1989)
13. Tokuda, K., et al.: Speech parameter generation algorithms for HMM-based speech synthesis. In: ICASSP. Proc. IEEE Int. Conf. on Acoustics, Speech, and Signal Processing, Istanbul, June 5-9, 2000, vol. III, pp. 1315–1318. IEEE Computer Society Press, Los Alamitos (2000)
14. http://hts.sp.nitech.ac.jp/?Publications
15. Imai, S., Sumita, K., Furuichi, C.: Mel log spectrum approximation (MLSA) filter for speech synthesis. Trans. IECE J66-A, 122–129 (1983)
16. Eichner, M., Wolff, M., Ohnewald, S., Hoffmann, R.: Speech synthesis using stochastic Markov graphs. In: Proc. IEEE Int. Conf. on Acoustics, Speech, and Signal Processing, Salt Lake City, pp. 829–832 (May 7-11, 2001)
17. Strecha, G., Eichner, M.: Low resource TTS synthesis based on cepstral filter with phase randomized excitation. In: Proc. XI. International Conference Speech and Computer (SPECOM), St. Petersburg, pp. 284–287 (June 25-29, 2006)
18. Eichner, M., Wolff, M., Hoffmann, R.: Voice characteristics conversion for TTS using reverse VTLN. In: ICASSP. Proc. IEEE Int. Conf. on Acoustics, Speech, and Signal Processing, Montreal, May 17-21, 2004, vol. I, pp. 17–20. IEEE Computer Society Press, Los Alamitos (2004)
19. Bell, A., Gregory, M.L., Brenier, J.M., Jurafsky, D., Ikeno, A., Girand, C.: Which predictability measures affect content word Duration. In: PMLA. Proc. ISCA Workshop on Pronunciation Modeling and Lexicon Adaptation for Spoken Language, Estes Park, CO, pp. 1–5 (September 14-15, 2002)
20. Jurafsky, D., Bell, A., Gregory, M., Raymond, W.D.: The effect of language model probability on pronunciation reduction. In: Proc. IEEE Int. Conf. on Acoustics, Speech, and Signal Processing, Salt Lake City, pp. 801–804 (May 7-11, 2001)

21. Werner, S., Eichner, M., Wolff, M., Hoffmann, R.: Towards spontaneous speech synthesis - Utilizing language model information in TTS. IEEE Trans. on Speech and Audio Processing 12(4), 436–445 (2004)
22. Werner, S., Wolff, M., Hoffmann, R.: Pronunciation variant selection for spontaneous speech synthesis - Listening effort as a quality parameter. In: Proc. IEEE Int. Conf. on Acoustics, Speech, and Signal Processing, Toulouse, May 14-19, 2006, vol. I, pp. 857–860. IEEE Computer Society Press, Los Alamitos (2006)
23. Marx, G.: Entwicklung einer Methode zur numerischen Lautanalyse. PhD thesis, Univ. Halle-Wittenberg. Landbauforschung Völkenrode, Sonderheft 149 (1994)
24. TU Dresden, Institut für Akustik und Sprachkommunikation, Jahresbericht, p. 34 (1999)
25. Hoffmann, R., Richter, T.: Anwendung von Spracherkennern für die Klassifikation von Schnarchlauten. DAGA, Aachen, 766–767 (March 18-20, 2003)
26. Tschöpe, C., Hirschfeld, D., Hoffmann, R.: Klassifikation technischer Signale für die Geräuschdiagnose von Maschinen und Bauteilen. 4. In: Tschöke, H., Henze, W. (eds.) Symposium Motor- und Aggregateakustik, Magdeburg, June 15-16, 2005. Motor- und Aggregateakustik II. Renningen: expert Verlag (2005)
27. Tschöpe, C., Hentschel, D., Wolff, M., Eichner, M., Hoffmann, R.: Classification of non-speech acoustic signals using structure models. In: ICASSP. Proc. IEEE Int. Conf. on Acoustics, Speech, and Signal Processing, Montreal, May 17-21, 2004, vol. V, pp. 653–656. IEEE Computer Society Press, Los Alamitos (2004)
28. Kordon, U., Wolff, M., Hussein, H.: Auswertung von Korotkoff-Geräuschsignalen mit Verfahren der Mustererkennung für die Blutdruckmessung am aktiven Menschen. DAGA, Braunschweig, 719–720 (March 20-23, 2006)
29. Wolff, M., Kordon, U., Hussein, H., Eichner, M., Hoffmann, R., Tschöpe, C.: Auscultatory blood pressure measurement using HMMs. In: ICASSP. Proc. IEEE Int. Conf. on Acoustics, Speech, and Signal Processing, Honolulu, April 16-20, 2007, pp. 16–20. IEEE Computer Society Press, Los Alamitos (2007)
30. Eichner, M., Wolff, M., Hoffmann, R.: Instrument classification using HMMs. In: ISMIR. Proc. 7th International Conference on Music Information Retrieval, Victoria, pp. 349–350 (October 8-12, 2006)
31. Isačenko, A.V., Schädlich, H.J.: Untersuchungen über die deutsche Satzintonation. Studia Grammatica. Akademie-Verlag, Berlin (1964)
32. Isačenko, A.V., Schädlich, H.J.: A model of standard German intonation. The Hague Paris, Mouton (Janua Linguarum, Series Practica, 113) (1970)
33. Mehnert, D.: Grundfrequenzanalyse und -synthese der stimmhaften Anregungsfunktion. PhD thesis, TU Dresden (1975)
34. Mehnert, D.: Analyse und Synthese suprasegmentaler Intonationsstrukturen des Deutschen. Habil. thesis, TU Dresden (1985)
35. Mixdorff, H., Fujisaki, H.: Analysis of voice fundamental frequency contours of German utterances using a quantitative model. In: ICSLP. Proc. Int. Conference on Spoken Language Processing, Yokohama, (September 18-22, 1994)
36. Mixdorff, H.: Intonation patterns of German - quantitative analysis and synthesis of F0 contours. PhD thesis TU Dresden (1998)
37. Jokisch, O., Kordon, U.: Generierung von Grundfrequenzverläufen in einem Sprachsynthesesystem mit neuronalen Netzen. 6. Konf. Elektronische Sprachsignalverarbeitung, Wolfenbüttel, 113–119 (September 4-6, 1995)
38. Jokisch, O., Hirschfeld, D., Eichner, M., Hoffmann, R.: Multi-level rhythm control for speech synthesis using hybrid data driven and rule-based approaches. In: ICSLP. Proc. Int. Conf. on Spoken Language Processing, Sydney, pp. 607–610 (November 30-December 4, 1998)

39. Jokisch, O., Mixdorff, H., Kruschke, H., Kordon, U.: Learning the parameters of quantitative prosody models. In: ICSLP. Proc. Int. Conf. on Spoken Language Processing, Beijing, 645–648 (October 16-20, 2000)
40. Mixdorff, H., Jokisch, O.: Evaluating the quality of an integrated model of German prosody. Intern. Journal of Speech Technology 6(1), 45–55 (2003)
41. Kruschke, H., Koch, A.: Parameter extraction of a quantitative intonation model with wavelet analysis and evolutionary optimization. In: ICASSP. Proc. IEEE Int. Conf. on Acoustics, Speech, and Signal Processing, Hongkong, April 6-10, 2003, vol. I, pp. 524–527. IEEE Computer Society Press, Los Alamitos (2003)
42. Jokisch, O., Hofmann, M.: Evolutionary optimization of an adaptive prosody model. In: ICSLP. Proc. Int. Conf. on Spoken Language Processing, Jeju, Korea, pp. 797–800 (October 4-8, 2004)
43. Kruschke, H.: Simulation of speaking styles with adapted prosody. In: Matoušek, V., Mautner, P., Mouček, R., Tauser, K. (eds.) TSD 2001. LNCS (LNAI), vol. 2166, pp. 278–284. Springer, Heidelberg (2001)
44. Jokisch, O., Kruschke, H., Hoffmann, R.: Prosodic reading style simulation for text-to-speech synthesis. In: Tao, J., Tan, T., Picard, R.W. (eds.) ACII 2005. LNCS, vol. 3784, pp. 426–434. Springer, Heidelberg (2005)
45. Engel, T.: Robuste Markierung von Grundfrequenzperioden. Diplomarbeit, TU Dresden (2003)
46. Raidt, S.: Cross-language comparison of two approaches to modelling prosody. Studienarbeit, TU Dresden/ICP Grenoble (2002)
47. Jokisch, O., Ding, H., Kruschke, H.: Towards a multilingual prosody model for text-to-speech. In: ICASSP. Proc. IEEE Int. Conf. in Acoustics, Speech, and Signal Processing, Orlando, pp. 421–424 (May 13-17, 2002)
48. Jokisch, O., Kühne, M.: An investigation of intensity patterns for German. In: EUROSPEECH. Proc. 8th European Conf. on Speech Communication and Technology, Geneva, pp. 165–168 (September 1-4, 2003)
49. Hofmann, M., Jokisch, O.: Optimization of MFNs for signal-based phrase break prediction. In: Proc. 3rd Intern. Conference on Speech Prosody, Dresden, (May 2-5, 2006)
50. Kühne, M., Wolff, M., Eichner, M., Hoffmann, R.: Voice activation using prosodic features. In: ICSLP. Proc. Int. Conf. on Spoken Language Processing, Jeju, Korea, pp. 3001–3004 (October 4-8, 2004)

VideoTRAN: A Translation Framework for Audiovisual Face-to-Face Conversations

Jerneja Žganec Gros

Alpineon Research and Development, Ulica Iga Grudna 15
1000 Ljubljana, Slovenia
jerneja.gros@alpineon.si

Abstract. Face-to-face communication remains the most powerful human interaction. Electronic devices can never fully replace the intimacy and immediacy of people conversing in the same room, or at least via a videophone. There are many subtle cues provided by facial expressions and vocal intonation that let us know how what we are saying is affecting the other person. Transmission of these nonverbal cues is very important when translating conversations from a source language into a target language. This chapter describes VideoTRAN, a conceptual framework for translating audiovisual face-to-face conversations. A simple method for audiovisual alignment in the target language is proposed and the process of audiovisual speech synthesis is described. The VideoTRAN framework has been tested in a translating videophone. An H.323 software client translating videophone allows for the transmission and translation of a set of multimodal verbal and nonverbal clues in a multilingual face-to-face communication setting.

Keywords: nonverbal communication, facial expressions, speech-to-speech translation, translating videophone.

1 Introduction

In the last decade, users have continually oscillated between the impersonal nature of technology offering anonymous electronic communication and the intimate reality of human relationships. No question, technology is the great enabler. But, paradoxically, now the human bit seems to be more, not less, important than ever before [1].

There are many situations—often those involving escalating conflict, sensitive feelings, high priority, important authority, or a great deal of money—that demand people to take the time and trouble to get into the same room to exchange information. Or at least they try to simulate face-to-face communication when individuals are in remote locations using videophones or web-phones [2].

Face-to-face behaviors have two important elements: verbal and nonverbal. According to various investigations, verbal communication accounts for less than 30% of communication, and nonverbal elements represent at least the remaining 70%. Nonverbal communication—communication that does not use words—takes place all the time. Smiles, frowns, who sits where at a meeting, the size of the office, how long someone keeps a visitor waiting—all these communicate pleasure or anger,

A. Esposito et al. (Eds.): Verbal and Nonverbal Commun. Behaviours, LNAI 4775, pp. 219–226, 2007.

friendliness or distance, power and status. Animals are particularly talented senders of nonverbal messages. If you have been around a friendly dog, you have experienced the animal's pushing its head under your hand. The message is crystal clear without words. "Pet me," the dog seems to be saying.

Eye contact, facial expressions, gestures, posture, voice, appearance—all these nonverbal clues influence the way the message is interpreted, or decoded, by the receiver.

In order to automatically facilitate face-to-face communication among people that speak different languages, we propose a framework for audiovisual translation of face-to-face communication, called VideoTRAN. There are many subtle cues provided by facial expressions and vocal intonation that let us know how what we are saying is affecting the other person. Transmission of these nonverbal cues is very important when translating conversations from a source language into a target language.

To our knowledge, no such attempt has been made so far. Speech-to-speech translation enables subtitling of phone conversations only. The SYNFACE project made it possible to facilitate telephone communication for hard-of-hearing people: a synthesized talking face controlled by the telephone voice channel allows hearing-disabled users to better understand phone conversations by lip-reading [3], [4].

The organization of this chapter is as follows. The following section introduces the VideoTRAN conceptual framework of translations of audiovisual face-to-face conversations. A simple method for audiovisual alignment in the target language is proposed and the process of audiovisual speech synthesis is described. The VideoTRAN framework has been tested in a novel demonstrator, a translating videophone, which is presented next. This allows for the transmission and translation of a set of multimodal verbal and nonverbal clues in a multilingual face-to-face communication setting.

2 The VideoTRAN Audiovisual Translation Framework

The VideoTRAN framework is an extension of our speech-to-speech translation research efforts within the VoiceTRAN project [5]. The VideoTRAN system architecture consists of three major modules:

1. *AudioVisual speech analysis*: automatic speech recognition in the source language enhanced by lip-reading visemes, enables segmentation of the source language video signal into units, corresponding to audio representations of words.
2. *Verbal and video alignment*: audiovisual alignments in the target language are achieved through: a) machine translation for the translation of verbal communication and b) video alignment for nonverbal conversation elements.
3. *Audiovisual speech synthesis* in the target language also adds to the intelligibility of the spoken output, which is especially important for hearing-disabled persons that can benefit from lip-reading and/or subtitles.

The underlying automatic speech recognition, machine translation, and speech synthesis techniques are described in [6], [7]. There are, however, major open research issues that challenge the deployment of natural and unconstrained face-to-face conversation translation systems, even for very restricted application domains, because state-of-the-art automatic speech recognition and machine translation systems are far from perfect. In addition, in comparison to translating written text, conversational spoken messages are usually conveyed with relaxed syntax structures and casual spontaneous speech. In practice, a demonstrator is typically implemented by imposing strong constraints on the application domain and the type and structure of possible utterances; that is in both the range and the scope of the user input allowed at any point of the interaction. Consequently, this compromises the flexibility and naturalness of using the system.

The remainder of this section describes the audiovisual alignment and the audiovisual speech synthesis in the target language in greater detail.

2.1 Target Language Audiovisual Alignment

In most speech-to-speech translation tasks, especially if the two languages are not closely related, the word order in the source language can differ significantly from the word order of aligned words in the target language. Below is an example for word alignments of two phrases in the source language (SL) English and the target language (TL) Slovenian:

```
SL>  He  was  really  upset.  PAUSE.  But  why?

TL>  Res je  bil  razburjen.  PAUSE.  Zakaj  vendar?
```

The changed word order in the target language requires changes in the video sequence, unless the entire phrase has been pronounced with the same facial expression, apart from lip and jaw movements involved in the production of verbal speech.

If face expression changes do occur within a phrase as part of nonverbal communication, we propose the following simple video-sequence recombination method for alignment of the audio and the video signal in the target language. We base our video alignment method on prominent words, which are often reflected by significant changes in facial expressions. Experimental evidence shows that upper-face eye and eyebrow movements are strongly related to prominence in expressive modes [10], [11]. We trace facial expressions through upper-face action units (AUs) associated with the eyes and eyebrows in the Facial Action Coding System (FACS) system [8], [9]. Eyebrow action units, for instance, have action unit labels 1, 2, and 4: AU1—Inner Brow Raiser, AU2—Outer Brow Raiser, AU4—Brow Lowerer.

When more than one action unit is present, the combination of action units is listed in ascending order; for example, AU1+2 expresses a combination of the inner and outer brow raisers. Initially, AUs are manually labeled on test conversation recordings. Later in the project, automatic recognition of action units will be implemented [12].

We assume that the alignment pair of a prominent word in the source language will again be a prominent word, which is conveyed with the same facial expression and prosodic markedness as the prominent work in the source language. To prove this assumption, a parallel corpus of bilingual audiovisual conversations is needed.

First we segment the video signal in the target language into short video clips and align them with the recognized words in the source language. We annotate each video clip with a facial expression code, which can be N (neutral), an action unit (AU), or a transition in case of a facial expression onset (N-AU) or offset (AU-N). Further, we mark the words in the source language where a new facial expression occurred as prominent words, shown in bold below:

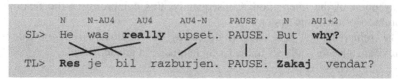

Following the assumption that prominent words match in both languages, we can derive the recombination of the video clips for the target language in the following way. First we annotate the facial expressions (AUs) of prominent words and the words on phrase boundaries in the target language according to the corresponding aligned facial expressions (AUs) in the source language:

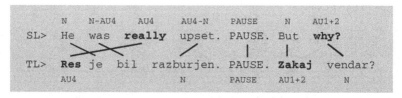

In the second step, facial expressions for the remaining words are predicted. If a prominent facial expression in the source language started with an onset (offset) on the previous (next) word, the same procedure is followed in the target language:

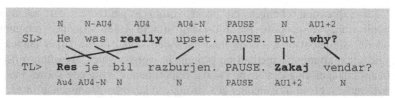

If the transition onsets into (or offsets out of) prominent facial expressions are not present in the original video signal, transition trajectories between the facial movements have to be modeled for transient features, such as nasolabial furrows, crows-feet wrinkles, and nose wrinkles.

The presented video-sequence recombination method for alignment of the audio and the video signal in the target language has several restrictions. It works best for frontal views with limited sideward head rotation only; in other cases perspective alignments should be used.

2.2 AudioVisual Speech Synthesis

The video alignment method based on matching prominent words described in the previous section provides the translation of only nonverbal elements between the source language and the target language. Lip and jaw movements involved in the production of verbal speech have to be modeled separately and integrated into the final video sequence.

Speech-synchronous face animation takes advantage of the correlation between speech and facial coarticulation. It takes the target language speech stream as input and yields corresponding face animation sequences. In our first experiment, we performed rudimentary modeling of lip movements only. The mouth region is located and replaced by an artificial lip controlled by the lip-relevant MPEG-4 Facial Animation Standard [13] viseme facial animation parameters, as shown in Figure 1. In order to allow for coarticulation of speech and mouth movement, transitions from one viseme to the next are defined by blending the two visemes with a weighting factor.

Fig. 1. VideoTRAN faces after processing. The mouth region in the image is covered by a rectangle with an artificial mouth, which is controlled by visemes and moves synchronously with the uttered phonemes.

During non-verbal periods such as pauses, grunts, laughing, the artificial mouth is replaced by the original video signal. As an alternative to artificial lip models, manipulation of video images of the original speaker's lips can be used [14]. The resulting speaking voice can also be adapted to that of the original speaker by applying voice transformation techniques.

3   The VideoTRAN Videophone Client

The VideoTRAN demonstrator under development is an H.323 client softphone with videophone capabilities. It is built around the CPhone open-source voice-over-IP (VoIP) solution [15]. It is based on the OpenH.323 and Trolltech PWLib libraries. Standard G.711 audio codec and the H.261 video codec are supported. It supports full duplex audio and bi-directional video.

The audiovisual processing of the first analysis unit or phrase inevitably introduces a short delay into the conversation. The audio stream is replaced by utterances in the target language, whereas the video stream is cut into clips and recombined according MT anchors corresponding to prominent words (significant AUs), as described in section 2.1. If the audio duration of a segment in the target language is longer than the source-language segment duration, the video signal is extrapolated to fit the target-language audio duration. Otherwise, the video signal is cut off at the end of the target language audio. A transitional smoothing at the video concatenation points still needs to be implemented. During nonverbal speech segments such as pauses, grunts, laughing, the original audio and video signals are brought back into the foreground.

Fig. 2. Screenshot of the VideoTRAN VoIP software client. To the right of the window with the video image, utterances in both the source language (recognized utterances) and the target language (translated utterances) are displayed.

A simple user-friendly user interface enables to set up video calls. To the right of the window with the video image, utterances in both the source language, i.e. the recognized utterances, and the target language, i.e. translated utterances, are displayed, as shown in Figure 2.

VideoTRAN is a fully H.323-compliant video conferencing solution compatible with other H.323 video conferencing clients and devices; for example, Microsoft NetMeeting, OhPhone, and GnomeMeeting. The VideoTRAN concept can also be ported to web-phones and hardware VoIP videophones.

4 Conclusions

Face-to-face communication remains the most powerful human interaction, electronic devices can never fully replace the intimacy and immediacy of people conversing in the same room, or via a videophone. In face-to-face conversation, there are many subtle cues provided by facial expressions and vocal intonation that let us know how what we are saying is affecting the other person. Therefore the transmission of these nonverbal cues is very important when translating conversations from a source language into a target language.

We have presented the VideoTRAN conceptual framework for translating audiovisual face-to-face conversations. It provides translations for both verbal and nonverbal components of the conversation. A simple method for audiovisual alignment in the target language has been proposed and the process of audiovisual speech synthesis has been described. The VideoTRAN framework has been tested in a translating videophone demonstrator: an H.323 software client translating videophone allows for the transmission and translation of a set of multimodal verbal and nonverbal clues in a multilingual face-to-face communication setting.

In order to evaluate the performance of the proposed face-to-face conversation translation approach, a combination of speech-to-speech translation performance metrics and facial expression performance metrics will be used.

The VideoTRAN concept allows for automatic face-to-face tele-conversation translation. It can be used for either online or offline translation and annotation of audiovisual face-to-face conversation material. The exploitation potentials of the VideoTRAN framework are numerous. Cross-cultural universal features in the form of gestures and postures can be transmitted and translated along with the facial expressions into the target language.

Acknowledgements

Part of the work presented in this paper was performed as part of the VoiceTRAN II project, contract number M2-0132, supported by the Slovenian Ministry of Defence and the Slovenian Research Agency.

References

1. Roebuck, C.: Effective Communication. American Management Association (1999)
2. Begley, A.K.: Face to Face Communication: Making Human Connections in a Technology-Driven World. Thomson Learning, Boston, MA (2004)
3. Spens, K.-E., Agelfors, E., Beskow, J., Granström, B., Karlsson, I., Salvi, G.: SYNFACE: a Talking Head Telephone for the Hearing Impaired. In: Proceedings of the IFHOH 7th World Congress. Helsinki, Finland (2004)
4. Agelfors, E., Beskow, J., Karlsson, I., Kewley, J., Salvi, G., Thomas, N.: User Evaluation of the SYNFACE Talking Head Telephone. In: Miesenberger, K., Klaus, J., Zagler, W., Karshmer, A.I. (eds.) ICCHP 2006. LNCS, vol. 4061, pp. 579–586. Springer, Heidelberg (2006)
5. VoiceTRAN project website: http://www.voiceTRAN.org
6. Žganec Gros, J., Gruden, S., Mihelič, F., Erjavec, T., Vintar, Š., Holozan, P., Mihelič, A., Dobrišek, S., Žibert, J., Logar, N., Korošec, T.: The VoiceTRAN Speech Translation Demonstrator. In: Proceedings of the IS-LTC 2006. Ljubljana, Slovenia, pp. 234–239 (2006)

7. Žganec Gros, J., Gruden, S.: The VoiceTRAN Machine Translation System. In: Interspeech 2007. Antwerpen, Belgium (Submitted to 2007)
8. Ekman, P., Friesen, W.V.: Facial Action Coding System. Consulting Psychologists Press, Palo Alto, CA (1978)
9. Ekman, P., Friesen, W.V., Hager, J.C. (eds.): Facial Action Coding System. Research Nexus. Network Research Information, Salt Lake City, UT (2002)
10. Krahmer, E., Ruttkay, Z., Swerts, M., Wesselink, W.: Perceptual Evaluation of Audiovisual Cues for Prominence. In: Proceedings of the 7th International Conference on Spoken Language Processing (ICSLP 2002), Denver, CO, pp. 1933–1936 (2002)
11. Beskow, J., Granström, B., House, D.: Visual Correlates to Prominence in Several Expressive Modes. In: Proceedings of the Interspeech 2007. Pittsburg, PA, pp. 1272–1275 (2006)
12. Tian, Y.L., Kanade, T., Cohn, J.F.: Facial Expression Analysis. In: Li, S.Z., Jain, A.K. (eds.) Handbook of Face Recognition, Springer, NY (2007) (in press)
13. Pandzic, I., Forchheimer, R.: MPEG-4 Facial Animation - the Standard, Implementation and Applications. John Wiley & Sons, Chichester, England (2002)
14. Ezzat, T., Geiger, G., Poggio, T.: Trainable Videorealistic Speech Animation. In: Proceedings of the ACM SIGGRAPH 2002, San Antonio, TX, pp. 388–398. ACM Press, New York (2002)
15. Cphone project, http://sourceforge.net/projects/cphone

Spoken and Multimodal Communication Systems in Mobile Settings

Markku Turunen and Jaakko Hakulinen

University of Tampere, Department of Computer Sciences
Tampere Unit for Computer-Human Interaction
Speech-based and Pervasive Interaction Group
33014 University of Tampere, Finland
`firstname.lastname@cs.uta.fi`

Abstract. Mobile devices, such as smartphones, have become powerful enough to implement efficient speech-based and multimodal interfaces, and there is an increasing need for such systems. This chapter gives an overview of design and development issues necessary to implement mobile speech-based and multimodal systems. The chapter reviews infrastructure design solutions that make it possible to distribute the user interface between servers and mobile devices, and support user interface migration from server-based to distributed services. An example is given on how an existing server-based spoken timetable application is turned into a multimodal distributed mobile application.

1 Introduction

Speech is one of the key aspects in mobile interaction technology: mobile phones have enabled ubiquitous speech communication and speech enables users to interact with information technology while their hands and eyes are occupied (e.g., while users are walking, performing everyday tasks, or driving a car). Furthermore, spoken interaction compensates the problems of small or missing displays and keyboards found on typical mobile devices, such as mobile phones, smartphones, personal digital assistants, and portable digital music players. In overall, speech can be an efficient and natural modality for interaction in mobile settings. While mobile phones are ubiquitous, and spoken interaction is used heavily in everyday communication between humans, there are not many mobile speech applications in everyday use. However, the interest towards mobile spoken and multimodal dialogue applications has increased. For example, many dedicated workshops have been arranged recently (ISCA Workshop on Multi-Modal Dialogue in Mobile Environments 2002, COLING 2004 Workshop on Robust and Adaptive Information Processing for Mobile Speech Interfaces, and MobileHCI 2006 & 2007 workshops on "Speech in Mobile and Pervasive Environments"). In addition, various applications and research prototypes have been introduced during the past few years.

1.1 Speech-Based and Multimodal Mobile Applications

Rather sophisticated speech interfaces can be implemented even with regular phones. First commercial spoken dialogue applications were such telephone based systems

A. Esposito et al. (Eds.): Verbal and Nonverbal Commun. Behaviours, LNAI 4775, pp. 227–241, 2007.

[6]. The ubiquity of mobile phones has made these server-based applications available while users are on the move. For example, public transport information services are usually designed to be used while traveling [30]. In these applications, mobile context defines the nature of interaction: dialogues may be interrupted because the users concentrate on their primary tasks, and there may be sudden, loud background noises etc. These interface issues should be taken into account in the design, development and evaluation of such applications.

In conventional telephone systems all information is processed by the server machines. This limits the interface since speech and telephone keys are the only available modalities. Lately, mobile devices have become rather powerful with a possibility to run custom applications. This has enabled multimodal and distributed applications. Multimodality can bring many advantages to speech-based interaction, as presented already by the famous Put-That-There system [2]. In a study of Weimer and Ganapathy speech inputs made a dramatic improvement in the interface based on hand gestures [36]. Similar results have been reported in other studies as well [11]. Common arguments favoring multimodality state that they prevent errors, bring robustness to the interface, help the user to correct errors or recover from them, and add alternative communication methods to different situations and environments [5]. Multimodal interfaces may also bring more bandwidth to the communication and it is possible to simulate other modalities, for example in the case of disabled users [29]. Disambiguation of error-prone modalities using multimodal interfaces is the main motivation for the use of multiple modalities in many systems. Error-prone technologies can compensate each other, rather than bring redundancy to the interface and reduce the need for error correction [18]. Since mobile environments are error-prone (noise etc.) multimodal interaction can be more efficient than speech-only interaction.

Multiple modalities can be used in several ways in mobile applications. One can approach multimodality by adding speech to an interface to compensate the problems of small displays. For example, Hemsen [12] has introduced several ways to incorporate speech in multimodal mobile phone applications to overcome the problems of small screens. On the other hand, we can start from a speech-only interface and increase its usability with additional modalities (e.g., graphics and haptics) and information sources (e.g., positioning information) when available. The transient nature of speech can be overcome by using static text, while maps can provide spatial information, and displays and keyboards can provide privacy for interaction in public situations. Finally, we have rich multimodal applications with several equally important modalities. Typical examples are "point and speak" interfaces, such as those developed by Sharon Oviatt et al. [19].

At the infrastructure level, we can distinguish between three main types of mobile spoken dialogue systems. First, there are numerous server-based systems accessed with dumb devices (typically mobile phones). Second, there are systems that are running entirely in mobile terminals, such as personal digital assistants [13, 15], and systems simulated with PC hardware [12]. Third, there are systems that distribute the processing between servers and mobile clients (e.g., smartphones). The distribution enables more advanced user interfaces, since all available interface elements in the mobile device can be used, while resource heavy operations, such as speech recognition, can take place in powerful server machines.

Most current mobile multimodal speech interfaces are distributed because of insufficient resources and missing technology components of mobile devices. Speech recognition, in particular, requires significant hardware resource, not available in typical mobile devices, and thus it is commonly implemented on the server side. Distributed speech recognition, where audio preprocessing front end is placed in the mobile device, and actual recognition takes place on the server, has the advantage of reducing the amount of data transmitted over a network, so industry has worked for a standard solution for such an approach [21]. Dialogue management, and in some cases, speech synthesis, can take place on a server as well. In addition, many applications need external information sources, such as databases. In some cases, e.g., in military applications [7], the entire infrastructure must be dynamic.

In this chapter, the work done with design and development of mobile multimodal speech applications is presented. In the following sections, service infrastructures for distributed spoken and multimodal user interfaces are reviewed. A concrete example shows how an existing server-based spoken dialogue timetable system is turned into a multimodal mobile system by using the solutions presented. The solutions make it possible to distribute the dialogue in flexible ways both to the server and mobile devices, and we are able to gradually move more responsibilities to the mobile devices as technology advances make it possible. The chapter ends with conclusions and discussion of future aspects of mobile speech-based and multimodal applications.

2 Mobile Service Infrastructure

Today, more and more applications are modeled using the Service-Oriented Architecture (SOA) approach [9], where loosely coupled and interoperable services are running on networked environments. For mobile speech-based and multimodal services, it is an efficient model to distribute the processing between servers and mobile devices. Figure 1 illustrates one possible setup for a SOA oriented mobile speech system infrastructure. It consists of several terminals with varying components, such as text-to-speech synthesis (TTS), dialogue management (DM), automatic speech recognition (ASR), and GPS positioning, servers for varying tasks, and databases. When multiple services are available, a lookup service becomes necessary [26]. IP-based communication is used between the different devices and generic XML-based interfaces are used between the three layers of technology components. For example, dialogue description languages such as VoiceXML [37] and SALT [25] can be used to exchange dialogue descriptions between the servers and the terminal devices. In addition, the database and the service interfaces can act as proxies to cache commonly used information. Here, the SOA framework forms the basis for the design and development of mobile spoken and multimodal systems. Next, different models to distribute the user interface are presented.

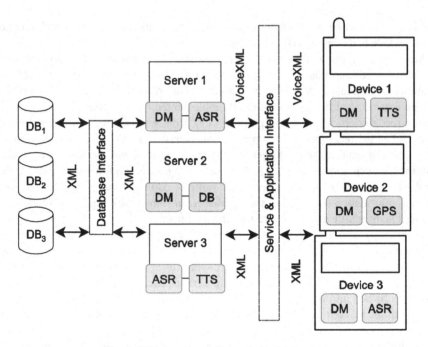

Fig. 1. SOA-based mobile service infrastructure

2.1 Models for Distributed Mobile Spoken Dialogue Systems

In order to implement mobile applications with efficient multimodal user interfaces, and use efficiently the resources of terminal devices and servers, we need to distribute the tasks, such as speech recognition and dialogue management, between the servers and the mobile devices. In other words, we need a suitable model for distribution. There are many ways to distribute multimodal dialogue processing between a mobile device and a server. These affect user interface solutions, since distribution results in certain delays etc., which make some interface solutions inappropriate. Next, current distribution models are reviewed, and a generic model for distribution is presented.

2.1.1 Client-Server Systems

In client-server systems the client calls one or more servers for specific tasks, such as speech recognition and speech synthesis. Many client-server architectures include a central HUB or a facilitator to connect the resources of the server and the mobile clients together. This is illustrated in Figure 2A. Many mobile multimodal systems have been implemented with this approach. For example, LARRI [4] is a wearable computing system that uses Galaxy-based HUB architecture [27] on the server side, and separate components for GUI and audio I/O on the mobile client side. All resource intensive tasks, such as dialogue management and speech recognition, are performed on the server side. A very similar approach has been used in the MUST guide to Paris [1].

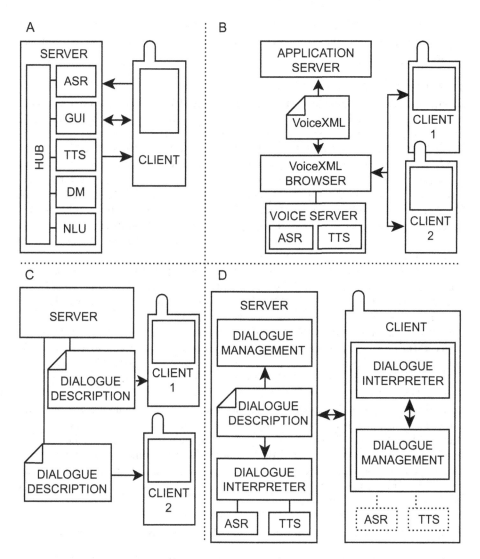

Fig. 2. Distributed system models

2.1.2 Voice Browsers

The second popular approach for implementing distributed applications is based on markup languages and browsers that enable mobile devices and server-based applications to communicate at the level of dialogue descriptions. The most widespread solution is VoiceXML [37], which has become an industry standard. The success of VoiceXML itself is one proof of the applicability of markup languages in describing dialogue tasks. In a typical VoiceXML setup, a mobile device (a regular mobile phone in most cases) contacts a VoiceXML browser via telephone network. The browser handles all connections to voice services (ASR, TTS) and back-end applications that reside on the server. Since regular telephones are used by default, the distribution in

VoiceXML systems takes place between servers: the application server handles the overall dialogue, while the VoiceXML browser handles single dialogue descriptions. Figure 2B illustrates this setup.

2.1.3 Dialogue Description Systems

In the VoiceXML architecture illustrated in Figure 2B, all computational resources are located on the server machines. This makes it possible to use dumb client devices with basic input/output capabilities. In multimodal systems we must process part of the dialogue locally in the mobile devices, and use their resources (e.g., TTS, display). Many such solutions are based on mobile clients that are able to run simple dialogue tasks generated by the server. The most well-known description language for speech-based systems is VoiceXML [37]. Dynamic generation of VoiceXML-based dialogue descriptions are used in various systems [20, 8]. Recent work with mobile applications includes converting static VoiceXML documents to ECMAScript code to make them compact enough for embedded devices [3], and altering the dialog flow for limited processing capabilities of the mobile devices [22].

VoiceXML is designed for speech-based systems. There are various markup languages targeted for multimodal interaction. These include XISL [14], SALT [25] XHTML+Voice [38], and MML [23]. They have slightly different approaches, but often the basic principle is the same. For example, XHTML+Voice extends a graphical HTML-based syntax with the voice communication markup taken from the VoiceXML framework to enable multimodal interaction. The distribution of tasks between the server and the client is similar to that of VoiceXML. The generic User Interface Markup Language (UIML) [35] has also been used in mobile multimodal systems [28, 16].

Typically, the mobile device receives a description of a dialogue fragment the server has generated, processes it, and provides the results back to the server. This is illustrated in Figure 2C. This way only an interpreter for the markup language in question needs to be implemented for each device and implementation of new applications requires programming only on the server side. The markup language may contain program code (such as ECMAScript code in the case of VoiceXML) to be processed locally on the mobile device.

2.2 Generic Model for Distributed Mobile Multimodal Speech Systems

In order to achieve maximal flexibility and efficiency in mobile speech applications, the system framework should support distribution of system components, efficient sharing of available resources, and distribution of dialogue tasks. This means that dialogue components should be able to run on both the server and client sides, both local and shared resources can be accessed when necessary, and the dialogue tasks are represented with a common dialogue description language that both the server and client devices are able to execute.

Figure 2D introduces a generic distribution model for mobile systems. The architecture contains dialogue management components both on the server and client sides. The dialogue management components generate dialogue descriptions containing all the information needed to carry out dialogue tasks (e.g., menu selections, correction dialogues, confirmations). The dialogue tasks can be carried out either on the server or the client device, since the client and the server use the available resources to actualize the tasks, and communicate when necessary. In this way, the resources available in each environment can be used optimally as devices that know their resources make the decisions how the descriptions are actualized. It is crucial to allow flexible sharing of resources. For example, if we do not have a speech recognizer on the mobile device, the dialogue interpreters need to communicate in order to share the server-based ASR component. Since both the server and the mobile device are capable of running the dialogue description, we can achieve the required level of flexibility.

Markup languages for dialogue descriptions, and their dynamic utilization in particular, are crucial in the distribution model presented. When we use a markup language to describe the information needed in interaction tasks, we can achieve both the optimal use of resources and consistency. Low-level tasks, e.g., the selection of optimal output medium, can be distributed to devices that handle the tasks regarding their capabilities. Overall coordination of high-level tasks is kept in the part of the system that generates the descriptions, and computationally demanding methods for dialogue management can be used. This also enables the system to be distributed physically and makes it possible to change the client devices used even during a single dialogue if needed. Next, we will describe a bus timetable application that uses the presented model to distribute the dialogue management tasks between a server and a smartphone.

3 Mobile Multimodal Timetable Service

Stopman is a task-oriented spoken dialogue system that provides timetables for each of the about 1200 bus stops in Tampere City area in Finland. The system offers basic functionality in a system-initiative manner (the system asks specific questions), while the rest of the functionality is available with a user-initiative interface (the user requests further information). The Stopman system has been publicly available since August 2003, and multiple usability evaluations have been conducted to the system to make it more efficient and pleasant to use [31]. Concluding from the usage experiences, long listings and spoken menus were frequent problems. Users found them boring and complicated, and they easily forgot what was said previously. Next we present how these problems can be address with a multimodal distributed interface to be used with smartphones.

Figure 3 illustrates two interfaces of the Stopman application: a conventional telephony interface implemented solely on a server (Figure 3, left-hand side), and a distributed multimodal interface on a smartphone (Figure 3, right-hand side). The interaction is similar except that the local resources of the smartphone are used in the multimodal system, while in the telephony interface, only speech and touch tones are used to interact with the system.

The smartphone interface differs from the telephony interface so that display, joystick and keypad are used to support speech inputs and outputs. In addition to spoken prompts, menus and supporting information is displayed on the screen. Users can use speech inputs, or use telephone keypad for navigation and selections. Menu items and global options can be selected using the joystick or the keypad like in the telephony

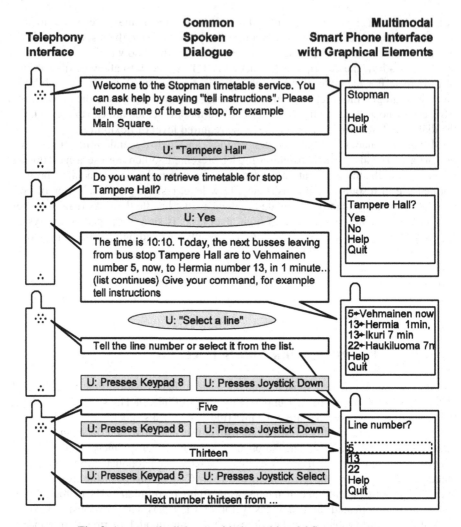

Fig. 3. An example dialogue with the multimodal Stopman system

version. The selected option is highlighted, and its value is spoken. This kind of multimodality can help users especially in noisy outdoor conditions, where it may be hard to hear system utterances and speech recognition might be unacceptable poor. Graphical information can also help the users in maintaining a mental model of the system status, if the user must do something else, for example, to step into a bus, while using the system. Telephone keys can be used together with speech inputs and outputs in two different ways. First, mobile phones with a loudspeaker or a handsfree set can be used like personal digital assistants, e.g., the mobile phone is held in hand, not against the ear. Second, experienced users (such as visually impaired users) are able to use the keypad efficiently while pressing the phone against the ear.

As shown in Figure 3, the spoken prompts and the displayed graphical contents are not the same. Instead, the content is designed to suit each output modality. It is efficient to display only the essential information on the screen, whereas more words are needed in order to make the spoken prompts understandable, fluent and less likely to be misheard. However, the conveyed information is the same. The use of display could be made even more efficient by using icons and animations, for example.

3.1 Dialogue Markup

The Stopman system uses VoiceXML to describe the distributed dialogue fragments. As said, VoiceXML is designed for speech-based interaction. Other modalities can be supported by including additional information in the VoiceXML descriptions as variables or comments. Example 1 presents a form with four alternative options taken from the example dialogue illustrated in Figure 3. The prompt field (line 3) describes what is said to the user, the display variable (line 4) describes what should be presented visually, and the option fields (lines 5 - 8) describe the possible input options. The prompt and display elements both convey the necessary information, i.e., they are redundant, but not the same literally. This is important, for example, if there is no display or the sounds are turned off. Since speech recognition takes place in the server, option fields may or may not cover all the possible inputs, i.e., the server-based recognition may have a larger choice of actions than the menu-based interface in the mobile device.

```
[ 1] <form>
[ 2]   <field>
[ 3]     <prompt>Do you want timetables for stop Tampere
               Hall?</prompt>
[ 4]     <var name="display" value="Tampere Hall?" />
[ 5]     <option>Yes</option>
[ 6]     <option>No</option>
[ 7]     <option>Help</option>
[ 8]     <option>Quit</option>
[ 9]   </field>
[10] </form>
```

Example 1: An example dialogue description (see Figure 3 for a realization).

It is noteworthy that the dialogue description does not tie the interface to any particular device. Depending on the capabilities of the used devices, the distribution of tasks between the server and the mobile device are handled differently by the corresponding dialogue interpreter components. This is because the resources of different devices are asymmetrical, e.g., one might have a speech synthesizer but no display, while another device has a display but no local TTS engine. When as much as possible is processed locally, the interface is responsive and we can also use the input and output capabilities of difference devices, such as touch screens and loudspeakers, to their full extent. The level of distribution depends on the used devices and their capabilities. This is different from the standard VoiceXML architectures where the distribution is static. Next, the technical solutions used to enable such dialogue management distribution are discussed. The underlying system architecture is presented briefly, followed by a detailed description of the distribution process in the Stopman systems.

3.2 Server System Architecture

In most conventional speech systems components are structured in a pipeline fashion (i.e., they are executed in a sequential order) although this kind of pipes-and-filters model is considered suboptimal for interactive systems [10]. These systems can be very bulky in mobile and distributed settings. Earlier work in distributed system architectures includes different variations of client-server approaches (see Figure 2A for an example). Two most well-known architectures used in speech applications are the Galaxy-II/Communicator architecture [27] and the Open Agent Architecture [17]. These architectures offer the necessary infrastructure components for server-based applications, but they assume that the client devices have separate system architectures, e.g., they do not offer support for mobile devices such as smartphones.

The Jaspis architecture [32] is a generic system architecture for speech-based applications. The architecture contains both server and mobile versions of the agent-based Jaspis architecture used for many desktop and server-based spoken dialogue systems, Stopman being one of these [33].

The Jaspis architecture offers building blocks for speech systems in the form of three kinds of software components called agents, evaluators, and managers. Managers are used to coordinate the agents and the evaluators. The functionality of the system is distributed across numerous compact agents, and multiple evaluators are used to dynamically reason which agent to activate in each situation. For example, a task can be handled with one set of agents when the user interacts with a speech-only device, while another, but not necessarily a distinct, set of agents can be used when the user switches to a device capable of multimodal interaction.

The server version of the Jaspis architecture runs on top of the J2SE (Java 2 Standard Edition) platform. A mobile version of the Jaspis architecture [34] runs on J2ME platforms (Java 2 Micro Edition), such as Series 60 mobile phones. The design of the mobile version follows closely the design of the original architecture, thus enabling technology transfer from server based applications to distributed mobile environments.

In comparison to J2SE, the J2ME platform contains several limitations. J2ME, and more precisely, the Mobile Information Device Profile (MIDP) 2.0 combined with the Connected Limited Device Configuration (CLDC) 1.0, supports only a subset of J2SE's libraries and APIs. Midlets have certain restrictions, such as that all graphical user interface elements and their events are accessed via a shared display object. A very similar approach is used in Java applets. It should be noted that this is not technical issue alone. Instead, it should be taken into account in the design of multimodal speech applications, and heterogenic applications running on different devices.

Devices supporting the J2ME platform are usually constrained with limited performance and memory. However, with basic Series 60 mobile phones (e.g., Nokia 6600 and 6630), it was possible to implement the multimodal version of the Stopman system. Next, we describe how dialogue distribution is implemented in the Stopman application using the generic distribution model and the Jaspis architecture.

3.3 Distribution in the Stopman System

In the original telephone version of the Stopman system (illustrated in Figure 3), all components are running on a server equipped with a Dialogic D/41JCT-LS telephony card. The users call the system with regular mobile phones. The multimodal smartphone version (as illustrated in Figure 3) is based on the generic distribution model as presented in the previous section (illustrated in Figure 2D). The role of the server in this model is to handle high-level dialogue management by generating the extended VoiceXML descriptions described earlier. The mobile device contains an interpreter for executing the VoiceXML descriptions with additional multimodal information. The resulting distributed system architecture is illustrated in Figure 4.

Figure 4 depicts the components used to distribute dialogue tasks in Stopman. The architecture is based on the generic distribution model [24]. In this model, the dialogue management system (1 in Figure 4) produces the VoiceXML descriptions of dialogue tasks (2), such as menus or prompts that should be presented to the user (see Figure 3 for concrete examples). The distribution of tasks takes place in the Communication Management subsystem that is implemented as a modular structure where the devices are easily changeable without a need to alter the rest of the system. The description generated by the dialogue management is handled with the handler devices (3, 4) that use available resources (speech recognition, speech synthesis, display, keys, etc.) to complete the task.

Communication Management subsystem in Jaspis contains abstract devices that are used to carry out tasks. Devices represent abstractions of resources that can handle tasks. Devices can also be combined, i.e. they can use other devices to complete the task. For example, a telephone synthesizer is a device that can handle a request to synthesize text and play the result via a telephony card. Separate components, called engines, implement the interfaces to the actual resources such as telephony cards, speech recognizers, synthesizers, and communication with smartphones (for the sake of clarity, Figure 4 is simplified, e.g., some engines are omitted). I/O Agents process the results the devices return. For example, I/O Agents implement natural language understanding functionality. I/O Evaluators decide when the communication management is done, i.e. when to provide the results back to the dialogue management.

There are different description handler devices for different terminal devices. In Figure 4 there is one telephony device (3), and one smartphone device (4a) on the server side. Both devices are combined devices, i.e. they delegate sub-tasks to other devices. The basic functionality of both combined devices is that they get a VoiceXML description as their input, and return a speech recognition result or a menu selection as a result. All other components of the server system, including natural language understanding, dialogue management, timetable database, and natural language generation components are the same, no matter which device is used.

In the case of standard telephony environment (5), all resources (synthesizers, recognizers, and telephony cards) are on the server. In the smartphone environment (6), the logic of handling the dialogue descriptions is divided between the mobile device and the server. Thus, the combined device (4a) is different from the one in the telephony version (3). Dialogue descriptions are handled with components placed on the smartphone, where a local handler (4b) manages the process. As a result, the

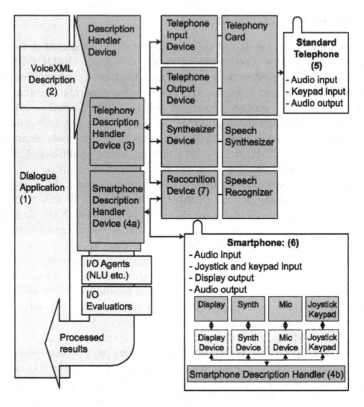

Fig. 4. Distributed system-level architecture

smartphone returns an audio input or a menu selection. After this, speech recognition is done if needed in the server using the same device as in the telephony version (7). In this way, the I/O Agents that perform natural language understanding can be the same in both versions.

As illustrated in Figure 4, both the standard telephone device (3) and the smartphone device (4a) are based on the same generic dialogue description device. In this way, the device dependent and device independent parts of processing are kept separate, and the system can be easily extended with new devices. At the same time, since the resources of mobile devices grow, some components running currently on the server can be moved to the mobile terminal device. This is possible because of the common system architecture.

4   Conclusions

In this chapter, the issues related to the design and development of mobile multimodal speech applications were discussed. Many successful telephone-based spoken dialogue systems have been developed during the recent years. Expanding the interaction to multimodality and making the systems distributed can make the interaction more efficient and natural. However, we face many challenges in this process due to technical limitations. The chapter presented solutions to the key challenges, such as distribution of dialogues.

A generic infrastructure for mobile speech-based and multimodal applications was presented. The infrastructure follows the Service-Oriented Architecture approach, i.e., loosely coupled and interoperable services run on networked settings. This kind of structure makes it possible to efficiently distribute the processing between servers and mobile devices. A model to distribute dialogue management tasks to mobile devices was presented. The model results in a manageable structure where the consistency and continuity of dialogue can be reached by using a suitable architecture, even if the devices used for interaction need to change.

An example application that uses the distribution of dialogue management tasks to mobile devices was presented together with a system architecture showing that the architecture and the distribution models are feasible for building distributed multimodal spoken speech applications.

New mobile computing environments, such as pervasive and ubiquitous computing raise new challenges for spoken and multimodal dialogue systems and interaction design. In pervasive computing environments, the dialogue can occur in different places and can be temporally discontinuous because the user is moving in the environment. This means that the devices used for communication might also change, even within a single dialogue. The key features of the pervasive speech applications are the distributed and concurrent nature of dialogues, rich multimodality, multilinguality and the active role of the computer. These are examples of the challenges that need to be addressed in the further development of spoken and multimodal mobile dialogue systems.

References

1. Almeida, L., Amdal, I., Beires, N., Boualem, M., Boves, L., den Os, E., Filoche, P., Gomes, R., Knudsen, J.E., et al.: The MUST guide to Paris: Implementation and expert evaluation of a multimodal tourist guide to Paris. In: IDS2002. Proceedings of the ISCA tutorial and research workshop on Multi-modal dialogue in Mobile environments, Kloster Irsee, Germany (2002)
2. Bolt, R.: "put-that-there": Voice and gesture at the graphics interface. Computer Graphics 14(3), 262–270 (1980)
3. Bühler, D., Hamerich, S.W.: Towards VoiceXML Compilation for Portable Embedded Applications in Ubiquitous Environments. In: Proceedings of Interspeech 2005, pp. 3397–3400 (2005)
4. Bohus, D., Rudnicky, A.: LARRI: A language-based maintenance and repair assistant. In: IDS 2002. Proceedings of the ISCA tutorial and research workshop on Multi-modal dialogue in Mobile environments, Kloster Irsee, Germany (2002)
5. Cohen, P., Oviatt, S.: The Role of Voice in Human-Machine Communication. In: Roe, D., Wilpon, J. (eds.) Voice Communication Between Humans and Machines, pp. 34–75. National Academy Press, Washington D.C (1994)
6. Cox, R.V., Kamm, C.A., Rabiner, L.R., Schroeter, J., Wilpon, J.G.: Speech and language processing for next-millennium communications services. Proceedings of the IEEE 88(8), 1314–1337 (2000)

7. Daniels, J.J., Bell, B.: Listen-Communicate-Show(LCS): Spoken Language Command of Agent-based Remote Information Access. In: Proceedings of the first international conference on Human language technology research (2001)
8. Di Fabbrizzio, G., Lewis, C.: Florence: a Dialogue Manager Framework for Spoken Dialogue Systems. In: Proceedings of ICSLP 2004, pp. 3065–3068 (2004)
9. Douglas, B.: Web Services and Service-Oriented Architectures: The Savvy Manager's Guide. Morgan Kaufmann Publishers, San Francisco (2003)
10. Garlan, D., Shaw, M.: An Introduction to Software Architecture. In: Ambriola, V., Tortora, G. (eds.) Advances in Software Engineering and Knowledge Engineering, Series on Software Engineering and Knowledge Engineering, vol. 2, pp. 1–39. World Scientific Publishing Company, Singapore (1993)
11. Hauptman, A., McAvinney, P.: Gestures with speech for graphic manipulation. International Journal of Man-Machine Studies 38, 231–249 (1993)
12. Hemsen, H.: Designing a Multimodal Dialogue System for Mobile Phones. In: Proceedings of Nordic Symposium on Multimodal Communications, 2003 (2003)
13. Hurtig, T.: A Mobile Multimodal Dialogue System for Public Transportation Navigation Evaluated. In: Proceedings of MobileHCI 2006, pp. 251–254 (2006)
14. Katsurada, K., Nakamura, Y., Yamada, H., Nitta, T.: XISL: A Language for Describing Multimodal Interaction Scenarios. In: Proceedings of ISCA Tutorial and Research Workshop on Multi-Modal Dialogue in Mobile Environments (IDS 2002), Kloster Irsee, Germany (2002)
15. Koskinen, S., Virtanen, A.: Public transport real time information in Personal navigation systems for special user groups. In: Proceedings of 11th World Congress on ITS, 2004 (2004)
16. Larsen, A., Holmes, P.D.: An Architecture for Unified Dialogue in Distributed Object Systems. In: Proceedings of TOOLS 26 - Technology of Object-Oriented Languages (1998)
17. Martin, D.L., Cheyer, A.J., Moran, D.B.: The Open Agent Architecture: A frame-work for building distributed software systems. Applied Artificial Intelligence: An International Journal 13(1-2), 91–128 (1999)
18. Oviatt, S.: Mutual disambiguation of recognition errors in a multimodal architecture. In: CHI 1999. Proceedings of Conference on Human Factors in Computing Systems, pp. 576–583. ACM Press, New York (1999)
19. Oviatt, S., Cohen, P.R., Wu, L., Vergo, J., Duncan, L., Suhm, B., Bers, J., Holzman, T., Winograd, T., Landay, J., Larson, J., Ferro, D.: Designing the User Interface for Multimodal Speech and Pen-based Gesture Applications: State-of-the-Art Systems and Future Research Directions. Human Computer Interaction 15(4), 263–322 (2000)
20. Pakucs, B.: VoiceXML-based dynamic plug and play dialogue management for mobile environments. In: IDS 2002. Proceedings of ISCA Tutorial and Research Workshop on Multi-Modal Dialogue in Mobile Environments, Kloster Irsee, Germany (2002)
21. Pearce, D.: Enabling new speech driven services for mobile devices: an overview of the proposed etsi standard for a distributed speech recognition front-end. In: proceedings of AVIOS 2000 (2000)
22. Rajput, N., Nanavati, A.A., Kumar, A., Chaudhary, N.: Adapting Dialog Call-flows for Pervasive Devices. In: Proceedings of Interspeech 2005, pp. 3413–3416 (2005)
23. Rössler, H., Sienel, J., Wajda, W., Hoffmann, J., Kostrzewa, M.: Multimodal Interaction for Mobile Environments. In: Proceedings of International Workshop on Information Presentation and Natural Multimodal Dialogue, Verona, IT (2001)
24. Salonen, E.-P., Turunen, M., Hakulinen, J., Helin, L., Prusi, P., Kainulainen, A.: Distributed Dialogue Management for Smart Terminal Devices. In: Proceedings of Interspeech 2005, pp. 849–852 (2005)
25. SALT. Speech Application Language Tags (SALT) Forum (2006), http://www.saltforum.org/

26. Schmandt, C., Lee, K.H., Kim, J., Ackerman, M.: Impromptu: Managin Networked Audio Applications for Mobile Users. In: Proceedings of MobiSys 2004, pp. 59–69 (2004)
27. Seneff, S., Hurley, E., Lau, R., Pao, C., Schmid, P., Zue, V.: Galaxy-II: a Reference Architecture for Conversational System Development. In: Proceedings of ICSLP 1998, pp. 931–934 (1998)
28. Simon, R., Jank, M., Wegscheider, F.: A Generic UIML Vocabulary for Device- and Modality Independent User Interfaces. In: Proceedings of WWW2004, pp. 434–435 (2004)
29. Smith, A., Dunaway, J., Demasco, P., Peischl, D.: Multimodal Input for Computer Access and Augmentative Communication. In: Annual ACM Conference on Assistive Technologies, pp. 80–85. ACM Press, New York (1996)
30. Turunen, M., Hurtig, T., Hakulinen, J., Virtanen, A., Koskinen, S.: Mobile Speech-based and Multimodal Public Transport Information Services. In: Proceedings of MobileHCI 2006 Workshop on Speech in Mobile and Pervasive Environments, 2006. (2006a)
31. Turunen, M., Hakulinen, J., Kainulainen, A.: An Evaluation of a Spoken Dialogue System with Usability Tests and Long-term Pilot Studies: Similarities and Differences. In: Proceedings of Interspeech 2006, pp. 1057–1060 (2006b)
32. Turunen, M., Hakulinen, J., Räihä, K.-J., Salonen, E.-P., Kainulainen, A., Prusi, P.: An architecture and applications for speech-based accessibility systems. IBM Systems Journal 44(3), 485–504 (2005a)
33. Turunen, M., Hakulinen, J., Salonen, E.-P., Kainulainen, A., Helin, L.: Spoken and Multimodal Bus Timetable Systems: Design, Development and Evaluation. In: Proceedings of 10th International Conference on Speech and Computer - SPECOM 2005, pp. 389–392 (2005b)
34. Turunen, M., Salonen, E.-P., Hakulinen, J., Kanner, J., Kainulainen, A.: Mobile Architecture for Distributed Multimodal Dialogues. In: Proceedings of ASIDE 2005 (2005c)
35. UIML. UIML specification (2006), http://www.uiml.org/specs/uiml3/ DraftSpec.htm
36. Weimer, D., Ganapathy, S.: A Synthetic Visual Environment with Hand Gesturing and Voice Input. In: Proceedings of CHI 1989, ACM Press, New York (1989)
37. VoiceXML. VoiceXML specification (2006),
    http://www.w3c.org/TR/2004/ REC-voicexml20-20040316/
38. XHTML+Voice. W3C., XHTML+Voice Profile 1.0 (2006),
    http://www.w3.org/TR/xhtml+voice/

Multilingual Augmentative Alternative Communication System

Pantelis Makris

Cyprus Neuroscience and Technology Institute, Nicosia, Cyprus
makrisp@cytanet.com.cy

Abstract. People with severe motor control problems, who at the same time lack of verbal communication, use alternatively non verbal communication techniques and aids which usually combine symbols, icons, drawings, sounds and text. The present paper describes completely configurable multilingual software that can contribute to the above group's needs as it facilitates access to a personalized computerized system which provides options for non verbal-written communication. This system incorporates enhanced or new features like acronymic writing, single switch access, word and phrase prediction, keyboard layout configuration, scanning of word and phrase lists and makes communication through internet (email and chatting options) possible. More over the system records all keystrokes, all words and acronyms used and provides valuable data for research on the best possible configuration of the system. What makes the system more innovative is the possibility it provides to users to send their emails and to network through internet chatting, with others.

Keywords: Augmentative Alternative Communication (AAC), severely handicapped, multilingual, configurable, acronyms, email, chatting.

1 Introduction

Approximately 1.3% of all individuals in the United States, share significant communication disabilities to the extent that they cannot rely on their natural speech to meet their daily communication needs [5]. Other researchers have reported a similar percentage in Europe. For instance, a study [7] estimates that 1.4% of the total population in the United Kingdom experience communication disorders. These individuals require various symbols, aids, strategies and techniques [2] offered by an Augmentative and Alternative Communication (AAC) system to succeed in some kind of communication. The term "AAC aid/device" is used to describe methods of helping people who find it hard to communicate by speech or writing.

According to Beukelman & Mirenda [5] AAC aid refers to a *"device, either electronic or non-electronic that is used to transmit or receive messages"*. AAC users are mostly people suffering from severe motor control and oral communication disorders, just like people with cerebral palsy, motor neuron disease, muscular dystrophy, aphasia, apraxia, Alzheimer dementia etc. They vary in age, socioeconomic, ethnic and racial backgrounds. As Light, [12] suggests these people use AAC to communicate in four areas of communicative interactions: for expressing

A. Esposito et al. (Eds.): Verbal and Nonverbal Commun. Behaviours, LNAI 4775, pp. 242–249, 2007.

their needs/wants, for information transfer, for social closeness and social etiquette. Beukelman & Mirenda [5] add to these areas the need for internal communication or self dialogue.

AAC as described by the American Speech-Language-Hearing Association (ASHA), involves attempts to study and, when necessary, to compensate for temporary or permanent impairments, activity limitations and participation restrictions of persons with severe disorders of speech-language production and/or comprehension, including spoken and written communication [2]. AAC combines many different methods of aided or unaided communication systems. Systems like signing and gestures, which do not need any extra bits and pieces to be produced and interpreted, are called *unaided systems* as ISAAC denote on their website [10]. Others use what are called aided systems like picture charts, books and special computers. In practice, regardless of the system used, AAC can help communicatively impaired people understand what is said to them as well as produce, write and communicate successfully what they want either by aided or unaided systems.

For the successful communication of these people lots of different AAC aids were developed and vast research goes on in the area on systems which combine text, symbols, icons, photos, animation, video clips and sounds all of them aiming at facilitating communication and message transferring but also at interpreting messages received from different sources like from friends on face to face communication, teachers in formal class situation, friends from a distance through written or recorded messages, from everyday interaction with the community and the society in general. The interpretation of these messages depends, at a great deal, on the user's personality and idiosyncrasy as Robinson & Griffith [19] report. Moreover Mollica [17] insists that users' mood, their passion and eagerness as well as their age, their neurological condition in relation to their communication, language and cognitive level are decisive for the effective use of AAC systems. Perhaps the most decisive factor for successful communication is their patience and their willingness and effort for communication.

It is estimated that AAC users put excessive effort to succeed in interpreting and also in producing messages, with the help of AAC systems. Their efforts to communicate with the outside world, in a relatively fast and effective way, often end in distress and disappointment. The alternative communication tools they currently employ are not fast enough or are laborious to use [15].

The speed of message production is crucial for them as they try to maintain any sort of communication. These people, especially those who are literate (can read and write), are also concerned with their possibilities to get connected to the virtual space. An area that is of great interest to them is them being in touch with the rest of the world through the internet. Communication methods through internet, for the benefit of AAC users, are still at a primitive stage, at least in most European countries and the users' need for social interaction at a wider range as well as with multicultural groups make it worthy for study and research in that area [18, 20].

The present paper outlines a multilingual augmentative communication system (**MACS**) that the writer has developed aiming to provide a flexible system to the Greek speaking AAC users, originally, but finally a system that can support AAC users of any nationality.

2 MACS – PES (Multilingual Augmentative Communication System)

MACS is a software that was developed, at first, to help Greek speaking users for everyday communication of their basic needs and wants. Originally called PES (which means speak) in Greek, it stands for multisensory communication system. Its original objective to provide a communication aid was modified very quickly when the BETA version was given to users for trial and comments. The very first version included, among other tools, a module for sending emails. At a second stage receiving emails was another thought but recently users have asked for chatting options, claiming that their possibilities of networking with the rest of the world on the virtual space are limited, if any.

Based on this feedback, a new system was designed to fulfill the new needs as described by the users themselves. Although the focus shifted to the networking modules of the software, there is a very careful design and considerable improvements on the scanning methods, the keyboard layout, the word pattern prediction, the linguistic prediction, the phrase-sentence prediction and in general, the possibility of highly flexible personalization of the software to each individual's needs.

The aim of this paper is to describe MACS and to provide to the reader the research points raised in an effort to inquire on the contribution of an AAC system, like MACS, to the networking of AAC users to multicultural, multilingual groups on the virtual space of the internet. MACS (PES) has been designed as a result of the vast experience of the researcher in special education and his personal involvement with the development of similar communication systems. The researcher strongly believes in making available multilingual software and he has prior experience in designing and developing similar software.

The lack of an AAC tool in most Eastern European countries and the Middle East solidifies the need for a multilingual capability of such software. In this sense, the proposed system is expected to meet the expectations of both the researcher and the potential users. In conclusion, MACS software will ultimately be a multilingual software and is expected to meet the needs of people with motor control and communication difficulties but also to support children and adults with other difficulties in writing and communicating (dyslexics, deaf, slow learners, etc).

2.1 The Basic Features of MACS

A wide variety of software and communication devices were surveyed before architecting the current design of MACS. Some of the many systems studied include Bliss symbols, Makaton system, Boardmaker (by Mayer Johnson), Widgit symbols, Grafis (Greek communication software), MAK400 [14], Wordpred [13], WordAid (by ACE Centre in UK), and WordQ (by Quillsoft). Adaptations and reconfigurations were attempted to mostly English AAC systems in an effort to customize them to the needs of Greek speaking AAC users. After studying thoroughly the different systems their best characteristics were listed and the design of MACS was decided to bring together the features, if possible of all the other systems. It was also thought to be a multilingual system which would ultimately serve the every day needs, of users from any nationality but mostly to provide a platform for communication through the internet. Consequently it was decided that the software should provide a more dynamic communication interface and a friendly environment that would be completely configurable and easily customizable to other languages. Significant effort was put to incorporate new prediction techniques, different speech production methods, to display completely customizable keyboard layouts, provide options for emailing and chatting on the internet. At this stage the software records various data and statistics like keystrokes, words used, new words and new acronyms written by the user, email addresses, ICQ contacts, speed of scanning, speed of writing, vocabulary used, keyboard layout used, most frequently used words, documents produced by the user. This data assists users in determining the most suitable configuration of the software. In conclusion the following features can be found on MACS.

2.2 Interface

Very friendly graphical user interface (GUI) completely configurable and easily customizable to other languages. Where possible there are help messages and prompts to the user. The original configuration is in English. Customization to a different language does not take more than thirty minutes and it is only needed to be done once. Settings and data from configuration procedures are stored and recalled each time the software is run.

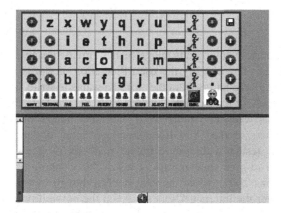

2.3 Personalization

The name of the user is recorded and pops up in emails, the speed of scanning can be adjusted to the users pace, font series can be selected, vocabulary and language of writing (Greek, English, Russian, etc.) to be used as well as keyboard layout can be configured to the users needs and wishes. Lists of everyday messages and acronyms can be updated, deleted or new ones can be created. Email addresses and chatting contacts are also recorded, deleted or updated. Sounds assigned to words of the vocabulary, to groups of messages or to the phrases from the acronyms can be recorded and associated to the text. Captions on the different controls and buttons can also be translated in different languages. All documents produced by the user are saved as separate files but they are also merged in one file. Data from this file are used to produce automatically new acronyms.

2.4 Keyboard Layout

There is an onscreen keyboard of five rows of eleven buttons each. Buttons have letters, symbols or icons on. The first four rows include buttons with the alphabet and some buttons have icons for delete, for space, for printing. One of these buttons carries the full stop character and there are also buttons with icons of arrows to move up and down from one row to the other. On the fifth row there are different buttons for different groups of messages like messages for wishes and wants, messages providing personal information, numbers, salutations and other topics. There is also a button for emails sending and a button for connection with chatting rooms.

2.5 Speech Production

Speech output is accomplished in two different ways. First, by using speech synthesis based on the syllabic structure of words. This method although still in a preliminary stage utilizes recorded segments of speech, like syllables, which are later synthesized (blended) to form words. This method applies mostly to phonetical (transparent) languages. The second method is by common speech synthesis as the software is supported by any sort of speech synthesis package.

2.6 Prediction

A lot of effort went into taking advantage of new prediction techniques, which are improving the speed of writing by the user. Prediction of words is activated by the time the user selects three letters from the word he wants to write. The two first letters are the two first letters of the word and the third letter is any letter from the remaining letters, i.e. if the user wants to type the word "morning" he has to write mo and any of the rest of the letters of the word like "mon" or "mor" or "mog" or "moi". The software has been tested with four different methods of prediction and the one adopted was found to give smaller lists of words for scanning and selection by the user (Makris, Athens 2007). More data are needed though to validate these results. Communication over the internet: Users are given the possibility to send and receive emails, get connected to chatting rooms and chat with friends. The tool is expected to be used as a data collecting engine for further research on acronyms.

2.7 Scanning

On screen keyboard is scanned (a cyan light goes from one cell to the next one). Scanning is linear and the speed of scanning can be changed at any moment. Changes in speed are recorded and each time the software runs the stored scanning speed is used. A single pressure switch or other types of switches can be connected to the computer for selection. For users who can tap the Space Bar or press Enter, switches don't need to be used.

2.8 Vocabulary

Some vocabularies are already included such as an English vocabulary and a Greek vocabulary. Users can produce their own vocabularies or lists of words and also their lists of acronyms. The software has a built in tool called Word Harvester which takes text documents and splits them automatically into word lists. The vocabulary to be used can be personalized. Words from vocabularies can be changed, deleted or new words can be added. If a word that a user wants to write does not exist in the vocabulary he is allowed to write the word, selecting each of its letters separately, and the word will automatically be transferred in user's vocabulary for future use.

2.9 Acronymic Writing

Users have the possibility to speed up their writing by building and using their own lists of acronyms. Acronyms use three letters to represent a whole phrase or sentence. For example "ews" will output "Excellent, wonderful, superb" or "mdf" will produce the phrase "My dear friend". In both cases of vocabulary use or of acronyms use MACS brings on a scanning list the most frequent words and or the acronyms for selection by the user.

2.10 Backup Module

Vocabularies, acronyms, keyboard layouts, documents, languages can be backed up for security reasons. The software is expected to be released later this year and given out for trial. Users are expected to evaluate the advantages of the system and provide feedback for improvements.

2.11 Advantages of the System

MACS is a simple, easy-to-use software that increases productivity, provides freedom, facilitates independence, self-confidence and motivation to the user and cares of his/her individual attributes, needs and interests. The program records keystrokes and their sequence as well as time intervals between keystrokes, counts words per minute, lists the most frequently used letters, the most frequently used acronyms and the most frequently used words, saves the speed and the direction of scanning, backs up the information of the keyboard layouts used and adds new words written by the user to the basic vocabulary. Information recorded on the frequently pressed keys help for the design of the optimum on screen keyboard for each individual user. Recordings from the system and data collected will be used for further research. Results will provide valuable information for improvements and better configuration of the software. New prediction techniques produce shorter lists for scanning. During prediction the program merges the existing vocabulary with the user's new words. Users can collect words from written documents with the use of a tool called Word Harvester and add them to their vocabulary. Vocabularies can easily be filtered and customized to users' needs.

The speed of scanning is customizable and saved each time it is changed, to be used the next time the user gets on the program. MACS is designed to serve users from any origin, it is multilingual and it can be translated into any language very easily. There is a possibility for the user to create and save his acronyms The user can send e-mails and chat with friends on the internet.

2.12 Additional Features

First letter of the user's writings becomes capital automatically. Same happens after a full stop. User can also have capital letters when writing names. MACS could be used also as a teaching tool and be a part of children's Individual Educational Plan (IEP) as it can easily be adapted to any age group. Vocabularies are plain text lists so the user can take any list of words and use it on his system. The software gives option to have every day communication messages grouped in different categories like:

Wishes: I would like to go to the cinema;
Personal: My name is Nick
Greetings: Hello, How are you?
Sundry: Numbers, questions, general information.

It also provides option for the user to use scanning or work without scanning. Scanning facilitates access and speeds up expressive writing. Has a backup option to backup all files and transfer them on others' systems Work directly within any Windows® 98 – XP standard application.

2.13 What Is New in the Software

Speech synthesis is produced with syllabic synthesis of speech, that is with blending of recorded speech segments. The software is customizable to any language. It has a configurable keyboard layout. Has a possibility to be used by Arabic speakers. There is an option for sending-receiving emails and chatting over the internet. It is usable across all ages.

3 Future Enhancements of MACS

Users' vocabulary to be used for communication among speakers of different languages. Option for SMS sending and receiving SMS messages.

References

1. Ainscow, E.K.: Developing Inclusive Schools. NFER bulletin (26) (2001)
2. American Speech-Language-Hearing Association.: Roles and responsibilittes of speech-language pathologists with respect to alternative communication: Position statements. Retrieved from http://www.asha.org/NR/rdonlyres/BA19B90C-4230-86A8–83B4E12E4365/ 0/v3PSaac.pdf
3. Barton, L.: Inclusive Education: romantic, subversive or unrealistic? International Journal of Inclusive Education 1(3), 231–242 (1997)
4. Biklen, D., Ferguson, D., Ford, A. (eds.): Schooling and Disability, pp. 108–140. National Society for the Study of Education, Chicago (1989)

5. Beukerman, D.R, Mirenda, P.: Augmentative Alternative Comuunication: Supporting children & adults with complex communication needs (2005)
6. Callaghan, T.C.: Early understanding and production of graphic symbols. Child Development 70, 1314–1324 (1999)
7. Enderby, P., Philipp, R.: Speech and language handicap: Towards knowing the size of the problem. British Journal of Disorders of Communication 25, 341–354 (1990)
8. Ferguson, P., Asch, A.: Lessons from Life: Personals and Parentals perspectives on school, childhood and disability (1989)
9. Heward, W.L.: Teen Faulty Notions about teaching and Learning that Hinder the Effectiveness of Special Education. The journal of Special Education 36, 186–205 (2003)
10. ISAAC.: What it is (2007), http://www.isaac-online.org/en/aac/what_is.html
11. Knapp, M.: Essentials of nonverbal communication. Holt, Rinehart & Winston, New York (1980)
12. Light, J.: Interaction involving individuals using augmentative and alternative communication systems: State of the art and future directions. Augmentative and Alternative Communication 4, 66–82 (1988)
13. Makris, P.: Modern Technology for the Communication and Education of the Communicatively Impaired and for People with motor Control Problems, The National Co federation of People with Special Needs, EYZHN, Panellinion Congress on Inclusion, Athens (December 2001)
14. Makris, P.: Augmentative Communication and Integration, 3rd Congress of the ICT Users: Technology in Education, Nicosia (2002)
15. Makris, P.: A Communication Device for Communicatively Impaired People with Motor Control Problems, CASTME Conference, Intercollege, Nicosia (2004)
16. Makris, P.: Multilingual Augmentative Communication System (MACS) and Integration, Paedagogiki Etairia, Athens (2007)
17. Mineo Mollica, B.: Representational competence. In: Light, J.C, Beukelman, D.R., Reichle, J. (eds.) Communicative competence for individuals who use AAC: From research to effective practice, pp. 107–145 (2003)
18. Peck, C., Donalson, J., Pezzoli, M.: Some benefits non-handicapped adolescents perceive for themselves form their social relationships with peers who have severe handicaps. Journal of the Association for Persons with Severe Handicaps 15(4), 241–249 (1990)
19. Robinson, J., Griffith, P.: On the scientific status of iconicity. Sign Language Studies 25, 297–315 (1979)
20. Wilson, J.: Doing justice to inclusion. European Journal of Special Needs Education 15(3), 297–304 (2000)

Analysis and Synthesis of Multimodal Verbal and Non-verbal Interaction for Animated Interface Agents

Jonas Beskow, Björn Granström, and David House

Centre for Speech Technology, CSC, KTH, Stockholm, Sweden
{beskow,bjorn,davidh}@speech.kth.se

Abstract. The use of animated talking agents is a novel feature of many multimodal spoken dialogue systems. The addition and integration of a virtual talking head has direct implications for the way in which users approach and interact with such systems. However, understanding the interactions between visual expressions, dialogue functions and the acoustics of the corresponding speech presents a substantial challenge. Some of the visual articulation is closely related to the speech acoustics, while there are other articulatory movements affecting speech acoustics that are not visible on the outside of the face. Many facial gestures used for communicative purposes do not affect the acoustics directly, but might nevertheless be connected on a higher communicative level in which the timing of the gestures could play an important role. This chapter looks into the communicative function of the animated talking agent, and its effect on intelligibility and the flow of the dialogue.

Keywords: ECA, animated agent, audiovisual speech, non-verbal communication, visual prosody.

1 Introduction

In our interaction with others, we easily and naturally use all of our sensory modalities as we communicate and exchange information. Our senses are exceptionally well adapted for these tasks, and our brain enables us to effortlessly integrate information from different modalities fusing data to optimally meet the current communication needs. As we attempt to take advantage of the effective communication potential of human conversation in human–computer interaction, we see an increasing need to embody the conversational partner using audiovisual verbal and non-verbal communication in the form of animated talking agents. The use of animated talking agents is currently a novel feature of many multimodal experimental spoken dialogue systems. The addition and integration of a virtual talking head has direct implications for the way in which users approach and interact with such systems [1]. However, techniques for analyzing, modeling and testing this kind of interaction are still in a stage of rapid development.

Effective interaction in dialogue systems involves both the presentation of information and the flow of interactive dialogue. A talking animated agent can provide the user with an interactive partner whose goal is to take the role of the human agent. An effective agent is one who is capable of supplying the user with relevant information,

A. Esposito et al. (Eds.): Verbal and Nonverbal Commun. Behaviours, LNAI 4775, pp. 250–263, 2007.

can fluently answer questions concerning complex user requirements and can ultimately assist the user in a decision-making process through the flow of conversation. One way to achieve believability is through the use of a talking head where information is transformed into speech, articulator movements, speech-related gestures and conversational gestures. Useful applications of talking heads include aids for the hearing impaired, educational software, audiovisual human perception experiments [2], entertainment, and high-quality audiovisual text-to-speech synthesis for applications such as news reading. The use of the talking head aims at increasing effectiveness by building on the user's social skills to improve the flow of the dialogue [3]. Visual cues to feedback, turntaking and signalling the system's internal state are key aspects of effective interaction.

The talking head developed at KTH is based on text-to-speech synthesis. Audio speech synthesis is generated from a text representation in synchrony with visual articulator movements of the lips, tongue and jaw. Linguistic information in the text is used to generate visual cues for relevant prosodic categories such as prominence, phrasing and emphasis. These cues generally take the form of eyebrow and head movements which we have termed "visual prosody" [4]. These types of visual cues with the addition of e.g. a smiling or frowning face are also used as conversational gestures to signal such things as positive or negative feedback, turntaking regulation, and the system's internal state. In addition, the head can visually signal attitudes and emotions. More recently, we have been exploring data-driven methods to model articulation and facial parameters of major importance for conveying social signals and emotions.

The focus of this chapter is to look into the communicative function of the agent, both the capability to increase intelligibility of the spoken interaction and the possibility to make the flow of the dialogue smoother, through different kinds of communicative gestures such as gestures for emphatic stress, emotions, turntaking and negative or positive system feedback. The chapter reviews state-of-the-art animated agent technologies and some of their possible applications primarily in spoken dialogue systems. The chapter also includes some examples of methods of evaluating communicative gestures in different contexts.

2 KTH Multimodal Speech Synthesis

Animated synthetic talking faces and characters have been developed using a number of different techniques and for a variety of purposes for more than two decades. Historically, our approach is based on parameterised, deformable 3D facial models, controlled by rules within a text-to-speech framework [5]. The rules generate the parameter tracks for the face from a representation of the text, taking coarticulation into account [6]. We employ a generalized parameterisation technique to adapt a static 3D-wireframe of a face for visual speech animation [7]. Based on concepts first introduced by Parke [8], we define a set of parameters that will deform the wireframe by applying weighted transformations to its vertices.

The models are made up of polygon surfaces that are rendered in 3D using standard computer graphics techniques. The surfaces can be articulated and deformed under the control of a number of parameters. The parameters are designed to allow for intuitive interactive or rule-based control. The display can be chosen to show only the surfaces or the polygons for the different components of the face. The surfaces can be made (semi) transparent to display the internal parts of the model, including the tongue, palate, jaw and teeth [9]. The internal parts are based on articulatory measurements using MRI (Magnetic Resonance Imaging), EMA (ElectroMagnetic Articulography) and EPG (ElectroPalatoGraphy), in order to assure that the model's movements are realistic. This is of importance for language learning situations, where the transparency of the skin may be used to explain non-visible articulations [10] [11] [12] [13]. Several face models have been developed for different applications, some of them can be seen in Figure 1. All can be parametrically controlled by the same articulation rules.

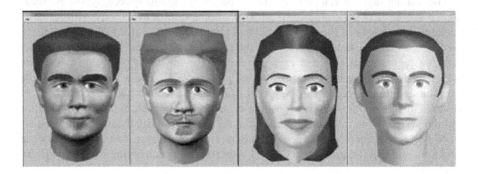

Fig. 1. Some different versions of the KTH talking head

For stimuli preparation and explorative investigations, we have developed a control interface that allows fine-grained control over the trajectories for acoustic as well as visual parameters. The interface is implemented as an extension to the WaveSurfer application (www.speech.kth.se/wavesurfer) [14] which is a freeware tool for recording, playing, editing, viewing, printing, and labelling audio data.

The interface makes it possible to start with an utterance synthesised from text, with the articulatory parameters generated by rule, and then interactively edit the parameter tracks for F0, visual (facial animation) parameters as well as the durations of individual segments in the utterance to produce specific cues. An example of the user interface is shown in Figure 2. In the top box a text can be entered in Swedish or English. The selection of language triggers separate text-to-speech systems with different phoneme definitions and rules, built in the Rulsys notation [5]. The generated phonetic transcription can be edited. On clicking "Synthesize", rule generated parameters will be created and displayed in different panes below. The selection of parameters is user controlled. A talking face is displayed in a separate window. The acoustic synthesis can be exchanged for a natural utterance and synchronised to the face synthesis on a segment-by-segment basis by running the face synthesis with phoneme durations from the natural utterance. The combination of natural and synthetic speech is useful for different experiments on multimodal integration and has been used in the Synface project [15]. In language learning applications this feature could be used to add to the naturalness of the tutor's voice in cases when the acoustic synthesis is judged to be inappropriate [16].

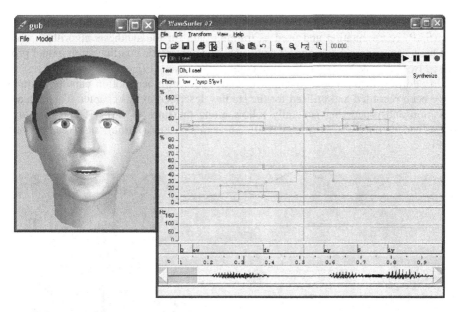

Fig. 2. The WaveSurfer user interface for parametric manipulation of the multimodal synthesis

3 Data Collection and Data-Driven Visual Synthesis

More recently, we have worked on data-driven visual synthesis using a newly developed MPEG-4 compatible talking head. A data-driven approach enables us to capture the interaction between facial expression and articulation. This is especially important when trying to synthesize emotional expressio ns (c.f. [17]).

To automatically extract important facial movements we have employed a motion capture procedure. We wanted to be able to obtain both articulatory data as well as other facial movements at the same time, and it was crucial that the accuracy in the measurements was good enough for resynthesis of an animated head.

We have used an opto-electronic motion tracking system – Qualysis MacReflex – to collect multimodal corpora of expressive speech. The Qualisys system allows capturing the dynamics of emotional facial expressions, by registering the 3D coordinates of a number of infrared-sensitive (IR) reflective markers, with sub-millimetre accuracy, at a rate of 60 frames/second.

In a typical session, a male native Swedish amateur actor was instructed to produce 75 short sentences with the six emotions happiness, sadness, surprise, disgust, fear and anger, plus neutral, yielding 7 x 75 recorded utterances.

A total of 29 IR-sensitive markers were attached to the speaker's face, of which 4 markers were used as reference markers (on the ears and on the forehead). The marker setup largely corresponds to MPEG-4 feature point (FP) configuration. Audio data was recorded on DAT-tape, and video was recorded using a mini-DV digital video camera. A synchronisation signal from the Qualisys system was fed into one audio channel of the DAT and DV to facilitate post-synchronisation of the data streams.

The recorded motion data was converted into an MPEG-4 facial animation parameter (FAP) representation and used as training data for the synthesis algorithms, that are based on principal component analysis and a parametric coarticulation model proposed by Cohen & Massaro [18]. For details, please see [19].

In addition to the above mentioned study, several other motion capture corpora have been recorded and utilised for the studies described in this chapter. The data acquisition and processing generally follow along the lines of earlier facial measurements carried out by Beskow et al. [20]. An example of a recording set-up can be seen in Fig. 3.

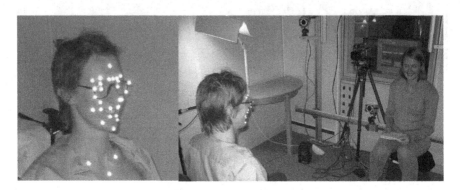

Fig. 3. Data collection setup with video and IR-cameras, microphone and a screen for prompts (right) and test subject with the IR-reflecting markers glued to the face (left)

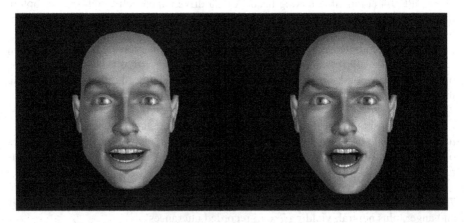

Fig. 4. Visual stimuli generated by data-driven synthesis from the happy database (left) and the angry database (right) using the MPEG-4 compatible talking head

The databases we have thus far collected have enabled us to analyze for example articulatory variation in expressive speech [17], visual manifestation of focal accent/prominence [21], and conversational cues in dialogue situations, in addition to providing us with data with which to develop data-driven visual synthesis. The data has also been used to directly drive synthetic 3D face models which adhere to the MPEG-4 Facial Animation (FA) standard [22] enabling us to perform comparative evaluation studies of different animated faces within the EU-funded PF-Star project [23][24]. Examples of the new head displaying different emotions taken from the database are shown in Figure 4.

4 Improving Intelligibility and Information Presentation

One of the more striking examples of improvement and effectiveness in speech intelligibility is taken from the Synface project which aims at improving telephone communication for the hearing impaired [25]. A demonstrator of the system for telephony with a synthetic face that articulates in synchrony with a natural voice has now been implemented as a result of the project.

Evaluation studies within this project were mainly oriented towards investigating differences in intelligibility between speech alone and speech with the addition of a talking head. These evaluation studies were performed off-line, e.g. the speech material was manually labelled so that the visible speech synthesis always generated the correct phonemes rather than being generated from the Synface recognizer which can introduce recognition errors. The results of a series of tests using non-sense VCV words and hearing-impaired subjects showed a significant gain in intelligibility when the talking head was added to a natural voice. With the synthetic face, consonant identification improved from 29% to 54% correct responses. This compares to the 57% correct response result obtained by using the natural face. In certain cases, notably the consonants consisting of lip movement (i.e. the bilabial and labiodental consonants), the response results were in fact better for the synthetic face than for the natural face [25]. This points to the possibility of using overarticulation strategies for the talking face in these kinds of applications. Results indicate that a certain degree of overarticulation can be advantageous in improving intelligibility [26]. The average preferred hyper articulation was found to be 24%, given the task to optimise the subjective ability to lip-read. The highest and lowest preferred values were 150 and 90% respectively with a standard deviation of 16%. The option of setting the articulation strength to the user's subjective preference is included in the Synface application.

Intelligibility tests have also been run using normal hearing subjects with similar results where the audio signal was degraded by adding white noise [25]. For example, for a synthetic male voice, consonant identification improved from 31% without the face to 45% with the face. A different type of application aimed at normal hearing persons is the use of a talking head in combination with targeted audio. To transmit highly directional sound, targeted audio makes use of a technique known as "parametric array" [27]. This type of highly directed sound can be used to communicate a voice message to a single person within a group of people (e.g. in a meeting situation or at a museum exhibit), minimally disturbing the other people. Within the framework of the EU project CHIL, experiments have shown that targeted audio combined with a talking head directed at the listener provides an efficient method of decreasing the disturbance by further lowering the audio intensity with retained and even increased intelligibility for the targeted listener [28].

5 Analyzing and Modelling Visual Cues for Prominence

5.1 Perception Experiments

In order to study the impact of visual cues on prominence we have carried out a series of experiments. The first concerns effects of eyebrow movements. In a previous study concerned with prominence and phrasing, using acoustic speech only, ambiguous sentences were used [29]. In the present experiment [4] we used one of these sentences:

1. När pappa fiskar stör, piper Putte *When dad is fishing sturgeon, Putte is whimpering*
2. När pappa fiskar, stör Piper Putte *When dad is fishing, Piper disturbs Putte*

Hence, "stör" could be interpreted as either a noun (1) (sturgeon) or a verb (2) (disturbs) ; "piper" (1) is a verb (whimpering), while "Piper" (2) is a name. In the stimuli, the acoustic signal is always the same, and synthesized as one phrase, i.e. with no phrasing prosody disambiguating the sentences. Six different versions were included in the experiment: one with no eyebrow movement and five where eyebrow rise was placed on one of the five content words in the test sentence. In the test list of 20 stimuli, each stimulus was presented three times in random order.

The subjects were instructed to listen as well as to look at the face. Two seconds before each sentence an audio beep was played to give subjects time to look up and focus on the face. No mention was made of eyebrows. The subjects were asked to circle the word that they perceived as most stressed/most prominent in the sentence.

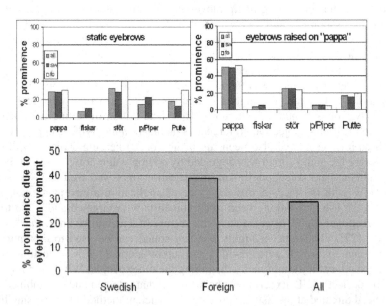

Fig. 5. Prominence responses in percent for each word. Subjects are grouped as all, Swedish (sw) and foreign (fo) (top). Mean prominence increase due to eyebrow movement (bottom).

The results are shown in Figure 5. Figure 5 (top, left) refers to judgements when there is no eyebrow movement at all. Obviously the distribution of judgements varies with both subject group and word in the sentence and may well be related to prominence expectations.

Figure 5 (top, right) displays the distribution when an eyebrow movement is occurring during the first word "pappa". A clear shift of responses to this word is evident. In Figure 5 (bottom) the mean increase due to eyebrow movement across all words can be seen. It is interesting to note that the Swedish speaking subjects with a different mother tongue showed a stronger dependence on the visual cues. It can be speculated that this group due to less familiarity with Swedish prosody relies more on visual aspects when they communicate in Swedish.

In another study [30] both eyebrow and head movements were tested as potential cues to prominence. Results from this experiment indicated that combined head and eyebrow movements are quite effective cues to prominence when synchronized with the stressed vowel of the potentially prominent word and when no conflicting acoustic cue is present.

5.2 Production Studies with Prominence in Several Expressive Modes

The types of studies reported on in the previous section have established the perceptual importance of eyebrow and head movement cues for prominence. These experiments do not, however, provide us with quantifiable data on the exact timing or amplitude of such movements used by human speakers such as can be found in e.g. [31][32]. Nor do they give us information on the variability of the movements in communicative situations. This kind of information is important if we are to be able to implement realistic facial gestures and head movements in our animated agents. In this section we present measurement results obtained from a speech corpus in which focal accent was systematically varied in a variety of expressive modes.

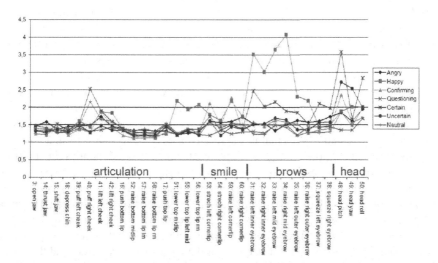

Fig. 6. The focal motion quotient, FMQ, averaged across all sentences, for all measured MPEG-4 FAPs for several expressive modes (see text for definitions and details)

The speech material used for the study consisted of 39 short, content neutral sentences such as "*Båten seglade förbi*" (The boat sailed by) and "*Grannen knackade på dörren*" (The neighbor knocked on the door), all with three content words which could each be focally accented. To elicit visual prosody in terms of prominence, these short sentences were recorded with varying focal accent position, usually on the subject, the verb and the object respectively, thus making a total of 117 sentences. The utterances were recorded in a variety of expressive modes including certain, confirming, questioning, uncertain, happy, angry and neutral. With the exception of angry, these were all expressions which are considered to be relevant in a spoken dialogue system scenario. The corpus is presented in more detail in [33], and the current study can be found in more detail in [21].

For recording the database, a total of 29 IR reflective markers were attached to the speaker's face, of which 4 markers were used as reference markers (on the ears and on the forehead). The marker setup, similar to that shown in Figure 3, largely corresponds to MPEG-4 feature point (FP) configuration. Audio data was recorded on DAT-tape, and video was recorded using a mini-DV digital video camera. A synchronisation signal from the Qualisys system was fed into one audio channel of the DAT and DV to facilitate post-synchronisation of the data streams.

In the present study, we chose to base our quantitative analysis of facial movement on the MPEG-4 Facial Animation Parameter (FAP) representation, because it is a compact and standardised scheme for describing movements of the human face and head. Specifically, we chose a subset of 31 FAPs out of the 68 FAPs defined in the MPEG-4 standard, including only the ones that we were able to calculate directly from our measured point data (discarding e.g. parameters for inner lip contour, tongue, ears and eyes).

We wanted to obtain a measure of how (in what FAPs) focus was realised by the recorded speaker for the different expressive modes. In an attempt to quantify this, we introduce the Focal Motion Quotient, FMQ, defined as the standard deviation of a FAP parameter taken over a word in focal position, divided by the average standard deviation of the same FAP in the same word in non-focal position. This quotient was then averaged over all sentence-triplets for each expressive mode separately.

As a first step in the analysis the FMQs for all the 31 measured FAPs were averaged across the 39 sentences. These data are displayed in Figure 6 for the analyzed expressive modes, i.e. Angry, Happy, Confirming, Questioning, Certain, Uncertain and Neutral. As can be seen, the FMQ mean is always above one, irrespective of which facial movement (FAP) that is studied. This means that a shift from a non-focal to a focal pronunciation on the average results in greater dynamics in all facial movements for all expressive modes. It should be noted that these are results from only one speaker and averages across the whole database. It is however conceivable that facial movements will at least reinforce the perception of focal accent. The mean FMQ taken over all expressive modes is 1.6. The expressive mode yielding the largest mean FMQ is happy (1.9) followed by confirming (1.7), while questioning has the lowest mean FMQ value of 1.3. If we look at the individual parameters and the different expressive modes, some FMQs are significantly greater, especially for the Happy expression, up to 4 for parameter 34 "raise right mid eyebrow". While much more detailed data on facial movement patterns is available in the database, we wanted to show the strong effects of focal accent on basically all facial movement patterns. Moreover, the results suggest that the specific gestures used for realization of focal accent are related to the intended expressive mode.

6 Visual Cues for Feedback

The use of a believable talking head can trigger the user's social skills such as using greetings, addressing the agent by name, and generally socially chatting with the agent. This was demonstrated by the results of the public use of the KTH August system [34][35]. These results led to more specific studies on visual cues for feedback such as [36] in which smile, for example, was found to be the strongest cue for affirmative feedback.

The stimuli used in [36] consisted of an exchange between a human, who was intended to represent a client, and the face, representing a travel agent. An observer of these stimuli could only hear the client's voice, but could both see and hear the agent. The human utterance was a natural speech recording and was exactly the same in all exchanges, whereas the speech and the facial expressions of the travel agent were synthetic and variable. The fragment that was manipulated always consisted of the following two utterances:

Client: "Jag vill åka från Stockholm till Linköping."
            ("I want to go from Stockholm to Linköping.")
Agent: "Linköping."

The stimuli were created by orthogonally varying six visual and acoustic parameters, using two possible settings for each parameter: one which was hypothesised to lead to affirmative feedback responses, and one which was hypothesised to lead to negative responses. The task was to respond to this dialogue exchange in terms of whether the agent signals that he understands and accepts the human utterance, or rather signals that he is uncertain about the human utterance. A detailed description of the experiment and the analysis can be found in [36]. Here, we would only like to highlight the strength of the different acoustic and visual cues. In Figure 7 the mean difference in response value (the response weighted by the subjects' confidence ratings) is presented for negative and affirmative settings of the different parameters. The effects of Eye_closure and Delay are not significant, but the trends observed in the means are clearly in the expected direction. There appears to be a strength order with Smile being the most important factor, followed by F0_contour, Eyebrow, Head_movement, Eye_closure and Delay.

This study clearly shows that subjects are sensitive to both acoustic and visual parameters when they have to judge utterances as affirmative or negative feedback signals. One obvious next step is to test whether the fluency of human-machine interactions is helped by the inclusion of such feedback cues in the dialogue management component of a system.

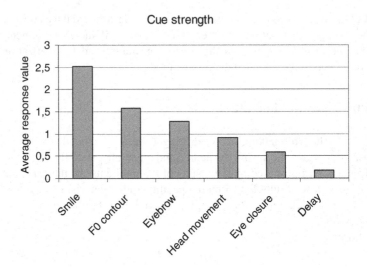

Fig. 7. The mean response value difference for stimuli with the indicated cues set to their affirmative and negative value

7 Future Challenges

In this chapter, we have presented an overview of some of the recent work in audio-visual synthesis, primarily at KTH, regarding data collection methods, modeling and evaluation experiments, and implementation in animated talking agents for dialogue systems. From this point of departure, we can see that many challenges remain before we will be able to create a believable, animated talking agent based on knowledge concerning how auditory and visual signals interact in verbal and non-verbal communication. In terms of modelling and evaluation, there is a great need to explore in more detail the coherence between audio and visual prosodic expressions especially regarding different functional dimensions. As we demonstrated in the section on prominence above, head nods which strengthen the percept of prominence tend to be integrated with the nearest candidate syllable resulting in audiovisual coherence. However, head nods which indicate dialogue functions such as feedback or turntaking may not be integrated with the audio in the same way. Visual gestures can even be used to contradict or qualify the verbal message, which is often the case in e.g. ironic expressions. On the other hand, there are other powerful visual communicative cues such as the smile which clearly affect the resulting audio (through articulation) and must by definition be integrated with the speech signal. Modelling of a greater number of parameters is also essential, such as head movement in more dimensions, eye movement and gaze, and other body movements such as hand and arm gestures. To model and evaluate how these parameters combine in different ways to convey individual personality traits while at the same time signalling basic prosodic and dialogue functions is a great challenge.

Acknowledgements

The work at KTH reported here was carried out by a large number of researchers at the Centre for Speech Technology which is gratefully acknowledged. The work has also been supported by the EU/IST projects SYNFACE and PF-Star.

References

1. Cassell, J., Bickmore, T., Campbell, L., Hannes, V., Yan, H.: Conversation as a System Framework: Designing Embodied Conversational Agents. In: Cassell, J., Sullivan, J., Prevost, S., Churchill, E. (eds.) Embodied Conversational Agents, pp. 29–63. The MIT Press, Cambridge, MA (2000)
2. Massaro, D.W.: Perceiving Talking Faces: From Speech Perception to a Behavioural Principle. The MIT Press, Cambridge, MA (1998)
3. Bickmore, T., Cassell, J.: Social Dialogue with Embodied Conversational Agents. In: van Kuppevelt, J., Dybkjaer, L., Bernsen, N.O. (eds.) Advances in Natural Multimodal Dialogue Systems, pp. 23–54. Springer, Dordrecht, The Netherlands (2005)
4. Granström, B., House, D., Beskow, J., Lundeberg, M.: Verbal and visual prosody in multimodal speech perception. In: von Dommelen, W., Fretheim, T. (eds.) Nordic Prosody: Proc of the VIIIth Conference, Trondheim 2000. Frankfurt am Main: Peter Lang, pp. 77–88 (2001)
5. Carlson, R., Granström, B.: Speech Synthesis. In: Hardcastle, W., Laver, J. (eds.) The Handbook of Phonetic Sciences, pp. 768–788. Blackwell Publishers Ltd., Oxford (1997)
6. Beskow, J.: Rule-based Visual Speech Synthesis. In: Proceedings of Eurospeech 1995, Madrid, Spain, pp. 299–302 (1995)
7. Beskow, J.: Animation of Talking Agents. In: Proceedings of AVSP 1997, ESCA Workshop on Audio-Visual Speech Processing, Rhodes, Greece, pp. 149–152 (1997)
8. Parke, F.I.: Parameterized models for facial animation. IEEE Computer Graphics 2(9), 61–68 (1982)
9. Engwall, O.: Combining MRI, EMA and EPG measurements in a three-dimensional tongue model. Speech Communication 41(2-3), 303–329 (2003)
10. Cole, R., Massaro, D.W., de Villiers, J., Rundle, B., Shobaki, K., Wouters, J., Cohen, M., Beskow, J., Stone, P., Connors, P., Tarachow, A., Solcher, D.: New tools for interactive speech and language training: Using animated conversational agents in the classrooms of profoundly deaf children. In: MATISSE. Proceedings of ESCA/Socrates Workshop on Method and Tool Innovations for Speech Science Education, pp. 45–52. University College London, London (1999)
11. Massaro, D.W., Bosseler, A., Light, J.: Development and Evaluation of a Computer-Animated Tutor for Language and Vocabulary Learning. In: ICPhS 2003. 15th International Congress of Phonetic Sciences, Barcelona, Spain, pp. 143–146 (2003)
12. Massaro, D.W., Light, J.: Read My Tongue Movements: Bimodal Learning To Perceive And Produce Non-Native Speech /r/ and /l/. In: Eurospeech 2003, Geneva, Switzerland, pp. 2249–2252 (2003)
13. Engwall, O., Bälter, O., Öster, A-M., Kjellström, H.: Designing the user interface of the computer-based speech training system ARTUR based on early user tests. Journal of Behavioural and Information Technology 25(4), 353–365 (2006)
14. Sjölander, K., Beskow, J.: WaveSurfer - an Open Source Speech Tool. In: Proc of ICSLP 2000, Beijing, vol. 4, pp. 464–467 (2000)

15. Beskow, J., Karlsson, I., Kewley, J., Salvi, G.: SYNFACE - A talking head telephone for the hearing-impaired. In: Miesenberger, K., Klaus, J., Zagler, W., Burger, D. (eds.) ICCHP 2004. LNCS, vol. 3118, pp. 1178–1186. Springer, Heidelberg (2004)

16. Engwall, O., Wik, P., Beskow, J., Granström, G.: Design strategies for a virtual language tutor. In: Kim, S.H.Ý. (ed.) Proc ICSLP 2004, Jeju Island, Korea, pp. 1693–1696 (2004)

17. Nordstrand, M., Svanfeldt, G., Granström, B., House, D.: Measurements of articulatory variation in expressive speech for a set of Swedish vowels. Speech Communication 44, 187–196 (2004)

18. Cohen, M.M., Massaro, D.W.: Modelling Coarticulation in Synthetic Visual Speech. In: Magnenat-Thalmann, N., Thalmann, D. (eds.) Models and Techniques in Computer Animation, pp. 139–156. Springer, Tokyo (1993)

19. Beskow, J., Nordenberg, M.: Data-driven Synthesis of Expressive Visual Speech using an MPEG-4 Talking Head. In: Beskow, J., Nordenberg, M. (eds.) Proceedings of INTERSPEECH 2005, Lisbon, Portugal, pp. 793–796 (2005)

20. Beskow, J., Engwall, O., and Granström, B.: Resynthesis of Facial and Intraoral Articulation from Simultaneous Measurements. In: Solé, M.J., D. R., Romero, J.(eds.) Proceedings of the 15th ICPhS, Barcelona, Spain, pp: 431–434 (2003)

21. Beskow, J., Granström, B., House, D.: Visual correlates to prominence in several expressive modes. In: Proceedings of Interspeech 2006, Pittsburg, PA, pp. 1272–1275 (2006)

22. Pandzic, I.S., Forchheimer, R.: MPEG Facial animation – the standard, implementation and applications. John Wiley & Sons, Chichester, England (2002)

23. Beskow, J., Cerrato, L., Cosi, P., Costantini, E., Nordstrand, M., Pianesi, F., Prete, M., Svanfeldt, G.: Preliminary Cross-cultural Evaluation of Expressiveness in Synthetic Faces. In: Proc. Affective Dialogue Systems (ADS) 2004, Kloster Irsee, Germany, pp. 301–304 (2004)

24. Beskow, J., Cerrato, L., Granström, B., House, D., Nordenberg, M., Nordstrand, M., Svanfeldt, G.: Expressive Animated Agents for Affective Dialogue Systems. In: Proc. Affective Dialogue Systems (ADS) 2004, Kloster Irsee, Germany, pp. 240–243 (2004)

25. Agelfors, E., Beskow, J., Dahlquist, M., Granström, B., Lundeberg, M., Spens, K.-E., Öhman, T.: Synthetic faces as a lipreading support. In: Proceedings of ICSLP 1998, Sydney, Australia, pp. 3047–3050 (1998)

26. Beskow, J., Granström, B., Spens, K.-E.: Articulation strength - Readability experiments with a synthetic talking face. TMH-QPSR, vol. 44, KTH, Stockholm, pp. 97–100 (2002)

27. Westervelt, P.J.: Parametric acoustic array. J. Acoust. Soc. Amer. 35, 535–537 (1963)

28. Svanfeldt, G., Olszewski, D.: Perception experiment combining a parametric loudspeaker and a synthetic talking head. In: Svanfeldt, G., Olszewski, D. (eds.) Proceedings of INTERSPEECH 2005, Lisbon, Portugal, pp. 1721–1724 (2005)

29. Bruce, G., Granström, B., House, D.: Prosodic phrasing in Swedish speech synthesis. In: Bailly, G., Benoit, C., Sawallis, T.R. (eds.) Talking Machines: Theories, Models, and Designs, pp. 113–125. North Holland, Amsterdam (1992)

30. House, D., Beskow, J., Granström, B.: Timing and interaction of visual cues for prominence in audiovisual speech perception. In: Proc. Eurospeech 2001, Aalborg, Denmark, pp. 387–390 (2001)

31. Keating, P., Baroni, M., Mattys, S., Scarborough, R., Alwan, A., Auer, E., Bernstein, L.: Optical Phonetics and Visual Perception of Lexical and Phrasal Stress in English. In: Proc. 15th International Congress of Phonetic Sciences, pp. 2071–2074 (2003)

32. Dohen, M.: Deixis prosodique multisensorielle: Production et perception audiovisuelle de la focalisation contrastive en Français. PhD thesis, Institut de la Communication Parlée, Grenoble (2005)

33. Beskow, J., Cerrato, L., Granström, B., House, D., Nordstrand, M., Svanfeldt, G.: The Swedish PF-Star Multimodal Corpora. In: Proc. LREC Workshop, Multimodal Corpora: Models of Human Behaviour for the Specification and Evaluation of Multimodal Input and Output Interfaces, Lisbon, Portugal, pp. 34–37 (2004)
34. Bell, L., Gustafson, J.: Interacting with an animated agent: an analysis of a Swedish database of spontaneous computer directed speech. In: Proc of Eurospeech 1999, pp. 1143–1146 (1999)
35. House, D.: Phrase-final rises as a prosodic feature in wh-questions in Swedish human–machine dialogue. Speech Communication 46, 268–283 (2005)
36. Granström, B., House, D., Swerts, M.G.: Multimodal feedback cues in human-machine interactions. In: Bernard, B., Isabelle, M. (eds.) Proceedings of the Speech Prosody 2002 Conference, pp. 347–350. Aix-en-Provence, Laboratoire Parole et Langage (2002)

Generating Nonverbal Signals for a Sensitive Artificial Listener

Dirk Heylen, Anton Nijholt, and Mannes Poel

Human Media Interaction Group
Department of Computer Science, University of Twente
The Netherlands
{heylen,anijholt,mpoel}@cs.utwente.nl

Abstract. In the Sensitive Artificial Listener project research is performed with the aim to design an embodied agent that not only generates the appropriate nonverbal behaviors that accompany speech, but that also displays verbal and nonverbal behaviors during the production of speech by its conversational partner. Apart from many applications for embodied agents where natural interaction between agent and human partner also require this behavior, the results of this project are also meant to play a role in research on emotional behavior during conversations. In this paper, our research and implementation efforts in this project are discussed and illustrated with examples of experiments, research approaches and interfaces in development.

1 Introduction

Most of the work on the generation of communicative behaviors of embodied conversational agents has been concerned with generating the appropriate non-verbal behaviors that accompany the speech of the embodied agent: the brows, the gestures, or the lip movements. The generation of the verbal and non-verbal behaviors to display when someone else is speaking, that is the behavior of a listening agent, has received less attention. A major reason for this neglect is the inability of the interpretation modules to construct representations of meaning incrementally and in real-time that is contingent on the production of the speech of the interlocutor. As many conversational analysts and other researchers of face-to-face interaction have shown, the behaviors displayed by auditors are an essential determinant of the way in which conversations proceed. By showing displays of attention, interest, understanding, compassion, or the reverse, the auditor/listener, determines to an important extent the flow of conversation, providing feedback on several levels.

In this paper we survey our work on listening behavior as it will be implemented in semi-autonomous embodied chat-bots that will be part of the Sensitive Artificial Listener (SAL) system. This system, developed in collaboration with Queens University, Belfast and used in the Humaine project (see http://www.emotion-net.research/), is used to elicit emotions and accompanying behaviors that occur in conversations. In the original system, a person is sitting in front of a camera and hears the voice of one of the "characters". The utterances by the characters are selected by

A. Esposito et al. (Eds.): Verbal and Nonverbal Commun. Behaviours, LNAI 4775, pp. 264–274, 2007.

an operator who can choose from a collection of pre-recorded phrases. They are indexed by the character they belong to, a pair of emotion dimension labels (positive/negative and active/passive) and by content category. They consist of general moves such as greetings, questions that prompt the persons interacting with SAL to continue speaking, and all kinds of reactions to what the persons are saying.

The scripts for each of the characters were developed, tested and refined in an iterative way. Each character has a number of different types of scripts depending on the emotional state of the user. So, for example, character Poppy has a script for the user in each of four emotional states - a positive active state, a negative active state, a positive passive state, a negative passive state. There are also script types relevant to the part of the conversation (beginning, main part) or structural state of the conversation (repair script). Each script type has within it a range of statements and questions. They cannot be context specific as there is no 'intelligence' involved. Many are clichés such as 'Always look on the bright side of things' (Poppy) or fillers such as 'Really' or prompts to keep the conversation going 'Tell me more'.

In the current system the operator chooses the particular utterances in accordance with the stage of the dialogue and the emotional state of the person. Each character has a different personality expressed through what they are saying and the way they say it and will try to bring the person in a particular emotional state by their comments; cheerful or gloomy, for instance. Our aim is to develop an agent version in which the voices are replaced by talking heads and the behaviors are partly decided upon automatically.

In this paper some modest steps that bring us closer to this goal are discussed. We describe the general contours of the project, the way we approach the subject, the set-up of experiments and some important implementation issues. In section 2 we provide some background on listening behavior research. Section 3 introduces the data that we are using and we give examples of research we perform on this data. This includes the annotation and analysis of listening behavior data and setting up of experiments based on observations of the data. After this, in section 4, we turn to the issue of designing a model of a semi-autonomous listening agent. Clearly, as may then have become clear from previous sections, no computational model showing all subtleties of listening behavior is available. Hence, in these general observations on possible architectural designs we have reserved a role for a human operator. Our research aims at making this operator superfluous. Some current implementation work that will make the operator-supported listening system more useful for experiments is explained in section 5.

2   Background on Listening Behavior for Embodied Agents

Listeners in face-to-face interactions are not only attending to the communicative signals being emitted by the speakers, but are sending out signals themselves in the various modalities that are available to them: facial expressions, gestures, head movements and speech. These communicative signals, operating in the so-called back-channel, mostly function as feedback on the actions of the speaker; providing information on the reception of the signals; propelling the interaction forward, marking understanding, or providing insight into the attitudes and emotions that the speech gives rise to.

Responses to talk by recipients can take many forms. They can take the form of a subsequent move in the next turn, but most of the behaviors of the non-talking participant in the conversation displayed during the turn of the speaker can count as some kind of "response", providing the speaker with feedback on perception, attention, understanding and the way in which the message is received in general: the change in the beliefs, attitudes and affective state of the recipient. These cues and signals enable the synchronization of the communicative actions (for instance turn-taking), grounding and the building of rapport.

There are several aspects to take into account that have been studied in the literature. The main studies of nonverbal behavior that paid attention to forms and functions of listening behavior on which we are basing our research are the following.

Synchronization of listener and speaker behaviour, signalling the degree of understanding, agreement or support, has been studied in, among others, [10]. More detailed studies have looked at the form and function of head movements in feedback, e.g. [6] and [11], and form and function of facial expressions, e.g., [3]. Finally, in [1] feedback requirements for establishing grounding in conversations are distinguished.

In order to be able to generate appropriate behaviors for a conversational agent in response to the speech of a human interlocutor we need a better understanding of the kinds of behaviors mentioned above, their timing, determinants, and their effects. As we stated before, most of the work on the generation of communicative behaviors of embodied conversational agents has been concerned with generating the appropriate nonverbal behaviors that accompany the speech of the embodied agent whereas the generation of the verbal and non-verbal behaviors to display during the production of speech by another actor, has been ignored in general. Besides the fact that most work on embodied conversational agents has focused on speaking behaviors, it also appears that not all expressive behaviors have received the same amount of attention. Language, facial expressions, gestures and gaze are the main kinds of expressive behaviors that have been studied so far. Posture and head movements, another group of nonverbal behaviors that are very informative about the intentions, attitudes, emotions and the mental state of interlocutors, in particular, "auditors", have been less widely studied.

Summarizing, the various feedback behaviours that our Sensitive Artificial Listener should display are not only varied in their form but also in their function. The timing of them is essential, as several forms occur in parallel with the utterance of the speaker (synchronous interaction). This poses a big challenge for constructing embodied agents that need to react instantly on the speech produced by speakers. Most of the work on reactive agents has based these reactions on superficial cues that are easy to detect. The listening agent developed at ICT [5], [13] produces feedback on the basis of head movements of the speaker and a few acoustic features [18]. Similar kind of input will be used in our SAL system in progress. Research on multimodal feedback signals in the context of the SAL project is also reported in [2], [7] and [8].

3 Data Collection and Analysis in AMI and Humaine

In order to learn more about the form, the distribution and the functions of feedback behaviors we look at the corpus collected in the AMI project (http://www.amiproject.org/) and the collection of interactions with the Wizard of Oz version of SAL (see http://www.emotion-research.net/). With two examples we illustrate the role these data collections have in our research.

3.1 Annotation of Listening Behavior

The first example illustrates our work on the analysis of head movements and their backchannel functions. The screenshot shown below (Fig. 1) shows some of the annotations that have been made for this reason on the AMI data. In this case, the annotations covered head movements, gaze position, facial expressions, a characterization of the function of the head movements and the transcripts. The characterization of the functions was based on the determinants listed in [7].

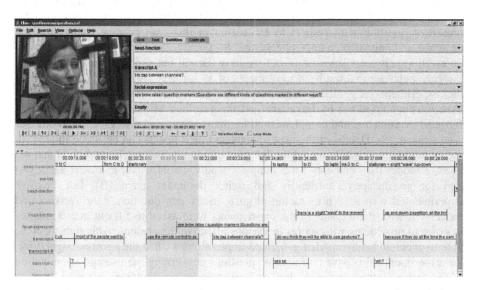

Fig. 1. Annotation tool for listening behavior in the AMI data

The following list provides the major functions that were used for head movements and back-channels.

- Cognitive determinants: thinking, remembering, hesitation, correction
- Interaction management: turn-regulation, addressing
- Discourse and information functions: deixis, rhetorical functions, question marker, emphasis
- Affect and Attitude: epistemic markers (belief, skepticism), surprise, etcetera.

Besides such hand-made annotations, we are using automatic procedures to extract features from the speech and head movements to be able to list in more detail the distribution of verbal and nonverbal backchannels. With an analysis of hundreds of fragments of listening behavior we hope to get a better picture of the association between head movements' properties and their functions, where the head movements can be quite tiny and the functions more refined than in most analyses currently available in the literature.

3.2 Impression Management

The personality of the four characters used in SAL comes out mainly in the kinds of things they say. The character Poppy, for instance, is cheerful and optimistic and will try to cheer up the interlocutors when they are in a negative state and be happy for them when they are in a positive state. Obadiah, on the other hand, is gloomy and passive and will say things with the opposite effect. The voices, created by (amateur) actors are also quite expressive.

When we are going to introduce talking heads in the SAL interface the choice of talking head should match these personalities, as should their nonverbal behaviors. An important question with respect to evaluation in this case is what impression the designed and animated characters generate. So far, we haven't put animators to work on creating particular animations, but we have carried out some experiments varying the gaze behavior and the head movements of a character and having participants in the experiment judge these behaviors. Our experiments were based on earlier experiments carried out by Fukayama [4] for gaze and Mignault and Chauduri [14] for head movements, and complemented by many other works on gaze, including our own work in [9]. Details of the experiments and their results can be found in [16]. In the experiments we made use of the Rutgers University Talking Head RUTH and we tried to model the behaviors for a happy, friendly, unobtrusive, extrovert agent (A) and for an unhappy, unfriendly and rather dominant agent (B). For this we experimented with head tilt, amount of gaze, mean gaze duration, gaze aversion and movement size. Participants in the experiments were asked to fill out questionnaires in order to provide us with scores in various affective dimensions. Although we were able to generate behaviors that generated impressions we had the agents designed for, the experiments also gave rise to new questions concerning the use and combination of the various impression variables. An issue that we are exploring in several studies (see also [2]) is the question of how complex expressions should be indexed by multiple functional variables at the same time.

4   Design of a Listening Behavior Model

In this section we report on the progress towards finding a uniform way to describe a model of a listening agent. The description is rather high-level, but it allows for various implementations, that is, different kinds of behavior models, depending on the kinds of experiments we want to carry out in the context of our SAL research. The description is done in terms of entity relation diagrams.

A listening agent receives sensor input from its environment and performs action output to the environment. Based on sensor input the agent decides which action to take. This is done in the following way:

1. The SENSOR INPUT is evaluated and MEANINGFUL EVENTS are detected;
2. MEANINGFUL EVENTS can be combined to form a new MEANINGFUL EVENT;
3. MEANINGFUL EVENTS may trigger a reaction from the agent, in other words, some MEANINGFUL EVENTS will cause the agent to act. A MEANINGFUL EVENT can be mapped to an ACTION PRIMITIVE;
4. The internal MENTAL STATE of the agent influences the action selection process of the agent. Depending on the state certain ACTION PRIMITIVES may or may not be selected when a MEANINGFUL EVENT occurs.

For the SAL project an operator (the Wizard) must be able to influence the agent's behavior, this makes the agent less autonomous, but gives more freedom in experimental settings.

In Fig. 2 we illustrate the choices in a diagram for the agent selection mechanism (read from left to right).

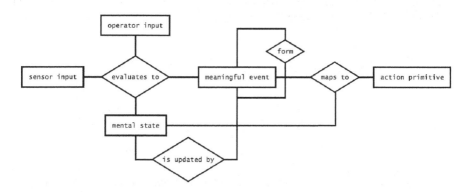

Fig. 2. Agent action selection mechanism

This is a simplified model that ignores some relations that will not be considered here. For example, a more realistic model lets the MENTAL STATE influence the SENSOR INPUT. Some other possibilities are OPERATOR INPUT directly triggering actions, etc.

Based on some exercises we are currently adapting this model. In these exercises we look at the current literature on responsive behavior and try to incorporate rules and algorithms into our framework. For example, we looked at the algorithms presented in [15] where measures of attention and interest based on gaze are used to decide if the speaker should continue the conversation. We also considered Maatman [12], who introduced rules such as "if the speech contains a relatively long period of low pitch then perform a head nod", or "if the human partner performs a head shake then mirror this head shake, etc., and we looked at rules presented by Thórisson [17], e.g., "look puzzled during an awkward pause". Attempts to incorporate these and similar rules into our framework necessarily led to refinements and extensions, for example, the addition of time and value attributes, the possibility to plan actions, the possibility to choose between contesting actions, etcetera.

We assume that ultimately this research line will allow us to implement a SAL system where the listening agent is equipped with a fixed set of action primitives (repertoire) and rules will be defined that decide if and when these actions should be performed.

5   A Remote Sensitive Artificial Listening System

While in section 3 and 4 of this paper we surveyed our research efforts to model listening behavior in a (semi-autonomous) listener agent, in this section we report about efforts to build an operator (Wizard) interface, where we can incrementally embed more knowledge about listening behavior, that is, elements of the model described in section 4, in order to reduce the task of the human operator. Hence, incrementally we want to automate the tasks of the operator by providing him with an interface and tools that slowly take over his tasks.

We realized a distributed version of the SAL system based on the client-server paradigm (see Fig. 3). Hence, the operator is no longer in the same room as the person interacting with SAL. This creates a true 'Wizard of Oz' system.

Fig. 3. Global setup for the remote SAL system

The distributed version of SAL consists of three components (Fig. 4): a central SAL server, a client at the respondent side and a client at the operator side. The system has an interface at both the operator and the respondent site. The current operator interface is depicted in Fig. 5.

Operator Interface. In the left pane the operator can see the status of the connection. The right pane called Interaction is for controlling the interaction. First there are four buttons for classifying the emotional state of the respondent into four categories; negative active (-ve act), positive active (+ve act), negative passive (-vi pass) and pragmatic (prag). Also there are buttons to select one of the four SAL characters; Poppy, Prudence, Obadiah and Spike. Under the buttons the operator can see the webcam recording of the respondent (not shown in the figure). The right part of the Interaction pane is dedicated to selecting one of the speaker scripts (WAV files) which is played at the respondent side. Speaker scripts of each speaker are divided into four ranges of replies that correspond to the four possible emotional states that the respondent can be classified into, which we name state scripts. The state scripts have some or all of the following three response categories of replies: 1. statement, 2.

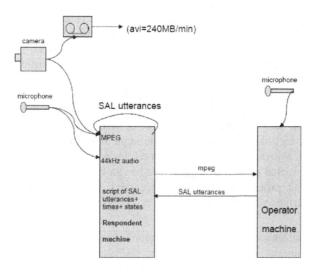

Fig. 4. The client-server architecture for the remote SAL system. The server is not depicted but arranges the connections between the operator and the respondent client.

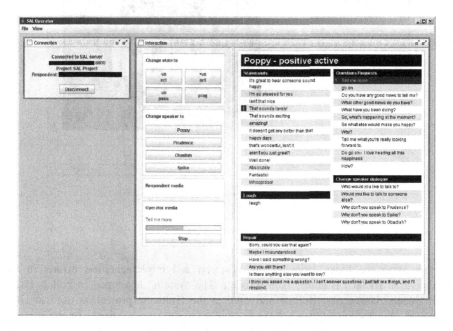

Fig. 5. The operator interface

question/request, and 3. change speaker dialogue. In addition there are start-up scripts, which appear at the start of the interaction with a character, and repair scripts.

Respondent Interface. To whom should the respondent address his or her speech and attention? Ultimately, the interface will show the (semi-)autonomous listening agent.

Presently, an important requirement is that it should have abstract visuals that catch the attention and the focus of the respondent and supports the mood and personality of the SAL speakers (see Figure 6). The visual image on the screen in the respondent interface changes as the SAL speakers change, and it should display the emotion in the voice of the SAL speaker on the simplest possible way. We can use or implement one or more basic algorithms for visuals that move and change color according to some parameters that can be extracted by speech recognition algorithms from the wav format of speaker scripts. Implementation of the visual display of the emotion in the SAL speaker's voice will take place after the implementation of more crucial parts of the remote SAL system. The above described design of the remote version of SAL has been implemented in Java using the Java Media Framework. The system supports plug-ins that can process interaction-related data, including recorded media, and enhance the interface with visualizations or extra operator options.

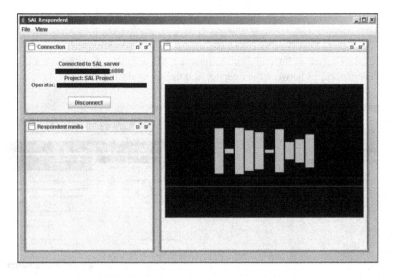

Fig. 6. The current respondent interface

6   Conclusions

In this paper we have surveyed our research and implementation efforts in the Sensitive Artificial Listening agent project. The system, developed in collaboration with Queens University, Belfast and used in the Humaine project, is used to elicit emotions and accompanying behaviors that occur in conversations. In the original system, a person is sitting in front of a camera and hears the voice of one of four possible characters. Goal of the research and implementation efforts is to replace the original system by a system where the voices are replaced by talking heads or embodied agents that not only generate the appropriate nonverbal behaviors that accompany speech, but that also display verbal and nonverbal behaviors during the production of speech by their conversational partner.

We discussed our settings for experiments and for data collection, annotation and analysis. Examples of experiments and the design issues for a listening behavior model were presented. Moreover, we introduced our current architecture of the system that can be used for experiments and in which results of research and experiments can incrementally be embedded.

Acknowledgements. We are grateful to our students, Ruben Kooijman and Boris Reuderink, for their work on this project. The research is supported by the FP6 EU Network of Excellence Humaine.

References

1. Allwood, J., Nivre, J., Ahlsén, E.: On the semantics and pragmatics of linguistic feedback. Journal of Semantics 9(1), 1–26 (1992)
2. Bevacqua, E., Heylen, D., Pelachaud, C.: Facial feedback signals for ECAs. In: Heylen, D., Marsella, S. (eds.) Proceedings AISB 2007 Symposium Mindful Environments, New Castle upon Tyne (April 2007)
3. Chovil, N.: Social determinants of facial displays. Journal of Nonverbal Behavior 15, 141–154 (1991)
4. Fukayama, A., Ohno, T., Mukawa, N., Sawaki, M., Hagita, N.: Messages embedded in gaze of interface agents - impression management with agent's gaze. In: Proceedings of CHI 2002, pp. 41–48. ACM Press, New York (2002)
5. Gratch, J., Okhmatovskaia, A., Lamothe, F., Marsella, S., Morales, M., van der Werf, R., Morency, L.-P.: Virtual rapport. In: Gratch, J., Young, M., Aylett, R., Ballin, D., Olivier, P. (eds.) IVA 2006. LNCS (LNAI), vol. 4133, pp. 14–27. Springer, Heidelberg (2006)
6. Hadar, U., Steiner, T., Rose, C.F.: Head movement during listening turns in conversation. Journal of Nonverbal Behavior 9, 214–228 (1985)
7. Heylen, D.: Head gestures, gaze and the principles of conversational structure. International Journal of Humanoid Robotics 3, 241–267 (2006)
8. Heylen, D.: Multimodal Backchannel Generation for Conversational Agents. In: van der Sluis, I., Theune, M., Reiter, E., Krahmer, E. (eds.) Proceedings of the workshop on Multimodal Output Generation (MOG 2007), Aberdeen, UK, pp. 81–92 (2007)
9. Heylen, D., van Es, I., van Dijk, B., Nijholt, A.: Controlling the gaze of conversational agents. In: van Kuppevelt, J., Dybkjaer, L., Bernsen, N.O. (eds.) Natural, Intelligent and Effective Interaction in Multimodal Dialogue Systems, pp. 245–262. Kluwer Academic Publishers, Dordrecht (2005)
10. Kendon, A.: Movement coordination in social interaction: some examples described. Acta Psychologica 32, 100–125 (1970)
11. Kendon, A.: Some uses of head shake. Gesture 2, 147–182 (2003)
12. Maatman, R.M.: Responsive behavior of a listening agent. Technical report, Institute for Creative Technologies (December 2004)
13. Maatman, R., Gratch, J., Marsella, S.: Natural behavior of a listening agent. In: Panayiotopoulos, T., Gratch, J., Aylett, R., Ballin, D., Olivier, P., Rist, T. (eds.) IVA 2005. LNCS (LNAI), vol. 3661, pp. 25–36. Springer, Heidelberg (2005)
14. Mignault, A., Chauduri, A.: The many faces of a neutral face: Head tilt and perception of dominance and emotion. Journal of Nonverbal Behavior 27, 111–132 (2003)

15. Pelachaud, C., Peters, C., Mancini, M., Bevacqua, E., Poggi, I.: A model of attention and interest using gaze behavior. In: Panayiotopoulos, T., Gratch, J., Aylett, R., Ballin, D., Olivier, P., Rist, T. (eds.) IVA 2005. LNCS (LNAI), vol. 3661, pp. 229–240. Springer, Heidelberg (2005)
16. Reuderink, B.: The influence of gaze and head tilt on the impression of listening agents. Manuscript, University of Twente (2006)
17. Thórisson, K.R.: Natural turn-taking needs no manual: Computational theory and model, from perception to action. Multimodality in Language and Speech Systems, 173–207 (2002)
18. Ward, N., Tsukahara, W.: Prosodic features which cue back-channel responses in English and Japanese. Journal of Pragmatics 23, 1177–1207 (2000)

Low-Complexity Algorithms for Biometric Recognition

Marcos Faundez-Zanuy[1], Virginia Espinosa-Duró[1], and Juan Antonio Ortega[2]

[1] Escola Universitària Politècnica de Mataró (Adscrita a la UPC)
08303 MATARO (BARCELONA), Spain
[2] Departament d'Enginyeria Electrònica, UPC Terrassa
faundez@eupmt.es, espinosa@eupmt.es, ortegar@eel.upc.edu
http://www.eupmt.es/veu

Abstract. In this paper we emphasize the relevance of low-complexity algorithms for biometric recognition and we present to examples with special emphasis on face recognition. Our face recognition application has been implemented on a low-cost fixed point processor and we have evaluated that with 169 integer coefficients per face we achieve better identification results (92%) than the classical eigenfaces approach (86.5%), and close to the DCT (92.5%) with a reduced computational cost.

1 Introduction

In common pattern recognition applications, usually, there are a limited number of classes and a great number of training samples; think for example in the recognition of handwritten digits (10 classes) from U.S. postal envelopes. This situation is absolutely reversed in biometrics [1], where we take normally three to five measures per person during the enrollment (three to five samples for training per class) and the people enrolled in the database is large (much more classes than samples per class). In this situations there area not enough training samples and the mean vector nor the covariance matrix can be estimated accurately. In fact, a small number of training samples is a desirable property of biometric systems. Otherwise the enrollment procedure for a new user will be time consuming and the system will lack of commercial value. Although speaker recognition [2] is a particular case where thousands of feature vectors are available, this is not the case in most of the other biometric traits such as face, signature, hand-geometry, fingerprint, etc. We have evaluated that some on-line signatures are as short as 50 samples. Hand geometry is based on some measures (finger length, width, perimeter, etc.) and a single feature vector is obtained per sample. Face recognition from a statistical approach considers each snapshot as a single feature vector. Thus it does not have too much sense to use a very sophisticated mathematical model and some simple approaches must be used. In addition, simple approaches usually require less memory and reduce the computational burden. This permits real time applications, even on a low-cost processor. Thus, some sophisticated models such as Hidden Markov Models (HMM) and Gaussian Mixture Models (GMM) [3] are not the most suitable tools when the number of training samples is not large.

A. Esposito et al. (Eds.): Verbal and Nonverbal Commun. Behaviours, LNAI 4775, pp. 275–285, 2007.

In [4-5] we addressed the problem of on-line signature recognition and we realized that the "classical" Vector Quantization (VQ) approach offered better performance than HMM and a similar performance to Dynamic Time Warping (DTW) with a reduced computational burden. Although DTW and VQ were successfully applied in the eighties for speech and speaker recognition applications, as the computational power was increased, more complex tools such as HMM provided better results. However on-line signature does not contain enough feature vectors for training a sophisticated statistical models, and simpler models can provide better results.

Face recognition problems have also been addressed by a method called eigenfaces [6] which in fact is a practical implementation of the Karhunen-Loeve (KL) transform. This transform has provided good results in several pattern recognition problems. However, it is not the most suitable for face recognition for a couple of reasons:

a) The transform is data dependent. Thus, the extracted features depend on the training image and some generalization problems can appear when dealing with new users and images not used during enrollment.

b) It is well known that simpler transforms such as DCT converge to KL when the block size to be transformed is large (>64 samples), and this is the case of face recognition. In fact, the most popular image compression standards JPEG and MPEG are not based on KL. They are based on DCT.

In this paper we will present an efficient and low-complexity face recognition approach based on Walsh Hadamard Transform (WHT). According to our experiments, WHT outperforms eigenfaces and provides similar results to DCT.

2   Face Recognition

Usually, a pattern recognition system consists of two main blocks: feature extraction and classifier. Figure 1 summarizes this scheme. On the other hand, there are two main approaches for face recognition:

Statistical approaches consider the image as a high-dimension vector, where each pixel is mapped to a component of a vector. Due to the high dimensionality of vectors some vector-dimension reduction algorithm must be used. Typically the Karhunen Loeve transform (KLT) is applied with a simplified algorithm known as eigenfaces [6]. However, this algorithm is suboptimal. Nowadays, with the improvements on computational speed and memory capacities, it is possible to compute the KLT directly, but computational burden and memory requirements are still important. In order to alleviate this problem we have resized the original images from 112×92 to 56×46 for the KLT results.

Geometry-feature-based methods try to identify the position and relationship between face parts, such as eyes, nose, mouth, etc., and the extracted parameters are measures of textures, shapes, sizes, etc. of these regions.

In this paper, we mainly focus on the study of the feature extraction for the face recognition using statistical approaches.

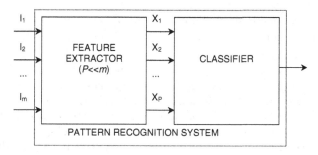

Fig. 1. General Pattern recognition system

2.1 Walsh Hadamard Transform

The Walsh-Hadamard transform basis functions can be expressed in terms of Hadamard matrices. A Hadamard matrix H_n is a $N \times N$ matrix of ± 1 values, where $N = 2^n$. In contrast to error-control coding applications, in signal processing it is better to write the basis functions as rows of the matrix with increasing number of zero crossings. The ordered Hadamard matrix can be obtained with the following equations [7]:

$$H(x,u) = \frac{1}{N}(-1)^{\sum_{i=0}^{n-1} b_i(x) p_i(u)}$$

Where:

$b_k(x)$ is the kth bit in the binary representation of x.

$$p_0(u) = b_{n-1}(u)$$

$$p_1(u) = b_{n-1}(u) + b_{n-2}(u)$$

$$p_2(u) = b_{n-2}(u) + b_{n-3}(u)$$

$$\vdots$$

$$p_{n-1}(u) = b_1(u) + b_0(u)$$

Where the sums are performed in modulo-2 arithmetic. For example, for $n=3$ the ordered Hadamard matrix is:

$$H_3 = \frac{1}{\sqrt{8}} \begin{bmatrix} 1 & 1 & 1 & 1 & 1 & 1 & 1 & 1 \\ 1 & 1 & 1 & 1 & -1 & -1 & -1 & -1 \\ 1 & 1 & -1 & -1 & -1 & -1 & 1 & 1 \\ 1 & 1 & -1 & -1 & 1 & 1 & -1 & -1 \\ 1 & -1 & -1 & 1 & 1 & -1 & -1 & 1 \\ 1 & -1 & -1 & 1 & -1 & 1 & 1 & -1 \\ 1 & -1 & 1 & -1 & -1 & 1 & -1 & 1 \\ 1 & -1 & 1 & -1 & 1 & -1 & 1 & -1 \end{bmatrix}$$

The two-dimensional Hadamard transform pair for an image U of $2^n \times 2^n$ pixels is obtained by the equation $T = H_n U H_n$. We have zero padded the 112×96 images to 128×128. Thus, in our experiments $n=7$.

[8] summarizes two measures that indicate the performance of transforms in terms of energy packing efficiency and decorrelation efficiency. It can be observed that the performance of the Walsh-Hadamard transform (WHT) is just a little bit worse than Discrete Cosine Transform (DCT) and Karhunen-Loeve Transform (KLT).

The WHT is a fast transform that does not require any multiplication in the transform calculations because it only contains ±1 values. This is very suitable for fixed point processors because no decimals are produced using additions and subtractions. Table 1 compares the computational burden of KLT, DCT and WHT [9]. It is interesting to observe that when dealing with DCT and WHT, basis functions are known in advance (they are not data dependent). In addition, it is important to emphasize that referent to performance gain, the transform choice is important if block size is small [9], say N<65. This is not our case, because we consider each image as a block of about 10000 components.

Table 1. Computational burden of KLT, DCT and WHT for images of size $N \times N$

Transform	Basis function computation	Image transformation
KLT	$O(N^3)$ (to solve 2 $N \times N$ matrix eigen-value problems)	$2N^3$ multiplications
DCT	0	$N^2 \log_2(N)$ multiplications
WHT	0	$N^2 \log_2(N)$ additions or substractions

Table 2 provides execution times using a Pentium 4 processor at 3GHz.

Table 2. Execution time for KLT, DCT and WHT

Transform	Basis function computation	Image transformation
KLT	347.78s	0.23s
DCT	0	0.0031s
WHT	0	0.0003s

We can define a zonal mask as the array $m(f_1, f_2) = \begin{cases} 1, & f_1, f_2 \in I_t \\ 0, & otherwise \end{cases}$, and multiply the transformed image by the zonal mask, which takes the unity value in the zone to be retained and zero on the zone to be discarded. In image coding it is usual to define the zonal mask taking into account the transformed coefficients with largest variances. Then the zonal mask is applied to the transformed image (or blocks of the image) and only the nonzero elements are encoded. In our case we will not take into account the variances of the transformed coefficients and we will just define the zonal mask in the following easy ways:

Rectangular mask: it will be a square containing N'xN' pixels
Sectorial mask: it will be a sector of 90° of a r radius circle.
Figure 2 shows one example of each situation.

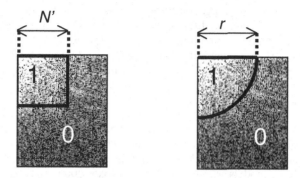

Fig. 2. Example of rectangular and sectorial masks

This definition lets to easily obtain the coefficients. The dimension of the resulting vector is N'xN' for the rectangular mask and, for the sectorial mask, the number of pixels meeting the following condition:

$$\vee f_1, f_2, \ if \ \sqrt{(f_1 - c_1)^2 + (f_2 - c_2)^2} < radius$$
$$then \ m(f_1, f_2) = 1; \ else \ m(f_1, f_2) = 0$$

where the coordinates of the center are the frequency origin ($c_1 = c_2 = 0$).

In our experiments we have obtained similar results with both kinds of masks. Thus, we have chosen the rectangular mask because it is easier to implement.

It is interesting to observe that in image coding applications the image is split into blocks of smaller size, and the selected transformed coefficients of each block are encoded and used for the reconstruction of the decoded image. In face recognition all the operations are performed over the whole image (it is not split into blocks) and all the computations are done in the transformed domain. Thus, it is not necessary to perform any inverse transform. On the other hand in image coding the goal is to reduce the amount of bits without appreciably sacrificing the quality of the reconstructed image, and in image recognition the number of bits is not so important. The goal is to reduce the dimensionality of the vectors in order to simplify the complexity of the classifier and to improve recognition accuracy.

3 Experimental Results

This section evaluates the results achieved using the WHT and compares them with the classical KLT, eigenface, and DCT methods.

3.1 Database

The database used is the ORL (Olivetti Research Laboratory) faces database [10]. This database contains a set of face images taken between April 1992 and April 1994 at ORL. The database was used in the context of a face recognition project carried out in collaboration with the Speech, Vision and Robotics Group of the Cambridge University Engineering Department.

There are ten different images of each of the 40 distinct subjects. For some subjects, the images were taken at different times, varying the lighting, facial expressions (open/closed eyes, smiling / not smiling) and facial details (glasses / no glasses). All the images were taken against a dark homogeneous background with the subjects in an upright, frontal position (with tolerance for some side movement).

3.2 Conditions of the Experiments

Our results have been obtained with the ORL database in the following situation: 40 people, faces 1 to 5 for training, and faces 6 to 10 for testing.

We obtain one model from each training image. During testing each input image is compared to all the models within the database (40x5=200 in our case) and the model close to the input image (using for instance the Mean Square Error criterion) indicates the recognized person.

3.3 Reduction of Dimensionality Using DCT, WHT and Eigenfaces

The first experiment consisted of the evaluation of the identification rates as function of the vector dimension. Thus, 200 tests (40 people x 5 test images per person) are performed for each vector dimension (92 different vector dimensions for DCT and WHT, and 200 for the eigenfaces and KLT method) and the corresponding identification rates are obtained. The possible vector lengths for the rectangular mask are $(N')^2 = 1, 4, 9, 16$, etc. For the eigenfaces and KLT methods we have just retained a number of eigenfaces ranging from 1 to 200. Figure 3 compares the achieved results.

Taking into account that we are looking for a low-complexity face recognition system, the classifier consists of a nearest neighbor classifier using the Mean Square Error (MSE) or the Mean Absolute Difference (MAD) defined as:

$$MSE(\vec{x}, \vec{y}) = \sum_{i=1}^{(N')^2} (x_i - y_i)^2$$

$$MAD(\vec{x}, \vec{y}) = \sum_{i=1}^{(N')^2} |x_i - y_i|$$

In our simulations better results are obtained using the MAD criterion. For instance, for the DCT algorithm and a vector dimension of 100 we achieved the following results:

- MSE criterion: identification rate= 91%
- MAD criterion: identification rate = 92.5%

Thus, we have chosen the MAD criterion in our simulations.

Table 3 shows the optimal number of coefficients for each transform, and the associated identification rate.

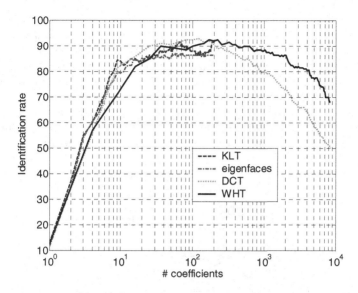

Fig. 3. Identification rate vs number of coefficients for several dimensionality reduction methods

Table 3. Maximum identification values for several transforms

Transform	# coefficients	Identification rate
Eigenfaces	52	87%
KLT	196	92%
DCT	121	93%
WHT	169	92.5%

It is important to observe that our new proposal, in addition to efficiency, presents another advantage over the classical eigenfaces method: the transformation is not data dependent, so it is not necessary to find any projection vector set. This same kind of solution is also preferred in image coding algorithms (JPEG, MPEG, etc.) that use DCT instead of KLT, because it is a fast transform that requires real operations and it is a near optimal substitute for the KL transform of highly correlated images, and has excellent energy compactation for images.

On the other hand, the KLT or its practical implementation (eigenfaces) implies that perhaps the set of projection vectors is too fitted to the training images that have been used to extract them, and can present poor generalization capabilities when representing the test images not used during training.

4 Practical Implementation

Face recognition problem using a fast and low-complexity recognition algorithm is: how can we reduce the variability between different image acquisitions? Fortunately, we can take advantage of a similar strategy applied for iris acquisition in some sensors, as described in [1]. It consists of a special glass, which performs as transparent glass in one direction and mirror in the other one. Figure 4 shows a representation of this proposed device. Basically, image acquisition is performed with a low-cost webcam hidden behind the glass. We have plotted an ellipse on the mirror surface, and the user just needs to fit the reflex of his face inside the contour. This solution provides same orientation and distance for all the acquisitions, making the posterior feature extraction and matching much more easily. Figure 5 shows some variations sources for captured images. Our proposed system can manage all of them except for occlusions.

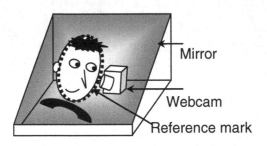

Fig. 4. Acquisition device

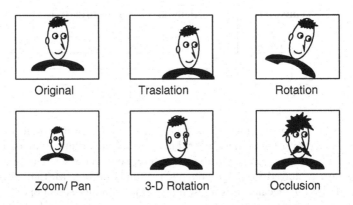

Fig. 5. Some variation sources in two-dimension image acquisition

Figure 6 presents the main constitutive blocks of a PC-based door-opening system, and figure 7 shows the physical aspect of the constructed gadget. This system has been installed, for evaluation purposes, in the same room that we controlled previously with a fingerprint system [13-14].

Main blocks are:

1. *Image acquisition device:* A low-cost webcam has been used to acquire snapshots of users. It is hidden below a special glass, which acts as mirror when looked at from outside. There is an ellipse plotted in the surface, with the goal to indicate the exact position of the reflected image on the surface.

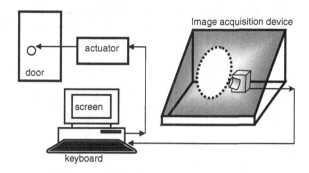

Fig. 6. Block diagram of the implemented system

Fig. 7. The door opening system

2. *Personal computer:* The core of the system is an ARM-core fixed-point processor. This solution is cheaper than using a standard PC, and more compact. In fact, the largest block of figure 7 is the power supply adapter.
3. *Screen:* It displays the result of the identification (if the user is recognized) and the entrance time. The screen is inside the room, but visible through a big glass.
4. *Keyboard:* Our system works on verification mode. Thus, the user needs to provide a Personal Identification Number (PIN) of four digits.

5. *Actuator (Door-opening device):* The computer just takes the decision to open or not the door. A standard device is needed similar to the manual remote door opening systems in our houses (entryphone).

Although it is not straight away to provide experimental identification rates using the whole system described in figure 6, we consider that it can provide reasonable identification rates when the user is enough trained and is able to interact with the system.

5 Conclusions

We have proposed a new approach to face recognition based on the Walsh-Hadamard transform, which can be easily implemented on a fixed point processor [11-12]. The experimental results reveal that it is competitive with the state-of-the-art statistical approaches to face recognition. Taking advantage of the minor differences of using different transforms (see [5] on page 517), emphasis is focused on this items:

a) We check that WHT performs reasonably good for identification when using small databases (ORL).

b) We check the differences on execution time, which justify the utility of WHT jointly with the possibility to implement it on a fixed point processor.

In addition, we have presented a whole system for face recognition based on the WHT algorithm.

Acknowledgements

This work has been supported by FEDER and MEC, TEC2006-13141-C03-02/TCM.

References

1. Faundez-Zanuy, M.: Biometric security technology. IEEE Aerospace and Electronic Systems Magazine 6, 15–26 (2006)
2. Faundez-Zanuy, M., Monte-Moreno, E.: State-of-the-art in speaker recognition. IEEE Aerospace and Electronic Systems Magazine 20(5), 7–12 (2005)
3. Reynolds, D.A., Rose, R.C.: Robust text-independent speaker identification using Gaussian mixture speaker models. IEEE Trans. On Speech and Audio Processing 3(1), 72–83 (1995)
4. Faundez-Zanuy, M.: Signature recognition state-of-the-art. IEEE Aerospace and Electronic Systems Magazine 20(7), 28–32 (2005)
5. Faundez-Zanuy, M.: On-line signature recognition based on VQ-DTW. Pattern Recognition 40, 981–992 (2007)
6. Turk, M., Pentland, A.: Eigenfaces for Recognition. Journal Cognitive Neuroscience 3(1), 71–86 (1991)
7. Gonzalez, R.C., Woods, R.E.: Digital image processing. Addison-Wesley, Reading (1993)
8. Gibson, J.D.: Digital compression for multimedia, principles and standards. Morgan Kaufmann, San Francisco (1998)

9. Jain, A.K.: Fundamentals of digital image processing. Prentice-Hall, Englewood Cliffs (1989)
10. Samaria, F., Harter, A.: Parameterization of a stochastic model for human face identification. In: 2nd IEEE Workshop on Applications of Computer Vision, Sarasota (Florida), IEEE Computer Society Press, Los Alamitos (1994)
11. Faundez-Zanuy, M., Espinosa-Duró, V., Ortega, J.A.: A low-cost webcam & personal computer opens doors. IEEE Aerospace and Electronic Systems Magazine 20(11), 23–26 (2005)
12. Faundez-Zanuy, M., Roure, J., Espinosa-Duró, V., Ortega, J.A.: An efficient face verification method in a transform domain. Pattern recognition letters 28(7), 854–858 (2007)
13. Faundez-Zanuy, M.: Door-opening system using a low-cost fingerprint scanner and a PC. IEEE Aerospace and Electronic Systems Magazine 19(8), 23–26 (2004)
14. Faundez-Zanuy, M., Fabregas, J.: Testing report of a fingerprint-based door-opening system. IEEE Aerospace and Electronic Systems Magazine 20(6), 18–20 (2005)

Towards Mobile Multimodal Telecommunications Systems and Services

Matúš Pleva, Ján Papaj, Anton Čižmár, Ľubomír Doboš, Jozef Juhár, Stanislav Ondáš, and Michal Mirilovič

Department of Electronics and Multimedia Communications, Technical University of Košice, Letná 9, 042 00 Košice, Slovak Republic
{Matus.Pleva,Jan.Papaj,Anton.Cizmar,Lubomir.Dobos,Jozef.Juhar, Stanoslav.Ondas,Michal.Mirilovic}@tuke.sk

Abstract. The communication itself is considered as a multimodal interactive process binding speech with other modalities. In this contribution some results of the project MobilTel (Mobile Multimodal Telecommunications System) are presented. It has provided a research framework resulting in a development of mobile terminal (PDA) based multimodal interface, enabling user to obtain information from internet by multimodal way through wireless telecommunication network. The MobilTel communicator is a speech centric multimodal system with speech interaction capabilities in Slovak language supplemented with graphical modalities. The graphical modalities are pen – touch screen interaction, keyboard, and display on which the information is more user friendly presented, and provides hyperlink and scrolling menu availability. The architecture of the MobilTel communicator and methods of interaction between PDA and MobilTel communicator are described. The graphical examples of services that enable users to obtain information about weather or information about train connection are also presented.

Keywords: multimodal, pocket PC, telecommunication, services, spoken language, human computer interaction.

1 Introduction

The main goal of this project is the research and development of mobile multimodal telecommunication systems, which allows access to information from different areas through mobile multimodal terminal and human - machine interaction with natural speech, with support of another mainly graphical modalities.

Modality is a path of communication between the human and the computer. Major modalities are vision and audition modality. Other modality which is usable on PDA devices is input touch modality (touch screen) as a sensor or device through which the computer can receive the input from the human. A system which integrates speech dialog, graphical user interface and a possibility to input a choice selecting from the list on touch screen could be called as multimodal.

MobilTel Communicator enables via multimodal multi-user interaction in Slovak language through telecommunication or IP network to find information in databases

A. Esposito et al. (Eds.): Verbal and Nonverbal Commun. Behaviours, LNAI 4775, pp. 286–293, 2007.

or Internet websites. The available modalities are speech, graphical user interface, stylus pen and keyboard on PDA device. The MobilTel Communicator is being developed as a multimodal extension to the IRKR [1] project (Smart Speech Interactive Interface) [2]. It means that a new TTM (Text-to-Multimodality) server was added and also a modified Audioserver for communicating with PDA audio devices.

The solution is based on using the web-browser installed in PDA as a GUI (Graphical User Interface) on PDA, and "thin" audio server for sending audio data from PDA to IRKR Audioserver and back. The solution's biggest advantage is that the final GUI is usable on every PDA device, with every OS which has a preinstalled compatible web-browser. Also on every other mobile devices or PC is the GUI interface available for testing and presentation.

In this contribution the architecture of the multimodal communicator solution and used technologies are described. Then an example of the multimodal service is depicted and finally the future work and new ides are listed for discussion.

2 Multimodal Communicator Architecture

The MobilTel communicator is a multimodal system based on a distributed 'hub-and-spoke' Galaxy architecture used in DARPA Communicator [3], [4].

Each module (server) seeks services from the HUB and provides services to the other modules through the Galaxy HUB process (Fig. 1).

It's based on easy Plug & Play approach, which means that plugging new servers is very easy and handful thanks to unified frame-based message communication structure with the HUB. Every communication goes trough the HUB, which can distribute the messages to more than one recipient and can also change the message or the structure of the frame and make a configurable log files.

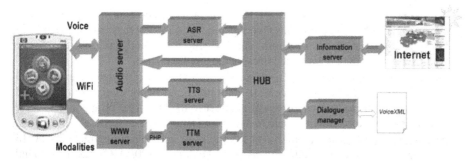

Fig. 1. Multimodal communication system architecture based on IRKR project architecture, with new TTM (Text To Multimodality) server for next modalities

Galaxy HUB process was developed in DARPA Communicator project [5], programmable by script files called "hub programs" (hub.pgm). Hub allows standardizing the communication between all other servers and the hub programs could manipulate duplicate or run simple scripts on the exchanged communication frames. This feature makes HUB the most powerful tool in this architecture. Changing the HUB program allows integrating new servers in the architecture. All servers could run on other platform or PC device because all frames between HUB and servers goes trough TCP/IP connection.

2.1 Servers of the Communicator

There are many servers in the system, and every one of them communicates with each other through the HUB. Only the audio data are transferred directly between the Audioserver and the TTS/ASR servers using the so called "broker channel" connection. The servers are the following:

- **ASR server** – There are two isolated words recognizers with thousands words capacity:
  1. The ATK (An Application Toolkit for HTK) based ASR module [6] and
  2. Sphinx-4 based ASR module [7], [8].

     - Acoustic models are context dependent (triphone), trained in a training procedure compatible with "refrec" [9], [10] trained on SpeechDat-SK [11], [12] and MobilDat-SK [13] databases. The MobilDat database was recorded according to IRKR project using GSM mobiles and the structure of the SpeechDat databases.
     - Only the ATK recognizer is commonly used. The Sphinx version of ASR was built for evaluation purposes.
- **Information (Backend) server** – IS server is capable of retrieving the information from web according to the Dialogue Manager (DM) requests, extracting the specified data and returning them in the XML format to the HUB. This server is capable to serve as many requests as the hardware can handle. It means that more backed servers are not necessary if there are more communicators running on one HUB system.
- **TTS server** - Diphone synthesizer is based on concatenation of diphones with Time Domain Pitch Synchronous Overlap and Add (TD-PSOLA) similar algorithm [14]. This server produces audio data which are directly transferred to the Audioserver and than played on corresponding audio device.
- **Dialogue manager server** - Based on VoiceXML 1.0 interpreter Fundamental components: XML Parser, VoiceXML interpreter and ECMAScript unit. The DM server is written in C++ with external wrapper to the hub [15]. Wrapper is a server responsible for converting the data to and from Galaxy frame standard.
- **Audio server** - Connects the whole system to the telecommunication or IP network, supports telephone hardware card - Dialogic D120/41JCT-LSEuro, sound card or VoIP connection (connection to PDA device). It uses a direct special connection with ASR and TTS server to transmit speech data (broker connection).
- **WWW server** – mainly Apache free web server which provides the GUI interface to the PDA device, transferring the dhtml (JavaScript+html) GUI interface produced with the PHP scripts running on the server. PHP scripts also allow the communication with TTM server using text files stored on the local filesystem.
- **TTM (Text To Multimodality) server** – provides next modalities, trough direct access to HUB with messages generated from files, and also logging messages

from HUB to another files. These files are monitored real-time and any other program or script can interact with the dialog of the communicator. In this case the PHP script running on the webserver monitors and generates these files and provides GUI interface to the PDA, with possibility to interact also by clicking on hyperlink, choosing from the scrolling menu or writing the option with the keyboard. Also the required information is user friendly graphically visualized (moving icons, pictograms, scrolling detailed list of train connections, etc.).

2.2 PDA-Side Services

On PDA side there are two main services running during the multimodal interaction:

1. Web browser – as graphical user interface (using the JavaScript and PHP to be a real-time service)
2. Voice audio server together with main control module. The audio server will be replaced with VoIP call client in the future.

The main control module is executing the corresponding GUI URL in default web browser in full-screen mode. The corresponding URL is transferred using the control TCP/IP channel, which is not implemented yet.

Voice is transferred through full duplex TCP/IP connections in pre-defined raw voice stream data format. Now the 8kHz 8 bit A-law format is used, because the speech recognition models were trained on corresponding format speech recordings database.

The GUI server is the default web browser in full-screen mode. Every screen is after the loading immediately redirected to the PHP script which is waiting for the voice interaction message from the HUB. If user interacts with pen or keyboard the screen is reloaded with updated content and the corresponding variables is also sent to the HUB. This procedure ensures that the interaction is updated in HUB and also in GUI webserver.

The voice dialog is written in VoiceXML language and the corresponding multimodal GUI dialog is written in HTML language using PHP and JavaScript. It means that every dialog changes should be implemented in VoiceXML and HTML files together.

The GUI server is able to run the dialog without the speech interaction for GUI testing purposes. But the required information is always acquired from the backend server trough the HUB messages. It means that the service is running only with the Galaxy architecture, also in testing mode.

3 Examples of Multimodal Services

There were two multimodal services developed until now:

1. Railway scheduler and
2. Weather forecast

Fig. 2. Example of the first screen service GUI

In these services is a combination of speech modality and other modalities, as we can see on the Fig.2. On first screen we can choose interactively clicking on the graphical representation of these two services: "Weather" and "Railway scheduler".

During the interaction the global choices could be chosen from the above menu:
- Home (first screen – choosing the service)
- Back (when we choose a false option – for example when we choose using voice recognition)
- Help (to present the help screen with the instructions for this phase of the dialog)
- Sound (to turn on/off the loudspeaker – if we do not need to hear the speech from TTS server – we are in noise environment)

3.1   Railway Scheduler Service

Railway scheduler provides information about train connections. We can select place from and where we want to travel, the date and time (default is the present time and today) when we want to travel (see Fig.3).

Selecting all these inputs we can get information about the closest train connection, price, name and type of the first connection train. If there is a need of using more

Fig. 3. Selecting the source, the destination city, time and the date of the journey

Fig. 4. The result of the railway scheduler service is better to see on the PDA screen. The user can then scroll the list of connection trains, and also choose the option to find the next connection. The speech communicator will also read all the information presented, but our memory is not able to store so much information on time. On PDA screen we have all information stored immediately.

connection trains there will be all trains presented below. Also the next possible connection button will provide the information about the next train. Information displayed on the dialog screens and the result screen is presented below (see Fig. 4).

3.2 Weather Service

Weather service provides information about weather forecast in the district towns of Slovakia [16]. We select the city from scrolling menu and the day (see Fig.5). We can also request the current weather information from the last hour.

Fig. 5. Selecting the city and day for the weather forecast service

The result for weather forecast is the maximal and minimal daily temperature and the weather state (rainy, sunny, etc.) presented like pictogram.

The actual weather information provides only current temperature during the past hour and also the air pressure. The time of the temperature observation is also presented (Fig. 6).

Fig. 6. Weather forecast (on the left) information presented on PDA screen and also the actual weather information (on the right)

4   Conclusion and Future Work

There is a new idea, to use some common interface also for speech communication. For example some types of VoIP technologies as SIP call client software. There are many functional SIP call clients on major operating systems and devices. For PocketPC PDA devices there is also well-known software product SJPhone tested and functional.

It means that it is possible to use common communication interfaces as SIP clients and web-browsers for speech and graphical modality. Only the problem of synchronizing these independent modalities remains and this is also a research goal of this project. Next goal is to evaluate the human computer interaction improvement by adding next modalities.

The next project activities will be oriented to optimizing and testing of demo version of the system. We will try to select optimal solution and increase the robustness by optimization of duplex voice transmission between PDA and multimodal server, optimization of GUI on the server and PDA side [17]. Next part of the project will be redesign and testing of the multimodal telecommunication services and optimization of multimodal dialog for services "Weather" and "Railway scheduler" according to first users' feedback.

In the final phase the demo version of multimodal version of communication system will be tested by freeing the communication for PDA devices connected to the laboratory WiFi AP (access point) and publishing the needed connection information to the students on the project website [18].

Acknowledgements

Research described in the paper was financially supported by the Slovak Grant Agency – APVV project MobilTel No. APVT-20-029004, and also by VEGA project No.1/4054/07.

References

1. Juhár, J., Ondáš, S., Čižmár, A., Rusko, M., Rozinaj, G., Jarína,R.: Development of Slovak GALAXY/VoiceXML Based Spoken Language Dialogue System to Retrieve Information from the Internet. In: Interspeech 2006 – ICSLP, Pittsburgh, USA, September 17-21 (2006) 485-488
2. http://irkr.tuke.sk/ Slovak testing dialog available on skype: irkr_pub
3. http://www.sls.csail.mit.edu/sls/technologies/galaxy.shtml
4. http://communicator.sourceforge.net/
5. http://communicator.colorado.edu/
6. Young, S. ATK: An application Toolkit for HTK, version 1.3, Cambridge University, January (2004)
7. Lamere, P., Kwok, P., Walker, W., Gouvea, E., Singh, R., Raj, B., Wolf, P.: Design of the CMU Sphinx-4 decoder, in Proc. Eurospeech 2003, Geneve, Switzerland, September (2003) 1181-1184
8. Mirilovič, M., Lihan, S., Juhár, J., Čižmár,A.: Slovak speech recognition based on Sphinx-4 and SpeechDat-SK, in Proc. DSP-MCOM 2005, Košice, Slovakia, Sept. (2005) 76-79
9. Lindberg, B., Johansen, F. T., Warakagoda, N., Lehtinen, G., Kačič, Z., Žgank, A., Elenius, K., Salvi, G.: A noise robust multilingual reference recognizer based on SpeechDat (II), in Proc. ICSLP 2000, Beijing, China (2000)
10. Lihan, S., Juhár, J., Čižmár, A.: Crosslingual and Bilingual Speech Recognition with Slovak and Czech SpeechDat-E Databases, In Proc. Interspeech (2005) Lisabon, Portugal, September (2005) 225 – 228
11. Winski R.: Definition of corpus, scripts and standards for fixed networks, Technical report, SpeechDat-II, Deliverable SD1.1.1., workpackage WP1, January (1997)
12. Pollak, P., Černocký, J., Boudy, J., Choukri, K., Rusko, M., Trnka, M.: SpeechDat(E) „Eastern European Telephone Speech Databases, in Proc. LREC 2000 Satellite workshop XLDB - Very large Telephone Speech Databases, Athens, Greece, May (2000) 20-25
13. Rusko, M., Trnka, M., Darjaa, S.: MobilDat-SK - A Mobile Telephone Extension to the SpeechDat-E SK Telephone Speech Database in Slovak, accepted for SPEECOM (2006) Sankt Peterburg, Russia, July (2006)
14. Darjaa, S., Rusko, M., Trnka M.: Three Generations of Speech Synthesis Systems in Slovakia, accepted for SPEECOM 2006, Sankt Peterburg, Russia, July (2006)
15. Ondáš, S., Juhár, J.: Dialogue manager based on the VoiceXML interpreter, in Proc. DSP-MCOM 2005, Košice, Slovakia, Sept. (2005) 80-83
16. Gladišová, I., Doboš, Ľ., Juhár, J., Ondáš, S.: Dialog Design for Telephone Based Meteorological Information System, in Proc. DSP-MCOM 2005, Košice, Slovakia, Sept. (2005) 151-154
17. GUI testing website http://147.232.47.73:8888/jar/index.html
18. MobilTel project website: http://mobiltel.tuke.sk/

Embodied Conversational Agents in Wizard-of-Oz and Multimodal Interaction Applications

Matej Rojc[1], Tomaž Rotovnik[1], Mišo Brus[2], Dušan Jan[2], and Zdravko Kačič[1]

[1] University of Maribor, Faculty of Electrical Engineering and Computer Science, Maribor, Slovenia
[2] Agito d.o.o., Ljubljana, Slovenia
{matej.rojc,tomaz.rotovnik,kacic}@uni-mb.si

Abstract. Embodied conversational agents employed in multimodal interaction applications have the potential to achieve similar properties as humans in face-to-face conversation. They enable the inclusion of verbal and nonverbal communication. Thus, the degree of personalization of the user interface is much higher than in other human-computer interfaces. This, of course, greatly contributes to the naturalness and user friendliness of the interface, opening-up a wide area of possible applications. Two implementations of embodied conversational agents in human-computer interaction are presented in this paper: the first one in a Wizard-of-Oz application and the second in a dialogue system. In the Wizard-of-Oz application, the embodied conversational agent is applied in a way that it conveys the spoken information of the operator to the user with whom the operator communicates. Depending on the scenario of the application, the user may or not be aware of the operator's involvement. The operator can communicate with the user based on audio/visual, or only audio, communication. This paper describes an application setup, which enables distant communication with the user, where the user is unaware of the operator's involvement. A real-time viseme recognizer is needed to ensure a proper response from the agent. In addition, implementation of the embodied conversational agent Lili hosting an entertainment show, which is broadcast by RTV Slovenia, will be described in more detail. Employment of the embodied conversational agent as a virtual major-domo named Maja, within an intelligent ambience, using speech recognition system and TTS system PLATTOS, will be also described.

Keywords: conversational agents, speech recognition, text-to-speech synthesis, speech-to-speech translation.

1 Introduction

Technologies such as embodied conversational agents and language technologies have great potential for providing user interfaces that will achieve similar properties as humans in face-to-face conversation and will enable users to communicate with machines using their natural communication skills [13]. Such interfaces being human-centred, personalized, and more entertaining have many potential applications such as

A. Esposito et al. (Eds.): Verbal and Nonverbal Commun. Behaviours, LNAI 4775, pp. 294–309, 2007.
© Springer-Verlag Berlin Heidelberg 2007

custom-mer care, e-commerce, e-learning, information delivery and services, entertainment, travelling environments, and personal assistants. This is in addition to recent applications within immersive virtual words in collaborative virtual environments.

This paper describes the technologies used to provide embodied conversational agents employed for human-machine-human or human-machine multimodal communication. Apart from the description of basic features of particular technology components two ongoing implementations of embodied conversational agents in human-computer interaction are discussed: Wizard-of-Oz and multimodal dialogue system. In Wizard-of-Oz application the embodied conversational agent is applied in a way that conveys the spoken information of the operator to the user with whom the operator communicates. Depending on the scenario of the application, the user may be aware or unaware of the operator's involvement. The operator can communicate with the user based on audio/visual or only audio communication. This paper describes an application setup, which enables distant communication with the user, where the user is unaware of the operator's involvement. A real-time viseme recognizer is needed to ensure proper response from the agent. In addition, implementation of the embodied conversational agent Lili hosting an entertainment show, which is broadcasted by RTV Slovenia, will be described in more detail. Also employment of the embodied conversational agent as a virtual major-domo within an intelligent ambience will be presented.

The remainder of the paper is organized as follows. Section 2 describes the basic features of the image synthesis system for defining embodied conversational agent. Section 3 describes speech recognition techniques used to allow spoken communication with the agents, whereas section 4 describes speech synthesis for spoken communication with the user. Section 5 provides the basic features of a speech-to-speech translation system that can be used in a multilingual virtual face-to-face conversation. The next section describes speech technology for those embodied conversational agents used for human-computer interaction in the Slovenian language. Section 7 presents three implementation examples. The last section draws the conclusions.

2 Image Synthesis for Embodied Conversational Agent

Graphics application for the embodied conversation agent was implemented in C# with the use of Managed DirectX API. Rendering utilizes vertex and pixel shaders to achieve vertex blending and effects, such as bump mapping, self-shadowing and subsurface scattering.

At the core of the graphics application is a scheduler that guarantees that animations and the camera and audio, stay in synchronization. The editor in the application allows a developer to predefine basic animations and the postures of the agent, which are then used as building blocks in the final composed animation. Examples of such building blocks are visemes, body postures and small elements such as smiles, brow movements, and blinking. The graphics application supports offline synchronization of animations with the audio, as well as online generation of behaviour in response to audio input.

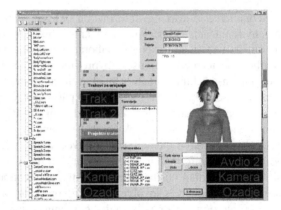

Fig. 1. Editor allows predefining basic animations and postures of the agent

In the offline synchronization we provide the audio file and accompanying text transcription to the application. With the use of the offline viseme recognizer, described later in the paper, the viseme animations are properly constructed and synchronized with the audio file. The user can further manually adjust any positioning of the visemes or refine some parts of the animation. In addition the user creates the nonverbal behaviour providing building blocks, or creating new animations if the existing ones do not cover their specific needs.

Online synchronization is designed for use without the need for operator involvement. All that is needed as input is the live audio stream. While the synchronization is done online, the image is displayed with some delay (typically 1-2 seconds) to allow for processing of the online viseme recognizer and scheduling of the animations. The application has complete control of the camera and animations. It will shuffle through different cameras, creating smooth transitions between views. At the same time the application procedurally generates animations that allow the agent to follow the camera with its gaze. The agent will also change its posture and employ other nonverbal behaviour such as looking around and smiling at the user.

3 Speech Recognition

This section presents two different speech recognition systems in multimodal interaction applications: offline and online.

3.1 Off-Line Viseme Recognition

In an offline system, speech is first recorded and then, together with orthographic transcription, sent to the viseme recognizer where realignment is performed between them. The result of the realignment process is a sequence of visemes with appended time marks. Each viseme has information about its starting time and duration. Visemes with time marks and original speech are then sent to the 3D model unit that synthesizes the conversational agent. The 3D model unit synchronizes the lip movements of the agent with input speech segments, based on information from the viseme recognizer. The structure of the system is presented in figure 2.

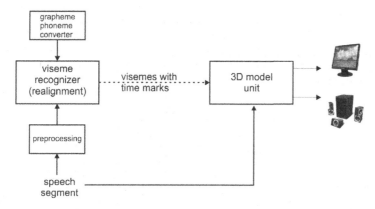

Fig. 2. Structure of the off-line viseme recognition system

3.2 On-Line Viseme Recognition

Several specific issues have to be considered, when transforming to a real-time online recognition system. Normally, a baseline speech recognizer obtains the result after the last frame of speech input has been processed. Since in the online system, the recognized visemes need to be aligned with speech and lip movements, a baseline version of the recognizer (standard offline recognizer) becomes unsuitable for this task. A primary goal was to minimize the amount of latency induced by the recognizer, and to make the remaining latency explicit, in order to obtain a better synchronization between the agent and the speech signal. Figure 3, therefore, presents an online system structure for automatic viseme generation and synchronization with a 3D model.

3.2.1 Latency

Latency is defined as the duration between the point of capturing the speech signal and the point when the recognizer output is emitted and visually manifested. There are four different kinds of latency sources in the speech recognition system:

- *Pre-processing latency*. A pre-processing module, which performs feature extraction, and represents the audio samples as frames. The first part of this latency presents the frame's length. In general however, this is short (typically 10ms). The second part is influenced by the higher order derivatives of the feature vectors (delta and acceleration coefficients), because it involves succeeding frames in order to be computed.
- *VoIP latency*. Distant communication with the user, and involves sending speech over TCP/IP network. An audio buffer is needed to ensure continuous audio flow. The size of the buffer depends on the size of individual audio packet that is sent over the network. This could be couples of 10 ms.
- *Search algorithm latency*. Decoding algorithms are crucial in building a low latency online recognizer. There are a lot of parameters which influence the decoder's speed (vocabulary size, context size, acoustic models size, speech environment, grammar ...).

- *Hypothesis latency.* A recognizer usually maintains a large number of partial hypotheses when searching for the final solution. If the recognizer needs to generate visemes 'on the fly', there is a high risk that the current promising hypotheses will later become the wrong one. An extra delay in producing final output is needed to maintain the accuracy of the basic speech recognizers.

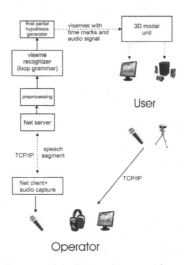

Fig. 3. Structure of the on-line viseme recognition system

4   Speech Synthesis

The following modules are normally used in the general architecture of any TTS system (figure 4): tokenizer, morphology analysis, part-of-speech tagger (POS), grapheme-to-phoneme conversion, symbolic and acoustic prosody module, unit selection module, concatenation, and acoustic module. Various language knowledge resources, e.g. morphological and phonetic lexica, linguistic rules, and acoustic speech database, can be used as the external language-dependent part. In the tokenizer module the text sentence is first broken into tokens. Special symbols, abbreviations, and numbers must be then converted into their corresponding word forms [14]. Then morphological analysis of the tokens is performed, usually assigning more than one POS tag to the tokens. By using a part-of-speech (POS) tagger in the following module, only one part-of-speech tag is assigned to each token, after the context has also been considered [1]. In the grapheme-to-phoneme conversion module, the phonetic transcriptions are assigned to the words, and the prosody modules follow. In some systems the symbolic and acoustic modules are merged, in others they are separated. In a symbolic prosody module, phrase breaks, prominence, and intonation patterns are usually predicted. The acoustic prosody module in the next step defines segment durations, pause durations, and F0 contours. The unit selection module uses off-line constructed acoustic inventory (usually found in any corpus-based TTS system). The acoustic inventory contains those unit candidates that are used for the conversion of input text into speech signal. Unit candidates must be found that are as close as possible to the desired prosody, as predicted by the prosody modules [2,3]. This task represents a big issue, especially in the case of corpus-based TTS systems, regarding time and space efficiency. In the acoustic processing module, the concatenation points are processed and a speech synthesis algorithm, such as TD-PSOLA, is usually used for generating the final speech signal [14,6].

Linguistic information must be flexibly and efficiently stored in any TTS system. Linguistic data processed in a TTS system are also very heterogeneous. TTS systems are involved in text analysis, syntactic analysis, morphology, phonology, phonetics, prosody, articulatory control, and acoustics. Therefore, it is desirable that different types of linguistic information use a single formalism. All TTS modules need external language resources. These must be separated from the system, in order to have a language-independent TTS engine. On the other hand, the access to language resources must be fast, in order to meet real-time requirements. Therefore, their representation must also be time and space efficient.

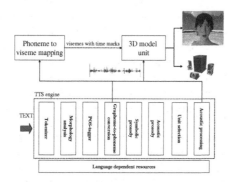

Fig. 4. Lip synchronisation using TTS engine

When using a conversational agent as a virtual major-domo, within an intelligent ambience, an ability to produce speech has to be given to the agent, therefore, a TTS system has to be integrated into the system. In synchronising speech with the agent's lips the use of a text-to-speech system makes the task a little easier than in the case of using a viseme recognizer. Namely, only a generated speech signal with corresponding grapheme-to-phoneme conversion has to be obtained, whereas phoneme-to-viseme mapping should be performed prior to lip synchronisation. Use of the TTS system in the process of lip synchronisation is presented in Figure 4.

As can be seen from Figure 4, the text is first sent to the TTS engine. Then all the processing steps are performed in order to obtain the corresponding phoneme string, and the speech signal. Both are sent to the phoneme-to-viseme mapping module. The phoneme-to-viseme mapping module is able to send usable output to the 3D model synthesis unit. Synchronization of the agent's lip movements using input speech segments is of great importance, in order to achieve adequate intuitiveness and naturalness of the embodied interface.

5 Speech-to-Speech Translation (S2ST) as an Interface in Multilingual Virtual Collaborative Environments

A lot of speech-to-speech translation (SST) systems have been developed over recent years. Nowadays, such systems represent one of the most challenging tasks for computational linguistics and speech technology research areas. Machine translation approaches integrate a variety of techniques from computational linguistics and computer science. Machine translation (MT) systems range from those applications used in real-world applications, to theoretical systems that explore new frontiers. Nevertheless, MT systems, unsurprisingly, have never yielded high-quality translations in unlimited domains, since MT requires the successful modelling of two languages, as well as modelling a translation relation between them.

On the other hand, immersive virtual worlds have witnessed intensive development over recent years because powerful computer graphics and wideband communication has found a place in the internet community. In connection with language technologies, especially speech-to-speech translation, possibilities have opened up for the development of numerous high-value added services within this collaborative virtual environment. When using a conversational agent in remote meeting application, in general, people speaking different languages could participate. In such situations, ASR and TTS engines must be incorporated into the speech-to-speech translation system (S2ST). The structure of such a system is illustrated in Figure 5. There are two different conversational agents, representing the two different users who participate in the conference (the number of agents is, in general, not limited to two). Each of them speaks a different source language. ASR, TTS and SMT (statistical machine translation module) are integrated into the system. In the case of user one, its language is recognized, translated, and synthesized from source language 1 into target language 2. In the case of the second user, his language is also recognized, translated and synthesized from source language 2 into target language 1. When source language 1 is equal to target language 2 and source language 2 is equal to target language 1, they are able to communicate in their mother tongues.

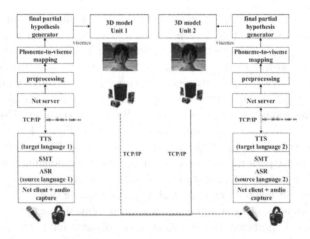

Fig. 5. Structure of the system with ASR, SMT and TTS

6 Speech Technology for Those Embodied Conversational Agents Used for Human-Computer Interaction in the Slovenian Language

In this chapter, the proprietary speech technology used for conversational agents in multimodal interaction applications will be presented in more detail. In the first part, an on-line viseme recognition system is presented in more detail and the second, describes the PLATTOS TTS, and the BABILON S2ST modules.

6.1 Speech Recognition System

The more important parts of the speech recognition system (ASR) used in the viseme recognition system are the pre-processing module, and a search algorithm with trained acoustic models.

6.1.1 Pre-processing
In the pre-processing module, FFT features are computed using a 10 ms analysis frame and a 25 ms Hamming window. The first and second derivative coefficients of the base melcepstral features and energy are appended in order to produce a thirty-nine dimensional feature vector. Also online normalization is used to reduce the influence of different acoustic channels.

6.1.2 Acoustic Models
For acoustic models, context-independent continuous-density hidden Markov models (HMM) with three emitting states and simple left-right topology are used. A Baum-Welch algorithm is used for robust parameter estimation [5]. For capturing different pronunciation styles of equal phonemes, we increase the number of Gaussian mixtures for the continuous hidden Markov model, to 64. A better coverage between the

Table 1. Definition of visemes for the Slovenian language

viseme number	name	Phones
0	sil,sp	/
1	PP	p,m,b
2	FF	f,v,w
3	kk	k,g,h
4	DD	t,d
5	CH	č,š,ž
6	SS	c,s,z
7	nn	n,l,r
8	RR	@r
9	J	j
10	aa	a
11	E	e
12	ih	i
13	oh	o
14	ou	u
15	eh	@

acoustic model and the corresponding speech segments is achieved this way. Models are estimated on SNABI speech database [7]. All phonemes (28) are replaced with visemes, as presented in Table 1. 16 different visemes are currently used.

6.1.3 Search Algorithm

A basic search algorithm uses the information provided by the acoustic and language models (in our case "loop" grammar) to determine the best word sequence:

$$\left[v_1^N \right]_{opt} = \arg\max_{v_1^N, N} \left\{ p\left(v_1^N\right) \cdot p\left(x_1^T \mid v_1^N\right) \right\} \tag{1}$$

$$\approx \arg\max_{v_1^N, N} \left\{ \prod_{n=1}^{N} \max_{s_1^T} \prod_{t=1}^{T} \left\{ p\left(x_t \mid s_t, v_1^N\right) \cdot p\left(s_t \mid s_{t-1}, v_1^N\right) \right\} \right\}, \text{ where}$$

$N \rightarrow$ number of visemes $T \rightarrow$ number of acoustic features

$v_n \rightarrow$ viseme n $x_t \rightarrow$ acoustic feature t (2)

$s_t \rightarrow$ state t of HMM $v_1^N = v_1, ..., v_N$ (viseme sequence)

$x_1^T = x_1, ..., x_T$ (sequence of acoustic features)

The search problem, described in Equation (2), can be efficiently solved by applying dynamic programming. A best-path solution exists by adoption of the Viterbi assumption as an optimality criterion. This solution is the sequence of visemes with highest probability. In the case of the on-line system, the most promising partial hypothesis needs to be produced. The next problem then arises: a partial hypothesis, which at a time point during the search process has the highest accumulated likelihood, can very well prove to be incorrect according to the probabilistic model, when additional input frames have been observed. This occurs when another partial hypothesis, which corresponds to a different path in the search space, as well as a different viseme sequence, takes the role of the currently best partial hypothesis. In order to solve this, the incorrectly emitted sequence must be corrected. We used a solution based on accepting a certain degree of hypothesis latency. Hypothesis latency is set dynamically to achieve the best ratio between accuracy and latency. Generation of output is continuously based on the viseme sequence that the currently best hypothesis corresponded to D frames earlier. The effect is that a best-path proving to be incorrect within D frames will not be manifested as errors in the output sequence. If the frame length D is sufficiently long, the on-line system will give exactly the same output as a basic recognition system. Another criterion when deciding to check for new partial hypothesis, is the score difference between the best and the next best score's of the current partial hypothesis. The larger the difference, the higher the probability of correct viseme sequence in partial hypothesis.

6.2 PLATTOS TTS System

For lip synchronisation using a TTS system a PLATTOS TTS system is used [12]. Its architecture enables efficient use in those applications with unlimited domain,

requiring multilingual or polyglot functionality. The integration of heterogeneous relation graphs (HRG) [10], a queuing mechanism, and finite-state machines provide a
powerful, reliable and easily maintainable TTS system. Flexible and language-
independent frameworks efficiently integrate all the algorithms used within the scope
of the TTS system. HRG graphs are used for linguistic information representation and
feature construction. Finite-state machines are used for time and space-efficient
lookup processes, for time and space efficient representation of language resources,
and the separation of language-dependent resources from a language-independent
TTS engine. The queuing mechanism consists of several dequeue data structures and
is responsible for the activation of all those TTS engine modules having to process the
input text. In the TTS system, all modules use the same data structure for gathering
linguistic information about input text. All input and output formats are compatible,
the structure is modular and interchangeable, it is easily maintainable and object oriented. PLATTOS TTS system architecture is shown in Figure 6.

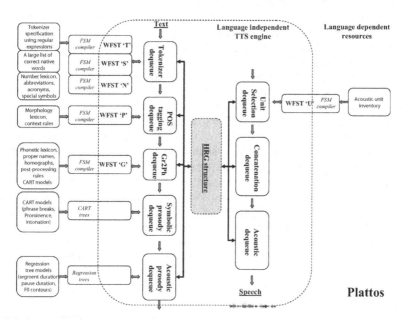

Fig. 6. The PLATTOS architecture (corpus-based TTS system), separated into language-
dependent and language-independent parts

The HRG structure gathers linguistic data for the corresponding sentence extracted
by modules of the TTS engine. The queuing mechanism consists of several dequeues
used for tokenizing, POS tagging, grapheme-to-phoneme conversion, symbolic prosody and acoustic prosody processing, unit selection, concatenation, and acoustic processing. Obviously, each module in the system is assigned to the corresponding
dequeue and the queuing mechanism takes care of flexible, efficient and easily maintainable data flow through the TTS system. The used mechanism also enables process
interruption after any dequeue in the system, and monitoring evaluation of the corresponding outputs (e.g. output from grapheme-to-phoneme conversion, POS tagging

modules, efficiency of the unit selection search algorithm etc.) [12]. The linguistic information from the database sentences stored in the form of HRG structure can also be used flexibly for performing re-synthesis experiments.

Since finite-state machines are time and space efficient, they are used for the representation of all language-dependent language resources. Either finite-state transducers or finite-state automata can be used. The FSM compiler must be used for compilation of regular expressions into the finite-state machine, construction of finite-state machine based tokenizers etc. When solving disambiguity problems, heuristically defined or trained weights can be assigned to FSM transitions and final states, yielding also weighted finite-state automata and transducers (WFSA, WFST) [8]. The tokenizer in Figure 6 is marked as 'T' in the TTS engine. Also two-level rules or rewrite rules can be used and compiled into finite-state machines by an FSM compiler. These rules can resolve e.g. any language-dependent disambiguity found in the input texts. Then follows finite-state automaton 'S' for storing large lists of valid words. It can be used e.g. by the spell-checking system, when it is included in the architecture. The POS-tagging module in general needs large-scale morphology lexicons. The overall performance of the TTS system depends on the time and space efficiency of each module. Therefore, the finite-state transducer 'P' can be used for time and space-efficient representation of such large-scale morphology lexicons. Some TTS systems also use rule-based POS-tagging algorithms (e.g. [1]). In this case, the POS-tagging rules can be compiled into finite-state machines, as described in [4]. Thus, common POS-tagging processing time only depends on the length of the input sentence and not on the size of the morphological lexicon, or the number of rules. The grapheme-to-phoneme conversion module has a significant impact on the final quality of the TTS engine, since it defines how to pronounce the input sentence. Many systems use large-scale phonetic lexicons for common words, proper names and even foreign words, found in the input text. All these resources can be represented by the finite-state transducer (FST) 'G', as seen in Figure 6. Machine-learned models can be used (e.g. CARTs, NN etc.) for processing unseen words. Decision tree models are used in the PLATTOS TTS system, since they represent efficient knowledge representation, regarding time and space requirements. Decision tree models are also used in the prosody modules (symbolic and acoustic prosody) for the prediction of phrase breaks, prominence and intonation event labels, segment durations, pauses between segments and the acoustic parameters of intonation events. It was shown that decision trees can also be represented by finite-state machines (labeled as WFST 'SP', WFST 'AP' in Figure 6) [9,15]. However, their compilation into finite-state machines only makes sense when they are going to be merged with other finite-state machines, as decision trees are already efficient knowledge representation structures. The unit selection search process represents, in corpus-based TTS systems, a significant time and space issue, because of the large unit search space. In this case, finite-state machines can be used for efficient access to unit candidates in the acoustic inventory. Tree-based clustering algorithms can also be used for the reduction of large search space, and the dynamic algorithms (e.g. Viterbi algorithm) can be used when searching for such unit sequences that have the best-match with the defined prosody for the input sentence. In the concatenation and acoustic modules, digital signal processing algorithms are used for the processing of concatenation points, and for adapting unit candidate's pitch and duration.

The dash-lined large rectangle denotes the language-independent PLATTOS TTS engine. The language-dependent resources are represented by using finite-state machine formalism, and CART models. Constructed FSMs and CART models are loaded into a PLATTOS TTS engine in a uniform way. These language-dependent models are constructed off-line by using corresponding tools [11]. As can be seen from Figure 6, the following language resources are needed: regular expressions for tokenizer construction and text normalisation, a large list of valid native words, number lexicon, an acronym lexicon and lexicon of special symbols, morphology lexicon, phonetic lexicons, homograph database and phonetic post-processing rules, prosodically annotated speech database (phrase breaks, prominence, intonation) used for training prosodic CART models, and an acoustic inventory constructed from the speech database. All this data has to be available for the target language in order to achieve the maximum performance of the whole system.

The PLATTOS TTS system is easily maintainable, allowing flexible migration to new languages, has efficient data flow throughout the whole system and between modules, and allows monitoring and performance evaluation after each module. The current level of optimisation performed in all modules of the system and representation of language resources doesn't affect the final quality of the synthesised speech. When the speech quality can be degraded, further optimisation on the system is still possible, resulting in a smaller footprint of the corpus-based TTS system. Using the PLATTOS TTS system, only language-dependent resources have to be prepared for the development of a text-to-speech synthesis system for a new language.

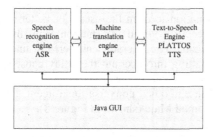

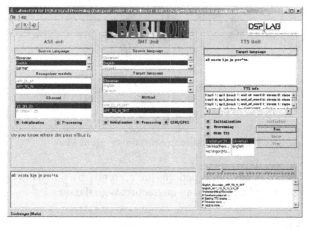

Fig. 7. BABILON speech-to-speech translation system for Slovenian/German and Slovenian/English pairs

6.3 BABILON Speech-to-Speech Translation System

The BABILON (S2ST) speech-to-speech translation system, in Figure 7, has currently been developed for the Slovenian/German and Slovenian/English language pairs and for limited application domains. It consists of three main modules: speech recognition engine, statistical machine translation module, and speech synthesis module (PLATTOS). All modules are integrated into the BABILON speech-to-speech translation system, which can be used by users through Java GUI. Speech processing modules are written in C++ program language and are integrated into the Java framework through JNI interfaces, in the form of dynamic libraries.

7 Implementation Examples

In this chapter some target applications based on the use of conversational agents are described in more detail. Within various on-going projects they are under constant improvement and are being further developed.

7.1 Wizard-of-Oz

The Wizard-of-Oz target application is based on the architecture presented in Figure 3. In this application, the operator uses a microphone and headphones to transmit/receive spoken information to/from the user. For better communication with the user, the operator also receives visual information from the place where the user communicates with the agent. The operator can perform unconstrained spoken conversation with the user, taking into account the delay caused mainly by the viseme recogniser. In current implementation the delay is around 750 ms. The user sees the operator in the form of an embodied conversational agent. In the described application, the agent has been named Maja (shown in Figure 8).

Fig. 8. Embodied conversational agent Maja

A predefined set of behavioural patterns are currently used to assure natural behaviour of the conversational agent during interaction with the user.

7.2 Major-Domo

The aim of the ongoing major-domo project within the ambient intelligence is to develop intelligent ambience with the integration of a conversational agent employed for multimodal interaction with the user, in order to achieve similar properties as humans in face-to-face conversation. The system's architecture is presented in Figure 9. The system consists of GUI interface (Java) that integrates TTS, ASR, a dialogue manager, and the conversational agent Maja. The dialogue manager takes care of real-time human-computer interaction, conversational agent Maja speaks out load all system reports and messages, and the ASR module continuously recognizes users' speech through the bluetooth channel. The dialogue manager communicates with all devices regarding ambience through the I/O module (WLAN,LAN), and further through the power network. All devices in the intelligent environment should be connected to one master or one of more slave module devices. The whole system enables flexible and efficient full-duplex data exchange between the PC server and all devices in the intelligent ambience. It is possible to control devices using speech wherever and whenever inside the intelligent environment.

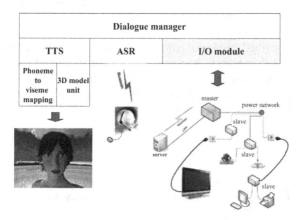

Fig. 9. Major-domo target application used in intelligent ambience

7.3 Conversational Agent Lili

Lili is an embodied conversational agent leading an entertainment show. The show is broadcast by the national broadcaster RTV Slovenia every morning on the entertainment 'info' channel.

Lili communicates with the audience via emails and SMS messages, which are sent to her telephone number or e-mail address. During the show she reads SMS messages, sometimes answers questions sent by watchers, and announces different top music lists for all kinds of music. She also offers different games, quizzes, questionnaires and announces different information. In all cases speech is pre-recorded and transcribed. In the beginning lip synchronisation was performed manually, which proved to be a very tedious and time consuming task. The viseme recogniser is now used to perform speech segmentation and labelling. The developed tools allow rapid development of lip synchronised video sequences.

Fig. 10. Virtual conversational agent Lili. Courtesy Multimedia Centre of RTV Slovenia

8 Conclusion

Language technologies, together with the technology of embodied conversational agents, enables the development of interfaces which will make possible natural face-to-face conversational interaction with the users and will be able to accomplish a wide variety of tasks. In this paper we have presented a framework for the development of such interfaces, described implementation of embodied conversational agents, and components of needed speech technology. We further discussed practical issues of speech technology components implementation (viseme recogniser, text-to-speech synthesis, and speech-to-speech translation), as well as presented three examples of the deployment of embodied conversational agents.

References

1. Brill, E.: A Corpus-Based Approach to Language Learning. PhD thesis (1993)
2. Bulyko, I.: Unit Selection for Speech Synthesis Using Splicing Cost with Weighted Finite State Transducers. In: Proc. of Eurospeech (2001)
3. Bulyko, I., Ostendorf, M.: Joint prosody prediction and unit selection for concatenative speech synthesis. In: Proc. of ICASSP (2001)
4. Emmanuel, R., Schabes, Y.: Finite State Language Processing. The Massachusetts Institute of Technology (1997)
5. Gauvain, J.-L., Lamel, L.F., Adda, G., Adda-Decker, M.: Speaker-independent continuous speech dictation. Speech Communication 15, 21–37 (1994)
6. Holzapfel, M.: Konkatenative Sprachsynthese mit grossen Datenbanken. Ph.D. thesis (2000)
7. Kačič, Z., Horvat, B., Zögling Markuš, A.: Issues in design and collection of large telephone speech corpus for Slovenian language. In: Gavirilidou, V., Maria (ur.) (ed.) Second international conference on language resources and evaluation. Proceedings. Athens: European Language Resources Association, Athens, Greece, May 31- June 2, 2000, vol. 2, pp. 943–946 (2000)
8. Mohri, M.: On Some Applications of Finite-State Automata Theory to Natural Language Processing. Natural Language Engineering 1 (1995)
9. Mohri, M., Sproat, R.: An efficient compiler for weighted rewrite rules. In: 34-th Meeting of the Association for Computational Linguistics ACL 1996, Santa Cruz, California (1996)
10. Taylor, P., Black, A., Caley, R.: Heterogeneous Relation Graphs as a Mechanism for Representing Linguistic Information. Speech Communication 33, 153–174 (2001)

11. Rojc, M.: Time and Space efficient structure of multilingual and polyglot TTS system – architecture with finite-state machines, PhD thesis (2003)
12. Rojc, M., Kačič, Z.: Time and Space-Efficient Architecture for a Corpus-based Text-to-Speech Synthesis System. Speech Communication 49(3), 230–249 (2007)
13. Spens, K.-E., Agelfors, E., Beskow, J., Granström, B., Karlsson, I., Salvi, G.: SYNFACE, a talking head telephone for the hearing impaired. In: Proc. IFHOH. 7th World Congress, Helsinki, Finland (2004)
14. Sproat, R.: Multilingual Text-to-Speech Synthesis. Kluwer Academic Publishers, Dordrecht (1998)
15. Sproat, R., Riley, M.: Compilation of Weighted Finite-State Transducers from Decision Trees. In: Proceedings of the Thirty-Fourth Annual Meeting of the Association for Computational Linguistics, pp. 215–222 (1996)

Telling Stories with a Synthetic Character: Understanding Inter-modalities Relations

Guilherme Raimundo, João Cabral, Celso Melo, Luís C. Oliveira, Ana Paiva, and Isabel Trancoso

INESC-ID
Avenida Prof. Cavaco Silva - Taguspark
2780-990 Porto Salvo, Portugal
guilherme.raimundo@gaips.inesc-id.pt, ana.paiva@inesc-id.pt

Abstract. Can we create a virtual storyteller that is expressive enough to convey in a natural way a story to an audience? What are the most important features for creating such character? This paper presents a study where the influence of different modalities in the perception of a story told by both a synthetic storyteller and a real one are analyzed. In order to evaluate it, three modes of communication were taken into account: voice, facial expression and gestures. One hundred and eight students from computer science watched a video where a storyteller narrated the traditional Portuguese story entitled "O Coelhinho Branco" (The little white rabbit). The students were divided into four groups. Each of these groups saw one video where the storyteller was portrayed either by a synthetic character or a human. The storyteller's voice, no matter the nature of the character, could also be real or synthetic. After the video display, the participants filled a questionnaire where they rated the storyteller's performance. Although the synthetic versions used in the experiment obtained lower classifications than their natural counterparts, the data suggests that the gap between synthetic and real gestures is the smallest while the synthetic voice is the furthest from its natural version. Furthermore, when we used the synthetic voice, the facial expressions of both characters (the virtual and the real) were rated worse than with the real voice. This effect was not significant for the gestures, thus suggesting that the importance of building synthetic voices as natural as possible is extremely important as it impacts in the perception of other means of communication (such as the perception of the facial expression).

1 Introduction

Human society relies on all types of storytelling for all types of activities. From learning, to socializing, to creating one's own memories, stories are part of what makes us humans. Thanks to storytelling, our ancestors' culture was passed from generation to generation giving us meaning in the world [18]. The advent of new technologies has therefore lead to the emergence of new forms of storytelling (computer games, interactive stories in virtual environments) and even our communication is adapted to fit this new media for telling stories. As such, several

A. Esposito et al. (Eds.): Verbal and Nonverbal Commun. Behaviours, LNAI 4775, pp. 310–323, 2007.

researchers have been focusing in the interpretation of the audience reaction to storytelling systems, while others look into the storyteller's expression of the story [20][16]. In parallel, significant research has been done in the generation of stories and the processes by which new technologies can automatically create such stories [1][4].

Meanwhile the area of synthetic characters is maturing, and many different types of uses have been given to such characters. Synthetic characters have portrayed different roles for different types of applications, such as for example, tv presenters, football commentators or sales advisors. Various studies exist that evaluate synthetic characters in environments such as E-retail [22] and education [2]. In this paper, we will discuss the role of a synthetic character as a storyteller, giving some insights into the different modalities used and how they impact the perception of a story being told. This is done using not only a synthetic storyteller but evaluating it in relation to the same features in a human actor.

Thus, in order to measure the storyteller's performance we considered three means of communication used in the storytelling: gestures, facial expression and voice. Furthermore, we considered that story understanding, conveying of emotion, believability and satisfaction [19], are essential aspects in the performance of a storyteller. To compare performance between storytellers, four videos were created. In each of these, the storyteller could be a human actor or a 3D character, and the storyteller's voice could also be from the human actor or synthesized. One hundred and eight people participated in the study where each participant visualized one of these four videos and rated each communication mean in the four mentioned aspects. We wanted to investigate if there were significant differences between the storytelling ability of our character and the human actor, and the relations between the different means and modalities used. However, the results showed that the synthetic character's voice not only had a negative impact in the perception of the facial expressions in the synthetic character, but also in the real character. Participants rated the human actor's facial expressions lower, if the voice was synthetic (although the facial expressions were the same as with the real voice).

This paper is organised as follows: first we will describe the virtual storyteller and some of the technical features in there included. Secondly we will briefly describe the experiment carried out and finally, show the results obtained.

2   The Synthetic Storyteller

We wanted to build a synthetic storyteller inspired in the typical and yet quite engaging storytellers that, in front of an audience are able to tell stories in compelling and often appealing way. To do that, we have collected several stories told by an actor, and used these stories as the baseline for the creation of our synthetic storyteller.

However, to avoid the audience's expectations to be high we created a cartoon character that would resemble as an old grandfather, but not realistic (seeking

Fig. 1. Papous: the storyteller

inspiration in children's characters such as the Tweenies^{TM} [21] series). Figure 1 shows the character created.

Facial Expression - The facial expressions for Papous needed to be as natural possible. To do that, the fine animation control needed for the experiment was obtained through the use of control parameters. A control parameter is a value that has a maximum, minimum and associated semantic information. This information dictates what happens when the value of the parameter varies. For example the intensity of contraction of the major zygomatic muscle, the rotation angle of the left eye or the degree of joy the face expresses. The existing parameters can be divided into two sets: atomic and group. The parameters that are atomic contain all needed information to create the desired deformation. The engine built allows the use of three types of atomic parameters: pseudo-muscular, transformation and skinning. The pseudo-muscular parameters follow a deformation model based in Waters model [23] and emulate the behavior of the contraction of a muscle under the skin. In our synthetic storyteller, 37 pseudo-muscles were used. The transformation parameters simply apply a geometric transformation to a given geometric object. This type of parameters are used to control the rotation of the synthetic character eyes. The skinning parameters use a known animation technic that uses weighted mesh connected to virtual bones. This type of parameter is used for the tongue and jaw movement of the synthetic character. The group parameters (non-atomic) are used, as the name mentions, to group several control parameters together. These are usually used to create abstractions of resulting deformations from several parameters. Emotional expressions and visemes are two examples of group parameters. Visemes are the facial displays when a given phoneme is spoken. An interpolation

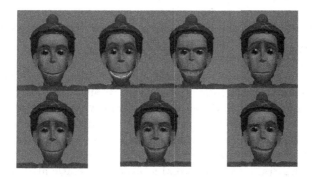

Fig. 2. Examples of the facial expressions of the character

between consecutive visemes is executed for viseme co-articulation. Figure 2
shows some of the expressions used for our storyteller.

Gestures - The gestures in the synthetic character were based in a articulated
modeled that is structured in a hierarchic architecture with three layers (similar
to [3] and [17]): geometry, animation and behavior. The model supports deterministic animation based in keyframes and non-deterministic animation that is
dynamically generated in real time through the use of inverse kinematics. Considering the deterministic animation, the geometry layer defines a skeleton, inspired
in the human, that is composed of 54 bones; the animation layer allows the execution and combination of animations which are defined over subsets of the
subjacent skeleton and keyframed based.; the behavior layer supplies scripting
abilities which allow the execution of complex animation sequences. Regarding
the non-deterministic animation, the geometric layer makes use of robotic ma-
nipulator members with 6 rotation junctions; the animation layer implements
the primitives of direct kinematic, inverse kinematic and inverse velocity; in the
behavioral layer the scripting is extended in order to allow the new primitives
of the non-deterministic animation.

The gestures' model permits gesticulation animation, i.e., the type of unconscious idiosyncratic movement with communicative meaning that occurs in the
context of a dialogue or narration [11]. The model is restricted to the upper body
since, according to McNeill [11], gesticulation occurs predominantly through the
arms and hands. Concretely, the model, was built upon the deterministic and
non-deterministic animation architecture allowing real time gesticulation defined
as an arbitrary sequence of positions, orientations and shapes of the hands.

For hand shapes the model allows the use of most static shapes from the
Gestural Portuguese Language [9]. Regarding hand's orientation and position,
the model allows, through the use of inverse kinematic, the animation of arbitrary
trajectories in the space that surrounds the synthetic character.

The gesture expression of the synthetic character in the story corresponds
to the application of a recording algorithm [10] for gesticulation transcription

to the human actor video and to the later conversion of this annotation into animation scripts. When the gesticulation done by the human actor was too complex, keyframed animations were created.

Voice - We needed to create a synthetic voice that would be synchronized with the real storyteller (and the virtual of course). As such, and in order to control the facial movements of the synthetic character in synchrony with the speech of the human actor, the natural phonetic signal was annotated. This process was performed in a semi-automatic manner. Since the actor wasn't obliged to follow a strict script, after the recording of the video, the performed story was transcribed. From this transcription several levels of automatic analyses were made that allowed to determine a possible phonetic sequence for the text. Following this process, also in a automatic manner, the sequence was aligned with the original speech signal [14]. Then it was considered the possibility that the speaker produced alternative pronunciations to the ones determined by the text analyses [14][15] resulting in a more accurate estimative of the performed phonetic sequence. Finally, the outcome of the automatic analyses was manually verified and some boundaries of phonetic segments were corrected.

For the synthesis of the synthetic voice it was also necessary to guarantee the synchronism between the speech signal and the video sequence. In order to achieve this goal it was necessary to impose that the duration of the synthetic phonetic segments was equal to the originals. Since the determination of the contour of the fundamental frequency is intimately related with the rhythm attribution, it was opted to impose the actor produced contour to the synthetic voice. The synthetic voice creation is made with a diphone synthesizer based in Linear Predictive Coding with a male voice. The synthesizer was developed at INESC-ID and uses as reference the original durations and produced speech with constant fundamental frequency.

We have at our disposal speech synthesizers with selection of variable dimension units which supply better quality synthesis. However, they were not used because they do not allow the same flexibility for the production of the synthetic signal. This signal was processed later on in order to have the same intonation of the speech produced by the human actor. Since the actor used a falsetto voice and the synthesizer uses a neutral voice, the variation of the fundamental frequency necessary to be used in the synthetic voice surpassed many times the 1.5 factor which usually is considered as an acceptable limit of distortion. In order to minimize this effect, a new technique named PSTS, was developed to alter the duration and fundamental frequency of the speech signal [5][6]. This technic also allows changing the speech signal parameters associated with the vibration form of the glottis. This is important for the production of speech with certain emotions. The way this parameters are changed in order to transmit those emotions is a current working topic [7]. Therefore, in this present study, the emotions present in the speech signal are transmitted solely by the variation of the rhythm and intonation.

3 Method

Our experiment was designed, so that each participant visualized one of four videos where the storyteller narrated the traditional Portuguese story "O Coelhinho Branco". After the visualization, the performance of the storyteller was evaluated through a questionnaire. The experiment followed an independent sample design, with each participant being assigned to a unique combination of the independent variables. There are 12 dependent variables in the experiment corresponding to the combinations of the 3 communication means (gestures, facial expression and voice) with the 4 analyzed aspects (story understanding, conveying of emotion, believability and satisfaction). These were measured through the use of a questionnaire explained below.

3.1 Design

The experiment was designed to use two independent variables: Character and Voice. Each of these was composed by a real level (human actor, human actor voice) and a synthesized level (3D-Papous character and synthesized voice). The real version uses the recording of a human actor while telling the story. The synthetic version uses a 3D character that is a blend between an old man and a tweenie [21]. And two other versions use a real with a synthetic variable. Both characters can be seen on Figure 3.

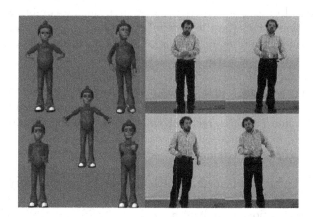

Fig. 3. Examples of the synthetic character and human actor telling the story

So that both versions of the character supplied the same knowledge to the participants, the semantic information transmitted by human actor gestures and facial expression was annotated. This annotation was then used in the creation of the synthetic character gestures and facial expressions. Regarding facial expression, the six basic emotions of Ekman [8] (Joy, Sadness, Anger, Surprise, Disgust and Fear) were taken into account. Particular facial area movements, such as the eyebrows, that are used to convey or reinforce currently spoken information, were also annotated. Concerning gestures, the focus of annotation resided in the gesticulation, i.e., in the unconscious and idiosyncratic movement that carries some communicative meaning [11]. To bring this annotations to life a character animation engine was created. This engine pays special attention to the processes of animation of facial and body expression in humanoid characters. In fact, it is not only capable of playing hand made deterministic animation but also allows a finer and more expressive control of isolated character parts.

3.2 Participants

The study had the participation of 108 students of computer science from Instituto Superior Técnico. From them, 89 were male and 19 female. Their ages varied between 18 and 28 years old with an average of 21 years and 10 months. The participants had no previous knowledge of the experiment objectives, knowing only that it was related to storytelling in virtual environments.

3.3 Material

For the video visualization, computers with 19" LCDs were used along with headphones for the audio. Each video had the duration of 7 minutes and 29 seconds and showed one level of each independent variable. For the evaluation of the video by the participants a questionnaire was created. This questionnaire is composed of 12 statements that result from the combination between the communication means (gestures, facial expression and voice) and considered aspects (story understanding, conveying of emotion , believability and satisfaction). Therefore, each statement is an assertion about one aspect of one of the means of communication. The participants rated the statements through a Likert scale with values between 1 and 7. Choosing the value 1 meant total disagreement with the statement, value 4 neither disagreement nor agreement with the statement and value 7 total agreement with the statement. Although the order of the statements in the questionnaire was obtained in a randomly fashion, we show them here sorted by communication mean and considered aspects.

1. The facial expressions helped in the understanding of the story
2. The storyteller's face expressed the story emotions
3. The facial expressions were believable
4. I liked the facial expressions
5. The gestures helped in the understanding of the story
6. The gestures expressed the story emotions
7. The gestures were believable
8. I liked the gestures
9. I understood everything the storyteller said
10. The voice expressed adequate emotions regarding the story
11. The voice was believable
12. I liked the voice

3.4 Procedure

The four possible combinations between the independent variables formed the sample groups displayed in Table 1.

Table 1. Sample Groups

	Real Character	Synthetic Character
Real Voice	RCRV	SCRV
Synthetic Voice	RCSV	SCSV

Each participant was assigned randomly to one of the four groups complying only with the restriction of equal participant numbers between groups. Thus, each sample group was constituted of 27 elements. At the beginning of each visualization the questionnaire was briefly explained to the participant. It was mentioned that the participant should read the questionnaire introduction before the video visualization and that he should fill out the rest of the questionnaire after the visualization.

4 Results

This section presents the results obtained by the carried out study. The data is depicted in Annex in tables 2, 3 and 4. These tables show the percentage of negative (disagreement with the statement), neutral (neither agreement nor disagreement with the statement) and positive (agreement with the statement) ratings and the results obtained through an analysis of variance. The statistical tests used are explained also in annex. Since the amount of gathered data is relatively high we opted to present the main results in a hierarchical order. First we will consider the variation of the independent variables. For each level of the independent variables we will then focus on a particular communication mean. Within each communication mean we present the results for each considered aspect. Second, we take into account the interaction effect between the independent variables. Last we present the results from the Mann-Whitney analysis.

Differences between Real and Synthetic Character

Facial Expression - Significant differences were found in the rating of facial expression for story understanding ($H = 7.48$, $df = 1$, $p = 0.006$), conveying of emotion ($H = 7.13$, $df = 1$, $p = 0.008$), believability ($H = 12.79$, $df = 1$, $p < 0.001$) and satisfaction ($H = 10.46$, $df = 1$, $p = 0.001$). In all aspects the synthetic character facial expression received lower ratings than the human actor.

Gestures - In the rating of the gestures a significant difference was found for the believability aspect ($H = 8.26$, $df = 1$, $p = 0.004$), having the synthetic character less believable gestures than its real counterpart. No significant differences were found for story understanding ($H = 1.12, df = 1, p = 0.290$), conveying of emotion ($H = 1.61, df = 1, p = 0.204$) and satisfaction ($H = 3.66, df = 1, p = 0.056$) aspects.

Voice - As expected, no significant differences were found for story understanding ($H = 2.40, df = 1, p = 0.121$), conveying of emotion ($H = 0.001, df = 1, p = 0.979$), believability ($H = 0.105, df = 1, p = 0.746$) and satisfaction ($H = 0.004, df = 1, p = 0.950$) of the voice when varying the nature of the character.

Differences between the Real and Synthetic Voice

Facial Expression - Significant differences were found in the rating of facial expression for story understanding ($H = 3.89, df = 1, p = 0.049$), conveying of emotion ($H = 6.64, df = 1, p = 0.010$), believability ($H = 5.87, df = 1, p = 0.015$) and satisfaction ($H = 9.92, df = 1, p =0.002$). In all aspects, facial expression received lower ratings when the synthesized voiced was used.

Gestures - We found no significant differences in the evaluation of gestures when varying the nature of the voice (as shown in Table 3).

Voice - There is a high significant difference ($p < 0.001$) for all considered aspects of the voice with the synthesized voice having lower ratings than the real voice.

Interaction Effect between Character and Voice

We found no significant interaction effect between Character and Voice for all statements (as can be seen in Table 3) . Though, it should be noticed that statement 9, concerning the story understanding trough the voice communication mean, has an interaction effect value ($p = 0.059$) close to significant.

Difference between Real and Synthetic Character only considering the Real Voice sample groups

Facial Expression - There is a significant difference for the story understanding ($U = 239, p = 0.026$) and believability ($U = 252, p = 0.045$) aspects, with the character obtaining lower ratings for the 3D character. No significant difference was found for conveying of emotion ($U = 303, p = 0.270$) and satisfaction ($U = 258, p = 0.058$) aspects.

5   Discussion

5.1   Analysis

In a general manner it can be concluded that the synthetic versions used in the experiment obtain worse classifications than their real counterparts. The data suggests that the synthesized gestures are the closer to the human version and that the synthesized voice has the furthest distance to the performance of the human actor. An interesting result is that the rating of the facial expression is affected not only by its real or synthetic nature but also by the nature of the voice used.

Facial Expression - For all dependent variables, the synthesized facial expression has a significant lower rating than the real one. Of particular interest is that the rating of this communication means is strongly affected not only by the visual expression but also by the voice. In fact, the use of synthesized voice has a significant negative effect when rating the facial expression. To isolate this effect, a statistical test was performed where only the human actor voice was used. With it we concluded that for the expression of emotions and for the satisfaction of this communication means, the difference between the real and synthetic storyteller was no longer significant. This fact suggests that these rank averages in particular are more affected by the synthetic voice. As is shown in statement 2 of Table 2, by only considering the human voice we have that the positive percentage rating is of 85.2% for the RCRV video and of 70.4% for the SCRV video. This 14.8% difference is a bit less than the half of the difference between the videos RCSV and SCSV where the percentage of positive ratings drops from 81.5% to 48.2%. By consulting statement 4 of the same table we encounter a similar behavior in what concerns the rating of facial expression satisfaction.

Gestures - Regarding gestures, only one significant difference was found in the rating of its believability. In this case the synthetic storyteller presents worse performance than the human actor. In the remaining ratings the data suggests that the synthetic gestures have a close performance to the real ones. It is also worthy of notice that gestures rating have always a majority of positive ratings (statements 5, 6, 7 and 8 of Table 2). Similarly to what happens in the facial expression, gestures also seem to be affected by the nature of the used voice, but this time in an inverse manner. Positive gestures ratings percentages have an increase or stay on the same value when the synthesized voice is taken into account. Unfortunately we did not achieve a significant difference when varying the voice nature, being the satisfaction rating the closest one to achieve such difference with a $p = 0.082$.

Voice - Through an analysis of the results, on the statement "I understood everything the storyteller said", we notice that there is a very close to significant value ($p = 0.059$) for the interaction between independent variables. This lead us to believe that this statement is not measuring what we intended. Therefore, we discarded this statement for analysis. In the remaining aspects, the voice was the medium that had a clearer significant difference between the real and the synthetic versions ($p < 0.001$), having the real voice higher ratings than its counterpart. Nevertheless, only the satisfaction regarding the synthetic voice obtained a majority of negative ratings (see statement 12 of Table 2). Both the emotion and believability aspect of the synthetic voice gathered a majority of positive ratings with values of 70.4% and 53.7% respectively.

5.2 Study Limitations

Like all studies this one is not without its limitation. By using subjective classifications from participants we may not be achieving the desired precision or obtaining data that is not representative of what we want to measure. Another problem at hand is that the sample used is only representative of the computer engineering students from Instituto Superior Tecnico population. To solve this issue the study should be extended to consider a larger number of participants with higher diversity.

5.3 Future Work

The creation of a precise measure of believability is a complex task that gives origin to a debate on its own. However, the achieved results show the impact

Table 2. Percentage of Positive, Neutral and Negative ratings

Statement#	%	Character		Voice		Video			
		Real	Virtual	Real	Virtual	RCRV	SCRV	RCSV	SCSV
1	Positive	70.4	42.6	63.0	50.0	77.8	48.1	63.0	37.0
	Neutral	13.0	14.8	13.0	14.8	14.8	11.1	11.1	18.6
	Negative	16.6	42.3	24.0	35.2	7.4	40.8	25.9	44.4
2	Positive	83.3	59.2	77.8	64.8	85.2	70.4	81.5	48.2
	Neutral	11.1	13.0	9.2	14.8	7.4	11.1	14.8	14.8
	Negative	5.6	27.8	13.0	20.4	7.4	18.5	3.7	37.0
3	Positive	77.8	50.0	72.2	55.6	81.5	63.0	74.1	37.0
	Neutral	16.6	13.0	14.8	14.8	18.5	11.1	14.8	14.8
	Negative	5.6	37.0	13.0	29.6	0.0	25.9	11.1	48.2
4	Positive	75.9	44.4	70.4	50.0	81.5	59.3	70.4	29.6
	Neutral	11.1	24.1	16.6	18.5	11.1	22.2	11.1	26.0
	Negative	13.0	31.5	13.0	31.5	7.4	18.5	18.5	44.4
5	Positive	83.3	75.9	79.6	79.6	85.2	74.1	81.5	77.8
	Neutral	7.4	5.6	5.6	7.4	7.4	3.7	7.4	7.4
	Negative	9.3	18.5	14.8	13.0	7.4	22.2	11.1	14.8
6	Positive	87.0	64.8	72.2	79.6	81.5	63.0	92.6	66.7
	Neutral	7.4	11.1	9.3	9.3	11.1	7.4	3.7	14.8
	Negative	5.6	24.1	18.5	11.1	7.4	29.6	9.7	18.5
7	Positive	75.9	57.4	66.7	66.7	74.1	59.3	77.8	55.6
	Neutral	13.0	14.8	9.2	18.5	14.8	3.7	11.1	25.9
	Negative	11.1	27.8	24.1	14.8	11.1	37.0	11.1	18.5
8	Positive	77.8	63.0	63.0	77.8	66.7	59.3	88.9	66.7
	Neutral	13.0	16.6	16.6	13.0	22.2	11.1	3.7	22.2
	Negative	9.2	20.4	20.4	9.2	11.1	29.6	7.4	11.1
9	Positive	87.0	77.8	94.4	70.4	96.3	92.6	77.8	63.0
	Neutral	3.7	1.8	1.9	3.7	3.7	0.0	3.7	3.7
	Negative	9.3	20.4	3.7	25.9	0.0	7.4	18.5	33.3
10	Positive	81.5	83.3	94.4	70.4	92.6	96.3	70.4	70.4
	Neutral	7.4	9.3	3.7	13.0	7.4	0.0	7.4	18.5
	Negative	11.1	7.4	1.9	16.7	0.0	3.7	22.2	11.1
11	Positive	68.5	74.1	88.9	53.7	92.6	85.2	44.5	63.0
	Neutral	11.1	9.2	11.1	9.3	7.4	14.8	14.8	3.7
	Negative	20.4	16.7	0.0	37.0	0.0	0.0	40.7	33.3
12	Positive	53.7	51.9	77.8	27.8	81.5	74.1	25.9	29.6
	Neutral	16.7	14.8	18.5	13.0	18.5	18.5	14.8	11.1
	Negative	29.6	33.3	3.7	59.2	0.0	7.4	59.3	59.3

of the voice in the facial expression appreciation is complex and thus worthy of future studies. A dedicate study may conclude if the relation uncovered by the study really exists in the direction that the data indicated. Another topic for a future study is related to the acceptance of the synthetic voice. Contrarily to what happens with the figurative representation of the character, it appears that the users are expecting that the synthetic character to have a human voice. This experience is certainly due the long exposure of cartoon characters which speech borrowed from human performers. In fact, voices of cartoon characters are often a selling ticket in cartoon movies. This means that we accept figurative representations to stylize humans, animals and even objects but we demand (or expect) human-like speech. The fact that the figurative representation does not possess the physical mechanism that allow the production of such acoustic signal, does not seem to affect in its believability. A synchronized labial movement with the speech is sufficient for the viewer to expect a human like vocal signal. A study concerning the acceptable level of distortion or of a stylized synthetic speech and the linking with different means of communication in characters (both gestures and facial expressions) which need to be accepted by the viewer are certainly important topics for further research.

Finally, we believe that the system and results obtained with the research here presented show that virtual storytellers provide a promising framework for studying how to convey emotions by voice, facial expression and gestures. The ideal storyteller should be able to start from a simple text, automatically add emotion tags, and convey the story with corresponding features in terms of the three means of communication. This work was a small contribution towards this still distant goal.

Table 3. Two-Way Non-Parametric ANOVA Test Results

Stat.#	Source	p	Mean Rank Real	Mean Rank Synthetic	Stat.#	p	Mean Rank Real	Mean Rank Synthetic
1	Character	0.006	62.56	46.44	7	0.004	62.90	46.10
	Voice	0.049	60.31	48.69		0.142	50.21	58.79
	Character*Voice	0.557				0.675		
2	Character	0.008	62.31	46.69	8	0.056	60.02	48.98
	Voice	0.010	62.04	46.96		0.082	49.49	59.51
	Character*Voice	0.453				0.693		
3	Character	<0.001	65.01	43.99	9	0.121	48.79	50.21
	Voice	0.015	61.62	47.380		<0.001	65.60	43.40
	Character*Voice	0.512				0.059		
4	Character	0.001	64.03	44.97	10	0.979	54.57	54.43
	Voice	0.002	63.78	45.22		<0.001	66.33	42.67
	Character*Voice	0.640				0.928		
5	Character	0.290	57.47	51.53	11	0.746	53.55	55.45
	Voice	0.919	54.21	54.79		<0.001	68.00	41.00
	Character*Voice	0.510				0.887		
6	Character	0.204	58.17	50.83	12	0.950	54.32	54.69
	Voice	0.626	53.09	55.91		<0.001	71.32	37.69
	Character*Voice	0.612				0.866		

6 Annex

Table 2 shows the percentage of negative (disagreement with the statement), neutral (neither agreement nor disagreement with the statement) and positive (agreement with the statement) ratings. This table displays the data organized by independent variable and video. Table 3 reveals the results obtained through an analysis of variance. The statistical test used is a two-way non-parametric analysis of variance described in [12]. The test is similar to a Kruskal-Wallis test extending it to consider two independent variables and possible interaction between them. Finally, Table 4 shows the results of a Mann-Whitney test between the RCRV and SCRV groups. In all tests it was considered that a difference was significant for $p < 0.05$.

Table 4. Mann-Whitney Test Results

		Statement #1	Statement #2	Statement #3	Statement #4
Mean Rank	RCRV	32.15	29.80	31.67	31.44
	SCRV	22.85	25.20	23.33	23.56
Mann-Whitney U		239	303	252	258
p (2-tailed)		0.026	0.270	0.045	0.058

Acknowledgments

This project was partially funded by the Portuguese Foundation for Science and Technology (POSI/SRI/41071/2001) and the EU funded Humaine Network of Excellence contract number 507422 of the IST programme.

References

1. Aylett, R., Louchart, S., Dias, J., Paiva, A., Vala, M.: FearNot! - An Experiment in Emergent Narrative. In: Panayiotopoulos, T., Gratch, J., Aylett, R., Ballin, D., Olivier, P., Rist, T. (eds.) IVA 2005. LNCS (LNAI), vol. 3661, pp. 305–316. Springer, Heidelberg (2005)
2. Baylor, A., Kim, Y.: Pedagogical Agent Design: The Impact of Agent Realism, Gender, Ethnicity, and Instructional Role. In: International Conference on Intelligent Tutoring Systems, Maceió, Brazil (2004)
3. Blumberg, B., Galyean, T.: Multi-Level Direction of Autonomous Creatures for Real-Time Virtual Environments. Computer Graphics (SIGGRAPH 1995 Proceedings) 30(3), 47–54 (1995)
4. Brooks, K.: Do Story agents use rocking chairs. In: ICM (1997)
5. Cabral, J., Oliveira, L.: Pitch-Synchronous Time-Scaling for High-Frequency Excitation Regeneration. In: Cabral, J., Oliveira, L (eds.) Interspeech 2005 (September 2005)
6. Cabral, J., Oliveira, L.: Pitch-Synchronous Time-Scaling for Prosodic and Voice Quality Transformations. In: Interspeech 2005 (September 2005)
7. Cabral, J.: Transforming Prosody and Voice Quality to Generate Emotions in Speech, MSc Thesis, IST, UTL (January 2006)

8. Ekman, P.: Facial Expressions. In: Dalgleish, T., Power, M. (eds.) Handbook of Cognition and Emotion, John Wiley & Sons Ltd, New York (1999)
9. Secretariado Nacional para a Reabilitação e Integração das Pessoas com Deficiência: Gestuário - Lígua Gestual Portuguesa 5ª edição
10. Melo, C., Paiva A.: A Story about Gesticulation Expression (under submission)
11. McNeill, D.: Hand and Mind: What gestures reveal about thought. The University of Chicago Press (1992)
12. Maroco, J., Bispo, R.: Estatística aplicada às ciências sociais e humanas. In: Climepsi (ed.), pp. 249–253 (2003)
13. Paulo, S., Oliveira, L.: Improving the Accuracy of the Speech Synthesis Based Phonetic Alignment Using Multiple Acoustic Features. In: Mamede, N.J., Baptista, J., Trancoso, I., Nunes, M.d.G.V. (eds.) PROPOR 2003. LNCS, vol. 2721, pp. 31–39. Springer, Heidelberg (2003)
14. Paulo, S., Oliveira, L.: Generation of Word Alternative Pronunciations Using Weighted Finite State Transducers. In: Paulo, S., Oliveira, L. (eds.) Interspeech 2005 (September 2005)
15. Paulo, S., Oliveira, L.: Reducing the Corpus-based TTS Signal Degradation Due to Speaker's Word Pronunciations. In: Paulo, S., Oliveira, L. (eds.) Interspeech 2005 (September 2005)
16. Pelachaud, C., Maya, V., Lamolle, M.: Representation of Expressivity for Embodied Conversational Agents. In: Workshop Balanced Perception and Action, Third International Joint Conference on Autonomous Agents & Multi-Agent Systems, New-York, julho (2004)
17. Perlin, K., Goldberg, A.: Improv: A system for scripting interactive actors in virtual worlds. Computer Graphics (SIGGRAPH 1996) 30, 205–218 (1996)
18. Roemer, M.: Telling Stories: Postmodernism and the Invalidation of Traditional Narrative. Rowman & Littlefield Publishers, Inc. (1995)
19. Sawyer, R.: The way of the Storyteller. In: Sawyer, R. (ed.) Penguin Books (1942)
20. Silva, A., Raimundo, G., Paiva, A., de Melo, C.: To tell or not to tell.Building an interactive virtual storyteller. In: Silva, A., Raimundo, G., Paiva, A., de Melo, C. (eds.) Proceedings of the Language, Speech and Gesture for Expressive Characters Symposium, AISB 2004, Leeds, Reino Unido, Abril de (2004)
21. Online reference Last access 23/02/2006
http://www.bbc.co.uk/cbeebies/tweenies
22. McBreen, H., Shade, P., Jack, M., Wyard, P.: Experimental assessment of the effectiveness of synthetic personae for multi-modal e-retail applications. Agents, 39–45 (2000)
23. Waters, K.: A muscle model for animation three-dimensional facial expression. In: Stone, M.C. (ed.) SIGGRAPH, pp. 17–24. ACM Press, New York (1987)

Author Index

Lecture Notes in Artificial Intelligence (LNAI)